Phobic and Obsessive-Compulsive Disorders

THEORY, RESEARCH, AND PRACTICE

THE PLENUM BEHAVIOR THERAPY SERIES
Series Editor: Nathan H. Azrin

Phobic and Obsessive-Compulsive Disorders

THEORY, RESEARCH, AND PRACTICE

Paul M. G. Emmelkamp

University of Groningen
Groningen, The Netherlands

PLENUM PRESS • NEW YORK AND LONDON

Library of Congress Cataloging in Publication Data

Emmelkamp, Paul M. G., 1949–
  Phobic and obsessive-compulsive disorders.

  (The Plenum behavior therapy series)
  Includes bibliographical references and index.
  1. Phobias. 2. Obsessive-compulsive neurosis. I. Title. II. Series. [DNLM: 1. Obses-
sive-compulsive disorder. 2. Phobic disorders. WM 178 E45p]
RC535.E45 1982   616.85′225   82-12362
ISBN 0-306-41044-3

RC535 .E451982

Emmelkamp, Paul M. G.,
1949–
Phobic and
obsessive-compulsive

© 1982 Plenum Press, New York
A Division of Plenum Publishing Corporation
233 Spring Street, New York, N.Y. 10013

Printed in the United States of America

Preface

In the last decade, the literature of phobic and obsessive-compulsive disorders has increased enormously. In view of this explosive growth it becomes increasingly difficult for the practitioner to keep abreast of important developments that have led to significant changes in treatment procedures. The purpose of this volume is to present a critical account of the current status of theory, research, and practice in the field of phobic and obsessive-compulsive disorders. More specifically, this book attempts to bridge the gap between theory, laboratory investigation, and application.

For purposes of clarity the volume has been divided into several parts. Parts I and II provide, it is hoped, a reasonably comprehensive account of the theory and research relevant to the etiology, assessment, and treatment of these disorders. Part I deals with phobic disorders and Part II with obsessive-compulsive disorders. The third part of the text is devoted to the clinical management of these disorders.

The opening chapter deals with phenomenology, classification, and prevalence of the various disorders. In addition, the status of analog research vis-à-vis clinical research is discussed.

The chapters on etiology discuss the many variables inherent in a comprehensive theory of the development of phobic (Chapter 2) and obsessive-compulsive behavior (Chapter 6). An explicit effort has been made to extend the discussion beyond the boundaries of learning theory. Attention is devoted to examining the contributions from other areas (e.g., biological, cognitive, psychoanalytical).

Issues related to the assessment of phobic and obsessive-compulsive disorders are dealt with in Chapters 3 and 7, respectively. These chapters help to clarify assessment conducted in the clinical trials discussed in subsequent chapters.

Chapter 4 presents an overview of the various cognitive-behavioral interventions for anxiety-based disorders. Here a detailed examination of the process involved in these interventions is provided, mostly based on analog research. A summary of research of each technique is described. Chapter 4 concludes with an attempt to formulate a unifying theory of fear reduction. This chapter is procedure oriented.

The clinical effectiveness of cognitive-behavioral and psychopharmacological approaches in the treatment of phobic disorders is reviewed in Chapter 5. Chapter 8 provides a detailed account of the present status of behavioral treatments of obsessive-compulsive disorders. A separate chapter (Chapter 9) is devoted to a critical overview of psychopharmacological treatment and psychosurgery with obsessional patients.

In Part III, considerable attention is given to the clinical management of phobic and obsessive-compulsive disorders. I have attempted to give readers some appreciation of the complexities of clinical interventions. Chapter 10 focuses on the clinical assessment and treatment planning, and emphasizes the important role of a functional analysis. The goal of the last chapters is to present clinical guidelines on how to apply exposure *in vivo* procedures on phobic (Chapter 11) and obsessive-compulsive patients (Chapter 12).

The present text is directed to both the practitioner and the researcher. The book will be found to be useful in the training of therapists and of interest also to experienced practitioners. In addition, parts of the book may serve as a useful supplemental text in courses on abnormal psychology and assessment. Researchers will find in the book a comprehensive and critical evaluation of research in this field. The extensive bibliography should assure the book's usefulness as a reference source. It is my hope that the subject matter of this volume will appeal to a wide audience of students in psychology and psychiatry, practitioners, and researchers.

I would like to thank several people for helping bring this book together. Most of all I wish to acknowledge the constant support and valuable suggestions from my colleague and wife Ank Benner. A significant contribution was also made by David Rabbie who assisted in the follow-up studies on obsessive-compulsives. Finally, I wish to express my profound gratitude to Greetje Hollander for generously assisting in the preparation of the entire manuscript.

PAUL M. G. EMMELKAMP

Contents

1

General Issues

Phobic and obsessive-compulsive disorders should be distinguished from normal fears and preoccupations. Most people experience fears but these usually do not require treatment. When fears become so disabling that they seriously affect life (e.g., fear of heights for a window-cleaner), they can be regarded as disorders. Phobia is a special type of fear in which responses are excessive. Like fears, phobias can occur in almost any situation but the cases seen in clinical practice have phobias in a limited number of situations. Preoccupations have to be distinguished from clinical obsessions. Preoccupations are different in that the themes concern every day worries that provoke little resistance.

Phobias can be defined as special kinds of fears that are out of proportion to the reality of the situation, can neither be explained nor reasoned away, are largely beyond voluntary control, and lead to avoidance of the feared situation (Marks, 1969). *Obsessions* are repetitive recurring thoughts—often but not necessarily anxiety inducing—that recur despite active attempts to ward them off. Obsessions may involve sexual themes, thoughts of causing physical harm to oneself or others, or obsessional fears of contamination. Obsessions are often—but not always—accompanied by urges and rituals. *Rituals* or *compulsions* are recurrent repetitive actions that usually serve to reduce anxiety and discomfort. The most common compulsive behaviors involve "cleaning" and "checking."

1. PREVALENCE AND CLASSIFICATION

1.1. Fears and Phobias

Fears are quite common among children. Miller, Barrett, and Hampe (1974) estimated children aged from 2 to 6 have about three

1

fears on the average, but the number of excessive fear reactions is small. Factor analytic studies (Miller, Barrett, Hampe, & Noble, 1972) of children's fears obtained three interpretable factors: (a) fear of physical injury, (b) fear of natural events such as storms and darkness, and (c) social stress, including fears of going to school, being criticized, and being separated from one's parents.

Most fears of children are passing episodes in a normal developmental process and disappear within a few months. Fears of injury and social anxiety usually do not dissipate as the child matures. Graziano, De Giovanni, and Gargia (1979) suggest that clinical fears be defined as those with a duration of over 2 years or with an intensity that is debilitating to the child. Table 1 presents fears that are associated with developmental periods.

The prevalence of clinical phobias among children is rare (Miller, Barrett, & Hampe 1974; Rutter, Tizard, & Whitmore, 1970). Graziano and De Giovanni (1979) reported that 6% of the children referred for behavior therapy were phobics. School phobia is the main phobic condition referred for treatment (Miller *et al.*, 1974) although its occurrence in the general population is less than 1%. Presumably, school phobia has such serious repercussions that parents must seek professional help.

In adolescence, social fears are the most common. Fears of blushing and fears of being looked at peaked in girls on the average about 2 years earlier than in boys (Abe & Masui, 1981).

Fears and phobias exist in a fairly high proportion of the adult general population but only a minor proportion of those who are affected ever consult health services. Agras, Sylvester, and Oliveau (1969) investigated the prevalence of fears and phobias in the general population. The total prevalence of phobias was estimated at 77/1,000 people. Only 9 out of 1,000 had seen a psychiatrist for treatment of a phobia. Thus, although severe fears are common among the general population, only a small percentage of "phobics" receive treatment.

In a subsequent study (Agras, Chapin, & Oliveau, 1972) the course of the phobias of a subgroup of the phobics studied by Agras *et al.* (1969) was investigated. None of the group had received treatment during the 5-year period. Most of the fears of children and adolescents had disappeared. At follow-up 100% were improved or symptom free. Of the adult group only 6% lost their phobic symptoms entirely. Moreover, 37% of the adult group showed a worsening of their main phobia. Those patients with a generalized main phobia (e.g., agoraphobia) had worse prognoses than the patients with specific phobias. This study confirmed the findings that children's fears often improve spontaneously.

Table 1. Developmental Fears at Different Age Levels[a]

Age	Fears
0–6 Months	Loud noises, loss of support
6–9 Months	Strangers
1st Year	Separation, injury, toilet
2nd Year	Imaginary creatures, death, robbers
3rd Year	Dogs, being alone
4th Year	Dark
6–12 Years	School, injury, natural events, social
13–18 Years	Injury, social
19+ Years	Injury, natural events, sexual

[a] From "Phobias of Childhood in a Prescientific Era" by L. C. Miller and E. Hampe, *Child Personality and Psychopathology: Current Topics* (Vol. 1). Copyright 1974 by Wiley & Sons. Reprinted by permission.

Though phobias are common in other psychiatric disorders, the frequency of phobic *disorders* in clinical practice is about 3% (Marks, 1969). Agoraphobia is the most common clinical phobia although other fears are much more frequent in the general population (Agras *et al.*, 1969). Agoraphobics constitute about 50–60% of all phobics seen in clinical practice (Agras *et al.*, 1969; Marks, 1969). The bulk of the remaining clinical phobias consists of illness phobias and social anxieties. Very few individuals with specific or "simple" phobias come for treatment; animal phobics are rarely seen.

The term *agoraphobia* refers to a syndrome in which the most characteristic feature is attacks of anxiety or panic in a variety of public places such as streets, crowds, stores, or busses. This causes "fear of fear" and leads to an avoidance of these situations. Agoraphobics become anxious when walking, shopping, going by bus, or visiting cinemas and churches. Most agoraphobics feel less anxiety when accompanied by a trusted person (partner) but they usually remain anxious, although to a lesser degree. The few agoraphobics who succeed in visiting churches, cinemas, and parties chose a chair near the exit. Although fear of open spaces is common among agoraphobics, it does not have the central function as was once thought. Marks and Bebbington (1976) suggested that "space phobia" is characterized by a fear of absent visuospatial support (open spaces) and by a fear of falling, unlike the fears of public places found in agoraphobia. Marks (1981a) proposed that this pseudoagoraphobic syndrome may be the result of disturbed integration of vestibuloocular reflexes. The features distinguishing space phobia from agoraphobia are shown in Table 2. It should be noted, however, that most agoraphobics fear open spaces too. Further controlled studies are needed to establish whether space phobia is indeed a separate syndrome with organic

Table 2. Features Distinguishing Space Phobia from Agoraphobia[a]

	Space phobia	Agoraphobia
1. Onset age	Old (mean 55 yr)	Young (mean 25 yr)
2. Fear of public places	Mild/absent	Mod/severe
3. Fear of open spaces	Mod/severe	Mild/severe
4. Fear of falling	Mod/severe	Mild/absent
5. Response to exposure *in vivo*	Slow, fragile	Good
6. Depression, free floating anxiety	Unusual	Common
7. Organic features	Usual	Rare

[a] From "Space 'Phobia': A Pseudo-Agoraphobic Syndrome" by I. Marks, *Journal of Neurology, Neurosurgery and Psychiatry*, 1981, *44*. Copyright 1981 by British Medical Journal. Reprinted by permission.

features that have to be distinguished from agoraphobia or is merely an agoraphobic variant.

Numerous factor analytic studies of self-reported fears have been conducted on normal populations. Apart from Torgersen's (1979), these analyses did not reveal an agoraphobic factor. Factor analyses of the Fear Survey Schedules of agoraphobics found a distinct agoraphobia factor consisting of fears of open spaces, crowds, and confined places (Arrindell, 1980; Hallam & Hafner, 1978).

Agoraphobia appears to be associated with "spontaneous" panic attacks (Marks, 1969), depression (Bowen & Kohout, 1979; Gardos, 1981; Jasin & Turner, 1980), somatic symptoms (Arrindell, 1980; Gardos, 1981), illness phobias (Bianchi, 1971; Buglass, Clarke, Henderson, Kreitman, & Presley, 1977), and hypochondriasis (Jasin & Turner, 1980).

Arrindell (1980) investigated the fears and associated symptoms of a large sample of phobics, all members of the Dutch society of phobic patients. The subjects completed a number of questionnaires including the Fear Survey Schedule (Wolpe & Lang, 1964) and the Symptom Check List (SCL-90-Derogatis, 1977). A higher order factor analysis revealed a "factorial definition" of agoraphobic (see Table 3). All nonphobic symptoms correlated significantly with the Agoraphobic-FSS factor. It should be noted that most of the nonphobic symptoms are associated with hyperventilation, which is related to agoraphobia (see p. 33).

Illness phobias, which are related to hypochondriasis, include fears of heart disease, cancer, and venereal diseases. Patients are extremely sensitive to sensation in their body (e.g., palpitations) and frequently (sometimes several times a week) visit their general practitioner for a check-up. Hyperventilation is also common in this group.

Clinical social anxiety or social phobia consists of disabling fears in social situations that cause patients to avoid such situations as much as

Table 3. Proposed Factorial Definition of Agoraphobia[a]

Nonphobic symptoms		Phobic symptoms	
Somatization (SCL-90)	FSS Factor II	Agoraphobia (SCL-90)	
Headaches	Being alone	Feeling afraid in open spaces or on the street	
Faintness or dizziness	Being in a strange place	Feeling afraid to go out of the house alone	
Pains in heart or chest	Crossing streets	Feeling afraid to travel on buses, subways or trains	
Pains in lower back	Falling	Having to avoid certain things, places or activities	
Nausea or upset stomach	High places on land	because they are frightening	
Soreness of muscles	Journeys by train, bus, car	Feeling uneasy in crowds, such as shopping or at a movie	
Trouble getting breath	Crowds	Feeling uncomfortable about eating or drinking in public	
Hot or cold spells	Large open spaces	Feeling afraid of fainting in public	
Numbness or tingling in	Being in an elevator		
parts of the body	Enclosed places		
Heavy feelings in arms	Airplanes		
or legs			
A lump in the throat			
Heart pounding or racing			
Trouble falling asleep			
Feeling weak in parts			
of the body			
Sleep that is restless			
or disturbed			
The idea that something			
serious is wrong with			
the body			

[a] From "Dimensional Structure and Psychopathology Correlates of the Fear Survey Schedule (FSS-111) in a Phobic Population: A Factorial Definition of Agoraphobia" by W. A. Arrindell, *Behaviour Research and Therapy*, 1980, *18*, 229-242. Copyright 1980 by Pergamon Press. Reprinted by permission.

possible. Clinical social anxiety is distinguished from the shyness and social anxiety many individuals experience by the intensity of the fears and the abnormal avoidance of social situations involved. A number of social phobics experience fears in any social situation, but in other patients, fears are limited to specific situations. For example, some patients fear that their hands will tremble when writing or holding a cup in front of others. Others may be afraid of blushing or of eating in public places.

There is a considerable overlap between social anxiety, agoraphobia, illness phobia, and anxiety states. Rather than consider them as distinct diagnostic categories, phobic symptoms are better viewed as lying in a number of different continua. The actual clinical diagnosis depends on the predominant features in a particular patient. The overlapping diagnostic groups are graphically depicted in Figure 1.

1.2. Obsessive-Compulsive Disorder

Obsessive-compulsive disorder is a rare condition; its prevalence in the general population has been estimated at .05% (Rüdin, 1953; Woodruff & Pitts, 1964). Obsessive-compulsive behavior (e.g., house-proud housewives; Cooper, 1970) is much more common in the general population. When obsessive-compulsive behavior becomes so severe that it

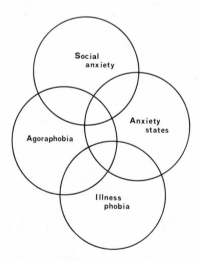

Figure 1. The overlap between agoraphobia, social anxiety, illness phobia, and anxiety states.

Table 4. Distribution of Obsessional Themes in Different Cultures

Content of obsession	Akhtar *et al.*	Rachman and Hodgson
Dirt/disease contamination	59%	55%
Agression/harm	25%	19%
Impersonal/orderliness	23%	35%
Religion	10%	10%
Sex	5%	13%

dominates one's life, it can be regarded as a disorder. Among psychiatric populations the incidence ranges from .1% up to 4.6% (Black, 1974), but the latter figure is probably an overestimation.

Obsessions and ritualistic activities are common among children in developmental phases but these usually disappear after some time. Obsessive-compulsive disorders among children are rare (Rapoport, 1982; Rutter *et al.*, 1970). Most obsessive-compulsive disorders start in the early 20s (Black, 1974). About 80% of patients report the onset before the age of 30.

There are now a number of studies reporting on the phenomenology of obsessive-compulsive disorders. The form and content of obsessions and compulsions appear to be strikingly similar in England (Rachman & Hodgson, 1980; Stern & Cobb, 1978), Scotland (Dowson, 1977), Germany (Zaworka & Hand, 1980), United States (Welner, Reich, Robins, Fishman, & van Dorn, 1976), Canada (Roy, 1979), and India (Akhtar, Wig, Verma, Pershod, & Verma, 1975).

About 80% of obsessional patients have obsessions as well as compulsions. A minority suffer from obsessions only. Pure rituals without accompanying obsessive thoughts are rare. Usually obsessions precede the rituals but sometimes the obsessive thoughts follow the performance of rituals, especially with obsessional doubting. The most common obsessional thoughts consist of fears of dirt and contamination. Harming obsessions are reported by about a quarter of the patients. Table 4 shows that the distribution of obsessional themes in England (Hodgson & Rachman, 1980) and India (Akhtar *et al.*, 1975) are essentially similar.

Factor analyses of obsessional questionnaires revealed several interpretable factors, which varied from study to study. However, all studies found two independent factors: "cleaning" and "checking" (Cooper & Kelleher, 1973; Hodgson & Rachman, 1977; Stern & Cobb, 1978; Zaworka & Hand, 1980). Cleaning compulsions are usually associated with contamination fears. Patients fear that they may become contaminated and therefore clean their house, themselves, and children. Whenever such a patient touches anything that might be contaminated (e.g., door knobs, other people, food), they have to wash their hands and arms, often for many minutes, or take a bath. With some patients, thoughts by themselves may provoke washing and cleaning rituals. Checking rituals may involve checking whether doors and windows are closed, and whether the gas is turned off. Whenever they leave their house a number of checkers will go back numerous times to see if everything is alright. Checking may also occur in other situations: for example, driving back to see if an accident has happened, going back to the office to see if anyone is locked up in a cupboard, and so forth. Both washing and checking rituals lead to avoidance of situations that are likely to provoke the rituals.

2. STATUS OF ANALOG AND CLINICAL RESEARCH

Behavior therapists claim that their clinical practices are based on experimental evidence. This seems to give behavior therapy a scientific reputation in the field of psychotherapy. However, the question arises whether behavior therapy as currently practiced is as scientifically based as behavior therapists assert. Swan and MacDonald (1978) found in a national survey of behavior therapists in the United States significant differences between behavior therapy as it is operationalized in research and behavior therapy as it is applied clinically.

Fear and anxiety are the target behaviors that received the most attention in the professional behavior journals of the 1970s (Ciminero, Doleys, & Williams, 1978). Such diverse behavioral procedures as systematic desensitization, flooding, aversion relief, biofeedback, covert reinforcement, and modeling have been claimed to be effective in the treatment of phobias. The interpretation and generalization of these findings, however, are frequently restricted because of study design characteristics (e.g., analog vs. clinical population). Most behavioral research has been of the analog type: Researchers have typically employed volunteers, usually students who had small animal phobias (e.g., of snakes) or social anxiety (e.g., speech anxiety; dating anxiety) as subjects. While some researchers selected only highly fearful subjects, others have used mildly or lowly fearful subjects. For instance, in a study by De Moor (1970) about one-third of the sample of "snake phobics" could touch the snake at the pretest; Melnick (1973) employed subjects with "dating anxiety" who dated less than twice a week.

Analog researchers usually excluded participants who had real psychological problems. To give just a few examples, subjects who were undergoing or had undergone any form of psychiatric treatment (e.g.,

Mathews & Rezin, 1977; Mealiea & Nawas, 1971) or who manifested emotional disorder or psychological difficulties (e.g., Barrett, 1969; Beiman, Israel, & Johnson, 1978; De Moor, 1970) have been excluded. However, it should be noted that subjects with psychological difficulties may be more similar to phobic patients than subjects without such problems.

Analog studies are often not internally valid. Several studies have demonstrated that demand characteristics can influence behavioral assessment in such studies. For instance, in a study by Emmelkamp and Boeke-Slinkers (1977a) the level of demand for approach behavior in a behavioral avoidance test was varied, using snake phobics as subjects. Both high-demand and low-demand subjects were regarded as "phobic" if they could not touch the snake with a gloved hand. On the basis of the results of the low-demand test, 16.9% of the subjects would have been classified as phobic and have qualified for treatment, whereas on the basis of the high demand test the percentage would only have been 6.8%. Thus, behavioral avoidance tests used in analog studies are easily in-fluenced by demand characteristics. Other studies also clearly indicate the influence of situational and instructional effects on behavioral assess-ment procedures (e.g., Barrios, 1978; Bernstein, 1974; Bernstein & Nietzel, 1973; Smith, Diener, & Beaman, 1974).

There are several important differences between clinical and analog populations. Phobic patients who apply for treatment in a clinical setting differ from controls and phobic students on various measures of psycho-pathology (Branham & Katahn, 1974; Hall & Goldberg, 1977; Olley & McAllister, 1974; Solyom, Beck, Solyom, & Hugel, 1974). In addition, subjects in analog and clinical studies may differ markedly with respect to approach contingencies (Hayes, 1976). Even though both types of subjects may show substantial avoidance behavior, phobic patients may experience much stronger approach contingencies than subjects in laboratory studies. Furthermore, the kind of phobias treated in clinical and analog studies differs widely. While analog researchers have typi-cally employed students with small animal phobias or social anxiety as subjects, agoraphobia forms the greatest category of phobias seen in clinical settings. Because of the differences between clinical and analog populations, the clinical value of such studies has been questioned (e.g., Cooper, Furst, & Bridger, 1969; Emmelkamp, 1981a).

Several investigators have argued that social anxiety (Borkovec, Stone, O'Brien, & Kaloupec, 1974; Curran, 1977; Heimberg, 1977) or mutilation anxiety (Beiman, O'Neil, Wachtel, Fugé, Johnson, & Feuer-stein, 1978) are both clinically more relevant target behaviors than small animal phobias. Although such arguments are sufficient to create a new pool of "patients," it is by no means clear why the results of treatment of shy students who volunteer for treatment are clinically more relevant than the results of treatment of their fellow students with snake phobias.

Borkovec *et al.* (1974) have suggested that speech and social anxiety are more desirable as target behaviors in analog studies since they are not susceptible to demand characteristics. However, data from studies by Blom and Craighead (1974) and Craighead and Craighead (1981) indicate that this assertion is incorrect. These data indicate that demand effects may significantly influence social anxiety as measured in these analog studies. As Craighead and Craighead (1981) state: "Generalizations from less fearful analogue speech-anxious populations to highly fearful clinical speech-anxious populations may be misleading" (p. 115).

Following Borkovec *et al.*'s (1974) proposition that social anxiety is a clinically relevant target, a large number of analog studies on social anxiety have been recently conducted (e.g., Arkowitz, 1977; Curran, 1977). Generally, investigators relied upon self-report instruments (e.g., social-anxiety questionnaire) for subject selection. Wallander, Conger, Mariotto, Curran, and Farrell (1980) assessed the comparability of four commonly used self-report selection instruments. There was a lack of convergence of these instruments and all instruments produced relatively independent subject samples: "Little was gained from knowing classification on one instrument in predicting classification on another" (Wallander *et al.*, p. 548). Thus, conclusions cannot be generalized from one analog population to another since different populations actually have been studied. Obviously, any conclusion to a clinical population is unwarranted.

I doubt seriously whether the hundreds of analog studies concerning anxiety and phobias have been of much value for developing and evaluating treatments for clinical patients. To take a concrete example, the most effective treatments currently available for the treatment of phobic and obsessive-compulsive patients (exposure *in vivo* techniques) have been developed in clinical studies. To date, analog studies about these techniques are almost lacking. This does not mean that I would recommend analog studies use exposure *in vivo* treatments. However, these results demonstrate that clinical researchers study different questions and follow quite different pathways, as compared to analog researchers.

The difficulty in generalizing results from analog studies to clinical patients is illustrated by the differential effectiveness of treatment with analog populations on the one hand and clinical populations on the other. For many years the behavioral treatment of phobias was dominated by systematic desensitization. In contrast with analog studies, where this procedure consistently has been found to be effective in improving minor fears, it has only small effects on social anxious and agoraphobic patients (see Chapter 5). Branham and Katahn (1974) compared desensitization and no treatment with both volunteer students and patients as subjects. Volunteers improved significantly more than patients. In their volunteer sample, desensitization was significantly superior to the control condition; whereas in their patient sample desensitization was no more effective than no-treatment. With cognitive modification procedures, the same picture arises. Cognitive modification procedures have been found to be quite effective with analog populations. However, recent studies at our department show that these procedures have clinically insignificant effects with agoraphobics and obsessive-compulsive patients (see Chapters 5 and 8). Other studies found differential effectiveness of biofeedback (Shepherd & Watts, 1974) and relaxation (Borkovec & Sides, 1979) for patients and for volunteers.

It is not my purpose to dismiss analog studies entirely. The relevancy of analog research depends on the type of questions with which one is interested. However, one cannot help but think that the choice between analog research or clinical research is much more determined by the setting in which one works than by the specific question under investigation. Generally, clinicians prefer clinical research, whereas researchers in university settings conduct analog studies. Unfortunately, in most universities, there are problems with respect to access to clinical patients. The professional rivalry between psychologists and psychiatrists seriously hinders progress in clinical research. Both psychiatry and psychology could profit from an association of clinical psychology with psychiatry.

The fact that so few clinical research studies are carried out may be due to the needs of researchers. An analog study into the effectiveness of treatments may be conducted within 3 months, whereas a clinical study usually takes at least 2 years. However, the output in terms of publications is the same. Thus, it is not surprising that researchers in university departments, who have to publish, prefer analog studies to clinical studies.

It has been suggested (Bandura, 1978) that analog research is more relevant than clinical research with respect to phobic individuals in the community who do not apply for treatment. However, this remains an experimental question. But even if results of analog research will prove to be relevant for numerous, yet unknown phobic individuals, this research would be socially relevant at best, which is obviously not the same as being clinically relevant. The clinical effectiveness of treatments can only be studied using clinical patients as subjects.

A clinical population as such does not warrant relevancy with respect to phobias. For instance, Dormaar and Dijkstra (1975) treated "social phobics," while for most patients social anxiety was not the main complaint. Another example of clinically irrelevant research was provided by Wolfe and Fodor (1977). They treated clinical patients who were hardly underassertive with assertive training. Obviously, the treatment of snake phobias using schizophrenics as subjects is as clinically irrelevant as using volunteer students.

It should be noted that drawing generalizations across different clinical populations is not justified. Clinical phobics are typically considered to be a homogeneous group. This uniformity myth has plagued behavioral research. Generally, outcome research has been technique rather than problem oriented. As we shall see much effort has gone into attempts to evaluate various techniques, but it is essential to note that there are important differences among various categories of phobic behavior. Therefore, conclusions cannot be generalized from one clinical population (e.g., social anxiety) to another (e.g., agoraphobia).

A related issue concerns the generalization of results of clinical trials to patients treated in routine clinical practice. It should be noted that treatment practices differ widely between patients treated in clinical trials and patients not treated in a research context. In experimental trials, patients have to follow intensive assessment procedures, including behavioral assessment and conversation with an assessor. Moreover, a functional analysis is not made, but patients are randomly assigned to treatment conditions. To what extent this might influence the clinical relevancy of this type of research is largely unknown and warrants further study.

Finally, with clinical phobics and obsessive-compulsives the phobias and obsessions often form only a part of the patient's problem. In a number of instances further treatment is indicated focusing on other problems. In our experimental trials, treatment is often continued after the experimental treatment has ended. To date, research on phobic and obsessive-compulsive patients has focused narrowly on the removal of these target behaviors (perhaps in an attempt to imitate the successful analog researchers). Thus, the relevancy of this type of research is also limited to these target behaviors.

PHOBIC DISORDERS

I

Etiology of Fears and Phobias

1. LEARNING THEORIES

The two-stage theory (Mowrer, 1960) of fear acquisition has been highly influential, and despite some serious criticisms (e.g., Bolles, 1970; Herrnstein, 1969; Rachman, 1976; Seligman & Johnston, 1973), it still plays a prominent part in current thinking of the development of fear reactions. Before embarking on the task of reviewing and evaluating the clinical value of this theory, I will give a brief summary of the theory and select a few of the major problems posed by more recent experimental work.

1.1. Two-Stage Theory

Mowrer explicitly distinguished between a classical conditioning process responsible for the conditioning of fear and an instrumental learning process responsible for the conditioning of the avoidance response. In the training procedure animals receive repeated pairings of a warning signal, for example, tone (CS), and an aversive stimulus, for example, shock (UCS). After some time the tone will acquire aversive properties and the animal will experience anxiety (CR) on tone presentation when no shock is applied. This phase of the experimental procedure represents the first stage of learning. Anxiety is attached to previously neutral cues through classical conditioning. In the second stage of learning, the animal terminates the tone by making escape responses, reducing thereby the anxiety it experiences. The termination or avoidance of aversive stimuli leads to negative reinforcement (anxiety reduction) thus strengthening the avoidance behavior. The second stage of learning involves operant conditioning. In summary, it is assumed that fear is acquired through a process of classical conditioning, and motivates avoidance behavior.

The assumption of the two-stage theory that avoidance is mediated by fear is neither supported by everyday experiences nor by experimental results. There is ample evidence that avoidance behavior can be acquired and maintained in the absence of fear as a mediating factor (Gray, 1975). A more serious difficulty for the theory is the failure of extinction to occur in avoidance responding. If the first stage of the theory is correct, it would be expected that rapid extinction of fear, and hence, of avoidance behavior should occur when the UCS is no longer present. However, there is abundant evidence that avoidance behavior, when established, is highly resistant to extinction despite the fact that conditioned fear itself must start to extinguish as soon as the shocks stop coming according to the extinction paradigm (e.g., Solomon & Wynne, 1954). Solomon and Wynne proposed that the failure to find extinction to occur could be accounted for by "partial irreversibility" and "anxiety conservation." More recently, modifications of the two-stage theory have been proposed which have a fairly substantial body of experimental evidence in their favor. These modifications involve the safety-signal theory and Herrnstein's (1969) theory of expectancies.

The safety signal theory assumes that it is not anxiety reduction *per se* but safety signals that positively reinforce avoidance behavior. This version differs from Mowrer's original theory in that it includes, besides the negative reinforcement (anxiety reduction), the onset of secondary rewarding stimuli (i.e., safety signals) as a potential source of reinforcement for avoidance behavior (Gray, 1975). Thus, the resistance to extinction of conditioned avoidance behavior is explained by the reinforcement of the avoidance behavior through the simultaneous presence of safety signals.

Research by Herrnstein and his colleagues led to another important modification of the two-stage theory (Herrnstein, 1969). In Mowrer's view avoidance behavior is maintained by the escape from the conditioned stimulus which is anxiety provoking and is thus reinforcing in its removal. Herrnstein (1969) argues that CS termination is an unnecessary feature of avoidance procedures. In a particularly well-designed study, Herrnstein and Hineline (1966) were able to demonstrate that the classically conditioned fear responses are not a requirement for the instrumental behavior. In their study, rats were offered a choice between two frequencies of being shocked at unpredictable intervals. Lever pressing resulted in the lower shock frequency but after some time control reverted to the schedule with the higher shock frequency until the animal's next lever press. Thus, animals could learn to choose being shocked at a lower frequency, rather than escape or avoid shock. Most animals learned to respond. Herrnstein (1969) argued that the reinforcement for avoidance behavior is a reduction in time of aversive stimulation. Further experiments suggested that the conditioned stimulus may function as a discriminative stimulus for the avoidance response rather than as a stimulus whose removal is inherently reinforcing as two-stage theory requires.

The alternative for the two-stage theory offered by Herrnstein is particularly interesting. First of all, it shows that avoidance behavior can be ruled by preferences rather than by anxiety *per se*. This could explain the persistence of avoidance behavior in the absence of fear as is sometimes seen in clinical cases. Further, it offers an explanation for the clinical finding that some obsessive-compulsive patients engage in anxiety inducing activities. This point will be discussed in Chapter 6.

Clinical observations have shown that the process learning theory is untenable as a uniform theory for the development of clinical phobias (Emmelkamp, 1979a). In this section studies on the development of clinical phobias will be discussed. The development and maintenance of obsessive-compulsive disorders will be dealt with in Chapter 6.

1.2. Classical Conditioning of Fear

Although the classical conditioning paradigm can be useful in the development of phobias after a traumatic experience, this paradigm is inadequate in explaining the *gradual* development of phobias, as is sometimes seen in patients. Moreover, phobic patients often do not seem to recall any traumatic experience. To date, three studies have obtained information about the acquisition of fears in analog populations (Fazio, 1972; Murray & Foote, 1979; Rimm, Janda, Lancaster, Nahl, & Dittmar, 1977). Research done by Rimm *et al.* (1977) showed that 16 out of 45 phobic volunteers reported direct experiences of a more or less traumatic nature (falling out of a tree; being attacked by a large dog). It should be noted, however, that the phobic subjects for this study were recruited from undergraduate students. The "phobias" of these subjects consisted of specific animal phobias ($n = 20$), specific situational phobias ($n = 20$), social anxiety phobias ($n = 4$), and claustrophobia ($n = 1$). Thus the bulk of the phobias were specific phobias. In a study by Fazio (1972) on the genesis of insect phobias, similar results were found. Murray and Foote (1979) studying the origins of snake phobia found very few frightening experiences with snakes in their phobic group: "There were only 3 subjects in this sample of 117 people who reported actually having been bitten by a snake and all of these were in the low fear group" (p. 491).

Most studies investigating the development of *clinical* phobias could not support a classical conditioning interpretation to account for the acquisition of fears (Buglass, Clarke, Henderson, Kreitman, & Presley, 1977; Goldstein & Chambless, 1978; Goorney & O'Connor, 1971; Lazarus, 1971; Liddell & Lyons, 1978; Solyom, Beck, Solyom, & Hugel, 1974).

Several studies have investigated the development of *agoraphobia*. Goldstein and Chambless (1978) found that the onset of the agoraphobia was marked by a conditioning event in only 4 out of 32 agoraphobics. In the Buglass *et al.* (1977) study, results showed that in only 7 out of 30 agoraphobics discrete events could be identified at the time of the onset of the agoraphobia. Also, only two of these events were "specific," meaning that the event occurred in the setting in which the patient was subsequently phobic. Essentially similar results were found by Solyom *et al.* (1974) and Bowen and Kohout (1979).

Several studies provide information with respect to the part played by classical conditioning in the acquisition of fears associated with *specific situations*. Grinker and Spiegel (1945) distinguished two types of origins in phobic reactions to combat stress. In the first type they were unable to find a traumatic experience, whereas in the second type the development of the phobia was precipitated by a definite trauma. Although their report is informative, their failure to present figures of the prevalence of both types of origins precludes more definite conclusions. Goorney and O'Connor (1971) investigated the development of anxiety associated with flying in 97 pilots and navigators of the Royal Air Force. In only 8% of their sample anxiety occurred shortly after, and were considered to be the result of, personal involvement in (or witnessing of) a flying accident. In another 13% anxiety commenced after a frightening experience during flight. If we consider both accidents and incidents as traumatic experiences in terms of classical conditioning, the acquisition of fear in only 21% of these cases could be explained along these lines. Similarly, Aitken, Lister, and Main (1981) found only 2 out of 20 phobic pilots to have experienced a significant flying accident as compared with 4 out of 20 controls.

Further negative results for a classical conditioning interpretation of fear were provided by a study by Liddell and Lyons (1978). Only 1 out of 10 patients who suffered from thunderstorm phobias reported a traumatic experience suggesting that the phobia was the result of conditioning.

To the best of my knowledge, only two studies of clinical specific phobias provide some support for the classical conditioning paradigm (Goldstein & Chambless, 1978; Lautch, 1971). In contrast with their findings on agoraphobics, Goldstein and Chambless (1978) found that the onset of the phobias of 17 out of 36 patients with specific phobias could be related to conditioning events. In the study by Lautch (1971) on dental phobic patients, clearcut conditioning events could be identified in all cases: "All 34 members of the phobic group had suffered what they deemed to have been a traumatic experience at the hands of the dentists on at least one occasion during childhood, whereas only 10 of the control group had done so" (p. 152). Further, all dental phobics except 4, who avoided dental treatment after the first traumatic experience, had a second traumatic experience as opposed to only 1 of the 34 control cases.

To summarize the studies reviewed so far, there is little evidence that classical conditioning is an important factor to account for the development of agoraphobia (Buglass *et al.*, 1977; Goldstein & Chambless, 1978; Solyom *et al.*, 1974). There is more evidence provided that classical conditioning of fear is involved in the development of specific phobias (Fazio, 1972; Goldstein & Chambless, 1978; Goorney & O'Connor, 1971; Grinker & Spiegel, 1945; Lautch, 1971; Rimm *et al.*, 1977). The latter conclusion, however, needs to be qualified by the finding that even with specific phobias in a substantial number of cases no traumatic experiences could be identified marking the onset of the phobia. Thus, it would seem reasonable to conclude that classical conditioning may play an important role in the development of specific phobias, although it is not a necessary factor.

The different findings in the Lautch (1971) study as compared to the other reports on the acquisition of specific phobias suggest that different classes of phobias may be associated with different types of origin. It is important to note that the traumatic experiences of the dental phobics were described as "physically painful, frightening, or as a feeling of an oncoming disaster." In addition, these patients were confined to the dental chair without any possibility of escape. It would seem reasonable to assume that these traumatic learning experiences (painful stimulus with no possibility of escape) are more similar to the typical classical conditioning experiments conducted in the laboratories than the traumatic experiences reported by patients with other specific phobias.

Above we concluded that classical conditioning is not a *necessary* factor in the development of specific fears. Now we may ask ourselves the question whether classical conditioning is a *sufficient* factor to account for the acquisition of specific fears. In my view, the answer is not affirmative. Other factors besides classical conditioning also seems to be necessary before a clinical phobia can develop. In the Aitken *et al.* (1981) and Lautch (1971) studies a number of control subjects reported the occurrence of traumatic experiences without developing a phobia. Obviously, one is forced to conclude that the presentation of a similar UCS was insufficient to produce conditioned fear in the latter cases. Vicarious learning could help to explain the different reactions of both types of subjects. Lautch found a history of an exaggerated fear of dental treatment among a number of family members of dental phobics as compared to controls. In addition, personality variables might also be predisposing factors for fear conditioning to occur. The dental phobics were found to be more neurotic and less extraverted than the controls. In contrast, Aitken *et al.* (1981) did not find any difference in personality tests between phobics and controls, though there were differences in skin conductance.

Although the reports reviewed above are suggestive, one should be careful with an interpretation, since such case reports are retrospective in nature. The question arises whether patients can recall anything specific related to the onset of the phobia many years later. We ourselves have repeatedly found that patients, who at first were unable to recall a traumatic event during the onset of the phobia, suddenly did report on such incidents during treatment. Similar experiences were reported by Boulougouris and Bassiakos (1973) and Marks, Viswanathan, Lipsedge, and Gardner (1972). Goldstein and Chambless (1978) point out that especially agoraphobics are unable to connect emotional responses to causative factors accurately.

A minimum requirement of the classical conditioning paradigm is that not only should a traumatic experience be identified, but also that the subject should have experienced pain or anxiety in the situation that subsequently led to his phobia. Unfortunately most studies reported on above did not provide data with respect to this point. Thus, the occurrence of traumatic incidents in the history of a phobic patient, which is in some way related to the development of the phobia, is by itself insufficient evidence that classical conditioning can be held responsible for the acquisition of fear.

Most damaging for the classical conditioning of the fear paradigm is the repeated failure to condition phobias. As early as 1920, Watson and Rayner succeeded in changing a healthy 11-months-old baby (little Albert) into a neurotic one by classical conditioning. The baby "was healthy from birth and one of the best developed youngsters ever brought to the hospital." The experimental procedure consisted of pairings of presentations of a white rat (CS) with a loud sound (UCS). The sound used was that made by striking a hammer on a suspended steel bar, a sound that had previously been found to produce fear and crying in Albert. The rat did not invoke fear before the start of the experiment. After seven joint stimulations the rat presented without sound led to anxiety: "The instant the rat was shown the baby began to cry. Almost instantly he turned sharply to the left, fell over on left side, roused himself on all fours and began to crawl away so rapidly that he was caught with difficulty before reaching the edge of the table." Further, the experimenters were able to demonstrate generalization of fear to previously neutral objects as a dog, fur coat, and cotton wool. Little Albert played an equally prominent role in the behavioral theories of fear development as did "little Hans" (Freud, 1909a) in the psychoanalytic theory.

Unfortunately, contrary to the results of the study by Watson and Rayner (1920) both Bregman (1934) and English (1929) failed to condition fear in infants. Studies done on the emotional response after aversion therapy are also relevant in this respect. Hallam and Rachman (1976) have pointed out that aversion therapy did not result in conditioned fear reactions after repeated conditioning trials. The usual outcome of the clinical application of aversion therapy is indifference to the CS rather than anxiety.

Several studies provide further evidence that traumatic experiences per se do not necessarily lead to the acquisition of fear. For example, a substantial number of the control subjects in the Lautch (1971) study failed to acquire dental fears despite the occurrence of a traumatic dental experience. Similarly, Aitken et al. (1981) and Goorney (1970) found that a number of aircrew had been involved in flying accidents without developing fears or phobias.

Further evidence indicating that traumatic experiences do not necessarily lead to conditioning of fears comes from studies of exposure to aerial bombardments, natural disasters, and internment in German concentration camps in World War II. Wilson (1942) reported on the psychiatric casualties following aerial bombardment. Of the 700 civilians who needed help at a first-aid post, only 6 required psychiatric hospital treatment. Thus, although these 700 persons had undergone a serious traumatic learning experience involving pain and anxiety, this did not lead to the acquisition of phobias in most cases. Lewis (1942) studied the increase in "neurotic illness" as a result of air raids in England. Interestingly, no striking increase was found. In study of the consequences of internment in German concentration camps, Matussek, Grigat, Haiböck, Halbach, Kemmler, Mantell, Triebel, Vardy, and Wedel (1971) found that "anxiety states" were reported by approximately 20% of the former victims (p. 46). Although 20% is still a substantial number, the finding that the extremely traumatic learning experiences in the Nazi concentration camps did not lead to more phobic reactions poses a serious problem for the classical conditioning interpretation of fear. Finally, an investigation of the psychological results of the experience of a cyclone (Parker, 1977) revealed that only 2 out of 34 evacuees had developed a storm phobia one year later.

In summary, the failure to condition fear in humans in a laboratory and the relatively low frequency of the occurrence of fears and phobias after traumatic learning experiences (aerial bombardments, internment, and natural disasters) indicate that classical conditioning is not a sufficient factor to account for the development of human fears and phobias.

1.3. Vicarious Learning

In an attempt to explain the development of fears that are not associated with traumatic learning experiences, one might argue that in these cases fears are acquired through vicarious learning. According to this paradigm, observing others experiencing anxiety in specific situations might lead to fear of those situations for the observer.

Indirect evidence in favor of a vicarious learning interpretation for the acquisition of phobias comes from studies demonstrating that children often share the fears of their parents. Particularly, mothers may be an important etiological factor in children's fears. The results of various older studies into the association between children's fears and the fears of their mothers are equivocal. Hagman (1932) studied the fears of 2–6-year-old children and found that fears were associated in mother and child. There was a correlation of .67 between similar fears of mother and child. However, the information he gathered might have been biased, since he used interviews with the mothers as his source of data. Lapouse and Monk (1959) studied the fears of children ranging from 8–12 years old and found mothers often underreporting fears of their children. No relationship between the fears of mother and child was found. Other data that supported a vicarious learning interpretation of fear were provided by Bandura and Menlove (1968). These authors reported a higher incidence of dog phobia in parents of children who were afraid of dogs than in parents of children without a dog phobia.

Recently, Windheuser (1977) attempted to investigate the relative contribution of vicarious learning and personality in the development of children's phobias. Phobic children and their mothers were compared with nonphobic children and their mothers. All children (ranging in age from 6 to 13) were clients of a child guidance counseling center. The phobias of the children consisted mainly of fears of animals, fears of medical and dental treatment, and fears of social situations. Both general anxiety and fears were assessed using similar questionnaires for mother and child. Results revealed that mothers of phobic children exceeded the mothers of nonphobic children significantly in the extent of their general anxiety as measured by the Manifest Anxiety Scale (Taylor, 1953). In addition, the analysis of the Fear Survey Schedule revealed a highly significant conformity of fears reported by mother and child in the phobic group. The association between the mother's and the child's fears was less pronounced in the nonphobic group. Taken together, these data suggest that vicarious learning is facilitated by a relatively high level of general anxiety in mother and child.

In summary, several studies indicate that mothers and children are frequently fearful of the same situation, which can be considered to support a vicarious learning interpretation of the etiology of children's fears. On the other hand, it should be noted that a relationship between fears of mother and child can also be the result of other processes than vicarious learning, for example, informational processes, genetic influences, or similar traumatic experiences.

Other indirect evidence in favor of the vicarious transmission of fear comes from retrospective patient reports. Several investigators of war neurosis found that some fears brought on by war experiences were caused by observing accidents of other soldiers (Grinker & Spiegel, 1945; Kipper, 1977). Kipper, in analyzing the circumstances surrounding the development of fears in soldiers in the Yom Kippur War, identified three sets of conditions under which these fears were acquired. The first set of conditions involved a sudden realization of danger. In the second group, fears developed "more or less accidentally." A third group of conditions "involved fears acquired vicariously while observing the unfortunate fate of fellow soldiers" (p. 218). Unfortunately, no figures were presented to indicate the percentage of cases in which vicarious learning might have been involved. Goorney and O'Connor (1971) studying anxiety associated with flying among the Royal Air Force aircrew in peacetime found that vicarious learning was involved in only a very few cases.

The studies by Fazio (1972) and Rimm et al. (1977) provide further evidence that vicarious learning might be responsible for the acquisition of fears in only a few cases: 13% of the subjects with an insect phobia (Fazio, 1972) and 7% of the subjects with other specific phobias (Rimm et al., 1977) reported vicarious learning experiences. Further, the Murray and Foote (1979) study presents "only marginal evidence of vicarious experiences in the acquisition of fear of snakes" (p. 491). Finally, in the Lautch (1971) study, a significant number of family members of dental phobics were found to have dental fears, which suggests that modeling might have been involved, although other processes may account equally for this finding.

My own clinical experience suggests that modeling plays a minor part in the development of clinical phobias. I cannot remember having met one agoraphobic patient who became phobic after seeing another individual being anxious while walking on the street or visiting supermarkets. However, in some socially anxious patients the fears might be, at least partially, the result of vicarious learning. To give an example of one such case, an orthodox religious patient became socially anxious after having observed her father publicly confessing a sin in a full church. Similarly, watching a person who is very anxious while giving a speech might lead to speech anxiety in the observer. There is also some clinical evidence indicating that vicarious learning plays a part in the development of obsessive-compulsive behavior.

Having shown that vicarious learning plays only a minor part in the development of clinical phobias, we may ask ourselves what evidence does support the proposition of Rachman (1977) that fears can be acquired through the transmission of information and instruction? This model of fear acquisition has the great advantage over two-stage theory and vicarious learning theory in that it provides a basis for explaining the development of fear in individuals who neither experienced a traumatic event nor observed this occurring to others. The findings of the study by Lautch (1971) cited previously can perhaps better be interpreted along this line than in terms of vicarious learning. Although there are some difficulties in interpreting the Lautch data, since no detailed information is provided, it seems unlikely that the dental phobics actually observed their family members undergoing dental treatment. It seems plausible that in most cases information about the anxiety was given directly to the dental phobic. In this regard, it is of some interest to note that a number of phobic patients have close relatives with similar problems. Marks and Herst (1970) found that 17% of phobics had family members with similar phobias. Further, 3 out of 10 thunderstorm phobics reported having family members with a history of similar excessive fears (Liddell & Lyons, 1978). While this may be taken to indicate that observational learning or informational processes are involved, genetic influences cannot be ruled out. How informational processes can influence the development of a phobia is clearly illustrated by the case of one of our agoraphobic patients. The mother of this patient suffered from some heart disease which did not upset the daughter very much. However, when the mother was told by her physician that she had better stay at home in order to prevent a heart attack, her daughter feared that she herself would die of a heart disease when walking outside, which resulted in a severe agoraphobia.

While there is some clinical evidence in support of the idea that informational processes may influence the development of phobias, the contribution of these processes is probably small. It seems to make more sense to hold that informational processes play a more dominant role in the acquisition of normal fears. According to Rachman (1977), "It is probable that informational and instructional processes provide the basis for most of our commonly encountered fears of every day life" (p. 384). Information-giving might be very important, particularly in the child's earliest years. Rachman speculated that some individuals are particularly prone to acquire fears by conditioning, while others acquire fears by transmission of information or vicarious learning. To date, no experimental evidence is available to support this position.

2. COGNITIVE FACTORS

Other influential theories concerning phobic behavior have been proposed by cognitively oriented therapists. In their view anxiety reactions are mediated by faulty cognitions or anxiety inducing self-instructions.

2.1. Negative Self-Statements and Irrational Beliefs

Two types of faulty thinking have been investigated: (a) negative self-statements and (b) irrational beliefs. Studies investigating the influence of self-instructions on anxiety indicated that negative self-statements may enhance arousal (May & Johnson, 1973; Rimm & Litvak, 1969; Rogers & Craighead, 1977; Russell & Brandsma, 1974). However, in a study with phobic subjects, Rimm et al. (1977) found that only half of the subjects reported, in vivo, thoughts preceding fear in the phobic situations. According to the cognitive theory, the thoughts should always precede the fear.

Irrational thinking is identified with Ellis (1962) who stated that phobics have a tendency to think irrationally and that these irrational beliefs produce their anxiety reactions. Several studies indicate that irrational beliefs are related to phobic anxiety (Galassi, Frierson, & Sharer, 1981; Golden, 1981; Goldfried & Sobocinski, 1975; Gormally, Sipps, Raphael, Edwin, & Varvil-Weld, 1981; Rimm et al., 1977). While the results of these studies might indicate that such irrational beliefs are causally linked to anxiety evocation, it is equally plausible that increased emotional arousal in certain situations may sensitize individuals to certain irrational expectancies (Goldfried & Sobocinski, 1975). The studies reviewed so far are of questionable relevance to clinical phobias, because none of these studies investigated the thoughts of phobic *patients*.

Recently, Sutton-Simon and Goldfried (1979) reported a study involving patients, although not necessarily phobic, who requested psychotherapy at a community clinic. In this study the relationship between two types of faulty thinking (irrational beliefs vs. negative self-statements) on the one hand and type of phobia (social anxiety vs. acrophobia) on the other was investigated. Results showed that social anxiety was correlated with irrational thinking only, while acrophobia was correlated with both types of faulty thinking.

2.2. Attribution Theory

Another influential theory that may be of importance to the etiology of phobias is the attribution theory of Schachter. Schachter and his colleague (Schachter & Singer, 1962) demonstrated that a person's interpretation of the nature of his bodily state of arousal can be modified by the explanations given to him by instructions. This raises the possibility that a person's mislabeling of his state of arousal may lead to the development of phobic reactions. Throughout this chapter various examples will be offered to illustrate that the cognitive response given to an internal reaction may account for the development of phobias.

3. BIOLOGICAL THEORIES

3.1. Preparedness

The assumption of equal conditionability as originally postulated in the conditioning theory of fear acquisition seems untenable. According to classical conditioning theory, any stimulus that is paired with an unconditioned stimulus that invokes pain or anxiety should result in a conditioned emotional reaction after a number of pairings. However, this assumption is no longer adequately defensible. Consider, for example, experiments of a kind in which one has attempted to condition fear in infants. Several such experiments have been reported and they show that the nature of the conditioned stimulus is of paramount importance for conditioning of fear to occur. English (1929) was unable to condition fear to a wooden toy duck but he succeeded in producing conditioned fear to a stuffed black cat. Bregman (1934) also failed to condition fear in infants. In this study the conditioned stimuli consisted of wooden shapes and colored cloths. Taken together, the variable results of the studies by Bregman (1934), English (1929), and Watson and Rayner (1920) seem to indicate that fears might be much more easily conditioned to animals and furry objects than to wooden objects, shapes, and cloths. This finding suggests that there might be an innate basis for some fear development. Marks (1969, 1977) suggested the concept of "prepotency" of certain stimuli to explain the development of some human phobias:

> Certain stimuli that do not spontaneously arouse fear may have a latent tendency to elicit it, with the result that the subject will learn to fear these stimuli much more quickly than others, and if the subject is already mildly afraid these stimuli can intensify the fear. (Marks, 1969, p. 15)

Along similar lines, Seligman (1971) views phobias as instances of highly "prepared" learning (Seligman, 1970; Seligman & Hager, 1972). According to Seligman the majority of clinical phobias concerns objects of natural importance to the survival of the species. In his view evolution has preprogrammed the human species to acquire phobias easily for potentially dangerous situations. Such prepared learning is selective, highly resistant to extinction, probably noncognitive, and can be acquired in one trial.

In recent years Öhman and his colleagues (Öhman, 1979; Öhman, Fredrikson, & Hugdahl, 1978) have tested the preparedness theory experimentally. These experiments will be discussed in some detail.

In their experiments normal nonphobic college students were conditioned to visual slides (CS) by means of electric shocks or loud noises as the UCS. To test the hypothesis that phobias comprise a nonarbitrary set of objects, they compared different conditioned stimuli: fear-relevant or potentially phobic stimuli (pictures of spiders or snakes) versus fear-irrelevant or neutral stimuli (pictures of flowers or mushrooms). It was found that conditioned electrodermal responses to fear-relevant stimuli showed much higher resistance to extinction than responses conditioned to neutral stimuli (Fredrikson, Hugdahl, & Öhman, 1976; Öhman, Eriksson, & Olofsson, 1975; Öhman, Erixon, & Löfberg, 1975; Öhman, Fredrikson, Hugdahl, & Rimmö, 1976). These findings support the preparedness theory. The effect of the stimulus content variable, however, was less clear cut during the acquisition phase.

In another experiment a different set of stimuli was used (Öhman & Dimberg, 1979). It was predicted that facial expression (angry vs. happy faces) would differ widely in conditionability with regard to an aversive electric shock (UCS). The slides of angry faces produced effects similar to those of the fear-relevant stimuli in the earlier experiments, whereas slides of neutral and happy faces were similar in effect to the previous neutral stimuli.

In a further experiment (Hodes, Öhman, & Lang, 1979) (1) "evolutionary" fear-relevant stimuli (snakes and spider), (2) "nonevolutionary" fear-relevant stimuli (revolvers and rifles), and (3) neutral stimuli (household objects) were used as the conditioned stimuli. As the preparedness theory would predict, it was found that the group with the evolutionary fear-relevant stimuli showed superior resistance to extinction than the other two groups. Essentially similar results were found by Hugdahl and Kärker (1981) who used electric outlets as fear-relevant stimuli.

In summary, the experiments so far reviewed clearly demonstrate that the stimulus content variable plays a major role with respect to resistance to extinction and far less so with respect to the acquisition phase, thus partially supporting the preparedness theory. Further evidence in favor of the preparedness theory was found in an experiment by Hugdahl and Öhman (1977). Instructions that no more shocks would be presented after the acquisition phase had a clear effect in the group with the neutral conditioned stimulus, but for the group with the fear-relevant stimulus there were no significant differences between the informed and noninformed groups during extinction. Thus, the subjects exposed to fear-relevant CS continued to respond although they knew that no more shocks would be presented. Further experiments using verbal threats (Hygge & Öhman, 1976) and modeling (Hygge & Öhman, 1976) have shown similar results, thus indicating that threat and a phobic model may function similar to the direct aversive stimuli used in the other experiments.

Despite the bulk of evidence in favor of preparedness provided by Öhman and his colleagues, the results of these studies need to be qualified in several ways. The studies in support of the preparedness theory have been conducted by one research group only. Cross-validation of this theory by other workers would be valuable, especially since the results of at least two studies (Reiss & McNally, 1980; Eelen, personal communication) were inconsistent with preparedness theory. Further, Carr (1979) has criticized the conditioned stimuli used in the studies by Öhman. He holds that the type of stimuli used differs in respects other than their evolutionary significance: "Snakes and flowers are drawn from two quite disparate classes of stimuli, namely animate and inanimate, and they differ greatly in terms of familiarity and likely frequency of previous unreinforced exposure" (p. 219). Although Öhman provides much evidence in support of the role of preparedness in laboratory fear conditioning, it is clearly a very bold claim to generalize these findings to human phobias. First, all subjects in their experiments were normal nonphobic college students. In the second place, the degree of aversiveness in their studies was minimal; the intensity of the aversive stimulus was decided by the subject. In the third place, subjects could withdraw from the experiment at any time. Thus, subjects had a high degree of control over the situation which is in sharp contrast with the development of clinical phobias, in which the feeling of loss of control might be of paramount importance. Last but not least, only psychophysiological data were used as the dependent variable. Phobic anxiety is usually conceptualized as three different systems: verbal reports, physiological responses, and overt behavior (Lang, 1971). These systems do not always covary (Rachman & Hodgson, 1974; Hodgson & Rachman, 1974). Further experiments should use self-report and behavioral data in addition to psychophysiological data as dependent variables.

What implications does the preparedness theory have for the *treatment* of clinical phobias? Rachman and Seligman (1976) reported on two clinical cases of phobias—a plant phobia and a phobia of brown things—which were clearly unprepared (lack of biological significance, rarity, and gradual acquisition) but both highly resistant to extinction. Rachman and Seligman (1976) argued that "unprepared phobias that reach the clinic may prove to be highly intractable to the gamut of behavior therapy, whereas behavior therapy may well be the treatment of choice for prepared phobias" (p. 338). De Silva, Rachman, and Seligman (1977) rated the preparedness of the content of phobias and obsessions of phobic and obsessive-compulsive cases. The majority of phobias was prepared. However, preparedness was *not* related to therapeutic outcome, which seriously weakens the clinical usefulness of the concept of preparedness. However, this study was retrospective; a controlled prospective study should be carried out before more definite conclusions can be drawn with respect to the usefulness of the preparedness theory and its implication for clinical phobias.

3.2. Genetic Factors

Studies investigating the contribution of a genetic component to anxiety have followed two strategies. The first type of studies has sought to investigate whether there is a higher family prevalence of anxiety in relatives than expected by chance. The second type of studies has compared anxiety in monozygotic (identical) and dizygotic (fraternal) twins. Studies into the family prevalence of anxiety generally have found first and second degree relatives of anxious patients to be at higher risk for anxiety neurosis than controls (e.g., Pauls, Crowe, & Noyes, 1979; Pauls, Noyes, & Crowe, 1979).

Studies investigating the family prevalence of phobic disorders provided inconclusive results. Buglass *et al.* (1977) found no striking difference between relatives of phobics and relatives of controls with respect to the frequency of phobic disorders. In contrast, in the Solyom *et al.* (1974) study, the relatives of phobics had a higher frequency of phobic disorders than did control relatives.

Results of the family studies have to be qualified. First, such studies provide only meager evidence of a genetic predisposition since environmental factors can account equally well for the differences found. Further, there is a serious risk of errors, especially overdiagnosis, when doing family studies in an unblind fashion (Cloninger, Martin, Clayton, & Guze, 1981). Therefore, the present discussion will confine its scope to a review of twin studies.

If it is observed that monozygotic twins are more similar than dizygotic twins with regard to anxiety, it is usually considered to be evidence of a genetic contribution, while differences in dizygotic twins generally are considered to be the result of differences in environmental factors. However, higher concordance in monozygotic twins may be caused by environmental factors as well. Social learning might be more similar for monozygotic twins than for dizygotic twins. Studies of monozygotic twins raised apart would provide more valuable data but these studies have not been conducted.

Several studies found a higher concordance in anxiety for monozygotic twins as compared to dizygotic twins (e.g., Slater & Shields, 1969; Young, Fenton, & Lader, 1971). Two studies are especially important with respect to a genetic contribution to phobias and will be discussed in some detail. In the first study (Young *et al.*, 1971) monozygotic ($n = 17$) and dizygotic ($n = 15$) twins completed the Middlesex Hospital Questionnaire (MHQ). Results indicated that monozygotics were more alike than dizygotics on all three anxiety subtests of the MHQ. The intraclass correlation coefficients among the monozygotic twins for the free floating anxiety, phobic anxiety, and somatic concomitants of anxiety were .56, .60 and .44, respectively, and .12, −.12 and −.06 for the dizygotic twins respectively. Thus, the results of this study suggest that fears might be influenced by hereditary factors.

In a more recent study (Torgersen, 1979) 50 monozygotic and 49 dizygotic pairs were compared with respect to their responses to a phobic fear questionnaire. Five factors resulted: (1) agoraphobia, (2) small animal phobias, (3) mutilation fears, (4) social anxiety, and (5) mixed fears (e.g., claustrophobia, heights, bridges). It was shown that monozygotic twins more often feared the same kind of situations than dizygotic twins. Taken together, this study demonstrated that the strength and the content of phobic fears, apart from agoraphobic fears, might be influenced by hereditary factors.

Results of these studies should be interpreted cautiously. The subjects in both the Young *et al.* (1971) and Torgersen (1979) studies consisted of a relatively unselected sample. Thus, strictly speaking, the studies provide some support for a genetic contribution to fears in normals rather than demonstrating a hereditary influence in clinical phobias. Further, it should be recalled that environmental factors cannot be ruled out.

3.3. Arousal and Fear Conditioning

In the classical conditioning theory of fear acquisition, the importance of the state of the organism is largely neglected. Studies conducted by Lader and his coworkers (Lader, 1967; Lader & Wing, 1966) indicated that there are important differences in the level of arousal of various subgroups of anxious and phobic patients. The series of studies demonstrated that agoraphobics and social anxious patients show only slightly less spontaneous skin conductance fluctuations than do patients with anxiety states. Specific phobics showed much less spontaneous fluctuations and their reaction was more or less comparable to that of normals. Another experimental finding was that patients with anxiety states, agoraphobics, and social anxious patients showed a slow rate of habituation to tones, while specific phobics and normals habituated rapidly. In discussing the results of these studies, Lader and Mathews (1968) suggested an interaction between level of arousal and conditioning. In the case of agoraphobic and social phobic patients the chronic state of overarousal is thought to be of greater importance than conditioning of anxiety to environmental stimuli, while in the case of specific phobics conditioning is proposed to be of more importance. Thus, Lader and Mathews ascribe a causative role to the high level of arousal found in agoraphobic and social anxious patients. As yet, we have little notion about the nature of the chronic state of overarousal. Although the primary pathology might be seen as a chronic state of overarousal, an alternate way of dealing with the problem would be to view the high arousal level as the result of the phobia. Although prospective studies might be particularly useful to investigate whether overarousal gives rise to agoraphobia and social anxiety or vice versa, there are inevitable doubts about the feasibility of such studies.

There is some evidence that arousal level might influence the efficiency of conditioning. Beech and his colleagues (Beech & Perigault, 1974; Asso & Beech, 1975; Vila & Beech, 1977, 1978) have argued that the state of the organism may play an important role in acquisition and extinction of phobic and obsessive-compulsive behavior. They predicted that individuals with a high level of adverse emotional arousal would show enhanced efficiency in acquiring a conditioned response to a noxious stimulus. Since fluctuations in level of arousal are characteristic of the menstrual cycle, it was hypothesized that premenstrually there would be greater efficiency in the acquisition of a conditioned response than intermenstrually. The findings of several experiments (Asso & Beech, 1975; Vila & Beech, 1977, 1978) show that conditioned responses are more readily acquired premenstrually than intermenstrually. The findings from the Asso and Beech (1975) study further indicate that phobic patients show an even greater vulnerability than normal controls.

A study by Hughdahl, Fredrikson, and Öhman (1977) demonstrates the importance of arousability in the acquisition of phobias. The results of their experiment suggest that individuals with a habitual high-arousal level are more susceptible to acquire phobias than are persons with low-arousal levels. Furthermore, Hugdahl *et al.* (1977) postulate that the effects of "arousability" and "preparedness" are additive: Evolutionary fear-relevant stimuli further increase an already high-arousal level.

3.4. Physical Factors

3.4.1. Hyperventilation

Hyperventilation which can result in palpitations, chest pains, sweating, "light headedness", neuromuscular irritability, and paraesthesia (Weimann, 1968) may be related to the onset of phobias. The main controversy over the etiology of the hyperventilation syndrome is whether the hyperventilation is a response to anxiety or a bad breathing habit with secondary production of anxiety (Hill, 1979; Pfeffer, 1978). Several studies (e.g., Garssen, 1980) indicate that stress may produce hyperventilation although only to a mild degree in normal subjects. Garssen (1980) reviewed the literature in this field and found a discrepancy between $PACO_2$ values generally found in normal subjects under stress and values found in patients with the hyperventilation syndrome, the values of the latter being much lower. It seems reasonable to assume that persons with a bad breathing habit, who have lowered $PACO_2$ values, are inclined to hyperventilate when confronted with stressful life events or when emotionally aroused. The concept of the vicious-circle effect may be helpful to understand the course of the hyperventilation after the first hyperventilation attack. According to Lachman (1972), once initiated, a psychosomatic event may produce stimuli that lead to reactions that rearouse or intensify the psychosomatic event and so on. A hyperventilation attack is usually accompanied with severe anxiety that by itself may provoke hyperventilation in the future. The vicious circle thus created is depicted in Figure 2.

There is probably a spectrum of phobic reactions associated with hyperventilation. At the one end are patients who, after a hyperventilation attack in a situation (e.g., store or being alone), avoid such situations. In the future this eventually may result in agoraphobia. Other persons do not avoid situations in which the hyperventilation attack occurred but start ruminating about diseases that may underlie their symptoms (e.g., heart disease, cancer). This might lead to illness phobias. Further, in a minority of social-anxious patients the onset of the phobia seems to be related to a hyperventilation attack. If a person gets a hyperventilation attack in front of others, he may start worrying about looking foolish which might lead to anxiety and avoidance of social situations.

In summary, it is proposed here that some persons are predisposed to react with hyperventilation when confronted with stress or anxiety. It is further suggested that anxiety associated with hyperventilation produces subsequent hyperventilation attacks and avoidance of situations in which persons anticipate that hyperventilation might occur.

3.4.2. Mitral Valve Prolapse Syndrome

There is now a growing body of evidence that mitral valve prolapse syndrome (MVPS) is related to anxiety neurosis (e.g., Crowe, Pauls, Venkatesh, Van Valkenburg, Noyes, Martins, & Kerber, 1979; Pariser, Pinta, & Jones, 1978). Mitral valve prolapse syndrome is a cardiological disease with symptoms similar to those of anxiety neurosis (e.g., chest pain, fatigue, dyspnea, palpitations, tachycardia, and anxiety).

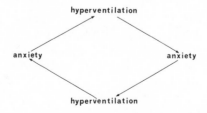

Figure 2. Vicious circle for hyperventilation development.

Kantor, Zitrin, and Zeldis (1980) suggested that MVPS might be related to agoraphobia. Female agoraphobics who experienced palpitations as a prominent part of their panic attacks and controls underwent a cardiac examination. Results of the study indicated that MVPS occurred significantly more frequently in agoraphobic women than in controls. Kantor *et al.* suggest that the palpitations and dyspnea associated with MVPS can lead to panic attacks and to agoraphobia: "Some patients respond to MVPS symptoms with fear and pronounced sympathetic arousal. This reaction further aggravates the symptoms by establishing a feedback loop" (p. 468). Besides agoraphobia, MVPS might be an equally important causative agent with illness phobias, particularly cardiac neurosis.

Alternatively, it could be argued that some phobics develop MVPS as a result of the stress on their heart caused by anxiety. It is important to note that not all MVPS patients develop anxiety or phobic reactions. MVPS is a common disorder occurring in about 10% of the population (Crowe *et al.*, 1979). Kane, Woerner, Zeldis, Kramer, and Saravay (1981) found that the majority of individuals with MVPS do not have phobic disorders or panic attacks which indicates that other factors are also important.

3.4.3. Menstrual Cycle

It is now a well established finding that many women do show changes in affect related to the premenstrual and the menstrual phases. After a thorough review of studies in this field Dennerstein and Burrows (1979) concluded:

> The majority of studies have found cyclical changes for negative moods. Irritability, restlessness, anxiety, tension, migraine, sleep disturbance, fatigue, impaired concentration, depression, and increased neurotic conflicts were reported more frequently during the premenstrual and menstrual weeks. (p. 84)

Further, in a study investigating the relationship between the menstrual cycle and hyperventilation, it was found that overbreathing in vulnerable periods of the menstrual cycle is more likely to cause symptoms than at other times (Damas-Mora, Davies, Taylor, & Jenner, 1980). These results, combined with the finding of Beech and his colleagues that women are particularly susceptible to acquire fears premenstrually, suggest that the menstrual cycle may play a part in the acquisition of phobias, since women are more vulnerable in particular phases of the cycle. Agoraphobics often experience exacerbation of the phobia during the premenstrual week, which is in keeping with this suggestion.

Although it is conceivable that the changes in arousal affect conditionability as suggested by the studies by Beech and his colleagues, an interpretation in terms of attribution theory seems also plausible. According to Schachter and Singer (1962) persons who are emotionally aroused will search in the environment stimuli that may "explain" their arousal, if they have no good immediate explanation themselves.

In line with attribution theory it is proposed that women may attribute the experienced physiological arousal that is caused by the menstrual cycle to environmental stimuli.

4. OTHER THEORETICAL CONTRIBUTIONS

4.1. Space Perception and Crowding

Recent developments in environmental psychology suggest that physical aspects of the environment may be related to the experience of anxiety and avoidance in normals. Studies on space perception and crowding may be of some relevance with respect to the development of agoraphobia, claustrophobia, and social anxiety. MacNab, Nieuwenhuijse, Jansweijer, and Kuiper (1978) had agoraphobic patients and normals judge perspective drawings depicting architectural spaces. They found that the variably perceived openness-enclosure of space was related to experienced anxiety both in normal subjects and agoraphobics: "the stronger the feeling of enclosure, the stronger are the feelings of displeasure, insecurity, suffocation" (p. 387). This finding suggests that the anxiety experienced by agoraphobics and claustrophobics may be related to experiences that are also aversive in normals.

In recent years there has been a growing interest in the effects of crowding on humans. Although most studies in this area indicate a link between crowding and the occurrence of aggressive behavior, there is also some evidence that crowding may lead to anxiety and social withdrawal (e.g., Mathews, Paulus, & Baron, 1979).

Gochman and Keating (1980) proposed an arousal–attribution model to explain the effects of crowding. They hypothesized that crowding could be mistakenly identified as the cause of noncrowding induced arousal: "the plausibility of a crowding attribution is enhanced by the widely held cultural belief that density negatively affects behavior. Thus, if the density level is high enough to ensure its relative salience, a crowding attribution provides a plausible explanation for the individual's arousal" (p. 159). Thus Gochman and Keating suggested that in crowded situations people may experience arousal that is in fact caused by factors unrelated to the density level. If the person is unaware of the actual source of arousal, then the arousal may erroneously be attributed to negative aspects of the crowded situation. This hypothesis was tested in a series of laboratory and field studies. The results of these studies provided support for the hypothesis that factors varying independently of density affect attributions to crowding.

The reader may wonder what these studies have to do with the development of clinical phobias. To illustrate the potential importance of these studies let me give a hypothetical example of how such attributions might affect phobic behavior. A woman who is in a state of marital distress experiences as a result of the marital conflict emotional arousal while shopping in a supermarket. According to the arousal–attribution model it is quite plausible that she attributes her arousal to the crowded supermarket rather than to her unhappy marriage. If this attribution is successful, then she will avoid supermarkets and other crowded areas in the future in order to prevent anxiety. Blaming crowding may provide a more acceptable explanation for the experienced arousal than facing her marital unhappiness and the possibility of a divorce. In my view, such misattribution may account for the development of agoraphobia in a number of cases.

4.2. Interpersonal Conflict

In my opinion (Emmelkamp, 1980a) behavioral interpretations of phobic behavior have been rather naive and can offer at best only a partial explanation of the condition. In addition to conditioning and cognitive factors, we have to search for other factors as well. A more comprehensive theory of phobia development should take into account the role of interpersonal conflicts. Further, it is suggested that the client's system might play an important part in the strengthening of the phobic behavior.

Several authors (e.g., Fry, 1962; Webster, 1953) suggested that partners of phobic patients are psychologically abnormal or do have phobic symptoms themselves. Two theories have been proposed to account for this finding—those of assortative mating and pathogenic interaction. The theory of assortative mating holds that persons of similar "constitution" are likely to marry each other. The theory of pathogenic interaction asserts that husbands and wives reciprocally influence one another. Controlled studies that have been conducted to test these theories have produced equivocal results. Agulnik (1970) studied psychological characteristics of phobic patients and their spouses and found no evidence that the partners of phobic patients were neurotic. Likewise, Buglass et al. (1977) found no evidence for assortative mating. Hafner (1977) however did find some evidence for assortative mating.

More has been written about the interpersonal problems of phobics, particularly agoraphobics. Several authors have stressed the importance of interpersonal conflict in the development of the phobic symptoms (Emmelkamp, 1979; Goldstein, 1973; Goldstein & Chambless, 1978; Goodstein & Swift, 1977; Hand & Lamontagne, 1976). Goldstein (1973) reported that 16 of 20 female agoraphobic patients felt strong urges to escape their relationship but were unable to do so at the time of the onset of the phobia. In his view, agoraphobics wish to flee the marriage, but cannot because of their fears of being alone. He proposed that the phobic symptoms are the result of psychological avoidance behavior in conflict situations that seem insolvable. In a subsequent study (Goldstein & Chambless, 1978) some evidence was provided that an agoraphobia onset occurs during times of high interpersonal conflict. Buglass *et al.* (1977) comparing family characteristics of agoraphobic couples and controls showed the groups to be strikingly similar. In their study couples were questioned about decision making. There was *no* significant difference between the two groups in any of the areas of decision making. Furthermore, ratings were made for two independent dimensions of the interactions between husband and wife during the interview: (1) assertion-compliance, and (2) affection-dislike. There was little difference between the assertion and affection scores of phobic and control wives. The husbands of phobics were somewhat less assertive than the husbands of controls. Although this study could not demonstrate differences in the marital relationship between phobic couples and controls, this should not be taken to indicate that interpersonal problems might not have played a part at the time of the onset of the phobia.

Finally the study by Aitken *et al.* (1981) is of some importance. They investigated whether marital conflicts were related to the development of flying phobia in aircrew. Seventy-five percent of the phobic group in contrast to 40% of controls had experienced marital or sexual problems. Moreover, the marital problems were rated as more severe in the phobic group.

In summary, there is some evidence that interpersonal conflict may lead to the development of phobias. A great deal of careful research has to be done in this area before more definite conclusions can be made pertaining to the part played by interpersonal conflicts.

4.3. Dependency

Several authors (e.g., Andrews, 1966) suggested that phobic persons are very dependent and it has been suggested that a parental overprotective concern for the child that is not necessarily affectionate may account for the development of phobias. (Bianchi, 1971; Terhune, 1949; Tucker,

1956; Webster, 1953). In a thought provoking paper, Fodor (1974) suggested that agoraphobia may be considered as a caricature of the female role in our western society. She holds that socialization, sex-role stereotyping, and sex-role conflict are responsible for the development of agoraphobia in women. Agoraphobia develops because the patients in infancy were reinforced for stereotypical female behavior (i.e., helplessness and dependency). In her view, interpersonal trappedness, particularly the feelings of being dominated with no outlet for assertion, might enhance the tendency to develop agoraphobia. As soon as a patient develops her symptoms, these behaviors are then reinforced by significant others in the woman's life because of her sex role.

Fodor's sex-role theory of agoraphobia is in keeping with the finding that most agoraphobics are females. However, the preponderance of female agoraphobics can also be explained by theories other than the "sex-role theory." First, Mitral Valve Prolapse Syndrome is more frequently found among women than among men. Since it has been suggested that this syndrome might be associated with agoraphobia (Kantor et al., 1980), this might partially explain the preponderance of female agoraphobics. Further, I have already discussed the finding that women during different phases of the menstrual cycle are particularly vulnerable to acquiring fears. In addition, the postpartum period is another period in which significant hormonal changes occur; the changes could easily be attributed to external sources rather than to the physical change itself. In this respect it should be noted that a number of patients acquire their phobia during this period.

Another explanation for the preponderance of female agoraphobics is that females are more willing to report phobias than males (see Katkin & Silver-Hoffman, 1976; Maccoby & Jacklin, 1974; Mack & Schröder, 1979; Speltz & Bernstein, 1976). After similar traumatic experiences, males are expected to continue working and are therefore automatically exposed to the phobic situations. Such exposure can result in the extinction of anxiety. Females, however, can more easily avoid such exposure. In this view, sex-role stereotyping is not such an important factor in the development of agoraphobia, but much more so in the maintenance of it.

Let us now look at studies that have investigated parental characteristics of phobic patients. Both Solyom, Beck, Solyom, and Hugel (1974) and Solyom, Silberfeld, and Solyom (1976) found the mothers of agoraphobics to be more overprotective than controls. On the other hand, Buglass et al. (1977) found no differences between agoraphobics and controls with respect to premorbid dependency. Parker (1979) studied parental characteristics of agoraphobics ($n = 40$) and social phobics

($n = 41$) using the Parental Bonding Instrument developed by Parker, Tupling, and Brown (1979). This questionnaire measured two dimensions: parental care and parental overprotection. The phobic patients scored their parents as less caring and as more overprotective than controls. Further analyses revealed that parental rearing practices may have differed for agoraphobics and social phobics respectively: "Social phobics scored both parents as low on care and high on overprotection, while agoraphobics differed from controls only in lower maternal care" (p. 559). Another striking contrast was that higher agoraphobic scores were associated with less maternal care and less maternal overprotection, while higher social phobic scores were associated with greater maternal care and greater maternal overprotection. This finding suggests that such parental characteristics as care and overprotection are differentially related to different types of phobias. Further studies are needed before more definitive conclusions can be drawn.

5. CONCLUDING REMARKS

There is little evidence that classical conditioning is involved in the development of clinical phobias. While there is some evidence that it might play a part in the development of specific phobias, in agoraphobia it plays only a minor part. The second stage of the two-stage theory of fear conditioning that holds that avoidance leads to anxiety reduction and thus strengthens the avoidance behavior has not been experimentally studied on phobics. However, patients usually relate that this is indeed the case. Further, experimental studies conducted on obsessive-compulsive patients generally support the second stage of the theory. These studies will be discussed in Chapter 6. Thus, while there is little evidence pertaining to the first stage of Mowrer's theory, it is plausible to assume that fear and avoidance are reinforced by anxiety reduction.

Although vicarious learning might be involved, its occurrence is probably infrequent and will account only for very few phobic cases. Informational processes might be important, but presumably more with respect to the acquisition of normal fears in children than clinical phobias.

While there is some evidence that hereditary factors might be involved, to date no firm conclusions can be drawn. Further studies using real phobic subjects are needed to establish the part played by hereditary factors. The interactions between hereditary factors and environmental influences are so very complex that studies into the family prevalence of anxiety and phobic disorders are of little value. Prospective studies that investigate the influence of differences in physiological arousal from birth on are needed to determine whether persons with a pathological arousal system are more likely to develop phobias (agoraphobia, social anxiety) than are others. Also, observation of parental rearing practices of such "high-risk children" might provide us with some information with respect to the interaction of environmental and biological variables. Presumably, not all persons with a pathological arousal system will develop phobias and such studies might give us some clues about important parental characteristics that might play a part in the development of the phobia. While overprotection might be important, the study by Parker (1979) suggests that other parental characteristics (e.g., lack of parental care) may be at least equally important.

While there is little evidence that classical conditioning is involved, in the majority of patients the phobia starts after negative life changes. For example, Solyom *et al.* (1974) list the following precipitating factors: fright, acute danger, serious illness, death of a relative or friend, domestic crisis, and unavoidable conflict. While clinical observation suggests that there is a clear relationship between life stress and the inception of the phobia, obviously this finding by itself does not offer a comprehensive theory of phobia development. While life stress might be related to the development of phobias, life stress is also associated with other disorders (e.g., depression, psychosomatic diseases). Further, many people do not develop phobias after experiencing similar negative life changes. This suggests that life stress may result in phobias only in particularly vulnerable persons. This vulnerability is the end result of an interaction between biological, environmental, and psychological variables.

An important psychological factor that might be involved is locus of control. Rotter (1966) has suggested that persons differ in the degree to which they perceive environmental reinforcers as being under their personal control, with internals perceiving these events as being under their control and externals perceiving reinforcers as being the result of luck, chance, fate, or powerful others. Johnson and Sarason (1978) suggested that internals and externals might respond differently to life change. They predicted that life change would have its most adverse effects on individuals who perceive themselves as having little or no control over such events. The results of their study indicated that locus of control orientation was a moderator variable in the relationship between life stress and anxiety and depression: "The results suggest that perhaps it is the individual who experiences high levels of (life) change but feels he/she has no control over events who is most susceptible to the effects of life stress" (p. 207). That locus of control is related to phobic anxiety was already demonstrated by Emmelkamp and Cohen-Kettenis (1975).

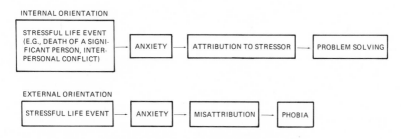

Figure 3. Relationship between life stress and phobic anxiety.

In their study a relationship was found between phobic anxiety and external locus of control. Taken together the findings of Johnson and Sarason (1978) and Emmelkamp and Cohen-Kettenis (1975), it is proposed that locus of control orientation may be an important variable in the development of phobias. Persons with an external control orientation experiencing anxiety attacks in a stressful period are likely to mislabel the anxiety and attribute it to external sources (e.g., crowded areas) or to a disease (e.g., heart attack). Some may even interpret it as a sign of going crazy. Thus they may perceive the experienced anxiety as being outside their control. The proposed model in which locus of control orientation is considered to be a moderator variable in the relationship between life stress and phobic anxiety is depicted in Figure 3.

The proposed model is presumably of more relevance with respect to the development of agoraphobia, social anxiety, and illness phobia than to specific phobias. However, there is some evidence that even here life stress might mark the inception of the phobias (Aitken *et al.*, 1981; Liddel & Lyons, 1978).

3

Assessment of Phobias

Measurements of phobic anxiety have included self-report, behavioral, and psychophysiological assessment. Self-report measures were designed to assess cognitive aspects of anxiety. A number of Fear Survey Schedules have been developed that provide the therapist with information about specific fears of the patient (see Lick & Katkin, 1976). The most frequently used procedure for assessing the behavioral component is the so called behavioral avoidance test. Snake phobics have to attempt picking up a snake, speech-anxious subjects have to give a speech before a small audience, etc. Psychophysiological recordings have been made when subjects were confronted with the feared objects either in imagination or in real life.

Several studies provided evidence that imagining a fearful scene produced increases in heart rate, respiratory rate, and skin conductance levels (e.g., Connolly, 1979; Grossberg & Wilson, 1968; Marks & Huson, 1973; Marzillier, Carroll, & Newland, 1979; McGlynn, Puhr, Gaynor, & Perry, 1973). However, subjective report of anxiety was usually a better discriminator between phobic and neutral images than were psychophysiological indices (e.g., Marks & Huson, 1973). Essentially similar psychophysiological responses have been found when the phobic stimulus was presented in real life (e.g., Watson, Gaind, & Marks, 1972; Stern & Marks, 1973; McGlynn et al., 1973; Sartory, Rachman, & Grey, 1977). Borkovec, Weerts, and Bernstein (1977) and Lick and Katkin (1976) recommended heart rate as the physiological measure of anxiety. Others, however, have suggested that physiological measurements directly concerned with cerebral functions (resting electroencephalogram and averaged evoked potentials) may be better correlates of anxiety (Tyrer & Lader, 1976).

1. THREE SYSTEMS THEORY

Following Lang's (1969, 1971) repudiation of the "lump theory" of fear, it has become commonplace to consider anxiety as a constellation of three different response channels: (1) cognitive-self-report, (2) behavior-motoric and (3) psychophysiological. At present, there are a number of studies (e.g., Bellack & Hersen, 1977; Hersen, 1973; Lang, 1968; Lamb, 1978; Leitenberg, Agras, Butz, & Wincze, 1971) that demonstrate that the intercorrelations among the three systems are typically low. This has led to the notions of desynchrony and discordance of fear measures. Rachman and Hodgson (1974) hypothesized that the three systems are partly independent (discordance) and may change independently from each other in the course of treatment (desynchrony).

In a thought provoking paper, Cone (1979) has challenged the notion of the "triple response mode." Cone called attention to basic flaws in the methodology of studies that investigated relationships among systems: "Research has varied both method of assessment and content area when computing correlations" (p. 87). For example, self-report can consist of such different statements as "I feel heart palpitations" or "I would like to run away." The former self-statement is more likely to be related to heart rate, whereas the latter is probably associated with behavioral indices. However, self-report of anxiety—irrespective of content—has usually been considered to refer to the "cognitive channel" thus neglecting the specific content of the self-statements. To quote Cone again: "It may be that the conclusions of response system independence (e.g., Lang, 1971) are premature and that a sorting out of behavior method confounds would lead to different interpretations" (p. 89).

Along similar lines, Lick, Sushinsky, and Malow (1977) hypothesized that the low relationship between the self-assessment of fear and actual behavior in a behavioral avoidance test situation could be increased by giving the subjects more information about the task they were required to perform in the laboratory test. Results of their study indicated that the correlation between self-report and avoidance measures of fear increases when self-report measures provide an accurate description of the fear-eliciting stimuli subjects encounter on an avoidance test. The authors concluded: "This suggests that the theoretical conception of anxiety emphasizing its inherent multidimensional nature (e.g., Lang, 1969) may have been somewhat premature, since the data base for this conceptualization did not rule out all methodological factors that could account for low correlations between measures tapping behavioral, cognitive, and physiological components of anxiety responses" (p. 201). Subsequent studies by Bandura and his colleagues demonstrated a high correlation between self-report ("efficacy expectations") and performance on a behavioral avoidance test (e.g., Bandura & Adams, 1977).

To summarize, lack of concordance between the different response systems is at least partly a function of methodological inadequacies associated with the measurement of the different "channels."

A final aspect of the issue of discordance between the three systems of fear concerns the reliability and validity of the measurement of each component by itself. Although the concurrent validity of self-report measures is satisfactory, the validity of psychophysiological indices of anxiety and standardized behavior tests is questionable. Generally, there is a low intercorrelation among different psychophysiological measures that purport to measure the same state of arousal (e.g., Marks & Huson, 1973; Hersen, Bellack, & Turner, 1978), which may be due to individual differences in physiological reaction patterns (Lacey, 1962). In addition, type of phobia may be related to a specific response pattern. For example, blood-injury phobics deviate from the generally observed pattern of heart rate increase when confronted with their phobic stimuli (Connolly, Hallam, & Marks, 1976). Blood phobics show heart rate deceleration rather than acceleration which can result in fainting. Individual differences in psychophysiological responding may also be due to personality characteristics. For example, repressors, who are persons with a defensive coping style were found to show a different psychophysiological reaction pattern than low- and high-anxious subjects (Weinberger, Schwartz, & Davidson, 1979).

Behavior therapists, suspicious of "introspective" self-report approaches, have overestimated the utility of behavioral avoidance tests. Evidence is accumulating that these tests are far from valid; performance on standardized behavior tests may be very different from actual behavior in everyday situations. For example, snake phobic subjects who touched a snake on a laboratory behavioral avoidance test, did not show improvement in the natural environment (Lick & Unger, 1977; Rosen, Glasgow, & Barrera, 1977). Similarly, laboratory assessment of social skills and social anxiety overestimated the amount of "real" therapeutic change (e.g., Arkowitz, Lichtenstein, McGovern, & Hines, 1975; Bellack, Hersen, & Lamparski, 1979). Thus, laboratory tests do not provide data that predict how subjects will function in naturalistic situations (Lick & Unger, 1977).

2. ASSESSMENT OF CLINICAL PHOBIAS

This section pertains to issues that are particularly relevant to assessment in studies with clinical phobias.

2.1. Rating Scales

Most researchers of clinical phobics have used the rating scales originally developed by Gelder and Marks (1966), or a latter modified version
by Watson and Marks (1971). The Gelder and Marks scale is a 5-point
scale, measuring phobic severity; separate ratings are made for main
phobia and other phobias. The Watson and Marks scale is a 9-point scale,
which measures both anxiety and avoidance for five fairly specific phobic
situations. Both scales can be scored by patient, therapist, and independent assessor.

Interrater reliability for the Watson and Marks scale has been found
to be satisfactory (see Emmelkamp, 1979). With respect to the Gelder
and Marks scale the data are inconclusive. Several studies found high
interrater reliability, but in other studies nonsignificant correlations between different raters were found. For example, Solyom, McClure,
Heseltine, Ledwidge, and Solyom (1972) found a lack of agreement between psychiatrists' ratings of phobias and patients' self-ratings; in the
Gillan and Rachman (1974) study, a similar lack of agreement was found
between psychotherapists' ratings on the one hand and patient and assessor ratings on the other hand. Lack of agreement between different
raters has not been reported in using the Watson and Marks scale. Presumably, the greater specificity of the latter scale enhances its reliability.

One disadvantage of both scales is that the scores of different
patients are not directly comparable: patients are rated for different
phobias. Both Emmelkamp, Kuipers, and Eggeraat (1978) and Watson,
Mullet, and Pillay (1973) have used the same five situations for all patients (agoraphobics) thus making the scores comparable across patients.
Of course, this approach is only useful with a homogeneous patient
population.

Researchers from the Oxford group have used a slightly modified
version of the original Gelder and Marks scale. A single rating of phobic
severity was made, while in the original Gelder and Marks scale, separate
ratings were made of "main phobia" and "other phobias."

Teasdale *et al.* (1977) compared this modified Gelder and Marks
scale and the Watson and Marks scale with 18 agoraphobics. High correlations were obtained between assessor ratings on the modified Gelder
and Marks scale and patient and assessor ratings on the Watson and
Marks scale. Moreover, transformed ratings on the Watson and Marks
scale were quite similar to ratings on the modified Gelder and Marks
scale except for the pretreatment measure. The findings of this study
suggest that ratings on the modified Gelder and Marks scale and the
Watson and Marks scale may not be all directly comparable.

It would be valuable for workers with phobic patients to use the same scale in the future. The Watson and Marks scale with five standard situations is recommended. For the assessment of agoraphobia the following situations were proposed (Emmelkamp, 1979): (1) walking away from hospital, (2) walking down a busy high street, (3) traveling on a bus, (4) shopping in a supermarket, and (5) sitting in a restaurant. These situations represent the cluster of agoraphobic fears and are relevant for most patients.

2.2. Behavioral Measures

In analog research with phobic subjects a behavioral avoidance test forms a condition *sine qua non* of the assessment procedures. However, it is much more difficult to assess clinical phobic patients behaviorally, because of the idiosyncratic character of the patients' phobias. Even with a relatively homogeneous subgroup of phobic patients as social phobics, patients might differ widely concerning the social situations which they fear.

2.2.1. Social Anxiety

Most studies with social-anxious patients have included behavioral tests. In most studies assessment was accomplished through role playing interactions in standardized real-life interaction tests (Argyle, Bryant, & Trower, 1974; Falloon, Lindley, McDonald, & Marks, 1977; Kanter & Goldfried, 1979; Hall & Goldberg, 1977; Marzillier, Lambert, & Kellett, 1976; Trower, Yardley, Bryant, & Shaw, 1978; Wolfe & Fodor, 1977). In the studies by Van Son (1978) the behavioral assessment consisted of an interpersonal role playing test with taped stimulus material.

Although role playing now appears to be increasingly popular as an outcome measure, the utility of these procedures is questionable. First, no single assessment procedure has been thoroughly validated. Second, it is generally assumed that behavior in these analog situations is quite similar to real-life behavior in the patients' natural environment. However, behavior in these tests may be only minimally related to social anxiety. For instance, Trower *et al.* (1978) reported that for their phobic patients the interaction test was not itself a phobic situation; most patients showed noticeable competency on this behavioral measure. Finally, a related problem of role playing is that the behavior of the patient is assessed in only one or a few standard situations. However, a situation that is relevant for one patient may be trivial for another and vice versa.

Scores in these situations are typically summed across individuals, thus neglecting the situational specificity of social anxiety. Several recent studies have demonstrated that role-played behavior may not accurately represent behavior in more naturalistic settings (e.g., Bellack, Hersen, & Lamparski, 1979).

Only a few studies with social phobics have attempted to test therapeutic changes in the patients' natural environment. In the study by Shaw (1976) subjects were asked to attempt the highest possible item on their hierarchy of phobic situations before and at the end of treatment. However, some items involved social situations which were difficult or impossible to arrange during behavioral testing.

Probably the most economical approach is to rely on patients' self-reports about their actual behavior in potentially phobic situations. Bryant and Trower (1974) developed the Social Situation Questionnaire, which provides an index of the patients' social participation in 30 everyday situations. Other researchers have made use of standardized social diaries (Marzillier *et al.*, 1976; Van Son, 1978). Such self-reports about behavior in potentially phobic situations might prove to be quite useful behavioral measures. Research needs to be undertaken into the reliability and validity of these questionnaires.

2.2.2. Agoraphobia

The behavioral assessment of agoraphobia is also not without problems. In our treatment outcome studies we have measured the time which agoraphobics could spend outside without undue anxiety; patients were instructed to walk alone on a route that was a difficult one and that ran in a straight line in a direction away from their homes or away from the hospital. Although this behavioral measure was time spent outside rather than distance walked, the measure of time is clearly related to distance.

Watson *et al.* (1973) used an almost similar behavioral test with their agoraphobics. Their test course ran away from the hospital and was divided into nine equal segments; patients had to note how far they had walked.

Correlation between this behavioral measure and phobic anxiety ratings have been found to be fairly high (Emmelkamp, 1980b; Emmelkamp & Mersch, 1982; Watson *et al.*, 1973). Furthermore, this behavioral measure was found to be relatively stable over time with untreated patients (Emmelkamp, 1974). A clear disadvantage of this measure is that only a part of the cluster of agoraphobic fears is measured behaviorally, although presumably the most important part.

Both Hand, Lamontagne, and Marks (1974) and Teasdale et al. (1977) have included other phobic situations in their behavioral tests with agoraphobics. Patients were instructed to go alone for up to 45 minutes as far as they could without undue anxiety into their two most frightening phobic situations. These situations included travelling on buses, going into open spaces, or shopping. The performance of patients was rated by an independent assessor. Because of the different situations in which patients are assessed, comparisons across patients become virtually impossible. Both Hand et al. (1974) and Teasdale et al. found this an unsatisfactory measure.

Another behavioral test with agoraphobics has been used by the Oxford group (Mathews et al., 1976, 1977). This test consists of a hierarchy of progressively more difficult items. At each testing patients are asked to complete as many items as they can. Results on this behavioral test correlated highly with phobic severity ratings by assessors but less so with patients' ratings (Mathews et al., 1976). Whether improvements on hospital behavioral measures parallel behavioral changes in the natural environment is largely unknown. Even if patients can walk away from the hospital without undue anxiety, this does not mean that they are automatically able to do the same from their homes. Structured diaries of patients' outdoor behavior might also be profitable.

Although demand characteristics have been found to have a substantial influence on the results of behavioral avoidance tests in analog studies, the effects of demand characteristics on behavioral assessment with clinical phobics have not been assessed. Different treatments might create different demands with posttesting. For example, "undue anxiety" might mean something quite different for a patient who has been treated with gradual exposure in vivo than it means for a patient treated by flooding in vivo. The latter patient is now instructed to come back on experiencing undue anxiety, while he or she has just learned to tolerate anxiety until it declined. The posttest instruction with such patients is rather paradoxical. Obviously, results at posttesting might be influenced to some extent by the implicit demands of the treatment received.

A major difficulty with behavioral tests is the reactivity of the assessment procedure: Repeatedly being exposed to the phobic situation, as is typically done with these tests, is therapeutic in itself. Repeated behavioral assessment interacts with treatment. Therefore, the amount of behavioral testing with one patient is clearly limited.

2.3. Concluding Remarks

At the present time the validity of behavioral tests with phobic patients is largely unknown. Thus, results of these tests should be interpreted cautiously. Indirect assessment of phobic anxiety and avoidance by means of rating scales (e.g., Watson & Marks, 1971) is quite useful. Fear questionnaires can also provide useful information for treatment planning and assessment of outcome. The fear questionnaire (Marks & Mathews, 1979) is recommended for this purpose. This questionnaire has the advantage above other fear survey schedules in that it was developed on a clinical phobic population. The form includes the 15 most common phobias and 5 associated anxiety-depression symptoms found in clinical practice. The phobia score is composed of agoraphobia, social, and blood-injury subgroups.

Finally, while psychophysiological assessment may be important to elucidate therapeutic processes, it is of little use as an outcome measure. The psychophysiological recording is very time consuming and costly, without substantially contributing to treatment decisions or treatment evaluation.

4

Cognitive-Behavioral Interventions

This chapter is procedure oriented as opposed to a focus upon various disorders to be remediated, which is the topic of Chapters 5 and 8. Here, the emphasis is on the processes underlying the various cognitive-behavioral procedures.

1. SYSTEMATIC DESENSITIZATION

Systematic desensitization (Wolpe, 1958) is probably the most well-known behavioral procedure to date. In systematic desensitization the patient is first trained in muscular relaxation; then he moves gradually up a hierarchy of anxiety-arousing situations while remaining relaxed at a pace determined by the patient's progress in overcoming his fear. Systematic desensitization may be applied either in imagination or *in vivo*, but most studies involve the imaginal variant.

In this section, research pertinent to the "construct validity" of systematic desensitization will be discussed. *Construct validity* in the context of therapy research reflects concern with the process involved in therapy. More specifically, construct validity raises the question of whether the outcome of therapy can be accounted for by the processes proposed by a theory (e.g., counterconditioning) or should be interpreted in terms of other constructs (e.g., expectancy of therapeutic gain).

Although numerous studies have demonstrated the effectiveness of systematic desensitization, at least in reducing circumscribed fears in analog populations, the theoretical underpinnings are still vague. Several theoretical explanations have been put forward, including reciprocal inhibition (Wolpe, 1958), counter-conditioning (Davidson, 1968), cognitive processes (Emmelkamp, 1975a), psychoanalytic interpretations (Silverman, Frank, & Dachinger, 1974), and relationship processes (Wolowitz, 1975).

1.1. Therapeutic Process

1.1.1. Reciprocal Inhibition and Counter-Conditioning

In his original presentation, Wolpe (1958) explained the effects of systematic desensitization in terms of reciprocal inhibition:

> If a response antagonistic to anxiety can be made to occur in the presence of anxiety-evoking stimuli so that it is accompanied by a complete or partial suppression of the anxiety responses, the bond between these stimuli and the anxiety responses will be weakened. (p. 71)

Presently, relaxation is widely used as a response to counter anxiety. Wolpe's original conception of desensitization was based heavily on Hull's concept of conditioned inhibition. Now the term countercondi- tioning is more often used to characterize systematic desensitization.

Both a reciprocal inhibition and a counterconditioning interpreta- tion hold that a graded hierarchy and an incompatible response (relaxation) are essential for successful desensitization of fear. However, desensitization with relaxation has been found to be equally effective as desensitization without relaxation (graded exposure). Marks (1975) re- viewed research in this area and found no evidence that relaxation en- hanced the effectiveness of imaginal exposure to the phobic stimuli. More recent studies also demonstrated that desensitization with relaxa- tion was no more effective than graded exposure to the hierarchy items (e.g., Goldfried & Goldfried, 1977; Ladouceur, 1978; Newman & Brand, 1980). Perhaps more to the point, studies with clinical phobics also found negative results with respect to relaxation in a systematic desensitization context (Agras *et al.*, 1971; Benjamin, Marks, & Huson, 1972; Gillan & Rachman, 1974). Borkovec and Sides (1979) found systematic desensiti- zation to be superior to graded exposure, but solely on subjective out- come measures.

According to Wolpe's formulation of systematic desensitization, anxiety must first be inhibited before avoidance behavior can be reduced. Leitenberg, Agras, Butz, and Wincze (1971) attempted to test this assumption with nine phobic patients. Heart rate and approach behavior were simultaneously assessed during treatment. Results indi- cated that anxiety reduction may be a consequence rather than a cause of behavioral changes. In some cases, heart rate decreased only after avoidance behavior was modified thus challenging the reciprocal inhibi- tion hypothesis.

In sum, there is no evidence that the effects of systematic desensitization should be interpreted in terms of reciprocal inhibition or counterconditioning.

1.1.2. Cognitive Processes

The contribution of cognitive factors to the process of systematic desensitization has remained a contested issue for more than a decade. There has been a continuous debate over the influence of cognitive factors, particularly expectancy of therapeutic gain, on systematic desensitization (e.g., Davison & Wilson, 1973; Emmelkamp, 1975a; Wilkins, 1979a). One strategy of evaluating the influence of cognitive (i.e., expectancy) factors to systematic desensitization is to compare desensitization with placebo conditions. However, most studies that have followed this strategy do not permit the drawing of any conclusion with respect to expectancy factors, because the credibility of the placebo controls has not been adequately assessed. Several studies (e.g., Borkovec & Nau, 1972; McGlynn & McDonell, 1974; Nau, Caputo, & Borkovec, 1974) have demonstrated that the "expectancy of improvement" produced by a placebo therapy must be assessed rather than assumed. In many cases placebo rationales have not been as credible as the rationale of systematic desensitization. Simply designating a technique as "placebo" does not ensure that subjects will find it believable (Lent, Crimmings, & Russell, 1981). Nevertheless, it is noteworthy that a number of studies could not detect any difference in effectiveness between systematic desensitization and placebo conditions (e.g., Donovan & Gershman, 1979; Holroyd, 1976; Kirsch & Henry, 1977; Lick, 1975; Marcia, Rubin, & Efran, 1969; McGlynn, 1971; McGlynn, Gaynor, & Puhr, 1972; McGlynn, Reynolds, & Linder, 1971; McReynolds, Barnes, Brooks, & Rehagen, 1973; Tori & Worell, 1973). Further, Gelder *et al.* (1973) found no differences between systematic desensitization and placebo as far as patients with specific phobias were concerned.

A different approach to the study of the influence of expectancy on treatment outcome is to vary instructional sets. Two strategies can be distinguished (Emmelkamp, 1975a). First, subjects who are given a therapeutically oriented instructional set are compared with subjects who are led to believe that they are participating in experimental procedures concerned with physiological reactions. Studies that have followed this strategy generally found a clear expectancy effect. Second, all subjects are informed that they are to receive therapy, but instructions concerning the anticipated outcome are varied (positive, neutral, or negative). Studies following this paradigm have produced conflicting results. However, as noted earlier (Emmelkamp, 1975a) "it is inappropriate to conclude that expectancy does not play an important part in the systematic desensitization procedure, because all subjects had received a therapeutic instruction" (p. 5). These therapeutic instructions may lead to expectations for improvement regardless of what the subject is subsequently told. In addition, regardless of instructions given by the experimenter, systematic desensitization may be experienced at face value as a treatment.

Several alternative explanations have been proposed to explain the expectancy effects, particularly experimenter bias (Wilkins, 1973) and demand characteristics (Borkovec, 1973). In his review of expectancy studies Wilkins (1973) concluded that the studies reporting an expectancy effect involved therapists who were not blind to the experimental manipulations, whereas in studies failing to demonstrate an expectancy effect therapists were blind. However, several studies have found expectancy effects with experimenters who were unaware of the expectancy manipulations applied to the subjects (Emmelkamp & Straatman, 1976; Emmelkamp & Walta, 1978; Rosen, 1974; Sullivan & Denney, 1977). Thus experimenter bias does not adequately explain the differences found in expectancy studies.

Borkovec (1973) proposed that subject characteristics could explain the contradictory results among expectancy studies. In a retrospective analysis of expectancy studies he suggested that the studies failing to find an expectancy effect employed fearful subjects, whereas studies demonstrating expectancy effects employed low fearful subjects. The post hoc classification fearful-low fearful subjects, as used by Borkovec (1973), has been criticized by Emmelkamp (1975b); his reanalysis of the studies reviewed by Borkovec indicates that several studies that did find expectancy effects involved highly fearful subjects. More recently, several studies found expectancy effects regardless of the phobic level of the subjects (Emmelkamp & Boeke-Slinkers, 1977b; Sullivan & Denney, 1977). Thus, contrary to Borkovec's (1973) hypothesis, highly fearful subjects were no less susceptible to expectancy effects than were low fearful subjects.

Finally, assessment in most expectancy studies has been limited to self-report and behavioral tests. Thus, it could be argued that expectancy might influence subjective and behavioral components of fear, but not the physiological component. Indeed, Borkovec (1973) and Rappaport (1972) failed to obtain expectancy effects on physiological indices of anxiety. Other studies, however, demonstrated expectancy effects on physiological measures (Beiman, 1976; Borkovec & Sides, 1979; Grayson & Borkovec, 1978; Kirsch & Henry, 1979; Lick, 1975). In addition, Donovan and Gershman (1979) found no differences between systematic desensitization and a placebo condition on two out of three physiological indices. Thus, expectancy influences have been demonstrated on both subjective, behavioral, and psychophysiological indices of anxiety.

Recently, Wilkins (1979b) pointed out some fundamental problems with the conceptualization of expectancy factors. He questioned the role of expectancy as an "interpretive artifact" and he stated: "The only class of expectancies from which independency has not been demonstrated is a class from which demonstration of independence is tautologically impossible" (p. 843). As argued by Bootzin and Lick (1979), Wilkins confused designs to answer questions about theoretical mechanisms with designs to demonstrate effectiveness. Contrary to claims made by Wilkins (1979b), systematic desensitization has not been found to be superior to credible placebo treatments. To date, at least ten studies have found placebo to be as effective as systematic desensitization.

In summary, expectancy factors appear to play an important role in systematic desensitization. It is still questionable whether systematic desensitization is not merely an effective placebo procedure. In order to investigate to what extent desensitization produces an effect independently of expectancy factors, the procedure should be compared with pseudo-therapies with the same credibility and face validity (Emmelkamp, 1975a).

1.1.3. Relationship Factors

The role of the therapeutic relationship has been an area of great theoretical controversy among different schools of psychotherapy. Classic learning theory approaches have viewed relationship factors as far less relevant to the therapeutic endeavor relative to other psychotherapeutic schools. Systematic desensitization was originally thought to be relatively devoid of relationship processes. As we have seen, the use of conditioning and learning principles was postulated as the sole reason for its effectiveness.

Morris and Suckerman (1974a; 1974b) set out to test the hypothesis that systematic desensitization is a function of therapist warmth versus a function of counterconditioning. In two analog studies, they demonstrated that subjects treated in "warm therapist" conditions improved significantly more than those in "cold therapist" conditions. This finding was replicated by Ryan and Moses (1979).

Some (e.g., Wolowitz, 1975) have interpreted these results as indicating that the therapeutic relationship is a necessary and sufficient factor for producing therapeutic change with systematic desensitization. However, in a study by Esse and Wilkins (1978) unempathetic imagery presentations still produced significantly greater avoidance reduction than the establishment of an empathetic relationship without imaginal exposure to the phobic stimuli.

In brief, analog studies demonstrate that therapist factors (i.e., therapist's warmth) affect the outcome of systematic desensitization but most of the variance in outcome should be attributed to exposure to phobic stimuli rather than to therapist factors.

1.1.4. Psychoanalytic Interpretation

Silverman et al. (1974) hypothesized that part of the effectiveness of systematic desensitization resides in the fact that it activates an unconscious fantasy of merging (i.e., the therapist as mother substitute), an activation which is made particularly likely by the use of the muscle relaxation procedure. To test this hypothesis, they compared two variants of systematic desensitization with insect phobic subjects. Instead of using relaxation as incompatible response, subjects were given subliminal exposures of either a symbiosis gratification stimulus (Mommy and I are one) or a neutral stimulus (People walking). The group that received subliminal exposure to the symbiotic gratification stimulus manifested more improvement than the group with the neutral stimulus, thus supporting their hypothesis that effectiveness of systematic desensitization resides in its activation of unconscious merging fantasies.

Emmelkamp and Straatman (1976) replicated the study of Silverman et al. (1974) with special reference to demand characteristics, using snake phobic volunteers as subjects. In this experiment, Mommy and I are one was used as symbiotic gratification stimulus and Snake and I are one as neutral stimulus. It was assumed that to subjects with snake phobia this stimulus would be more relevant than the stimulus "people walking." Results indicated that systematic desensitization with a symbiotic gratification stimulus was not more effective than desensitization with a neutral stimulus. Rather, it was shown that subjects receiving the neutral stimulus improved more on the behavioral avoidance test. The difference in outcome with the Silverman et al. (1974) study may be explained by the fact that the neutral stimulus Snake and I are one was experienced as more relevant than the stimulus Mommy and I are one.

A more recent study (Condon & Allen, 1980) also failed to replicate the study by Silverman et al. (1974). Three groups of subjects were exposed to one of the tachistoscopically presented stimuli (1) Mommy and I are one, (2) Daddy and I are one, or (3) a random combination of letters. The stimulus Daddy and I are one was chosen because it should temporarily increase fear according to psychoanalytic theory. Subjects in all conditions showed significant improvement thus challenging the psychoanalytic predictions.

Taken together the results of studies which attempted to replicate Silverman *et al.*'s finding, there is *no* support for a psychoanalytic reinterpretation of the effectiveness of systematic desensitization.

1.1.5. Imaginal versus In Vivo Exposure

Wolpe's (1963) statement that "there is almost invariably a one to one relationship between what the patient can imagine without anxiety and what he can experience in reality without anxiety" receives little support. A transfer gap between what a client could imagine without feeling anxiety and what he could deal with *in vivo* without feeling tension has been reported a number of times (e.g., Agras, 1967; Barlow, Leitenberg, Agras, & Wincze, 1969; Hain, Butcher, & Stevenson, 1966; Meyer & Crisp, 1966; Sherman, 1972). Clients who had been successfully desensitized in imagination nevertheless proved to react with anxiety when they were confronted with the phobic stimuli *in vivo*.

Several studies have directly compared systematic desensitization in imagination and *in vivo*. Results indicate that *in vivo* exposure was far more effective (Dyckman & Cowan, 1978; Barlow *et al.*, 1969; Litvak, 1969; Sherman, 1972). It is noteworthy that much effort has gone into studying imaginal desensitization and almost no studies have been conducted with respect to systematic desensitization in real life. Presumably, the consensual delusion that imaginal desensitization is equivalent to *in vivo* desensitization originated in the conceptualization of desensitization in conditioning terms and has been reinforced for years by the lack of tests with real clinical patients.

1.2. Systematic Desensitization and Relaxation as Coping Skills

In contrast with classical systematic desensitization which is aimed at a "deconditioning" of anxiety, self-control procedures are aimed at teaching patients active, generalized anxiety-coping skills. During the 1970s several procedures to teach patients coping skills had been devised. A common characteristic of these self-management procedures was the emphasis on *in vivo* exposure. Patients learned procedures that they had to apply in the anxiety-arousing situations. Generally, it was assumed that these procedures had a broader applicability in that they also dealt with nontargeted anxieties.

1.2.1. Systematic Desensitization as Self-Control

Instead of a passive conditioning conceptualization, Goldfried (1971) argued that systematic desensitization should be viewed as a self-control procedure in which clients are taught to exert voluntary control over their feelings of anxiety. Several modifications of the standard systematic desensitization procedure were recommended by Goldfried. First, relaxation is conceptualized as a coping skill; second, different fears are placed within a single multidimensional hierarchy; third, clients are instructed to stay in the imaginal situation, when anxiety occurs, and to cope with anxiety by relaxing it away; and finally, clients have to apply relaxation skills in real-life anxiety-provoking situations.

Since self-control desensitization focuses on applying relaxation coping skills whenever proprioceptive cues of anxiety or tension are perceived, the effects of this procedure should transfer across anxiety arousing situations. As far as targeted anxieties are concerned, self-control desensitization has been found to be equally effective as traditional desensitization (Deffenbacher & Parks, 1979; Spiegler, Cooley, Marshall, Prince, Puckett, & Skenazy, 1976; Zemore, 1975) or more effective (Denney & Rupert, 1977). The results of studies that investigated the effects of self-control desensitization on generalization measures have provided conflicting results. Several studies (Deffenbacher & Parks, 1979; Deffenbacher, Michaels, Michaels, & Daley, 1980; Zemore, 1975) found transfer of treatment effects across anxiety arousing situations, whereas others did not (Denney & Rupert, 1977; Spiegler et al., 1976; Harris & Bennett-Johnson, 1980). More importantly, however, in neither study was self-control desensitization found to be superior to standard desensitization with respect to nontargeted anxiety reduction.

Goldfried and Goldfried (1977) compared two self-control desensitization procedures with speech-anxious subjects: one with a hierarchy relevant to speech anxiety and the second involving a hierarchy totally unrelated to public speaking situations. No differential effectiveness was found between the two self-control desensitization conditions, which suggests that the learning of an active coping skill is an important factor with self-control desensitization.

1.2.2. Relaxation as Coping Skill

Several other self-management procedures have been developed in which clients are trained in relaxation as a coping skill. Clients are trained to recognize the physiological cues of tension and to apply relaxation whenever tension is perceived. Three different procedures have been studied: applied relaxation (Deffenbacher, 1976), anxiety management

(Suinn & Richardson, 1971; Suinn, 1976), and cue-controlled relaxation (Russell & Sipich, 1973).

In *anxiety management* training, the client imagines a single highly anxiety arousing situation and actively attempts to relax away anxiety feelings. In *applied relaxation*, clients have to apply relaxation to stressful and anxiety provoking situations in real life. *Cue-controlled relaxation* is aimed at enabling the individual to achieve a state of relaxation in response to a self-produced cue, having paired that cue with relaxation. Following relaxation training the client subvocalizes the cue word (e.g., "calm", or "relax") with each exhalation.

A fundamental assumption shared by all these relaxation techniques is that if patients learn an active coping skill, they can apply it in a variety of anxiety-arousing situations in daily life. In contrast to self-control desensitization, no hierarchy of anxiety arousing situations is used. At present, there is no evidence that any one of these techniques is more effective than others (Barrios, Ginter, Scalise, & Miller, 1980).

Several studies indicate that relaxation presented as a coping skill is more effective than standard relaxation exercises (Chang-Liang & Denney, 1976; Goldfried & Trier, 1974; Hutchings, Denney, Basgall, & Houston, 1980).

Deffenbacher and Shelton (1978) found anxiety managment to be slightly more effective than standard systematic desensitization. When systematic desensitization was presented as a self-management procedure, however, relaxation (also presented as a coping skill) was about equally effective (Bedell, Archer, & Rosman, 1979; Deffenbacher, Mathis, & Michaels, 1979; Deffenbacher *et al.*, 1980).

It should be noted, that the positive results of self-management relaxation procedures may be attributed to expectancy factors. Both Marchetti, McGlynn, and Patterson (1977) and McGlynn, Kinjo, and Doherty (1978) compared cue-controlled relaxation with an equally credible placebo treatment and could not find any difference in effectiveness. There is no evidence that these relaxation procedures produce therapeutic gains to a degree greater than that effected by a credible placebo procedure. Finally, clinical studies are lacking: All studies reviewed here used analog populations, usually students with speech-anxiety or test-anxiety.

2. FLOODING PROCEDURES

Flooding procedures can be subdivided according to cues presented (psychodynamic cues vs. "symptom-contingent" cues). In this section a brief description of these flooding techniques will be given and then research will be reviewed with respect to variables that are related to success of flooding.

2.1. Description of Procedures

2.1.1. Implosive Therapy

The implosive therapy was developed by Stampfl and Levis (1967; 1968). Implosive therapy has been claimed to be based on the principle of extinction. During treatment the therapist presents a *complex* of conditioned stimuli to the patient without primary reinforcement and without allowing an avoidance response. The therapist tries to maximize anxiety throughout treatment, which eventually leads to "extinction." Sessions are continued until a significant reduction in anxiety is achieved. Not only is it essential to the implosive approach that the "symptom-contingent" cues are presented, but also that the patient is exposed to aversive stimuli assumed to be underlying the patient's problems ("hypothesized-sequential cues"). *Hypothesized cues* are defined as "those which are not directly correlated with symptom onset but which represent 'guesses' as to the remaining components of the avoided CS complex" (Levis & Hare, 1977, p. 321). These hypothesized cues may concern such dynamic themes as aggression, guilt, punishment, rejection, loss of control, and oral, anal, or sexual material. For a detailed account of the implosive theory the interested reader is referred to Levis and Hare (1977).

So far, only one study has compared implosive therapy with psychodynamic cues versus implosive therapy without such cues (Prochaska, 1971). Both procedures were found to be about equally effective. Almost all controlled studies (both with analog and with clinical populations) have conducted implosive therapy without such psychodynamic cues. Since the therapeutic procedures used differ considerably from the implosive therapy as originally developed by Stampfl, the term flooding will be used throughout this chapter.

2.1.2. Flooding

Apart from the psychodynamic cues, flooding therapy for phobias got wide attention from behavior therapists. Flooding can be carried out in imagination or *in vivo* but the earlier studies and clinical applications consisted of imaginal flooding. With flooding in imagination the patient has to imagine situations and experiences that he finds the most frightening for a prolonged period of time. To illustrate this treatment approach, here an example of such a scene used with one of our agoraphobics:

> Imagine that you are going out of the front door of this house. You walk through the front garden and then you are in the street. You turn left and walk in the shopping center where you have to go and buy something. Imagine it as well as you can: the houses you walk past, the cars that rush past you. You are walking there alone and you are going in the direction of the railway crossing. The bars are down and you have to wait. A group of people is standing there waiting and they look at you. You find it very disturbing, this waiting, and you hop a bit from one leg to the other. At last the bars are going up, you walk on, and arrive in the shopping center. It is fuller there; there are more and more people. You begin to feel rather bad now. You become dizzy. You feel it in your legs. But you nevertheless walk on, because there is nowhere you can go there on the street, you cannot flee inside anywhere. Now you have to cross the street. There is a string of cars and you run between them. On the other side of the street there are still more people. Now you are feeling completely dizzy. Your legs are heavy. But there you are walking in the middle of the pavement and there is nowhere you can go. You begin to panic and you think, "I want to go away," "I want to go home," but you cannot go home. You hold onto a gate for a while, but you can't manage anymore. You are sweating terribly, you take another couple of steps and then you fall. You fall there in the middle of the street. People come and stand all around you and are wondering what has happened. And there you lie, in the middle of the street.

2.2. Therapeutic Process

2.2.1. Duration of Exposure

One of the most important variables in determining the effectiveness of flooding appears to be the duration of exposure to the stimulus variable within each session. Too early termination of flooding sessions may lead to an exacerbation instead of a reduction of fear. In fact, the patient is then allowed to escape the fearful situation (either in imagination or *in vivo*) which may lead to an immediate anxiety reduction (negative reinforcement).

The effects of duration of exposure in imaginal flooding was investigated by Chaplin and Levine (1980). With continuous exposure, imaginal flooding material was presented twice without interruption for a total of 50 min. In the interrupted condition a 10-min intertrial interval separated the two 25-min presentations. Continuous flooding was superior to interrupted flooding. Other analog studies resulted in equivalent findings (Girodo & Henry, 1976; McCutcheon & Adams, 1975; Miller & Levis, 1971).

To date, two clinical studies have been reported that investigated this particular issue. Stern and Marks (1973) compared short (4 half-hour) sessions with long (two-hour) sessions. Prolonged sessions were clearly superior to shorter ones when exposure was *in vivo* but not with imaginal exposure. Similarly, Rabavilas, Boulougouris, and Stefanis (1976) found prolonged exposures *in vivo* (80 min) to be superior to short (10 min) exposure *in vivo*.

It is noteworthy that in most studies with clinical patients much longer exposure duration has been used than has typically been done in analog research. In the analog studies flooding sessions lasted from 20 to 60 min. In contrast, in clinical studies where flooding has been found to be effective, flooding lasted up to several hours.

2.2.2. Processes of Anxiety Reduction

2.2.2.1. Flooding in Imagination. The process of anxiety reduction during flooding in imagination sessions has been studied in several studies. Foa and Chambless (1978) assessed *subjective* anxiety throughout flooding in imagination with agoraphobic and obsessive-compulsive patients. Patients were instructed to imagine the scenes described by the therapist as vividly as possible. Flooding sessions lasted 90 min. Patients had to indicate their anxiety every 10 min on a scale of 0–100 SUDS. Figure 4 shows the mean SUDS of the agoraphobics during second and last (eighth) treatment sessions. The results of this study showed that habituation of subjective anxiety occurs within sessions. Most often it follows a curvilinear pattern. In addition, evidence was provided for habituation across sessions. It is interesting to see that in the Foa and Chambless study subjective anxiety starts to decline only after 50 min, whereas in most analog studies the duration of exposure during flooding is often much shorter.

Several studies investigated whether habituation of physiological arousal occurred during flooding in imagination. Generally, after an initial increase in arousal, arousal decreases, thus showing a curvilinear habituation curve. Such results were found on heart rate (Mathews & Shaw, 1973; Orenstein & Carr, 1975; Watson *et al.*, 1972) and on skin conductance measures (Mathews & Shaw, 1973; McCutcheon & Adams, 1975).

2.2.2.2. Flooding *in Vivo*. In a study by Stern and Marks (1973) subjective anxiety and heart rate were monitored during exposure *in vivo* with agoraphobics. There was little decrement in heart rate and subjective anxiety during the first hour of exposure. During the second hour

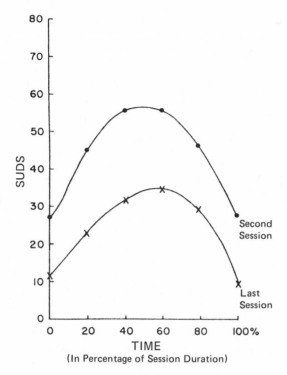

Figure 4. Mean subjective anxiety ratings during second and last flooding sessions with agoraphobics (*n* = 6). (From "Habituation of Subjective Anxiety during Flooding in Imagery" by E. B. Foa and D. L. Chambless, *Behaviour Research and Therapy,* 1978, *16,* Fig. 3. Copyright 1978 by Pergamon Press. Reprinted by permission.)

heart rate and subjective anxiety declined (see Figure 5). Studies on specific phobics also found habituation of physiological arousal and subjective anxiety during prolonged exposure *in vivo* (Nunes & Marks, 1975; Watson *et al.*, 1972). Here, heart rate was found to decrease much earlier than with agoraphobics.

In the Watson *et al.* (1972) study flooding in fantasy evoked less tachycardia than exposure *in vivo.* Even after habituation to imaginal stimuli had occurred, patients responded with much tachycardia when exposed to the phobic stimuli *in vivo.*

2.2.2.3. Biochemical Changes. Curtis and his colleagues studied biochemical changes during flooding *in vivo* with subjects who had phobias to small animals and insects. There was some evidence that anxiety induced by flooding led to growth hormone response (Curtis,

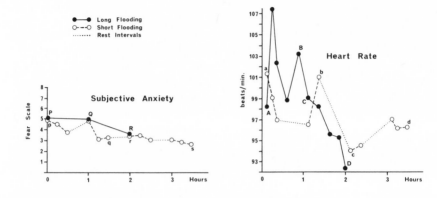

Figure 5. Changes during flooding *in vivo:* subjective anxiety (*n* = 16) and heart rate (*n* = 15). (From "Brief and Prolonged Flooding: A Comparison in Agoraphobic Patients" by R. Stern and I. M. Marks, *Archives of General Psychiatry,* 1973, *28,* Fig. 4. Copyright 1973 by the American Medical Association. Reprinted by permission.)

Nesse, Buxton, & Lippman, 1979). However, flooding did not lead to change in prolactin levels (Nesse, Curtis, Brown, & Rubin, 1980); further almost no cortisol elevations (Curtis, Buxton, Lippman, Nesse, & Wright, 1976) were found. Normally, biochemical changes are shown in response to stressors on these indices. In discussing their findings, Nesse *et al.* (1980) suggest that the notion of an undifferentiated "stress" response needs to be reconsidered: "We suspect that endocrine responses to stressors are not general but are quite specific depending on the exact nature of the stressor" (p. 30). This suggestion is in line with data of Appleby, Klein, Sachar, and Levitt (1981) that indicate that the stress of a panic attack may be biochemically distinct from other forms of physical and psychological stress.

    2.2.2.4. Cognitive Changes. Although cognitive changes are presumably of paramount importance in the process of flooding, these factors have received relatively little attention.

    To date, three studies have been reported that attempted to assess the influence of expectancy of therapeutic gain on flooding in imagination by varying instructional sets. Borkovec (1972) found a significant expectancy effect: although flooding resulted in a decrease of physiological arousal, only subjects with therapeutic instructions showed an improvement on the behavioral measure. Dee (1972) investigated the effect of therapeutic instruction on flooding: positive expectancy appeared to facilitate anxiety reduction. Finally, Segal and Marshall (1980) compared flooding under different therapeutic instructions with placebo. Subjects were led to believe that treatment was either very helpful (positive) or untested (neutral), or ineffective (negative). Although the instructional manipulation was ineffective since these attitudes were found to change over time, flooding was no more effective than placebo (see Figure 6). All four groups improved significantly on subjective ratings of discomfort, approach behavior, and heart rate. However, none of these measures revealed a significant between-group difference. Similarly, Gelder *et al.* (1973) found no differences between placebo and flooding as far as specific phobias were concerned.

Sorgatz and Prümm (1978) investigated whether fake physiological feedback enhanced success of flooding. In their flooding-analog study subjects who were informed about their progress by means of fake physiological feedback improved significantly more than subjects who viewed these signals as distracting and without further purpose.

As to the influence of expectancy on flooding *in vivo*, no experimental studies have been conducted. The data of correlational studies are inconclusive. Emmelkamp and Wessels (1975) found a positive correlation between agoraphobics' expectancy of therapeutic gain at the start of the treatment and success of exposure *in vivo*. However, these results are in contradiction with those of Stern and Marks (1973) who found no significant correlation between expectancy and improvement.

In sum, flooding in imagination has not been shown to be effective independently from nonspecific variables as expectancy of therapeutic gain. It should be noted, however, that very few studies have addressed

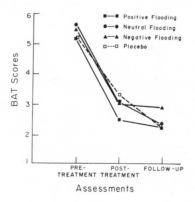

Figure 6. Scores on the behavioral avoidance test. (From Segal & Marshall, 1980. Reprinted by permission of the authors.)

this issue, and, apart from the study by Gelder *et al.* (1973), all were of analog nature. Conclusions with respect to the influence of such non-specific factors on flooding applied to clinical patients are unwarranted.

2.3. Anxiety Evocation

Another continuing debate in the flooding literature concerns the stimulus content during flooding. Some therapists have used actual depictions of the feared situation. Others employed depiction of horrifying scenes, often including adverse consequences to the patient, based on the notion that anxiety evocation was necessary before extinction could occur. For example, during flooding one can have a car-phobic patient imagine that he is driving a car on a busy motorway or have him imagine that he is involved in a terrible car accident.

Even if adverse consequences to the subject are excluded, the content of a flooding scene may differ considerably. For instance, flooding scenes can contain either coping statements or helplessness statements (Mathews & Rezin, 1977). In other studies (e.g., de Moor, 1970) even reassuring statements with snake-phobic subjects have been used: "You really never looked at a snake. Now, look at it. A long body thinner at the ends. One end is the tail, it's a pointed one. The other end is the head, a very little head with two piercing eyes, a little mouth and a very little forked tongue flicking in and out. Look at it. *That's what a snake is all about*" (p. 49). Flooding along these lines may be better conceived of as cognitive restructuring. Unfortunately, in most studies the details of the flooding procedures used are not reported. This makes cross-study comparisons virtually impossible.

2.3.1. Horrifying versus Neutral Cues

Several studies compared flooding with and without horrifying scenes. The results of these studies are equivocal. While Foa, Blau, Prout, and Latimer (1977) found that the subjects who had been treated by flooding with horrifying cues improved significantly more with respect to interference of their fear in everyday life as compared with pleasant flooding and no-treatment control subjects, other studies found pleasant flooding to be more effective (Mathews & Shaw, 1973; Marshall, Gauthier, Christie, Currie, & Gordon, 1977).

Stimulus content with flooding in these studies may have been confounded by the degree of helplessness depicted in the scenes: With horrifying themes subjects were depicted as being helpless. For instance in the scenes used by Mathews and Shaw (1973) the subjects are described as being covered by spider webs and powerless to escape. Mathews and Rezin (1977) compared horrifying versus pleasant and coping versus no-coping rehearsal in a 2 × 2 factorial design. Pleasant themes led to more anxiety reduction than horrifying themes especially on the avoidance measure. Coping rehearsal had most effect combined with horrifying themes.

Summarizing the studies reviewed so far, it may be concluded that the inclusion of horrifying stimuli during flooding in imagination does not enhance effectiveness. Rather, it seems that flooding with pleasant scenes is more effective, at least with respect to anxiety reduction. In addition, coping statements may increase the effectiveness of flooding when horrifying stimuli are used. However, these conclusions must be qualified in several ways. In the first place, all studies were of the analog type. Thus, generalization of the results to the population of clinical patients seems unwarranted. Secondly, Mathews and Rezin (1977), Mathews and Shaw (1973) and Marshall *et al.* (1977) used taped stimulus material. It is quite possible that during taped flooding scenes, cognitive avoidance on the part of the subject is more likely when horrifying cues are presented than when pleasant scenes are offered. If cognitive escape and avoidance occurs during flooding, habituation of anxiety may be prevented and this theoretically may even lead to an exacerbation of fear. There is some evidence that actual verbal presentations of imaginal phobic stimuli elicit more physiological arousal than taped presentations (DeScipkes & Rowe, 1978).

It seems to me that flooding should always use realistic themes: Patients should be able to imagine themselves in the depicted situations. The point at issue here is that for some patients horrifying cues may be quite realistic, whereas for others these cues may be quite unrealistic and therefore can be easily avoided by internal statements like "that isn't real; that will not occur to me." If we allow that flooding themes should be realistic in order to prevent cognitive avoidance, it follows that flooding treatment should be tailor made. Let me illustrate my point by a clinical example. In our flooding treatment with agoraphobic patients, we have included such "horrifying scenes" as feeling dizzy, getting a panic attack, fainting, and people looking at the patient and making comments about him or her while lying down. Also we have patients imagine that they are taken to a mental hospital. However, only those horrifying cues were used of which the patient was really afraid. Thus, patients who feared going insane were flooded on this theme, whereas flooding for patients who feared being observed in public consisted of such scenes. Thus, even within a relatively homogeneous population of phobic patients, the situations patients are really afraid of might differ from patient to patient. Therefore, flooding scenes should be adapted to the individual fears.

Now turning back to the analog studies, the horrifying themes used seem to have been quite unrealistic for most of the spider-phobic or rat-phobic subjects. For instance, as already mentioned, the spider phobics in the Mathews and Shaw (1973) study had to imagine that they were covered by webs with no possibility of escape. I wonder how many spider phobics are really afraid of this. In fact, Mathews and Shaw (1973) found no differences between horrifying cues and realistic cues in terms of self-reported anxiety *during* flooding, which seems to emphasize my point.

Before meaningful conclusions can be drawn with respect to the contribution of horrific cues to flooding in imagination, studies are needed in which *realistic* flooding themes with and without horrific cues are compared with each other: The content of these scenes must be based upon the patient fears. In addition, treatment has to be given by a live therapist to prevent any possible cognitive avoidance behavior on the part of the subject.

2.3.2. Anxiety Evocation during Exposure In Vivo

Several studies have investigated the effects of anxiety evocation during exposure *in vivo*. In the early days of exposure *in vivo*, guidelines for conducting treatments were derived from implosion and flooding theory and it was thought to be essential that anxiety should be maximized during exposure *in vivo* before extinction or habituation could occur. In the first controlled study that included flooding *in vivo* with phobic patients (Marks, Boulougouris, & Marset, 1971) therapists tried to evoke anxiety deliberately during exposure *in vivo*. Hafner and Marks (1976) allocated 12 agoraphobics randomly across high-anxiety and low-anxiety conditions. In the high-anxiety condition, patients were encouraged to confront their symptoms during exposure *in vivo*; therapists' reassurance was minimized. Instead, throughout the exposure *in vivo* procedure the therapist tried to induce anxiety by such statements as: "Imagine yourself feeling worse and worse, giddy, sweaty, nauseated, as if you are about to vomit any moment . . . you fall to the floor half conscious, people gather round you, someone calls for an ambulance" (p. 77). In the low-anxiety condition, patients were allowed to distract themselves; and they were even encouraged to do relaxation exercises. No anxiety-inducing statements were made by the therapists. Patients in the high-anxiety condition experienced more anxiety and panic attacks than patients in the low-anxiety condition. However, *no* differences were found in improvement in either condition. Thus, deliberately inducing anxiety during exposure *in vivo* did not enhance improvement.

In an analog study by Kirsch, Wolpin, and Knutson (1975) speech-anxious college students were treated by several variants of exposure *in vivo*. Results of this study revealed that delivering a speech without anxiety provocation was more effective than when anxiety was deliberately provoked by a "booing" audience.

2.4. Exposure In Imagination versus Exposure *In Vivo*

Several clinical studies have been conducted comparing flooding in imagination with flooding *in vivo*. Both Stern and Marks (1973) and Watson, Mullett, and Pillay (1973) found flooding *in vivo* to be superior to flooding in imagination. However, the results of these studies are difficult to interpret since flooding in imagination was conducted by means of a tape-recorder. Moreover the design was unbalanced: Fantasy sessions always preceded *in vivo* sessions, thus delayed effects of flooding in imagination could not be ruled out.

In a study by Emmelkamp and Wessels (1975) three different flooding procedures were compared: (1) 90 min of flooding *in vivo*, (2) 90 min of flooding in imagination, and (3) 45 min of flooding in imagination immediately followed by 45 min of flooding *in vivo*. After four flooding sessions all groups received self-controlled exposure *in vivo*, a procedure to be discussed later on. Patients were agoraphobics. With flooding *in vivo* patients had to walk outside alone uninterruptedly for 90 min in a straight line from their home. Patients were not allowed to avoid this situation. When they became anxious they had to stay in the situation until anxiety declined. With flooding in imagination the patient had to imagine the most frightening situations, for example, sitting in a hall full of people, walking alone on the streets, or traveling by train or bus. The third condition consisted of a combination of these two procedures. Results at the intermediate test indicated a slight effect of flooding in imagination. Prolonged exposure *in vivo* proved to be superior to flooding in imagination, whereas the effects of the combined procedure were in between those of exposure *in vivo* and exposure in imagination (see Figure 7). Flooding in imagination led to a significant *increase* in anxious mood. During self-controlled exposure *in vivo*, after flooding in imagination, patients improved on nearly all the variables to a much greater extent than during the previous treatment.

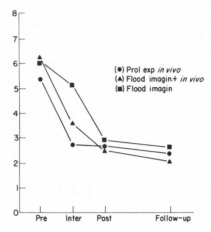

Figure 7. The effects of flooding *in vivo*, flooding in imagination, and combined flooding on phobic anxiety / avoidance. After the intermediate test each treatment group received self-controlled exposure *in vivo*. (From "Flooding in Imagination vs. Flooding *in Vivo:* A Comparison with Agoraphobics" by P. M. G. Emmelkamp and H. Wessels, *Behaviour Research and Therapy,* 1975, *13,* Fig. 3. Copyright 1975 by Pergamon Press. Reprinted by permission.)

To date, only one study (Mathews *et al.*, 1976) found *no* differences between the effects of treatments involving exposure to either imaginal or real phobic situations. There are, however, several important differences between this study and the Emmelkamp and Wessels study that might explain the conflicting results (Emmelkamp, 1977a). First, the way in which the exposure procedures were carried out may be quite different in both studies. In the imaginal treatment Emmelkamp and Wessels (1975) used only those scenes that aroused most anxiety; in the exposure *in vivo* treatment also the most difficult situations for each client were used. In contrast, with both exposure *in vivo* and in imagination, Mathews *et al.* (1976) presented situations from a hierarchy in graded order from the least to the most difficult. Along a continuum of approach to phobic stimuli, the exposure procedures of Mathews *et al.* resemble desensitization (without relaxation), whereas for the Emmelkamp and Wessels (1975) procedures, the term "flooding" seems to be more appropriate. Furthermore, patients in the Emmelkamp and Wessels study were taken off drugs; in the Mathews *et al.* (1976) study, 29 out of 36 patients were taking psychotropic medication, mostly minor tranquillizers. Thus, it seems that the anxiety experienced during treatment in the Mathews *et al.* study was less than in the Emmelkamp and Wessels study.

Practice at home (exposure *in vivo*) between treatment sessions may be another important difference in these studies. In the Emmelkamp and Wessels study, *no* homework assignments were given before the intermediate test. Moreover, treatment was 3 times weekly, which leaves little room for self-exposure *in vivo*. In contrast, Mathews *et al.* treated their patients only once a week; patients were instructed to practice at home between the imaginal treatment sessions. Also, at each session an agreement was reached between therapist and patient on an item that the patient had to practice at home. Mathews *et al.* state "*considerable emphasis* was placed on the patients' own efforts, to the extent of selecting a target for home practice each week, and requiring a diary to be kept of practice attempts." A check of diaries completed by the patients revealed that, on the average, they went out once a day throughout treatment. Thus, Mathews *et al.* seem to have compared exposure *in vivo* with a combination of exposure *in vivo* and imagination.

In the Emmelkamp and Wessels study exposure *in vivo* led to a reduction of 2.9 scale points (anxiety and avoidance main phobia) after four sessions in about one and one half weeks; in the Mathews *et al.* study even smaller gains (2.2 scale points) were achieved after 4 months of treatment and 16 treatment sessions (clients rating: results are presented on a 0–8 scale). The difference in outcome cannot be easily explained by different patient selection criteria since the groups of patients seemed actually quite similar. Both studies used chronic agoraphobics: if there was any difference between the patient population, the patients in the Emmelkamp and Wessels study were presumably more severe cases. Only patients with agoraphobia of at least 2 years duration were included (Mathews *et al.* criterion was at least 1 year). Furthermore, Emmelkamp and Wessels included patients who were unable to visit the institute because of their phobia: all their patients were treated in their homes. In the Mathews *et al.* study these patients were excluded. Assuming that patient groups were quite similar, procedural differences are presumably responsible for the difference in outcome.

Johnstone, Lancashire, Mathews, Munby, Shaw, and Gelder (1976) reported the results of measures taken during treatment in the Mathews *et al.* (1976) study. On measures of the immediate effects of treatment, exposure *in vivo* had consistent positive effects, whereas imaginal flooding had little or no effect. These results suggest that the long-term effects after imaginal flooding were indeed due to the exposure *in vivo* in between treatment sessions.

In conclusion, flooding *in vivo* has been found to be far more effective than flooding in imagination.

2.5. Flooding versus Systematic Desensitization

Numerous studies have been carried out comparing systematic desensitization with flooding. The main features of these studies are summarized in Table 5.

2.5.1. Analog Studies

Most analog studies have yielded equivocal results. Research in this area is encumbered by vague theoretical notions and terminological confusions concerning flooding. Therefore, straightforward comparisons across studies are rather difficult. The procedural and methodological flaws in these studies were discussed elsewhere (Emmelkamp, 1982a). There is no evidence that systematic desensitization is superior to flooding or vice versa. The methodological and procedural flaws are so grave and the procedures used so far removed from clinical practice that most efforts that have been done in this area seem to be a waste of time.

2.5.2. Clinical Studies

The results of two studies (Boudewyns & Wilson, 1972; Hussain, 1971) are difficult to evaluate due to methodological flaws and the conclusions based on these studies are not warranted (Emmelkamp, 1982a).

When both systematic desensitization and flooding were carried out in imagination, generally no differences were found (Crowe, Marks, Agras, & Leitenberg, 1972; Shaw, 1976; Solyom, Heseltine, McClure, Solyom, Ledwidge, & Steinberg, 1973). When treatment consisted of a combination of imaginal and *in vivo* exposure, conflicting results were reported.

In a study reported by Boulougouris, Marks, and Marset (1971) and Marks, Boulougouris, and Marset (1971) both treatments involved six 50-min sessions of imaginal exposure followed by two 70 min sessions of exposure *in vivo*. Flooding proved to be more effective than desensitization, especially with agoraphobics. In a study by Gelder, Bancroft, Gath, Johnston, Mathews, and Shaw (1973) no differences between flooding and desensitization were found. Their treatments involved three information sessions and eight imaginal sessions followed by four *in vivo* sessions.

The differences in outcome of these studies can perhaps best be explained by the differences in exposure *in vivo* that patients received. In the Marks *et al.* (1971) study, exposure *in vivo* was firmly forceful during flooding, but relaxed during desensitization (Marks, 1975). However,

Table 5. Flooding versus Systematic Desensitization[a]

Study	Population	Treatment	Sessions (min)	Mode of treatment presentation	Results
		A. Phobic Patients			
Crowe, Marks, Agras, & Leitenberg (1972)	Mixed ($n = 14$)	Flooding SD[b] Reinforced practice (block design)	4×50	L[o]	$3 > 2$[c] (behavioral measure)
Gelder, Bancroft, Gath, Johnston, Mathews, & Shaw (1973)	18 Agoraphobics 18 Other phobics	Flooding SD Nonspecific control	$15 \times 45 - 60$	L	$1 = 2$[d] $1 \& 2 > 3$ (agoraphobics)
Hussain (1971)	Agoraphobics or Social phobics ($n = 40$)	Flooding-thiopental Flooding-saline SD-thiopental SD-saline (crossover)	6×45	L	$1 > 2, 3, \& 4$
Marks, Boulougouris, & Marset (1971)	9 Agoraphobics 7 Specific	Flooding SD (crossover)	$8 \times 50 - 70$	L	$1 > 2$
Shaw (1976)	Social phobics ($n = 30$)	Flooding SD Social Skills	10×60 10×60 10×75	L	$1 = 2 = 3$
Solyom, Heseltine, McClure, Solyom, Ledwidge, & Steinberg (1973)	39 Agora/social phobics 11 Other phobics	Flooding SD Aversion relief Phenelzine Placebo	12×60 12×60 24×30 6×60 6×60	L	$1 > 2$ (FSS only) $3 > 1, 2, 4 \& 5$ (psychiatric rating) $4 > 5$ (psychiatric rating)

Table 5. (Continued)

Study	Population	Treatment	Sessions (min)	Mode of treatment presentation	Results
		B. Analog studies			
Barrett (1969)	Snake phobia	Flooding SD No-treatment	± 2 ± 12	L	1 = 2 1 & 2 > 3 1 more efficient
Borkovec (1972)	Snake phobia	Flooding SD Placebo No-treatment	4 × 50	L	1 = 2
Calef & MacLean (1970)	Speech anxiety	Flooding SD No-treatment	5 × 60	L	1 = 2 1 & 2 > 3
Cornish & Dilley (1973)	Test anxiety	Flooding SD Counseling No-treatment	4 × 40	T[f]	1 = 2 1 & 2 > 4
De Moor (1970)	Snake phobia	Flooding SD No-treatment	5 × 20	L	1 = 2 1 & 2 > 3
Hekmat (1973)	Rat phobia	Flooding SD Semantic desensitization Pseudo-desensitization	2 × 40 5 × 40	L	2 & 3 > 1 4 > 1 (behavioral measure) 2 & 3 > 4
Horne & Matson (1977)	Test anxiety	Flooding SD Modeling	10 × 60	L	1, 2 & 3 > 4 & 5 (test anxiety) 3 > 2 > 1 (test anxiety)

Study	Disorder	Treatments	Design		Results
		Study skills No-treatment			2, 3 & 4 > 1 & 5 (grade point average)
Marshall, Gauthier, Christie, Currie, & Gordon (1977)	Snake phobia	Flooding SD Placebo No-treatment	3 × 40	L	1 > 2 1 & 2 > 3 & 4 3 = 4
Mealiea & Nawas (1971)	Snake phobia	Flooding Implosive SD Placebo No-treatment	5 × 30	T	3 > all others (behavioral measure) 1 = 5 (behavioral measure) 2 & 4 > 5 (behavioral measure) 1 = 2 = 3 = 4 = 5 (self-report)
Mylar & Clement (1972)	Speech anxiety	Flooding SD No-treatment	5 × 60	T	1 = 2 1 & 2 > 3
Smith & Nye (1973)	Test anxiety	Flooding SD No-treatment	7 × 45	L	1 = 2 (test anxiety) 2 > 1 (other measures)
Suarez, Adams, & McCutcheon (1976)	Surgical operation	Flooding SD No-treatment	3 × 30	?	1 = 2 (behavioral measure) 2 > 1 (self-report)
Willis & Edwards (1969)	Mouse phobia	Flooding SD Placebo	± 4 × ?	L	2 > 1 & 3 1 = 3

[a] Adapted from Emmelkamp (1982a).
[b] SD = Systematic Desensitization.
[c] a > b = Treatment a superior to treatment b.
[d] a = b = Treatment a about equally effective as treatment b.
[e] L = treatment presented by life therapist.
[f] T = treatment presented by tape.

Gelder *et al.* state that "differences in procedures were found more difficult to maintain" and "little attempt was made to apply specific desensitization or flooding measures while practice was going on" (p. 448). Moreover, the different results might be explained by different amounts of self-exposure *in vivo* in between treatment sessions. In the Marks *et al.* study there was less time between sessions for an effect to develop from self-exposure than in the Gelder *et al.* study: Marks *et al.* treated patients three times a week rather than once a week as Gelder *et al.* did.

That exposure *in vivo* was indeed an important aspect of the treatments of Gelder *et al.* was shown by a secondary analysis of process variables in their treatments (Mathews, Johnston, Shaw, & Gelder, 1973). It was found that anxiety anticipated in the real-life phobic situation did not change consistently until the start of the *in vivo* exposure phase (see Figure 8). The results of this study suggest that the imaginal part of the treatment is redundant, at least with respect to anxiety anticipated in real-life situations.

Summarizing the studies with phobic patients it can be concluded that desensitization in imagination and flooding in imagination are about

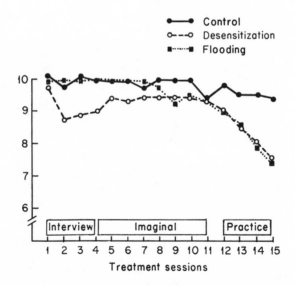

Figure 8. Mean scores of anxiety estimated for phobic situations "in real life" for each treatment group. (From "Process Variables and the Prediction of Outcome in Behaviour Therapy" by A. M. Mathews *et al., British Journal of Psychiatry,* 1973, *123,* Fig. 4. Copyright 1973 by the British Journal of Psychiatry. Reprinted by permission.)

equally effective (or equally ineffective). Further, exposure *in vivo* appears to play an important part: The differential effectiveness found may be due to the way exposure *in vivo* was carried out.

3. SELF-CONTROLLED EXPOSURE *IN VIVO*

Although in systematic desensitization it is assumed that anxiety must first be inhibited before avoidance behavior can be reduced, in self-controlled exposure *in vivo* the avoidance behavior is changed directly, which may eventually lead to a decrease in anxiety (Leitenberg, Agras, Butz, & Wincze, 1971). Working within an operant conditioning paradigm, Leitenberg and his colleagues demonstrated that graded exposure *in vivo* in an anxiety arousing situation was successful in the treatment of a variety of clinical phobic cases (Agras, Leitenberg, & Barlow, 1968; Agras, Leitenberg, Barlow, & Thomson, 1969; Agras, Leitenberg, Wincze, Butz, & Callahan, 1970) and in the treatment of such common fears as fear of heights, fear of snakes, fear of painful electric shock, and (in young children) fear of darkness (Leitenberg & Callahan, 1973). This treatment procedure has been called successive approximation, reinforced practice, or shaping.

Let me illustrate this treatment approach with three case studies of agoraphobics described by Agras, Leitenberg, and Barlow (1968). The patients had to walk a one-mile "course" from the clinical research center to downtown. Patients were told: "We would like to know how far you can walk by yourself without undue anxiety. We find that repeated practice in an structured situation often leads to progress." The therapist timed the duration of each walk. Systematic praise (positive reinforcement) given contingent upon progress in distance walked was introduced, removed, and reintroduced in sequential phases of the experiment with each patient. Results of one of these single case experiments are presented in Figure 9. Social reinforcement (praise by the therapist) led to an increase in the distance walked. Removing the reinforcement led to worsening. Finally, reintroduction of social reinforcement led to improved performance. Results of these three single-case studies suggested that reinforcement for improved performance was responsible for the improvements achieved.

3.1. Comparison with Other Treatments

Several studies have compared successive approximation with other behavioral treatments. Successive approximation proved to be more

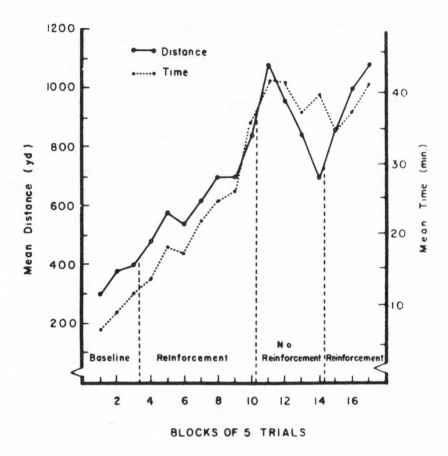

Figure 9. The effect of reinforcement and nonreinforcement on the performance of an agoraphobic patient. (From "Social Reinforcement in the Modification of Agoraphobia" by W. S. Agras, H. Letenberg, and D. H. Barlow, *Archives of General Psychiatry*, 1968, *19*, Fig. 2. Copyright 1968 by the American Medical Association. Reprinted by permission.)

effective than systematic desensitization in imagination with phobic volunteers (Barlow, Agras, Leitenberg, & Wincze, 1970; McReynolds & Grizzard, 1971) and with phobic patients (Crowe, Marks, Agras, & Leitenberg, 1972). Successive approximation and flooding were found to be about equally effective with phobic patients, including agoraphobics (Crowe *et al.,* 1972; Everaerd, Rijken, & Emmelkamp, 1973).

3.2. Therapeutic Process

3.2.1. Reinforcement versus Feedback

In successive approximation reinforcement and feedback have been confounded, since patients are given both social reinforcement and contingent feedback for time spent in the phobic situation. In order to investigate the relative contribution of feedback and reinforcement, Emmelkamp and Ultee (1974) compared successive approximation and self-observation using agoraphobics as subjects. With both procedures the patient had to walk a course leading in a straight line from the patient's home with instructions to turn back on experiencing undue anxiety. With successive approximation the patient was informed by the therapist about the time he had stayed away after each trial; in addition, the patient was reinforced whenever there was an increase in the time outside. The differences between successive approximation and self-observation are that during the latter procedure the patient observes his progress by recording the time that he is able to spend outside (feedback), and that he is never reinforced by the therapist. The patient had to record the duration of each trial in a notebook. No difference in effect was found between successive approximation and self-observation: Thus, verbal praise contingent upon achievement did not enhance the effects of graduated exposure plus feedback.

Figure 10 presents the data from the experimental treatment of a severe agoraphobic patient (Emmelkamp, 1982b). In the first phase of this experiment the patient was treated with self-observation. In the second phase the therapist gave systematic praise contingent upon an increase in the time walked. Finally, the self-observation condition was reintroduced. As shown in this figure, treatment led to a steady increase in the time the patient was able to walk outside along a course from his home, irrespective of treatment condition. Thus, there is no evidence that systematic praise adds to the effects of feedback.

The effectiveness of graduated exposure plus feedback has further been demonstrated in analog (Becker & Costello, 1975) and clinical studies (Emmelkamp, 1974; 1980b; Emmelkamp & Emmelkamp-Benner, 1975; Emmelkamp & Wessels, 1975; Leitenberg, Agras, Allen, Butz, & Edwards, 1975).

3.2.2. Role of Feedback

Whether feedback enhanced the effectiveness of graduated exposure was studied by Rutner (1973) in an analog study involving rat

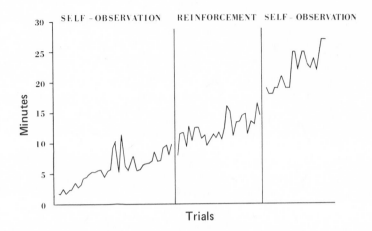

Figure 10. The effect of feedback and reinforcement on the performance of an agoraphobic patient. (From "Exposure *in Vivo* Treatments" by P. M. G. Emmelkamp, in A. Goldstein and D. Chambless (Eds.), *Agoraphobia: Multiple perspectives on theory and treatment.* Copyright 1982 by Wiley. Reprinted by permission.)

fearful volunteers as subjects. Treatment consisted of self-controlled exposure to a live rat. Each subject was instructed to look into a box containing a rat, and to keep viewing the rat for as long as the subject could before releasing a handle that terminated the trial. A total of 35 experimental trials were conducted. Four experimental conditions were created: (1) exposure only, (2) exposure plus self-monitored feedback, (3) exposure plus therapeutically oriented instruction, and (4) exposure plus therapeutically-oriented instruction with feedback. Results indicated that feedback did enhance the effectiveness of self-controlled exposure, while no significant effects were found for either the therapeutically oriented instruction or the interaction factor. Thus, results of this study showed the importance of precise trial by trial feedback in self-controlled exposure *in vivo*.

3.2.3. Self-Control Of Exposure Time

With both successive approximation and self-observation procedures, the exposure time is controlled by the patient. Whether such self-control enhances the effects of graduated exposure *in vivo* was studied by Hepner and Cauthen (1975) using snake phobic volunteers as subjects. Graduated exposure under subject control with feedback was compared to graduated exposure under therapist control with feedback. Self-control of exposure time proved to be superior to therapist control in reducing avoidance behavior. Presumably, a cognitive process of enhancement of self-attribution of personal competence is associated with self-controlled exposure *in vivo*.

3.3. Concluding Comment

In summary, self-controlled exposure *in vivo* has been found to be quite effective in clinical trials. There is no evidence that reinforcement enhances the effectiveness of this procedure. Results of analog studies indicate that both feedback and self-control of exposure time are important factors and both enhance the effectiveness of graduated exposure *in vivo*.

4. MODELING

With modeling treatment, phobic individuals view a model that performs approach behavior toward a phobic stimulus. The effects of modeling treatments are usually explained in terms of vicarious learning (Bandura, 1969). By viewing the model performing bold behavior, the anxiety in the observer is assumed to extinguish vicariously.

Modeling procedures have been successfully applied in the treatment of phobias. However, it should be noted that almost all studies in this area have dealt with analog populations (most often animal phobias). Thus, the utility of modeling procedures with clinical phobic cases remains to be demonstrated.

Modeling procedures vary in several aspects: The model may be presented in live ("overt modeling"), displayed on film ("symbolic modeling"), or imagined covertly ("covert modeling"). In addition, guided participation *in vivo* after observing the therapists' approach behavior has become known as participant modeling.

4.1. Therapeutic Processes

No meaningful modeling procedure can be applied devoid of exposure to the phobic stimulus. Thus, it is questionable whether the effects of modeling should be ascribed to vicarious learning processes. Rather, an explanation in terms of exposure is equally plausible. Several studies have sought to test whether modeling was more effective than mere exposure to the phobic stimuli. These studies have provided conflicting results. Rankin (1976) found modeling more effective than mere exposure after anxiety was reduced through prior exposure to the phobic stimulus; modeling was no more effective than exposure when both were presented as the first treatment.

Results of other studies comparing modeling and exposure procedures (including systematic desensitization) are difficult to evaluate since modeling was often mixed with relaxation and narratives. Denney and Sullivan (1976) attempted to separate the effects of modeling and relaxation: Several variants of exposure and modeling were compared. Modeling alone was more effective than mere exposure to the phobic object. However, when both exposure and modeling were combined with relaxation and narratives, modeling was no more effective than exposure. In my opinion, the results of this study might be interpreted in terms of treatment generated "expectancies." It is quite possible that modeling subjects believed they were receiving a valid treatment, whereas exposure only subjects did not. On the other hand, when exposure was made equally credible as a treatment procedure by adding relaxation and narratives, the effects of modeling did not surpass the effects of exposure. Unfortunately, expectancy ratings are lacking. The above hypothesis suggests that the effects of modeling may be ascribed to placebo factors rather than to vicarious learning. Current research efforts have not yet provided sufficient evidence to rule out an interpretation of modeling effects in terms of a cognitive-expectancy model.

4.2. Covert Modeling

During covert modeling, clients imagine rather than watch models approach and handle fearful stimuli. The covert modeling studies have been reviewed by Kazdin and Smith (1979) and will not be repeated here. Briefly, although several studies found covert modeling effective in comparison with control conditions, in other studies control conditions were found to be equally effective.

4.3. Participant Modeling: Exposure *in Vivo*

Participant modeling involves two stages: the therapist initially models approach behavior to the phobic stimulus, followed by the therapist guiding the subject's participation through progressively more demanding tasks. Participant modeling has been found to be far more effective than modeling alone (Bandura, Adams, & Beyer, 1977; Blanchard, 1970; Lewis, 1974; Ritter, 1969) and covert modeling (Thase & Moss, 1976).

The participant modeling approach consists of two components: (1) modeling and (2) gradual exposure *in vivo*. To date there is no evidence that the modeling component is an essential feature of this approach. Bourque and Ladouceur (1980) compared five different performance based treatments: (1) participant modeling (PM), (2) participant modeling without therapist physical guidance (PMWC), (3) modeling plus exposure *in vivo* (M + R), (4) therapist-controlled exposure *in vivo* (TCE), and (5) self-controlled exposure *in vivo* (CCE). Subjects were acrophobics who were recruited through advertisements placed in community newspapers. Results on the behavioral avoidance test are shown in Figure 11. Clearly, modeling does not enhance treatment effectiveness, since the results failed to delineate any differences among the various treatments.

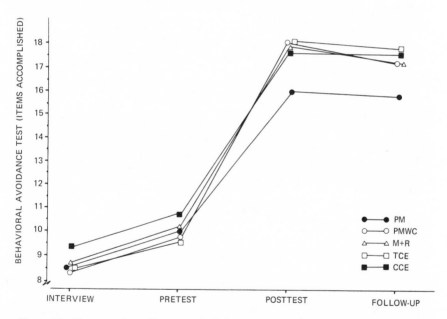

Figure 11. Mean number of items on the behavioral avoidance test accomplished by each group during the various assessment sessions. Modeling conditions [participant modeling (PM), participant modeling without therapist physical guidance (PMWC), and modeling plus exposure in vivo (M + R)] are not superior to plain exposure *in vivo* [Therapist-controlled (TCE) and self-controlled (CCE)]. (From "An Investigation of Various Performance-Based Treatments with Acrophobics by P. Bourque and R. Ladouceur, *Behaviour Research and Therapy*, 1980, *18*, Fig. 1. Copyright 1980 by Pergamon Press. Reprinted by permission.)

As the authors point out: "Since both graduated exposure conditions are devoid of vicarious aids it is difficult to conceive that modeling exerted a substantial effect in the modeling-plus-response rehearsal condition" (p. 167). The most parsimonious explanation to account for the equivalent changes seems to be a common component in the different treatment—exposure *in vivo*.

Several recent studies have contributed toward further clarification of the role of exposure *in vivo* in participant modeling. Results of these studies (Bandura, Jeffery, & Gajdos, 1975; Smith & Coleman, 1977) indicate that self-directed practice enhances the effectiveness of participant modeling. In the Smith and Coleman (1977) study rat-phobic volunteers were assigned to one of three groups. After treatment by means of participant modeling, subjects received either self-directed treatment with varied rats, or continued with participant modeling. Both self-directed practice conditions led to greater fear reduction to generalization stimuli than did the participant modeling condition. The results of this study indicate that successful performance in real life situations might be more important than modeling.

4.4. Concluding Remarks

Whether modeling potentiates the effects of exposure procedures is still a question for further study. Moreover, the relative contribution of modeling may depend on the target behavior under study. Even though modeling presumably will be of limited value with acrophobics and agoraphobics, it might be more important in the treatment of social-anxious patients, who lack adequate social skills. Further, the need for additional work with clinical patients is underscored. Modeling therapies applied to clinical phobic patients are currently based on extrapolations from laboratory data and require further examination in clinical cases.

5. COVERT REINFORCEMENT

The procedure of covert positive reinforcement, originally developed by Cautela (1970) has been applied to phobic cases. Covert positive reinforcement refers to a procedure in which the patient is required to imagine himself or herself performing a behavior that the patient is unlikely to commit followed by a covert reinforcement. Thus, the phobic individual is asked to imagine that he or she is performing approach behavior in an anxiety-arousing situation. The client is subsequently instructed to imagine a pleasant scene (reinforcing stimulus) contingent on the vivid imagination of approach behavior. The procedure is conceptualized in operant terms:

> This technique draws from the abundant information available from experimental work on positive reinforcement that indicates that when a positive reinforcer is made contingent upon a specified response, the probability of that response reoccurring will increase. (Cautela & Wall 1980, p. 154)

Cautela (1973) suggested that manipulating covert events might be therapeutically equivalent or even superior to modification of the overt behavior. Apart from a few clinical case studies, all controlled studies concern analog populations.

5.1. Therapeutic Process

Several studies found covert positive reinforcement more effective than no-treatment control groups (Bajtelsmit & Gersham, 1976; Finger & Galassi, 1977; Guidry & Randolph, 1974; Hurley, 1976; Kostka & Galassi, 1974; Ladouceur, 1974; 1977; 1978; Marshall, Boutilier, & Minnes, 1974) and attention-placebo groups (Flannery, 1972; Guidry & Randolph, 1974; Ladouceur, 1977; 1978; Marshall *et al.*, 1974). However, in the Bajtelsmit and Gershman (1976) study covert positive reinforcement was found to be no more effective than placebo. Comparative evaluations of covert reinforcement and systematic desensitization have found both procedures to be about equally effective (Kostka & Galassi, 1974; Ladouceur, 1978; Marshall *et al.*, 1974).

5.1.1. Operant Conditioning

The theoretical rationale in terms of operant conditioning has been seriously questioned. Results of several studies indicate that covert reinforcement is not a crucial element of this procedure, since omitting the reinforcer or noncontiguous presentation of the reinforcer led to similar outcome (Bajtelsmit & Gershman, 1976; Hurley, 1976; Ladouceur, 1974; 1977; 1978; Marshall *et al.*, 1974). Results of these studies cast doubt on the operant model paradigm underlying this procedure. The rationale of covert positive reinforcement was seriously challenged by the finding of Bajtelsmit and Gershman (1976): Covert reinforcement following anxious behavior was equally effective as when it followed the desired behavior. According to the operant model, reinforcement of anxiety should have led to an increase instead of to a reduction of anxiety.

5.1.2. Imaginal versus In Vivo Exposure

The most parsimonious explanation for the effects of covert positive reinforcement appears to be exposure to the phobic stimuli. Two studies (Engum, Miller, & Meredith, 1980; Flannery, 1972) tested the relative effectiveness of covert reinforcement presented either after imaginal or after *in vivo* exposure; *in vivo* exposure was found to be the most effective.

5.1.3. Expectancy of Therapeutic Gain

There is some evidence that the imaginal covert reinforcement procedure is influenced by expectancy factors. Engum *et al.* (1980) manipulated demand that stressed the likelihood of success of the covert reinforcement procedure. Subjects who were told that the effects of treatment were unknown improved significantly less than subjects with a high expectation of therapeutic gain when exposure was imaginal. Expectancy did not influence outcome with exposure *in vivo*.

5.2. Concluding Comment

There is no evidence that covert reinforcement achieves its effects through operant reinforcement. The experimental evidence available at present suggests that the therapeutic mechanisms should be interpreted in terms of exposure to phobic stimuli and expectancy of therapeutic gain.

Finally, it is important to recall that controlled *clinical* studies are lacking. While therapists may be tempted to use covert techniques out of curiosity (Engum *et al.*, 1980), treatment based upon these grounds seems ethically troublesome.

6. BIOFEEDBACK

Biofeedback procedures are often applied in the treatment of anxiety or phobic states. In this section an overview will be given of the research that has been conducted in this area. Most of the research has concerned electromyographic feedback and heart rate feedback.

6.1. Electromyographic Feedback

A number of researchers have investigated whether electromyographic biofeedback (EMG) results in a reduction of anxiety symptoms. Studies involving normal volunteers as subjects have produced equivocal results. Several studies (Coursey, 1975; Haynes, Moseley, & McGowan, 1975; Reinking & Kohl, 1975) found EMG feedback superior to relaxation instructions as far as changes in EMG level were concerned; no differences were found on other measures. However, other studies found EMG feedback no more effective (Schandler & Grings, 1976) or even less effective than relaxation procedures (Beiman, Israel, & Johnson, 1978).

Several controlled studies have been conducted with anxious patients as subjects. Both Canter, Kondo, and Knott (1975) and Townsend, House, and Addario (1975) found EMG feedback superior to control conditions, when EMG was taken as the primary dependent variable. As far as anxiety symptoms were concerned, *no* significant differences between EMG and relaxation (Canter *et al.*, 1975) and between EMG and group psychotherapy (Townsend *et al.*, 1975) were reported. Recently, Raskin, Bali, and Peeke (1980) compared EMG feedback, relaxation therapy, and transcendental meditation. Again, EMG feedback was not found to be superior to the other relaxation therapies. Clinical outcome was poor irrespective of treatment condition. Further, no evidence was provided to support the assumption that muscle relaxation was related to outcome.

The effects of drugs (diazepam) and EMG feedback were compared by Lavallee, Lamontagne, Pinard, Annable, and Tetreault (1977). Forty outpatients suffering from chronic anxiety were divided across four conditions: (1) EMG feedback plus diazepam, (2) EMG feedback plus drug placebo, (3) EMG placebo plus diazepam, and (4) EMG placebo plus drug placebo. Treatment in the EMG placebo condition was identical to that of the EMG feedback group except that no tone was heard by the subjects. They were asked to relax but were not given specific instructions on relaxation techniques. Results are illustrated in Figure 12.

Both EMG feedback and diazepam resulted in significant changes in EMG levels, whereas the placebo group improved the least on this measure. The interpretation of the results on the anxiety measure are difficult to discern, since the authors failed to perform a between-group statistical analysis. However, inspection of Figure 12 reveals that in the long run the placebo group improved most. Thus, the conclusion of the authors that "EMG feedback seems to offer a worthwhile treatment for anxiety reduction" (p. 70) does not appear to follow from their study. If anything, the EMG placebo plus drug placebo group had the best outcome at follow-up with respect to anxiety, which was the original target of treatment.

It is noteworthy that Jessup and Neufeld (1977) could not demonstrate a significant change on the EMG measure in a study involving

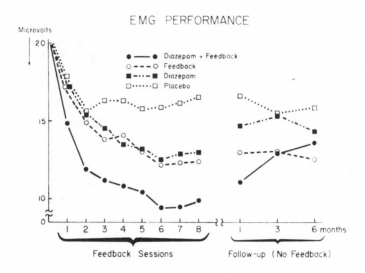

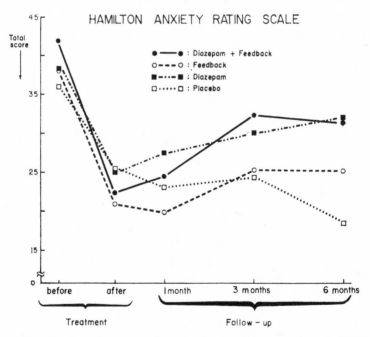

Figure 12. Effect of EMG feedback, diazepam, and placebo on EMG performance and anxiety. Although EMG feedback results in improved EMG performance, placebo treatment is equally effective in reducing anxiety. (From "Effects on EMG Feedback, Diazepam, and Their Combination on Chronic Anxiety" by Y. J. Lavallee *et al., Journal of Psychosomatic Research,* 1977, *21,* Fig. 1. Copyright 1977 by the Journal of Psychosomatic Research. Reprinted by permission.)

psychiatric patients. Perhaps even more significant, noncontingent tone presentation (control condition) led to significant changes on heart rate and anxiety measures, while EMG feedback (contingent tone) did not. A study by Romano and Cabianca (1978) examined the effectiveness of EMG-assisted systematic desensitization and systematic desensitization alone in the treatment of test anxiety. The use of EMG feedback did not appear to enhance the effects of treatment.

Both Counts, Hollandsworth, and Alcorn (1978) and Reed and Saslow (1980) investigated whether EMG biofeedback could enhance treatment by relaxation with test anxious individuals. The results of these studies indicated that biofeedback did not contribute to the effectiveness of cue controlled relaxation.

In summary, there is no evidence that EMG feedback has something to offer which other treatments (e.g., relaxation) do not. The few differences in favor of EMG feedback that have been found all concerned EMG level as the dependent variable. Although it has generally been assumed that high levels of frontal EMG are related to anxiety, a study by Burish and Horn (1979) indicates that this is not the case. Even though several arousal producing situations were successful in increasing arousal as measured by self-report and physiological measures, these situations had *no* effect on EMG levels.

6.2. Alpha Feedback

It has been suggested that increases in alpha densities or amplitudes could lead to experiences of relaxation and reductions in anxiety level (Hardt & Kamiya, 1978). For example, Hardt and Kamiya (1978) claimed that the reductions in trait anxiety were large enough to be useful in anxiety therapy.

Plotkin and Rice (1981) set out to test this hypothesis with subjects who were high in trait anxiety. Subjects were randomly assigned to training in either enhancement or suppression (placebo) of electroencephalogram (EEG) alpha activity. Both groups of subjects were informed that their particular training was considered an effective means of facilitating anxiety reduction. Results indicated that anxiety reduction was just as effectively produced with feedback training for decreased alpha levels as it was with training for increased alpha levels: "Anxiety reductions were unrelated to either the direction or magnitude of actual alpha changes, they were highly and positively correlated with the trainees ratings of perceived success at the biofeedback task" (p. 595) and they conclude: "the biofeedback context . . . may serve as a very powerful placebo that is highly effective in including experiential and behavioral changes" (p. 595).

In summary, there is no evidence that anxiety reduction should be attributed to the effects of alpha feedback training *per se*, since no clinical studies have been conducted.

6.3. Heart Rate Feedback

Gatchel and his colleagues have investigated whether heart rate biofeedback can be used in the treatment of speech anxiety. In the first study of this series (Gatchel & Proctor, 1976), heart rate control was found to be more effective than a no heart rate control condition both on physiological indices, self-report, and observers' ratings. There was also a near significant expectancy effect, indicating that improvement was at least partially due to expectancy factors. In a subsequent study (Gatchel, Hatch, Watson, Smith, & Gass, 1977) the relative effectiveness of heart rate feedback and muscle relaxation were assessed. Therefore the effects of (1) heart rate feedback, (2) relaxation, (3) relaxation plus heart rate feedback, and (4) false heart rate feedback (placebo) were compared in a between-group design. Results indicated that all treatments (including placebo) improved on self-report measures, with no differences among the groups. Only on physiological indices during the posttest speech situation the placebo group differed from the active treatment groups. Moreover, the combined procedure was found to be the most effective on this measure. Finally, the last study of this series (Gatchel, Hatch, Maynard, Turns, & Taunton-Blackwood, 1979) replicated the placebo effect found in the Gatchel *et al.* (1977) study. Results of this study demonstrated that false heart rate feedback was equally effective as true heart rate feedback and systematic desensitization on self-report indices and overt motor components of anxiety. Only on heart rate level, heart rate feedback was found to be more effective relative to desensitization and placebo. No significant group differences were found for skin conductance and EMG indices. Moreover, results indicated that the placebo effect was not short-lived, since identical results were obtained at one month follow-up.

Nunes and Marks (1975, 1976) investigated whether true heart rate feedback enhanced the effectiveness of exposure *in vivo*. In contrast with the studies by Gatchel and his colleagues, this study involved real patients with specific phobias. Although it was found that heart rate feedback substantially reduced heart rate, this effect did not generalize to skin conductance or to subjective anxiety. In addition to the studies by Nunes and Marks, some case reports have been published demonstrating the effectiveness of heart rate feedback with phobic patients (e.g., Blanchard & Abel, 1976, Wickramasekera, 1974; Gatchel, 1977). However, these studies have typically confounded exposure and biofeedback which prevents the drawing of any conclusion.

Finally, results of several studies indicate that heart rate feedback is more effective with low-anxious subjects than with high-anxious subects (Blankstein, 1975; Shepherd & Watts, 1974). The results of the Shepherd and Watts study are the more interesting, since they compared student volunteers with agoraphobic patients. It was found that agoraphobic patients did significantly worse than phobic students in decreasing their heart rate.

In summary, while heart rate feedback may lead to some control over heart rate, this does not lead to a greater reduction of subjective anxiety relative to control condition. Thus, feedback of heart rate seems to have little to offer in the treatment of anxiety. Furthermore, it should be noted that heart rate feedback during exposure to a phobic stimulus may even inhibit approach behavior, as was found in two analog studies with snake phobic volunteers (Carver & Blaney, 1977a, 1977b).

Already in 1974, Engel questioned the usefulness of heart rate feedback in the treatment of anxiety: "It may not be feasible to treat anxiety by teaching subjects to slow their heart rates since heart rate is merely one peripheral manifestation of anxiety and not the illness itself. If one taught an anxious patient to slow his heart, the end result could be an anxious patient whose heart beats slower" (p. 303). The present review suggests that this is indeed the case.

6.4. Concluding Remark

Despite claims made by the proponents of biofeedback, there is no substantial evidence that biofeedback is of any value in the treatment of anxiety-related disorders. The application of biofeedback in this area seems to have been more beneficial to the industry than to anxious and phobic patients.

7. COGNITIVE THERAPY

Behavior therapy is going cognitive. This is demonstrated by the vast increase of articles dealing with cognitive-behavior modification in the behavioral journals (Ledwidge, 1978). Most of the cognitive-behavior–modification studies have involved phobic or anxiety related problems. Now, at least 30 controlled studies in this area have been reported, but we are still far from a definitive evaluation of the usefulness of the cognitive approach for anxiety-related problems. First, almost all controlled studies involved analog populations, most often students, who were treated for relatively mild problems. Second, the category of cognitive-behavior modification contains such diverse treatment procedures as rational emotive therapy, systematic rational restructuring, self-instructional training, stress inoculation, attentional training, stimulus reappraisal, etc. Evaluation of these various procedures and cross-study comparisons is often complicated by inadequate report of the treatment procedures actually used. Third, almost two-thirds of these studies dealt with social-evaluative anxiety or unassertiveness; most of the others with test anxiety. It is interesting to note that only two studies dealt with snake phobias (Meichenbaum, 1971; Odom, Nelson, & Wein, 1978). The preponderance of social-evaluative anxiety and test anxiety as target behavior in the cognitive-modification studies might indicate that cognitive procedures are more useful with this type of anxiety than with other phobias.

7.1. Cognitive Restructuring and Self-Instruction

The cognitive behavior modification procedures can be divided roughly into two categories: (1) procedures that focus on insight into irrational beliefs and on challenging these beliefs, for example, rational emotive therapy (Ellis, 1962) and systematic rational restructuring (Goldfried, Decenteceo, & Weinberg, 1974); and (2) procedures that focus on the modification of the client's internal dialogue (for example, self-instructional training (Meichenbaum, 1975).

An important goal in both rational therapy and self-instructional training involves modification of dysfunctional thought patterns. A central assumption shared by proponents of both approaches is that the anxiety feelings result from maladaptive thoughts.

7.1.1. Rational Therapy

Ellis uses an A–B–C framework of rational emotive therapy. *A* refers to an *A*ctivating event or experience, *C* to the emotional or behavioral *C*onsequence, and *B* to the person's *B*elief about the activating event (A) that is assumed to lead to the consequence (C). In rational emotive therapy the therapist teaches the patients to differentiate between their rational and irrational beliefs. In a Socratic-like fashion the therapist challenges the underlying irrational beliefs.

Goldfried *et al.* (1974) placed rational emotive therapy within a behavioral framework. In systematic rational restructuring, patients' maladaptive internal sentences are systematically modified. Rather than attack the patient's irrational beliefs verbally and cajole the patient into thinking more logically as is typical for rational emotive therapy, the therapist starts with an explanation of the basic assumption underlying rational restructuring. Further, a list of various common irrational beliefs is presented. If the patient agrees with the basic assumption, a rational analysis of the individual's own specific target behavior is presented. Finally, the patient is instructed to modify his or her internal sentences. A hierarchy of increasingly more anxiety-arousing situations is constructed. Patients have to imagine these situations and to reevaluate their anxiety-producing self-statements rationally: Successful coping determines progression to the next item of the hierarchy.

7.1.2. Self-Instructional Training

With self-instructional training, patients are instructed to substitute positive coping self-statements for the anxiety-engendering self-statements. Generally, four stages are differentiated: preparing for, confronting, or handling a stressor, possibly being overwhelmed by a stressor, and, finally, reinforcing oneself for having coped. Examples of coping self-statements typically used in self-instructional training are provided in Table 6. During treatment sessions patients practice self-instructing. This is usually done in conjunction with relaxation. It should be noted, however, that with self-instructional training "insight" into negative or unproductive self-statements is often an integral part of the treatment procedure. Research on specific phobias, social-evaluative anxiety, and test anxiety as target behavior will be discussed separately. Even though there are some technical differences in both procedures, for present purposes no differentiation will be made between rational emotive therapy and systematic rational restructuring, since both procedures appear to be very similar.

7.2. Specific Phobias

Two studies have been conducted using snake-phobic volunteers as subjects. Meichenbaum (1971) compared various variants of videotaped modeling: (1) mastery model, (2) mastery model plus self-statements, (3) coping model, and (4) coping model plus self-statements. A coping model was found to be more effective than a mastery model. Self-statement did not enhance the effectiveness of the mastery model. With the coping models, the addition of self-statements yielded more positive results on the difficult tasks of the behavioral avoidance test only. Odom et al. (1978) compared (1) exposure in vivo (guided participation), (2)

Table 6. Examples of Coping Self-Statements Rehearsed in Self-Instructional Training [a]

Preparing for a stressor
  What is it you have to do?
  You can develop a plan to deal with it.
  Just think about what you can do about it. That's better than getting anxious.
  No negative self-statements: just think rationally.
  Don't worry: worry won't help anything.
  Maybe what you think is anxiety is eagerness to confront the stressor.
Confronting and handling a stressor
  Just "psych" yourself up—you can meet this challenge.
  You can convince yourself to do it. You can reason your fear away.
  One step at a time: you can handle the situation.
  Don't think about fear: just think about what you have to do. Stay relevant.
  This anxiety is what the doctor said you would feel. It's a reminder to use your coping
  exercises.
  This tenseness can be an ally: a cue to cope.
  Relax: you're in control. Take a slow deep breath.
  Ah, good.
Coping with the feeling of being overwhelmed
  When fear comes, just pause.
  Keep the focus on the present: what is it you have to do?
  Label your fear from 0 to 10 and watch it change.
  You should expect your fear to rise.
  Don't try to eliminate fear totally: just keep it manageable.
Reinforcing self-statements
  It worked: you did it.
  Wait until you tell your therapist (or group) about this.
  It wasn't as bad as you expected.
  You made more out of your fear than it was worth.
  You damn ideas—that's the problem. When you control them, you control your fear.
  It's getting better each time you use the procedures.
  You can be pleased with the progress you're making.
  You did it!

[a] From "Self-Instructional Methods" by D. H. Meichenbaum in F. H. Kanfer and A. P. Goldstein (Eds.) *Helping People Change.* Copyright 1975 by Pergamon Press. Reprinted by permission.

systematic desensitization, (3) cognitive restructuring, (4) verbal extinction, (5) placebo, and (6) no treatment. On the behavioral measure and fear thermometer, exposure *in vivo* was found to be superior to all other conditions. Cognitive restructuring was found to be more effective on the psychophysiological modality (heart rate) only.

Cognitive restructuring was found to be equally effective as prolonged exposure in imagination in a study by D'Zurilla, Wilson, and Nelson (1973) involving volunteers who were afraid of dead rats. Results of this study further indicated that systematic desensitization was no more effective than no treatment control.

Finally, a study by Girodo and Roehl (1978) should be mentioned. They compared (1) information giving, (2) self-instructional training, and (3) a combined procedure using volunteers with a fear of flying. Anxiety ratings obtained during a normal flight indicated that self-instructional training was no more effective than prior information giving.

7.3. Social-Evaluative Anxiety

In this section studies will be discussed which deal with speech anxiety, communication apprehension, interpersonal anxiety, dating anxiety, and unassertiveness.

7.3.1. Systematic Desensitization versus Cognitive Restructuring

7.3.1.1. Rational Therapy. Several studies have compared rational therapy with systematic desensitization and have provided conflicting results. In the studies by Di Loreto (1971) and Lent, Russel, and Zamostny (1981), systematic desensitization was found to be more effective than cognitive restructuring. In contrast, rational therapy proved to be more effective than self-control desensitization in the studies by Kanter and Goldfried (1979) and Shahar and Merbaum (1981). Further, Kanter and Goldfried (1979) found a combined treatment approach (rational therapy plus self-control desensitization) to be more effective than self-control desensitization, but *less* effective than rational restructuring alone.

7.3.1.2. Self-Instructional Training. Both Meichenbaum (1971) and Thorpe (1975) found self-instructional training to be superior to systematic desensitization with unassertive subjects. Weissberg (1977) compared (1) desensitization, (2) desensitization with coping imagery, and (3) self-instructional training plus desensitization. No consistent differences among the three treatments were found.

In summary, there is little evidence that rational therapy is more effective than systematic desensitization or vice versa. While there is some evidence that self-instructional training is superior to systematic desensitization, at least with unassertive subjects, this needs to be replicated before firm conclusions can be drawn.

7.3.2. Social Skills Training versus Cognitive Restructuring

Studies that examined the relationship between behavioral deficits and self-evaluation processes in the area of social anxiety and nonassertiveness found differences in the accuracy of self-ratings of social competence between high and low anxious subjects (Alden & Cappe, 1981; Clark & Arkowitz, 1975; Glasgow & Arkowitz, 1975). In addition, Golden (1981) found a relationship between social anxiety and irrational beliefs: subjects who endorsed irrational beliefs were high social-anxious as compared with individuals who did not report such beliefs. Similar results were reported with respect to nonassertiveness (Alden & Safran, 1978). Finally, Mandel and Shrauger (1980) found self-critical self-verbalizations to affect the extent of subsequent heterosocial approach behavior in shy males.

Taken together, the results of these (analog) studies indicate that social anxiety and nonassertiveness may be more related to dysfunctional cognitions than to a lack of behavioral competence. This suggests that cognitive restructuring procedures may have beneficial effects with "unassertive" populations.

Studies attempting to compare the relative efficacy of social skills training (including assertiveness training) and cognitive approaches have produced equivocal results. Most studies involving a comparison of skills training and cognitive modification found no significant differences between both procedures (Alden, Safran, & Weideman, 1978; Elder, Edelstein, & Fremouw, 1981; Fremouw & Zitter, 1978; Thorpe, 1975). Two studies (Linehan, Goldfried, & Goldfried, 1979; Tiegerman & Kassinove, 1977) found skills training to be slightly more effective than cognitive restructuring. Other studies found each procedure to results in specific effects. Gardner, McGowan, DiGiuseppe, and Sutton-Simon (1980) found cognitive therapy to be more effective in reducing scores on self-report measures, while skills training was more effective on the behavioral measure. Similarly, Glass, Gottman, and Shmurak (1976) found skills training more effective on behavioral indices (role-play test); here cognitive restructuring facilitated transfer of training to nontraining situations, while skills training did not.

7.3.2.1. Enhancing Effects of Cognitive Restructuring. Given the multifaceted aspects of social anxiety, it was only natural that researchers attempted to develop therapeutic packages that focused both on the dysfunctional cognitions and behavioral skills deficits. A number of investigators combined cognitive restructuring and social skills training in one therapeutic package.

Several studies found a combined cognitive-social skills treatment to be no more effective than either social skills training alone (Carmody, 1978; Glass *et al.*, 1976; Gormally, Varvil-Weld, Raphael, & Sipps, 1981; Hammen, Jacobs, Mayol, & Cochran, 1980; Tiegerman & Kassinove, 1977), or cognitive therapy alone (Glass *et al.*, 1976; Gormally *et al.*, 1980). In contrast, results of other studies indicate that a cognitive-social skill approach might be superior. For instance, Wolfe and Fodor (1977) compared (1) social skills training, (2) social skills training plus rational therapy, (3) a consciousness-raising group, and (4) waiting-list control with unassertive women in an outpatient clinical setting. Both skills training and the combined procedure were superior to the consciousness-raising group and waiting list control on the behavioral measure. Only the patients who had received rational therapy showed anxiety reduction. Derry and Stone (1979) also found a combined procedure to be more effective than social skills training alone. However, treatment in both the Wolfe and Fodor (1977) and Derry and Stone (1979) study involved two sessions only, which limits the conclusions to be drawn.

Finally, Linehan *et al.* (1979) found a combined cognitive-social skills treatment to be superior to rational therapy and skills training alone, but the majority of measures failed to confirm this at a statistically significant level.

In summary, studies comparing the effects of cognitive restructuring and skills training have produced conflicting results. Although a few studies indicate that cognitive modification might enhance the effectiveness of social skills training, results of these studies have to be qualified owing to either the small number of treatment sessions or inconclusive statistical evidence. Thus, it appears that cognitive interventions have not added significantly to the effectiveness of skills training approaches.

7.4. Test Anxiety

According to Liebert and Morris (1967) cognitive ("worry") and emotional (affective and physiological responses) components of test anxiety should be distinguished. There is now a fair amount of evidence to support the utility of such a distinction (Allen, 1980).

Interventions to reduce the unpleasant emotional arousal include systematic desensitization, flooding, imaginal exposure, and relaxation. A therapeutic approach that is aimed at the "worry" component is attentional training. Classification of cognitive restructuring processes for test anxiety is more problematic since often both components of test anxiety are dealt with: The component that is emphasized varies from study to study.

Cognitive restructuring has been found to be superior to systematic desensitization (Holroyd, 1976; Meichenbaum, 1972) and to imaginal exposure (Goldfried, Linehan, & Smith, 1978).

Several studies addressed the issue of whether a treatment approach aimed at both the cognitive and the emotional component of test anxiety was more effective than treatments that focused on one component only. Little and Jackson (1974) compared the following conditions: (1) attentional training (cognitive component), (2) relaxation training (emotional component), (3) attention training plus relaxation, (4) placebo, and (5) no-treatment control. Results indicated that the combined procedure was more effective than relaxation and attentional training by themselves.

Finger and Galassi (1977) also compared (1) attentional training, (2) relaxation, (3) attentional training plus relaxation, and (4) no treatment. Although all treatment resulted in beneficial effects, treatments did not differentially affect the cognitive component and the emotional component of test anxiety. Findings obtained with the two major self-report measures, "Emotionality" and "Worry," indicated that improvement resulted from each treatment, regardless of whether the treatment focused on the cognitive or the emotional component. Similar results were reported by Deffenbacher and Hahnloser (1981). Cognitive and relaxation groups were less "worried," "emotional," and anxious than controls, but did not differ from one another.

There is some evidence that focusing on the emotional component only, as is typically done with systematic desensitization and relaxation training, is not appropriate in the case of test anxiety. Results of laboratory studies (Hollandsworth, Glazeski, Kirkland, Jones, & Van Norman, 1979; Holroyd, Westbrook, Wolf, & Bradhorn, 1978) indicate that low and high test-anxious subjects exhibit almost similar arousal levels during testing. Although level of arousal during test-taking does not adequately discriminate effective and ineffective test-takers, the use of negative self-verbalizations may do so. Hollandsworth et al. (1979) found that low-anxious subjects labeled their arousal as facilitative, while high-anxious subjects viewed their arousal as debilitative. Hollandsworth et al. (1979) suggest that it may be more productive to train test-anxious subjects to relabel arousal as facilitative rather than attempt to reduce it using relaxation.

Kirkland and Hollandsworth (1980) questioned the importance of the anxiety-reduction focus of the cognitively based programs. In their cognitive skills acquisition program no emphasis was placed on arousal or anxiety reduction. Self-instructional training consisted of on-task statements (e.g., "I have plenty of time"; "Read the questions carefully") and positive self-evaluations. This program proved to be superior to cue-controlled relaxation and meditation. The authors suggest training for attention-focusing skills and deemphasizing the role of physiological arousal and they conclude: "Perhaps it is time to give the phrase test anxiety a respectful burial and talk about inadequate test performance in terms that more accurately describe what it is, namely, ineffective test taking" (p. 438). This rather bold statement seems to be unwarranted, since their sample consisted of nonclinical "test-anxious" subjects: Approximately one-third of normal nonanxious students served as "test-anxious" clients. Presumably, arousal plays a much more important role in clinical cases of test-anxiety. Unfortunately, none of the studies reviewed here used truly anxious patients.

7.5. Rational Therapy versus Self-Instructional Training

As already noted cognitive restructuring procedures differ in the emphasis on insight into irrational beliefs and the training of incompatible positive self-statements. Several studies have been conducted to investigate which component of cognitive restructuring was the most productive. In a study with speech-anxious teenagers, Thorpe, Amatu, Blakey, and Burns (1976) compared (1) general insight (discussion of Ellis's irrational beliefs), (2) specific insight (discussion of irrational ideas relevant to public speaking), (3) self-instructional training, and (4) a combination of specific insight and self-instructional training. Results indicated that insight (general and specific) contributes more to cognitive restructuring than self-instructional training or a combination of insight plus self-instructional training. However, the reverse was found by Glogower, Fremouw, and McCroskey (1978). Here, self-instructional training was found to be superior to specific insight into negative self-statements. In addition, it was found that a procedure which combined specific insight and self-instructional training was consistently more effective than any single procedure, although this difference did not reach significance. Finally, Carmody (1978) compared the effectiveness of two variants of assertive training. Results of this study indicated that assertiveness training plus rational therapy, along the lines of Ellis, was equally effective as assertiveness training plus self-instructional training.

In summary, studies comparing various components (i.e., insight vs. self-instructional training) have produced conflicting results. A related issue is whether during self-instructional training coping statements of a specific nature are more productive than more generalized coping statements. The relative contribution of specific coping statements and generalized coping statements was investigated by Hussian and Lawrence (1978), using test-anxious volunteers as subjects. Generalized coping statements included statements as: "When fear comes, just pause." Specific coping statements referred to test-taking and preparation, such as: "I know I'm well prepared for this test, so just relax"; or "The test is a challenge, nothing to get worked up over." Results of this study indicated that the test-specific statements were more productive than the generalized coping statements.

Sutton-Simon and Goldfried (1979) investigated the differential involvement of two forms of faulty thinking (irrational thinking vs. negative self-statements) in two types of anxiety (social anxiety vs. fear of heights). In contrast with social anxiety, which was significantly correlated with only irrational thinking, acrophobia was correlated with both irrational thinking and negative self-statements. Results of this study suggest that it might be more productive to match cognitive treatment procedures with types of faulty thinking rather than treating all anxiety related problems with an identical cognitive treatment package.

7.6. Interaction between Clients' Characteristics and Treatment

The literature on the outcome of cognitive therapy yields conflicting results. Generally, cognitive procedures have not been found to be superior to behavioral ones. The time seems to be ripe for investigators to stop subscribing to the myth of patient uniformity and to systematically match treatments to particular clients' characteristics. Three studies have been located to date that attempted to identify optimal matches between client and treatment procedures.

7.6.1. Psychophysiological Arousal

Shahar and Merbaum (1981) hypothesized that high physiological reactors would respond better to desensitization whereas weak reactors would achieve better therapeutic gains with cognitive restructuring. These hypotheses were only partially supported in their study with speech-anxious subjects.

Another attempt in this direction was reported by Gross and Fremouw (1980). These investigators assessed speech-anxious subjects both on cognitive, physiological, and behavioral measures while giving a 4-minute speech. This assessment yielded three subtypes of speech-anxious subjects: (1) cognitive dysfunctional, (2) psychophysiological, and (3) behavioral. Subjects were randomly assigned to cognitive restructuring and relaxation. Although subjects with low physiological responsivity performed poorly in progressive relaxation, there was a failure to support an interactional model for cognitive restructuring.

7.6.2. Cognitive Characteristics

Hammen et al. (1980) attempted to determine whether social skills training and cognitive-behavioral training were differentially effective for individuals having different cognitive characteristics. Contrary to expectations, no differential responsiveness to different treatments was found: cognitive therapy was not more effective with individuals endorsing high levels of dysfunctional cognitions. High levels of dysfunctional cognitions predicted poor outcome irrespective of treatment group.

In summary, while there is partial support for an interactional model for physiological responsivity, the studies failed to show interaction of treatment type and level of dysfunctional cognitions.

7.7. Concluding Remarks

Almost all studies in the cognitive area have involved analog populations. It is remarkable that the journal *Cognitive Therapy and Research*, which is devoted entirely to the cognitive approach, has not yet published one study involving real clinical phobic patients. To date, only a few studies have involved real clinical patients, and the picture that arises on basis of these studies is far less optimistic with respect to the cognitive approach. These studies will be dealt with in Chapters 5 and 8.

It is far from clear whether the beneficial effects of cognitive modification in the analog studies can be attributed to a modification of cognitive processes. Cognitive programs are designed to address specific targets (e.g., decrease of negative or irrational thoughts) which are assumed to lead to improvement of anxiety. It is questionable whether the cognitive programs have a specific impact on the target behaviors. Apart from a few exceptions subjects became less anxious as a result of treatment, but they did not improve differentially dependent on the kind of treatment they received. Only a few studies found a change in irrational beliefs after cognitive restructuring. Several studies found an equivalent reduction (Hammen *et al.*, 1980) or an even greater reduction of irrational beliefs (Alden *et al.*, 1978) after social skills training as compared to cognitive restructuring. Thus the effectiveness of the treatments may be unrelated to the specific skills trained in each treatment modality which raises questions with respect to the construct validity of cognitive approaches.

It is important to note that an alternative explanation in terms of "nonspecific" treatment factors (including clients' expectancies about therapeutic change) cannot be ruled out at the moment. For example, in a study by Craighead (1979) significant effects were found for a placebo condition on cognitive measures. Although self-instructional training was more effective than the placebo condition in decreasing the number of negative self-statements, positive self-statements were increased as effectively by the placebo condition. Nonspecific factors such as treatment generated expectancies and treatment credibility need to be controlled in future studies.

8. UNIFYING THEORY

It is clear that all procedures reviewed so far have beneficial effects in the treatment of fear and anxiety, at least in analog populations. The mechanisms by which these procedures achieve their results are, however, far from understandable. Although it is obvious that almost all procedures contain elements of exposure to phobic stimuli, this does not elucidate the therapeutic processes involved. Exposure is merely a description of what is going on during treatment and not an explanation of its process.

8.1. A Cognitive-Expectancy Model

In my opinion, the conditioning explanation presumed to underlie the various treatment techniques seems no longer tenable. Rather, cognitive processes appear to be more important. Elsewhere (Emmelkamp, 1975a) I have presented a cognitive-expectancy model to explain the effects of various behavioral treatments for anxiety and fear. This model emphasized *self-observation of improvement* and *expectancy of therapeutic gain*. All imaginal based treatments consist of exposure to the phobic stimuli. However, not exposure *per se* but self-observation of improvements seems to be the crucial factor. Through continuous exposure to the phobic stimuli, habituation may occur. Eventually, the patient observes that the imagining of fearful situations no longer arouses anxiety. However, this does not mean that the real-life phobic situation no longer arouses anxiety (e.g., Agras, 1967; Barlow *et al.*, 1969). There is a transfer gap between what patients can imagine without feeling anxiety and what they can do in real life without anxiety. In my opinion, self-observation of imagining phobic stimuli no longer arousing anxiety —combined with therapeutic suggestion that the patient has improved— prompts reality testing *in vivo*. Through successful performance in the real life situations habituation *in vivo* is eventually effected. Briefly, while exposure plays a role in the "first" and "second" stage of the treatment process, other important variables seem to be the patient's self-observation of improvement and the expectancy of therapeutic gain. Thus, the effects of exposure depend on the attitude and the set of the patient.

Other procedures as "self-control relaxation" and cognitive restructuring may work through a similar mechanism. Having learned a coping skill, patients are instructed to venture into the phobic situations *in vivo*. Self-observation of successful performance *in vivo* may lead to further cognitive changes and may motivate further coping efforts.

In a similar vein, Bandura (1977) has argued that behavioral treatments act through a common cognitive pathway. According to Bandura, behavioral procedures achieve changes in behavior by altering the level and strength of self-efficacy. Perceived self-efficacy affects how much effort a phobic individual will expend and how long he or she will persist in anxiety arousing situations: "The stronger the perceived self-efficacy, the more active the coping efforts" (Bandura & Adams, 1977, p. 288). There are a number of studies that support the hypothesized relationship between perceived self-efficacy and behavioral changes (Bandura & Adams, 1977; Bandura, Adams, & Beyer, 1977; Bandura, Adams, Hardy, & Howels, 1980). However, Barrios (1980) provided a more stringent test of the validity of the self-efficacy theory in a clinical sample and found efficacy expectations to be poor predictors of physiological and behavioral changes.

8.2. Imaginal versus *in Vivo* Exposure

There is now sufficient evidence that imaginal treatments are often redundant. Treatment may start directly with exposure *in vivo*. The routine use of imaginal procedures with phobic patients should be abandoned. Imaginal procedures are still the treatment of choice when real-life exposure is difficult to arrange (e.g., thunderstorm phobias), or when habituation in imagination is the primary aim of treatment (e.g., obsessional ruminations; see Chapter 8).

Within an imaginal exposure paradigm, suggestions have been made to improve the effects of the imagination procedures. Lang (1977, 1979) has proposed that imaginal material will have an emotional impact to the extent that the client processes important elements of the image. Lang (1977) suggests that it is important to differentiate between response propositions (e.g., "My palms are sweating," "I run away") and stimulus propositions contained in the emotional images. Thus imagery instructions can emphasize stimulus propositions (e.g., Imagine that you are in a room with a snake on the floor) without mentioning emotional responses or, alternatively, may be primarily made up of response propositions, which can be either emotional (e.g., "You feel anxiety," "You feel your heart racing") or behavioral (e.g., "You run away"). Lang proposed that this propositional conception of emotional imagery could clarify a number of conflicting issues in imagery therapy research. He argued that for imaginal treatment to be effective the image should contain the subject's response to the situation in addition to symbolic representation of the stimulus situation. It is the simultaneous presentation of both stimulus and response propositions that result in the emotion-eliciting image.

Several studies have explored the relationship between instructional manipulations and psychophysiological responses in imagery. While some support for Lang's hypothesis was provided (Lang, Kozak, Miller, Levin, & McLean, 1980) results of other studies were either equivocal (Anderson & Borkovec, 1980; Bauer & Craighead, 1979) or negative (Carroll, Marzillier, & Watson, 1980; Glenn & Hughes, 1978). However, even if there was more confirmatory evidence for Lang's theory, this probably would not result in a "come-back" of imaginal based procedures. It should be noted that, at least in the clinical studies, flooding imagery usually contained both stimulus and response propositions. Nevertheless, treatment so conducted was found to be far less effective than *in vivo* exposure.

8.3. Self-Directed Treatment

Based on the cognitive-expectancy model (Emmelkamp, 1975a) we predicted that self-directed treatment would have several advantages compared with therapist-directed treatments, since in the latter treatments patients may attribute their improvement to their therapist rather than to their own efforts. The few comparative clinical studies (with agoraphobics and obsessive-compulsives) indicate that self-directed treatment *in vivo* is at least as effective as therapist-directed treatment (Emmelkamp, 1974; Emmelkamp & Kraanen, 1977; Emmelkamp & Wessels, 1975). Moreover, there is some evidence that therapist-directed treatment followed by self-directed practice is more effective than either approach alone (Emmelkamp, 1974). Similar results were obtained by Kelly (1980) in an analog study with snake-fearful subjects.

Finally, results of analog studies comparing therapist-directed treatment (participant modeling) and self-directed treatment indicate the superiority of the self-directed approach (Bandura *et al.*, 1975; Smith & Coleman, 1977). Compared with subjects who received therapist-directed treatment, subjects who had the benefit of independent mastery experiences displayed greater fear reduction.

8.4. Concluding Remarks

In the early days, behavioral treatments for anxiety and fears were defined as the application of "established laws of learning" or were viewed to be based on "modern learning theories." The claim that these procedures are exclusively based on learning paradigms seems nowadays no longer tenable. The present review suggests that additional factors such as therapeutic relationship, expectancy of therapeutic gain, and self-observation of improvement play an important role. The preceding review indicates that *in vivo* procedures are more powerful than imaginal ones. Taken together, these data lead to the clinical emphasis on *in vivo* treatments and self-attributed success experiences to enhance therapeutic changes.

Treatment of Clinical Phobias

CONTROLLED STUDIES

In this chapter, research into the effects of treatment with clinical patients will be reviewed. After a brief review of controlled studies investigating the effects of psychotherapy, a detailed review is provided of the clinical effectiveness of behavioral treatments on agoraphobia, social anxiety, and sexual anxiety. Finally, the therapeutic effects of drugs on phobic disorders will be reviewed. The clinical application will be discussed in Chapters 11 and 12.

1. PSYCHOTHERAPY

Reports of psychoanalysts concerning the treatment of phobias involved theoretical essays on the dynamics of the patients; the effectiveness of treatment is rarely discussed (Emmelkamp, 1979a). However, Friedman (1950) reported that "after the dynamics of the case were worked through, many patients failed to recover." Other psychoanalysts, too, reported unsatisfactory results. Both Freud and Fenichel have used exposure *in vivo* in the treatment of phobic cases, which seems to have been forgotten by their followers. So writes Freud: "One can hardly ever master a phobia if one waits till the patient lets the analysis influence him to give it up. One succeeds only when one can induce them through the influence of the analysis . . . to go about alone and struggle with the anxiety while they make the attempt" (Freud, 1959).

Fenichel stated the same point perhaps even more clearly: "The analyst must actively intervene in order to induce the patient to make his first effort to overcome the phobia; he must induce the patient to expose himself to the feared experiences" (Fenichel, 1963, p. 215). One can only wonder why the suggestion of these authorities has not been taken seriously by their followers.

Several authors reported on the treatment of anxiety neurosis and phobias with psychotherapy (Errera & Coleman, 1963; Miles, Barrabee, & Finesinger, 1951; Robert, 1964; Terhune, 1949). These studies have serious methodological flaws such as no control groups, retrospective assessment of results, no independent assessment of results, and no homogeneous population. In addition, more often than not results are confounded by additional medication, electro-convulsive therapy (ECT), or unsystematic exposure *in vivo*, which precludes the drawing of any conclusion with respect to the effectiveness of psychotherapy.

Several studies have compared the effectiveness of psychotherapy and behavioral treatments. For present purposes, only prospective studies involving real clinical phobic patients will be discussed. Gelder and Marks (1966) were the first to conduct such a study. In their study systematic desensitization and psychotherapy were compared with severe agoraphobic inpatients. After 60–70 sessions no significant differences between the treatments were found. Overall improvement was small. In a subsequent study involving mixed phobic patients as subjects (Gelder, Marks, & Wolff, 1967) systematic desensitization proved to be more effective than individual or group psychotherapy at the posttest, despite the fact that desensitization patients received less treatment than the psychotherapy patients. In a following study in this series (Gelder & Marks, 1968) seven patients who were unimproved after the group psychotherapy were treated with desensitization. Patients improved three times as much after 4 months of desensitization than after 2 years of group psychotherapy. Finally, Dormaar and Dijkstra (1975) and Gillan and Rachman (1974) found systematic desensitization also to be superior to psychotherapy although in the Dormaar and Dijkstra study the between-group difference was not statistically significant.

In summary, systematic desensitization has been found to be more effective than psychotherapy when mixed phobic patients or social-anxious patients (Dormaar & Dijkstra, 1975) were concerned. With agoraphobics, systematic desensitization was no more effective than psychotherapy.

2. BEHAVIORAL TREATMENT OF AGORAPHOBIA

Systematic desensitization seems to have little to offer in the treatment of agoraphobia (Cooper, Gelder, & Marks, 1965; Evans & Kellam,

1973; Gelder & Marks, 1966; Gelder *et al.*, 1967; Marks *et al.*, 1971; Marks & Gelder, 1965; Yorkston, Sergeant, & Rachman, 1968). Studies that involved both agoraphobics and specific phobics generally found that systematic desensitization was more effective for specific phobics as compared with agoraphobics. In contrast with the foregoing studies, Gelder *et al.* (1973) found no differential effectiveness of desensitization for agoraphobics and for other phobics. However, most of the improvements found may be attributed to exposure *in vivo*: Most changes seemed to have occurred *after* systematic desensitization during 4 sessions of exposure *in vivo*.

Aversion relief also is of little value in the treatment of agoraphobia. Solyom, McClure, Heseltine, Ledwidge, and Solyom (1972) investigated the effects of this treatment on agoraphobics. Overall improvement was rather small. Patients rated their main phobia as unimproved.

As already discussed in Chapter 4, flooding in imagination is less effective than flooding or prolonged exposure *in vivo*. There is no evidence that flooding in imagination is more effective than systematic desensitization in imagination. Most studies that found favorable results for flooding in imagination have confounded imagination and *in vivo* exposure (e.g., Mathews, Johnston, Lancashire, Munby, Shaw, & Gelder, 1976). Briefly, the rather small effects of systematic desensitization, aversion relief, and flooding in imagination do not warrant widespread clinical application. In the last few years, research on agoraphobics has been concentrated on the development of exposure *in vivo* programs, which will be discussed in some detail.

2.1. Prolonged Exposure *in Vivo*

Although prolonged exposure *in vivo* may be applied with individual cases (e.g., Emmelkamp & Wessels, 1975) group exposure *in vivo* seems to offer several advantages. Besides the aspect of saving therapist time, groups may provide the patient with coping models and may lead to fewer dropouts. Studies comparing individual and group exposure *in vivo* found no clear differences in effectiveness (Emmelkamp & Emmelkamp-Benner, 1975; Hafner & Marks, 1976).

Various investigators in different centers have found prolonged exposure *in vivo* conducted in groups to be a very effective treatment for agoraphobics (Emmelkamp, 1980c; Emmelkamp *et al.*, 1978, 1979; Emmelkamp & Mersch, 1982; Hafner & Marks, 1976; Hand *et al.*, 1974; Teasdale *et al.*, 1977). Often dramatic improvements with respect to anxiety and avoidance are achieved even in a few days, but generally, a lack of continuing improvement has been found when treatment ends (e.g., Emmelkamp, 1980c; Emmelkamp & Mersch, 1981; Hafner & Marks, 1976; Teasdale *et al.*, 1977).

2.1.1. Group Cohesion

Hand *et al.* (1974) compared cohesive and uncohesive groups of agoraphobics. At follow-up it was found that cohesive groups improved more than uncohesive groups. However, Teasdale *et al.* (1977) could not replicate this finding. The role of cohesiveness in exposure groups is yet not clear. Although cohesiveness may be therapeutic in that patients motivate each other to struggle with their anxiety and to give up their avoidance behavior, in some groups cohesiveness may be counter-therapeutic. Patients in the latter groups may support each other in avoiding situations by spending their therapeutic time drinking coffee instead of doing their exercises. Therapists should be alert to the possibility of groups-avoidance.

2.1.2. Neighborhood Groups

Sinnott, Jones, Scott-Fordham, and Woodward (1981) selected agoraphobic patients for treatment by group exposure *in vivo* according to their residential geographic neighborhood. They hypothesized that a neighborhood-based program would be more effective than a clinic-based program since exposure tasks in the natural environment could lead to rewarding social contact which reinforces the likelihood of successful completion of homework assignments. In their study (1) neighborhood-based treatment, (2) clinic-based treatment, and (3) no-treatment control were compared. All exposure patients received homework assignments but the subjects in the neighborhood group were encouraged to use each other as "target destinations." There was some evidence that the neighborhood-based group was the most effective.

2.2. Self-Management Programs

In Andrews's (1966) view the phobic patient is characterized by dependency relationships with others and by a characteristic avoidance of activity that involves independent handling of difficult and fear-arousing situations. This lack of independency constitutes a fairly broad pattern of responses and not just a response to the phobic stimulus itself. Emmelkamp and Cohen-Kettenis (1975) found a significant correlation between external locus of control and phobic anxiety with agoraphobics. This suggests that an agoraphobic should be regarded as someone who can be characterized by an avoidance of anxiety-arousing situations due to a lack of internal control. In light of this consideration, acquiring self-control may be an important therapeutic goal for agoraphobics. If this reasoning is correct, then treatment for agoraphobics should focus on teaching generalizable coping skills.

Problems with respect to a lack of continuing improvement when formal treatment ends may be prevented by self-management programs in the patients' natural environment. An additional advantage of this approach is that the most severe agoraphobics, who are unable to visit a therapist, can be treated. To date, two treatment programs that are managed by patients in their own environment have been developed.

2.2.1. Dutch Program

The first self-management program was developed by Emmelkamp (1974). Treatment consisted of self-controlled exposure plus feedback (self-observation). After an instructional phase in the presence of the therapist, the patient had to carry on alone. The procedure involves a graduated approach by the patient in the actual feared situation. From the first session, the client had to enter the phobic situation. The client had to walk alone on a route through the city with instructions to turn back on experiencing undue anxiety. The client had to record the duration of each trial and to write this down in a notebook. Then, he had to enter the phobic situation in the same way. This procedure was repeated until the 90-min session was over. At the end of each session, the patient had to send the results to the therapist.

In a study by Emmelkamp (1974) the effects of the following treatments were compared: (1) self-observation, (2) flooding, (3) flooding followed by self-observation, and (4) no-treatment control. Each flooding session consisted of 45 min of flooding in imagination, immediately followed by 45 min of flooding *in vivo*. During self-observation, the therapist was present only at the first few sessions. At the following sessions patients had to practice alone. There was a total of 12 sessions. In the combined flooding/self-observation condition, the first three sessions involved flooding. After the intermediate test the patient was treated with the self-observation procedure. The therapist was present only at the first two sessions of the self-observation method.

In contrast to the control group all treatments resulted in significant improvements. Results on the behavioral measure are presented in Figure 13.

At the beginning of the treatment the patients were able to walk outside for an average of 11 min; at the posttest this period was on the

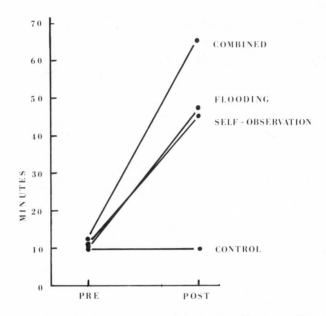

Figure 13. The effects of the treatment on the behavioral avoidance test. (From "Exposure *in vivo* Treatments" by P. M. G. Emmelkamp in A. Goldstein and D. Chambless (Eds.), *Agoraphobia: Multiple Perspectives on Theory and Treatment.* Copyright 1982 by Wiley. Reprinted by permission.)

average 10 min for the control group, 47 min for the flooding group, 45 min for the self-observation group, and 65 min for the flooding/self-observation group. No difference in effect was found between flooding and self-observation methods. Thus, provoking anxiety, as occurs in flooding, is not requisite for the successful treatment of agoraphobia, as gradual self-controlled exposure results in an equal improvement. Rapid exposure without retreat is not superior to an approach in which patients may retreat when they start to feel anxious.

The results of this study further indicated that the combined approach (flooding followed by self-observation) is more effective than each of the individual treatments. At the posttest, the combined treatment led to significantly greater improvement on the behavioral measure and the phobic anxiety scale—other phobias. Moreover, results at three months follow-up showed that the combined flooding/self-observation group continued to improve on the phobic anxiety scale—other phobias—and on the Fear Survey Schedule (Wolpe & Lang, 1964). This suggests that treatment results can be generalized to other phobic situations than those which had been dealt with during treatment.

The self-observation procedure has several advantages. Firstly, treatment costs the therapist much less time than flooding. The mean therapist time requirement was at least two times as great for the flooding condition as for the self-observation. Even more important, with the self-observation procedure the patient becomes less dependent upon the therapist; the therapist teaches a method which the patient has to apply on his or her own. One major difficulty with flooding procedures is that improvement generally does not persist when the treatment has come to an end (Gelder, 1977), although there is enough room left for further improvement. Results achieved with the combined self-observation procedure show that there is a continuing improvement after treatment ends.

The effectiveness of self-observation as a self-management procedure was further demonstrated in the studies by Emmelkamp (1980b); Emmelkamp and Emmelkamp-Benner (1975); Emmelkamp and Wessels (1975); and Emmelkamp and Kuipers (1979). In contrast with results found with prolonged exposure *in vivo* with this self-management program, most patients went on to make further gains during follow-up (Emmelkamp, 1974, 1980b; Emmelkamp & Kuipers, 1979).

2.2.2. Oxford Program

More recently, Mathews, Teasdale, Munby, Johnston, and Shaw (1977) developed another self-management program for agoraphobics. Their program differs from our program in that the patients' spouses were actively involved in planning and encouraging practice attempts. Furthermore, their patients had to remain in the phobic situation long enough for anxiety to decline, rather than to return on experiencing undue anxiety as is the case with self-observation.

A controlled investigation of the home-based treatment of Mathews *et al.* (1977) was reported by Jannoun, Munby, Catalan, and Gelder (1980). Agoraphobics were randomly allocated to either programmed practice or "problem solving" treatment. Both treatment formats were presented as self-help programs. With programmed practice, the patient was instructed to practice going out daily for at least an hour and the partner was taught how to cooperate and reinforce successful coping attempts. In the "problem solving" treatment no specific instructions were given to go out more often. Rather, treatment involved the couple's discussion of life stresses and problems for at least an hour a day.

The results revealed that programmed practice was superior to the problem-solving treatment. However, the results of one therapist's problems solving treatment was comparable to that of programmed practice. Results are presented in Figure 14. Jannoun *et al.* (1980) claim that the different outcomes of the problem-solving treatment cannot be accounted for by differential encouragement to go out more. As depicted in Figure 14 there was no increase in the number of hours spent away from home by the more successful of the problem-solving subgroups at the end of treatment. Rather, the data appear to indicate that anxiety reduction is essential for the treatment of phobia:

> It would appear that change in phobic behavior can be achieved either by instructing and encouraging the patient to enter the phobic situations after which phobic anxiety is reduced, or by reducing the patient's general anxiety first, which then makes it relatively easier for the patient to go into the situations. (Jannoun *et al.*, p. 304)

A second controlled investigation of the home-based program was reported by Mathews, Jannoun, and Gelder (1979). In this study the role of the partner was investigated. Patients were randomly allocated to treatment by home-practice alone or treatment by partner-assisted home-practice. While the partner condition was more effective at the posttest, it is interesting to see that the home-practice alone condition was the only one to show continuing improvement between posttest and follow-up.

The use of the partner in this program is questionable. By using the partner as cotherapist, the therapist may inadvertently reinforce the dependent relationship between patient and partner. For clinical purposes, it should be remembered that an important therapeutic goal for agoraphobics is to become independent of both therapist and family members. Whether the aid of the spouse as cotherapist may be useful in achieving this end needs to be ascertained for each case separately. It should be emphasized that it may be therapeutically wise to let the patient attribute improvement to his or her own efforts instead of to the therapist or family members. In any case, with marital distressed couples the spouse should not be mobilized as cotherapist.

2.3. Other Issues

2.3.1. Spaced versus Massed Exposure

Foa, Jameson, Turner, and Payne (1980a) compared 10 sessions of massed practice with 10 sessions of spaced practice in a cross-over design. In the massed practice condition, treatment was conducted on consecutive days, whereas in the spaced condition, sessions were held once a

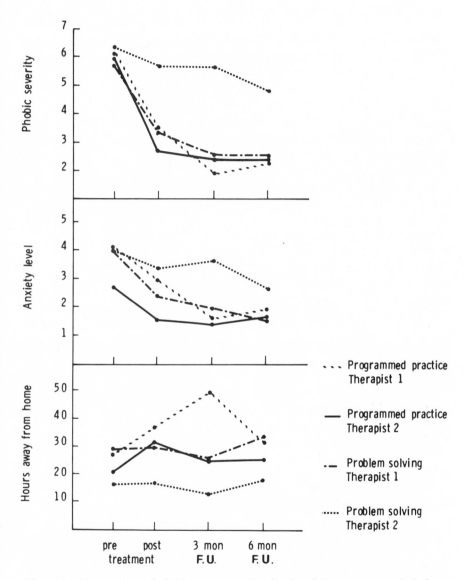

Figure 14. Mean ratings of phobic severity, anxiety level, and time out per week, before and after treatment and during follow-up. (From "A Home-Based Treatment Program for Agoraphobia: Replication and Controlled Evaluation" by L. Jannoun *et al., Behavior Therapy* 1980, *11*, Fig. 1. Copyright 1980 by Association for the Advancement of Behavior Therapy. Reprinted by permission.)

week only. Results indicated that massed practice was more effective than spaced practice. Foa *et al.* (1980a) suggest that the superiority of the massed condition may be due to the fact that massed practice provides less opportunity for accidental exposure between treatment sessions and for the reinforcement of avoidance or escape behavior.

2.3.2. Paradoxical Intention

Ascher (1980) compared graded exposure (self-controlled exposure *in vivo*) with "paradoxical intention." In the latter approach, the patients were instructed to go to the most difficult situation and to apply the "paradoxical instruction." They had to focus on the physiological experience of anxiety and "to try to increase this symptom in an attempt to court the anticipated disastrous consequence." Patients were instructed to remain until anxiety had declined. Ascher (1980) found paradoxical intention to be superior to graded exposure. However, several methodological flaws limit conclusions from being drawn. First, the design was unbalanced. Second, only behavioral assessment was used having unknown validity. Third, exposure time was not equated across techniques. Finally, numbers were small, five subjects in each group.

2.3.3. Breathing Exercises

Although agoraphobia is often associated with hyperventilation (see p. 33), it is unclear whether hyperventilation is a physiological determinant of agoraphobia or a somatic concomitant of anxiety experienced in phobic situations. Generally, treatment of hyperventilation attacks consists of rebreathing of the expired air or in holding one's breath in order to raise the lowered arterial carbon dioxide tension.

Visser (1978) investigated whether agoraphobics would benefit from breathing exercises. Since hyperventilation is due to an increased rate of respiration, deepened respiration, or both, patients were instructed to breathe normally. Patients were trained to breathe out passively and to insert a short rest period after each respiratory cycle. Breathing exercises led to normal breathing in the office but did not affect anxiety and avoidance behavior. While the results of Visser's study are negative with respect to improvement of the agoraphobic complaints, it might appear that breathing exercises *during* exposure *in vivo* could be beneficial to some agoraphobics. In most cases hyperventilation improved as a result of exposure *in vivo*. However, in resistant cases, specific attention to breathing is necessary.

2.3.4. Historically Portrayed Modeling

Emmelkamp and Emmelkamp-Benner (1975) investigated whether the effect of exposure *in vivo* could be enhanced by the introduction of a video-recording in which improved "ex-clients" related their experiences with the same treatment. This film may be regarded as a form of modeling in which model mastery of problems is portrayed historically rather than enacted currently (Bandura & Barab, 1973). Half the patients saw the video-recording immediately before treatment started. In this film, three "ex-patients" were interviewed about their experiences with the same treatment. Immediately before treatment started clients rated how much they expected to gain from therapy.

The video-recording did not enhance treatment effectiveness. It should be noted that historically portrayed modeling was presented by film. Thus, it is possible that historically portrayed modeling might be more effective when presented in real life. This could be accomplished by having former phobics assist in the treatment of new patients (Ross, 1980).

The negative results of historically portrayed modeling do *not* indicate that expectancy of the therapeutic gain does not influence treatment outcome with exposure *in vivo*. The explanation of the treatment to the patients may have induced high expectations from the treatment to which the video-recording could no longer contribute anything. After the rationale was explained patients in both conditions expected on the average that it was "likely" that they would be helped by the treatment and that they would be "much better" within "a few months." In addition, a significant relationship was found between expectancy and improvement on anxiety and avoidance scales.

2.3.5. Marital Complications

Two types of studies are relevant with respect to marital complications. First, a series of studies examined the influence of marital satisfaction on the outcome of behavior therapy. Second, a few studies addressed themselves to the issue of whether improvement of the phobic patient led to negative changes in the partner or the marital relationship.

2.3.5.1. Interpersonal Problems. Several studies investigated to what extent interpersonal problems affect the outcome of exposure in *in vivo* procedures. Hudson (1974), working with agoraphobics who received prolonged exposure *in vivo* treatment, found that patients from "sick families" showed much less improvement than patients from "well adjusted" families. Milton and Hafner (1979) treated 18 patients with prolonged exposure *in vivo* and found that patients whose marriages were rated as unsatisfactory before treatment improved less during treatment, and were significantly more likely to relapse during follow-up than those patients with satisfactory marriages. Bland and Hallam (1981) related the level of marital satisfaction with response to exposure *in vivo* treatment and found a significant difference between "good marriage" and "poor marriage" groups with respect to phobic severity. At a 3-month follow-up the "poor marriage" group showed a significantly greater tendency to relapse compared with the "good marriage" group. Interestingly, improvement was found to be associated with patient satisfaction with spouse. Spouse's dissatisfaction with the patient was *not* related to outcome of treatment. Emmelkamp divided agoraphobics into low and high marital satisfaction groups. All patients were treated with self-controlled exposure *in vivo*. After four treatment sessions, almost no significant differences between groups were found. Patients with low marital satisfaction improved as much as patients with high marital satisfaction. Neither at the posttest nor at 1-month follow-up was self-controlled exposure *in vivo* influenced by the interpersonal problems of agoraphobics. The finding of this study is in contrast to the findings of Bland and Hallam (1981), Milton and Hafner (1979), and Hudson (1974). The contradictory findings might be explained by a number of differences. First, in the Emmelkamp (1980b) study, treatment consisted of self-controlled exposure *in vivo* rather than prolonged exposure *in vivo*. Further, the assessment of marital satisfaction varied from study to study and may not be directly comparable. Finally, Emmelkamp (1980b) assessed only short term effects, whereas the differences in outcome between "good" and "bad" marriage groups tended to become greater at 3-month (Bland & Hallam, 1981) and 6-month (Milton & Hafner, 1979) follow-ups. Thus, while little differences may be found immediately after treatment, maritally dissatisfied patients may relapse and maritally satisfied patients may show further improvement several months after treatment.

In the studies reviewed so far, marital satisfaction was assessed before the start of treatment. It is conceivable that patients might find it difficult to admit dissatisfaction with their partner before a therapeutic relationship has developed. Therefore, a patient's account of the relationship in the course of treatment might give a more accurate picture of satisfaction with spouse than pretreatment indices of marital satisfaction. In a study by Emmelkamp and van der Hout (1982), the information with respect to marital satisfaction was gathered retrospectively from the therapists' files. It was hypothesized in advance that patients who complained about their partners during treatment were more likely to become treatment failures with exposure *in vivo* as compared with patients who did not complain about their partner. Results revealed that complaints about the partner did differentiate failures from successful cases.

2.3.5.2. Adverse Treatment Effects. Several studies investigated whether treatment had adverse effects on the patient's spouse and the marital relationship. Hand and Lamontagne (1976) reported that in some cases improvement of phobias was followed by a marital crisis. Hafner (1977) found that a deterioration of the most hostile husbands at follow-up coincided with a maximum improvement in their wives' phobic symptoms. Some spouses were adversely affected by their wives' improvement, but improved when their partner relapsed. Milton and Hafner (1979) reported that: "the marriages of nine (out of 15) patients appeared to be adversely influenced by their symptomatic improvement" (p. 807). However, inspection of their data (Table 1, p. 808) reveals a totally different picture: Both patients and their partners show an improvement rather than a deterioration on marital and sexual adjustment. Thus, the idea of a worsening of the marriage was based on clinical anecdotal material, rather than on the more objective measures used. In contrast to the conclusions of Milton and Hafner, Bland and Hallam (1981) found that phobia removal led to a reduction in the spouses' dissatisfaction with the patient. In summary, while clinical anecdotes suggest that phobic removal might lead to an exacerbation of interpersonal problems, little or no objective data are provided to support this idea.

2.3.5.3. Marital Treatment. Although a number of agoraphobics have problems with their partners, they often want treatment for their phobias instead of for these problems. In our experience, only few agoraphobics accept help for marital difficulties. Recently, Cobb, McDonald, Marks, and Stern (1980) compared marital treatment with exposure *in vivo*; subjects were both agoraphobics and obsessive-compulsives who also manifested marital discord. Results indicated that exposure *in vivo* led to improvements with respect to both the compulsive and phobic problems and the marital relationship, while marital therapy did not improve the phobic/obsessive-compulsive problems.

In evaluating the effects of exposure *in vivo* on agoraphobics one should realize that the treatment is an emotional strain on both patient and family. It is now clearly demonstrated that exposure *in vivo* may lead to a dramatic improvement with respect to phobia removal in even a few days. For some patients and their families these changes are realized too soon. After rapid phobia removal patients' self-concepts and the role each person has in the family system have to change just as quickly as the patients' newly acquired skills. This might be an impossible task for some patients and their families, especially in chronic cases. If help with these problems is refused by the patient or his family, it may be therapeutically wise to retard improvement in order to equalize changes of self-concept and family system with phobia removal. However, no data are available to indicate for which patient this approach might be valuable.

2.4. Cognitive Therapy

Agoraphobics often complain of anxiety-inducing thoughts. With a number of patients these "negative" cognitions change "spontaneously" as a result of treatment by exposure *in vivo*. For example, during exposure *in vivo* patients may notice that the awful things they fear, as fainting, getting a heart attack, or "going crazy," do not take place. However, while we have found these cognitive changes with a number of patients, clearly not *all* patients do change their cognitions during treatment and for some patients these cognitive changes are only short-lived.

Another point also deserves attention. Although patients are exposed to the phobic situation *in vivo,* real exposure may still be avoided by the patients through such thoughts as "There is a hospital, if something goes wrong, there will be help." Similarly, *after* treatment sessions some patients "reassure" themselves with statements as "Well, this time nothing did go wrong because I had a good day, but tomorrow I can get a real attack." Thus, patients may use private speech that interferes with real exposure to the anxiety-inducing situations. Although, as yet, no research has been conducted into the effects of such negative private speech, it is tempting to assume that such cognitive avoidance militates against the effects of *in vivo* exposure.

2.4.1. Controlled Studies

The last few years we have directed some research into cognitive change methods for agoraphobics. In our first study (Emmelkamp *et al.*, 1978) cognitive restructuring was compared with prolonged exposure *in vivo* in a cross-over design. Both prolonged exposure *in vivo* and cognitive restructuring were conducted in groups. Each procedure consisted of five sessions. Exposure *in vivo* was found to be far more effective than cognitive restructuring both on the behavioral measure and phobic anxiety and avoidance scales (see Figure 15). However, treatment was conducted in a relatively short time period (one week), which might be too short to result in significant cognitive changes. Moreover the use of the

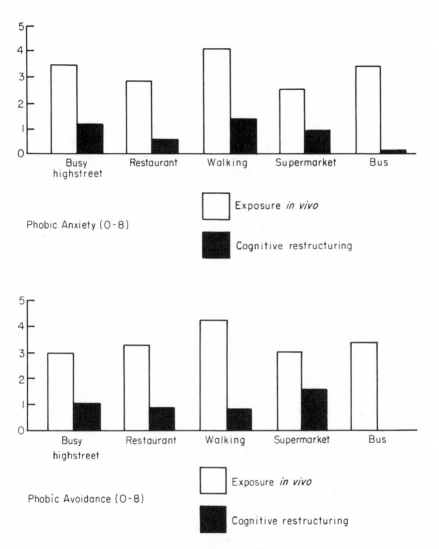

Figure 15. Mean change scores on phobic anxiety and avoidance scales. (From "Cognitive Modification versus Prolonged Exposure *in Vivo:* A Comparison with Agoraphobics by P. M. G. Emmelkamp *et al., Behaviour Research and Therapy,* 1978, *16,* Fig. 2. Copyright 1978 by Pergamon Press. Reprinted by permission.)

cross-over design precluded conclusions about the long-term effectiveness of our cognitive package.

In a following study (Emmelkamp & Mersch, 1982), three treatments were compared in a between-group design: (1) cognitive restructuring, (2) prolonged exposure *in vivo,* and (3) a combination of cognitive restructuring and prolonged exposure *in vivo.* Each session lasted 2 hours and each treatment consisted of eight sessions. During cognitive restructuring more emphasis was placed on insight into unproductive thinking than in the cognitive procedure used by Emmelkamp *et al.* (1978). In each session patients had to analyze their own feelings in terms of Ellis's ABC theory. In the combined procedure half of the time was spent on self-instructional training; the other half on prolonged exposure *in vivo.* During the latter phase of the combined treatment patients were instructed to use their positive self-statements during their *in vivo* exercises. The results on the behavioral measure and phobic anxiety and avoidance scales (Watson & Marks, 1971) are presented in Figures 16 and 17.

    At the posttest prolonged exposure *in vivo* and the combined proce-

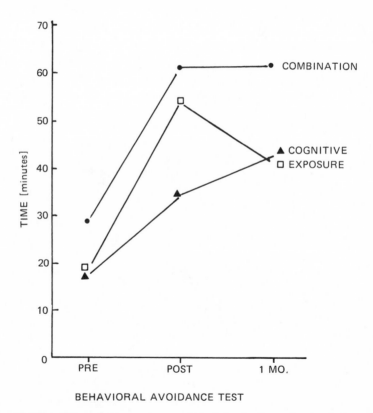

BEHAVIORAL AVOIDANCE TEST

Figure 16. The effects of the treatments on the behavioral test *(in vivo* measurement). (From Emmelkamp & Mersch, 1982.)

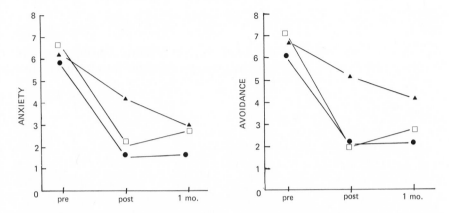

Figure 17. The effects of the treatments on the phobic anxiety and avoidance scales (self-ratings): (□) = exposure; (▲) = cognitive; (●) = combination. (From Emmelkamp & Mersch, 1982.)

dure (self-instructional training plus exposure *in vivo*) were clearly superior to cognitive restructuring on phobic anxiety and avoidance measures and on the behavioral measure, although the difference between exposure and cognitive restructuring on the latter measure was nonsignificant. At 1-month follow-up, however, the differences between the treatments had partly disappeared, due to a continuing improvement in the cognitive restructuring condition and a slight relapse in the exposure *in vivo* condition. Thus, although the short-term effects were similar to the results of the Emmelkamp *et al.* (1978) study, in the long run cognitive modification was about equally effective. Self-instructional training did not enhance the effects of exposure *in vivo*. On no variable was the combined procedure found to be more effective than exposure *in vivo*. Similar results were found in a study with obsessive-compulsive patients (Emmelkamp, van de Helm, van Zanten, & Plochg, 1980).

Interestingly, only cognitive-restructuring led to significant improvement at follow-up on depression, locus of control, and assertiveness (see Figure 18). However, since cognitive restructuring was found to be significantly more effective than the other two treatments on one of these measures (assertiveness) only, the findings that the cognitive restructuring group's report of depression, locus of control, and assertiveness improved across time requires some hesitancy in its interpretation. The improvements found on these questionnaires suggest that cognitive restructuring led not only to improvements on the target behaviors (i.e., phobic anxiety and avoidance), but to generalized behavior changes. It is tempting to assume that cognitive restructuring patients learned coping

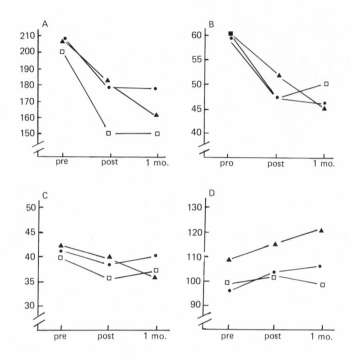

Figure 18. The effects of the treatments on the (A) Fear Survey Schedule, (B) Zung-Self-rating Depression Scale (SDS), (C) Locus of Control (I-E), and (D) assertiveness (ASES): (□) = exposure; (▲) = cognitive; (●) = combination. (From Emmelkamp & Mersch, 1982.)

skills which they did not only apply in phobic situations but in other situations as well.

A third study that evaluated the effects of cognitive restructuring was reported by Williams and Rappoport (1980). Agoraphobics were assigned to two conditions: (1) exposure *in vivo* plus self-instructional training and (2) exposure *in vivo*. Treatment was directed to their driving disabilities; other fears were not dealt with. Exposure *in vivo* was graded with increasing task difficulty. The lowest task was driving one block in a quiet residential neighborhood, and highest task was driving on a crowded urban freeway. After some practice in the office cognitive modification subjects were instructed to use positive self-statements during the exposure *in vivo* phase of treatment. The cognitive techniques used "were drawn from those most widely advocated by exponents of cognitive therapy, and were presented enthusiastically and repeatedly as an integral part of treatment." Results revealed that on the behavioral measure the noncognitive group gained significant benefit from treatment, while the cognitive group did not. Both groups improved on the Fear Questionnaire (Marks & Mathews, 1979). Interestingly, both the cognitive and noncognitive group showed a significant reduction in the number of phobic thoughts recorded during the behavioral test. The two groups showed significantly more coping thoughts at the posttest than the behavioral group. Thus, although cognitive therapy did result in patients using coping self-statements, these statements did not replace phobic thoughts.

The results of studies with clinical populations using cognitive procedures has not yet given the answer of the usefulness of the cognitive approach for clinical patients. Comparison of the results of the clinical studies leads to a few suggestions about effective parameters of cognitive restructuring. First, cognitive therapy conducted over a longer time interval might prove to be more effective than when conducted over a short period. One week of cognitive restructuring led to clinically insignificant results (Emmelkamp *et al.*, 1978), whereas after 2 months cognitive restructuring clearly led to clinically meaningful improvements in the Emmelkamp and Mersch study (1982).

Further, insight into unproductive thinking might prove to be more relevant than self-instructional training. In the Emmelkamp and Mersch study (1982) more emphasis was placed on insight into unproductive thinking than in the Emmelkamp *et al.* (1978) and Rappoport and Williams studies (1981). Several analog studies have been conducted to investigate which component of cognitive restructuring was the most productive, but these studies have produced conflicting results. To investigate the differential effectiveness of components of cognitive therapy Emmelkamp (1980c) compared rational emotive therapy with self-instructional training with agoraphobics as subjects. Treatment consisted of six sessions. Both components of cognitive restructuring led to some improvements but after six sessions these improvements were rather small. Neither of the two procedures was superior to the other on phobic anxiety and avoidance.

2.4.2. Concluding Remarks

To summarize, all studies on agoraphobics found exposure *in vivo* to be superior to cognitive restructuring immediately after treatment. Generally, cognitive restructuring led to a slight improvement on anxiety and avoidance. One study (Emmelkamp & Mersch, 1982) found cognitive restructuring almost as effective as exposure *in vivo*, but only in the long run, which was partly due to a relapse of the exposure *in vivo* group. It should be noted that a relapse after exposure *in vivo* is uncommon. One of the reasons to account for this partial relapse may be the fact that patients were not instructed to expose themselves *in vivo* as homework assignments as is usually done.

Emmelkamp *et al.* (1978) discussed a number of reasons why cognitive restructuring produced such poor results in the treatment of agoraphobics while others claim to have achieved such impressive results with similar cognitive modification procedures. First, most other studies were analog studies: The effects of treatments in analog studies might be more strongly influenced than in clinical trials by demand characteristics and expectancy of therapeutic gain. Further, it seems probable that the intelligence of the patients in clinical trials on the average will have been lower than that of the typical subjects in analog research (students). Cognitive restructuring might well be more effective with intelligent students used to thinking rationally than with less intelligent clinical populations. Finally, the degree of physiological arousal in anxiety-engendering situations, too, might differ considerably for agoraphobics and for subjects in analog studies. It is quite possible that cognitive restructuring constitutes an effective form of treatment for low physiological reactors (such as the subjects of analog studies) although such treatment is less effective with high physiological reactors (such as agoraphobics).

2.5. Assertiveness Training

It has been argued that agoraphobics are quite unassertive: They are not able to stand up for their rights and have often considerable difficulty in expressing their feelings adequately. Therefore, they are often dominated by significant others in their surroundings, especially by parents and husbands.

If we assume that agoraphobia may develop as a result of unassertiveness, then agoraphobics should profit from assertiveness training. To study the effectiveness of assertiveness training on agoraphobics we (Emmelkamp, van der Hout, & de Vries, 1982) recently compared the effectiveness of (1) assertiveness training, (2) prolonged exposure *in vivo*, and (3) a combination of assertiveness training and prolonged exposure *in vivo*. Patients were 21 subassertive agoraphobics who scored below the median on an assertiveness scale (Adult Self-Expression Scale; Gay, Hollandsworth, & Galassie, 1975): Thus, only low-assertive agoraphobics were used as subjects. The median was based on scores of agoraphobics in our previous clinical trials. Each session lasted 3 hours and each condition received ten sessions. Treatment was conducted in groups.

With assertiveness training, patients had to report on social situations in which they were unassertive or felt uneasy. During treatment sessions, these situations were discussed and a more adequate handling of these situations was trained through modeling by the therapist or by one of the other patients, and through behavior rehearsal. About half of the time was devoted to structured exercises as looking, giving a small speech, refusing requests, etc. In the combined treatment half of the time was devoted to assertiveness training, whereas the other half consisted of exposure *in vivo*. During the exposure *in vivo* phase of the combined treatment, patients had to practice the newly learned assertive skills.

As for the main measures (behavioral measurement and ratings for phobic anxiety and avoidance) exposure *in vivo* was found to be superior (see Figure 19). However, this difference was not always found to be statistically significant, due to the small number of patients in each condition. On the other hand, assertiveness training was found to be more effective on assertive measure (see Figure 20). The combined procedure was not more effective than each of the individual treatments on its own. The results of this study indicate that both forms of behavioral treatment have something to offer for subassertive agoraphobics. Exposure *in vivo* leads to rapid improvement with respect to anxiety and avoidance. On the other hand, assertiveness training leads to more improvement than exposure *in vivo* with respect to assertiveness. In another study (Emmelkamp, 1980b) we found that assertive and unassertive agoraphobics benefitted equally from exposure *in vivo*. Taken together, these data indicate that the most efficient therapeutic strategy is to start with exposure *in vivo* and proceed later to assertiveness training if necessary. It should be noted that several patients become more assertive as a result of exposure *in vivo*. Typically, these patients have been assertive prior to the onset of the agoraphobia. Presumably, the development of the agoraphobia had led to a lack of self-sufficiency and self-efficacy which finally resulted in unassertiveness.

Theoretically, it is interesting to see that several agoraphobics improve with respect to the anxiety and avoidance, without prior exposure *in vivo*. Similar results were found with obsessive-compulsive patients (Emmelkamp, 1982; Emmelkamp & van de Heyden, 1980; see Chapter 8). These data indicate that at least in some cases phobic anxiety may be overcome without any exposure to the phobic stimuli.

2.6. Patient and Process Variables as Predictors of Outcome

Several studies have looked for predictors of treatment outcome. Generally, pretreatment measures proved to be poor predictors of outcome (e.g., Hafner & Marks, 1976). Heightened physiological arousal

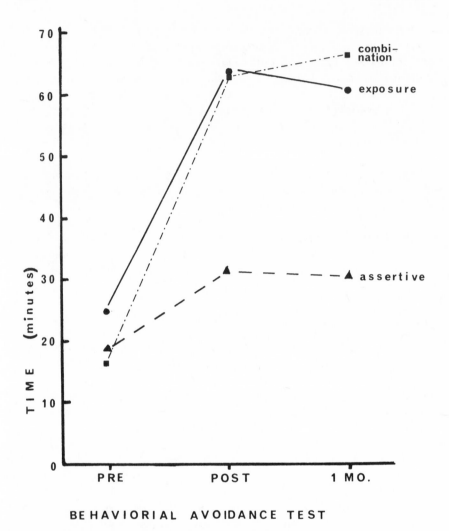

Figure 19. The effects of the treatments on the behavioral test (*in vivo* measurement). (From Emmelkamp, van der Hout, & de Vries, 1982.)

before treatment (Stern & Marks, 1973; Watson & Marks, 1971), initial severity of phobia (Stern & Marks, 1973), "emotional stability" and duration of phobia (Mathews, Johnston, Lancashire, Munby, Shaw, & Gelder, 1976), and expectancy of therapeutic gain (Emmelkamp & Emmelkamp-Benner, 1975; Emmelkamp & Wessels, 1975) may all be associated with outcome.

In a study of failures with exposure *in vivo* (Emmelkamp & van der Hout, 1982) initial severity, pretreatment depression, and nonassertiveness did not differentiate failures from successful cases. Further, no evidence was found that agoraphobics who had realistic fears (overvalued ideation) that they suffered from a serious disease, failed to benefit from treatment by exposure *in vivo*. Emmelkamp (1980b) also could not find a relationship between assertiveness and success of treatment by exposure *in vivo*.

Johnston, Lancashire, Mathews, Munby, Shaw, and Gelder (1976) found that predictive power improved as treatment progressed. However, they pointed out that "these correlations do not achieve useful levels until about eight weeks have passed, and this is rather too long for it to be of practical value" (p. 374). Emmelkamp and Kuipers (1979) looked for prognostic variables for result of treatment at 4-year follow-up. The following prognostic variables, measured at the start of treatment, were investigated: (1) duration of phobia, (2) locus of control, (3) social anxiety, and (4) depression. None of these variables showed a clear relationship with results at follow-up. Munby and Johnston (1980) correlated patients' scores on the main measure of agoraphobic severity prior to treatment with follow-up results (ranging from 5 to 9 years after treatment). The correlations showed that phobia ratings prior to treatment were poor predictors of long-term outcome.

In summary, few variables were found to predict treatment outcome. The few relationships that have been found between variables at

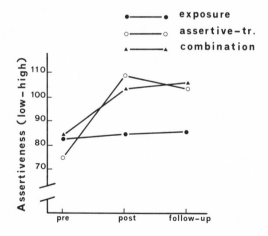

Figure 20. The effects of the treatments on assertiveness (Adult-Self-Expression Scale). (From Emmelkamp, van der Hout, & de Vries, 1982.)

the start of treatment and outcome can be partially explained by chance and have little clinical utility.

2.6.1. Parental Characteristics

Emmelkamp and van der Hout (1982) investigated whether parental characteristics were associated with failure of exposure *in vivo*. To assess the perceived parental characteristics agoraphobics had to complete the EMBU (Perris, Jacobsson, Lindström, von Knorring, & Perris, 1980). Failures were differentiated from successes on the "strictness" dimension: Failures perceived their mothers as more strict than did the patients whose treatment had been successful. The relationship between strictness of parental discipline and failure of treatment suggests that parental discipline might be an important prognostic factor.

The finding that perceived strictness of mothers' discipline was related to failure of exposure *in vivo* may have a bearing on the issue of the therapeutic relationship. It is conceivable that patients with such rearing experiences are particularly sensitive to the "strictness" of the therapist during exposure *in vivo*. This proposed "transference" is, of course, highly speculative but the findings are interesting enough to warrant further study.

2.6.2. Therapeutic Relationship

The relationship between therapist and patient has been neglected in the behavioral literature (De Voge & Beck, 1978), despite the finding of some studies in the early 1960s that the therapeutic relationship might be of paramount importance in the process of behavior therapy. For example, Meyer and Gelder (1963) pointed out that the therapeutic relationship might be crucial in the behavioral treatment of agoraphobia. After having given an account of the treatment by behavior therapy of five agoraphobics, they state that "the single factor which seems most relevant to the outcome of behavior therapy is this relationship" (p. 26).

Crisp (1966) attempted to assess the positive and negative feelings of the patient for his therapist throughout the behavioral treatment of 11 patients including agoraphobics. He found a consistent relationship between such "transference" feelings and the clinical course of the treatment: "the major clinical changes during treatment are often associated with or occasionally preceded by . . . appropriate change in 'transference'" (p. 182).

Generally, studies into the effects of various behavioral procedures with agoraphobics neglected the possible influence of the therapeutic relationship upon the outcome of therapy. Usually, patients were randomly assigned across various therapists in an attempt to control for a possible "therapist" factor. Mathews *et al.* (1973) compared flooding, desensitization, and control treatment and found no evidence that one therapist was more effective than another. They suggest that

> the personal qualities which appear to influence the results of counseling procedures are less important when the more precisely formulated techniques of flooding, desensitization and the special control treatment are used.

However, subsequent studies (Mathews *et al.*, 1976; Jannoun *et al.*, 1980) found a significant therapist effect, indicating that the improvements achieved could not be ascribed solely to technical procedures.

Emmelkamp and van der Hout (1982) investigated the influence of perceived therapists' qualities on the outcome of exposure *in vivo*. Subjects were agoraphobics who had participated in a group treatment. Patients had to complete the Relationship Inventory (Barrett-Lennard) as modified by Lietaer (1976). There was a significant relationship between outcome of therapy and such "good" therapist characteristics as empathy, positive regard, and congruity. Similar results were found in a study of Rabavilas, Boulougouris, and Perisssaki (1979). Phobic and obsessive-compulsive patients who had been treated with exposure *in vivo* rated the following therapists' qualities at follow-up: warmth, acceptance, respect, understanding, interest, liking, objectivity, and gratification of dependency needs. Results indicated that therapists' respect, understanding, and interest were positively related to outcome. However, gratification of patient's dependency needs was negatively related to outcome.

It is tempting to consider the results of these studies to be supportive of the view that therapists' characteristics play an important part in the behavioral treatment of agoraphobics. Alternatively, the patients' ratings of outcome and therapist may be reflections of the patients' overall satisfaction with the treatment. If the latter is true, one may not conclude that the therapists' characteristics were causal in effecting the favorable outcome since the favorable outcome of therapy might have influenced the patients' recall of their therapists' characteristics.

Further indications that the therapeutic relationship may influence treatment outcome came from interviews which Emmelkamp and van der Hout (1982) held with a number of patients who were considered to be treatment failures. Generally, failures found that the therapist did not show that they really understood their feelings.

Taken together, the therapeutic relationship seems to be of importance. For some patients it may take a considerable time before a "good"

therapeutic relationship develops. With this subgroup of patients premature exposure *in vivo* may at best be a waste of time and at worst a
"torment" which can lead to drop-out off treatment.

2.7. Follow-up

Follow-up in the various treatment outcome studies ranges from a
few weeks to one year. Long term follow-up after behavioral treatment
with phobic patients is relatively rare. Marks (1971) reported follow-up
data of 65 phobic patients, about half of whom were agoraphobics.
Patients had been treated in the trials of Gelder *et al.* (1967) and Marks,
Gelder, and Edwards (1968) with desensitization, hypnosis, and psychotherapy. At 4 years follow-up, 58% of the patients were rated as improved. Those who were originally desensitized showed the greatest
improvement.

Emmelkamp and Kuipers (1979) conducted a prospective follow-up
study with 70 agoraphobics who were treated at an average of 4 years ago
in the trials of Emmelkamp (1974), Emmelkamp and Ultee (1974),
Emmelkamp and Wessels (1975), and Emmelkamp and Emmelkamp-
Benner (1977). After the clinical trial a number of patients were further
treated individually. The number of treatment sessions averaged around
18 (clinical trials plus further treatment).

The results of the anxiety and avoidance scales at pretest, posttest
and follow-up are shown in Figure 21. It appears that the improvements
that were manifested during the treatment were maintained and partly
continued during follow-up. The improvement on the anxiety scale,
between posttest and follow-up, was significant. This could mean that in
the course of treatment with self-controlled exposure *in vivo,* the patient
developed a general strategy for coping with anxiety-arousing situations
that they can apply on their own. Results at follow-up revealed further
continuing improvement in depression. Patients did not report the
emergence of problems other than agoraphobia.

Marks found that 58% of the patients had improved at 4 years
follow-up (improvement indicates a change of 1 point or more on a
5-point scale). In the Emmelkamp and Kuipers (1979) study, 75% of the
patients turned out to have improved on the main phobia (anxiety and
avoidance combined). Improvement indicates reduction of main phobia
by two points or more on the 0–8 scale (Watson & Marks, 1971). The
superior results of Emmelkamp and Kuipers (1979) might be due to the
exposure *in vivo* procedures that were applied with all patients during
the treatment.

Other follow-up studies on agoraphobics were reported by McPherson, Brougham, and McLaren (1980) and Munby and Johnston (1980).

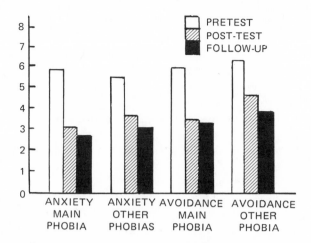

Figure 21. Mean scores on phobic anxiety and avoidance scales (pretest, posttest, follow-up). (From "Agoraphobia: A Follow-Up Study Four Years after Treatment" by P. M. G. Emmelkamp and A. Kuipers, *British Journal of Psychiatry*, 1979, *134*, Fig. 1. Reprinted by permission.)

Improvements brought about by the treatment were maintained over a follow-up period that ranged from 4 years (McPherson *et al.*) up to 9 years (Munby & Johnston). Unfortunately, no information is provided with respect to number of patients with whom treatment failed in the Munby and Johnston study.

It should be noted that results of behavioral treatment were variable. While behavioral treatment led to considerable improvements, relatively few patients were completely free of agoraphobic symptoms. For example, although 75% of our patients turned out to have improved at follow-up, improvement was far from complete. There proved to be a great variation in the improvement achieved. Some patients were symptom free, some were moderately improved, and a few patients did not benefit at all. Similarly, McPherson *et al.* (1980) reported that only 10% of the sample was completely symptom free: "the majority (66%) reported that their symptoms had stabilised at a level which, while occasionally causing them slight distress, could easily be tolerated and affected their every day lives only slightly, if at all" (p. 151).

3. BEHAVIORAL TREATMENT OF SOCIAL ANXIETY

In contrast with numerous analog studies that deal with social anxiety, speech anxiety, dating anxiety, unassertiveness, etc. (reviewed by Arkowitz, 1977; Curran, 1977), relatively few studies in the area of social anxiety have used real patients. Studies using social inadequates or unassertive patients are included in the present review, since most patients with social interaction difficulties experience anxiety in social situations (Hall & Goldberg, 1977).

Generally, three behavioral theories concerning the functioning of social anxiety can be distinguished: (1) conditioned anxiety theory, (2) skills-deficits theory, and (3) cognitive theory.

If patients have adequate social skills but are inhibited in social situations by conditioned anxiety, this anxiety has to be dealt with. For example, Wolpe (1958) holds that maladaptive fears inhibit the emission of assertive responses. Thus, according to this proposition techniques that are successful in reducing anxiety should lead to a concomitant increase in assertiveness. Others have argued that anxiety experienced in social situations is the result of inadequate handling of these situations. A patient may lack the skills to initiate conversations or to handle himself in groups. If it is assumed that such lack of social skills provokes anxiety, then anxiety may be overcome through social skills training. Finally, more recently, the maladaptive cognitions of social-anxious patients have been stressed. Social-anxious patients usually have worrying thoughts about current and anticipated social meetings. It is argued that faulty evaluation of one's performance in social situations or irrational beliefs mediate social anxiety. If anxiety is mediated by faulty thinking, cognitive therapy may result in alteration of such irrational beliefs and maladaptive self-statements and, hence, could lead to anxiety reduction.

3.1. Conditioned Anxiety versus Skills Deficit

3.1.2 Systematic Desensitization versus Skills Training

In this section studies investigating the effectiveness of systematic desensitization and social skills training are reviewed.

3.1.2.1. Systematic Desensitization. Several studies have investigated the effectiveness of systematic desensitization with social-anxious patients (Hall & Goldberg, 1977; Marzillier, Lambert, & Kellett, 1976; Shaw, 1976; Trower, Yardley, Bryant, & Shaw, 1978; Van Son, 1978). In general, limited clinical improvements were achieved. In only three studies was systematic desensitization compared with no-treatment conditions: In neither study was desensitization significantly more effective than controls. In addition, Dormaar and Dijkstra (1975) found no significant between-group differences between psychotherapy and desensitization. Finally, Kanter and Goldfried (1979) found systematic desensitization as self-control more effective than a waiting list-control, using social-anxious community residents as subjects; however, overall improvement was small.

Briefly, systematic desensitization is of limited value with social-anxious patients. Results of studies dealing with real patients contrast with those of studies using analog populations. In the latter studies desensitization has consistently been found to be effective in the treatment of social anxiety.

3.1.2.2. Social Skills Training. Social skills training seems to be of more value in the treatment of social anxiety. However, the evidence in favor of this approach is far from conclusive. Although several studies could not find consistent differences between systematic desensitization and social skills training (Hall & Goldberg, 1977; Shaw, 1976; Trower *et al.*, 1978 [social phobics]; Van Son, 1978 [social inadequates]), results of other studies indicate that social skills training may be superior (Marzillier *et al.*, 1976; Trower *et al.*, 1978 [social inadequates]; Van Son, 1978 [erythrophobics]).

3.1.3. Test of the Social Fear and Skill-Deficit Hypotheses

As we have seen, the conditioned anxiety hypothesis predicts that anxiety reduction should lead to an increase in assertion. However, two studies demonstrate that anxiety reduction was not automatically followed by a change in assertion. Trower *et al.* (1978) demonstrated that systematic desensitization had some effect on social fear of social phobics, but no treatment effects were shown on the objective behavioral indices of social skills. Recently, Marshall, Keltner, and Marshall (1981) evaluated the effects of assertiveness training and relaxation on assertiveness and social fear respectively. Subjects were social-anxious inmates from a penitentiary. Assertiveness training led to increased assertion but did not decrease social fear, while for inmates in the relaxation group social fear, but not assertion, was modified. Thus, assertiveness training and relaxation had specific and nonoverlapping effects. The results of this study support neither the conditioned anxiety hypothesis nor the skills-deficit hypothesis. According to the conditioned anxiety hypothesis, anxiety reduction should have led to an increase in assertion. Similarly, according to the skills-deficit hypothesis, effective assertiveness training should have led to a reduction in social fear.

3.1.4. Individual Response Patterns

The clinical studies reviewed so far grouped all social-anxious patients together and ignored the role of individual differences. In a particularly well-designed study Öst, Jerremalm, and Johansson (1981) attempted to match treatment to individual response patterns. Social-anxious out-patients ($n = 32$) were divided into two groups showing different response patterns; behavioral and physiological reactors. The patient's heart rate was recorded continuously during a conversation test. Patients with high heart rate but small overt behavior reactions during this test were classified as physiological reactors. On the other hand, patients with large behavioral reactions but little or no reaction on heart rate were classified as behavioral reactors. Within each group half of the patients were randomly assigned to treatment that focused on the behavioral component (social skills training) while the other half received treatment that primarily focused on the physiological component (applied relaxation). It was hypothesized that patients who were treated with a method that matched their response pattern would achieve better results than the group treated with the other method. The results generally supported the hypothesis. Thus, it seems therapeutically wise to match treatment to the individual needs of patients.

3.2. Cognitive Therapy

Relatively few studies have examined the effectiveness of cognitive therapy with clinically relevant populations. In the Kanter and Goldfried (1979) study, referred to earlier, the following treatment conditions were compared: (1) cognitive restructuring, (2) self-control desensitization, (3) cognitive restructuring plus self-control desensitization, and (4) waiting-list control. Cognitive restructuring proved to be superior to desensitization and control group. It is noteworthy that the combined treatment (cognitive restructuring plus desensitization) was *less* effective than cognitive restructuring alone.

Further evidence for the effectiveness of cognitive restructuring was provided by Wolfe and Fodor (1977). Results of their study indicated that both skills training and cognitive restructuring yielded improvements on the behavioral measure; cognitive restructuring, however, was the only condition which led to anxiety reduction.

3.2.3. Concluding Remarks

Both skills training and cognitive restructuring seem to be promising treatments for social-anxious patients, although further studies are certainly needed before more definitive conclusions can be drawn. The effectiveness of systematic and prolonged exposure *in vivo* has not been studied, presumably because such an exposure is difficult to arrange in real life situations. One should remember that both cognitive restructuring and social skills training contain elements of exposure *in vivo*. For instance, *in vivo* homework assignments are an integral part of Ellis's Rational Emotive Therapy:

> For unless phobic individuals act against their irrational beliefs that they must not approach fearsome objects or situations and that it is horrible if they do, can they ever really be said to have overcome such beliefs? (Ellis, 1979, p. 162)

Similarly, the effects of social skills training may be due to exposure *in vivo* to social situations. During treatment sessions patients are exposed to anxiety-arousing situations and have to give up their avoidance behavior, which eventually may lead to anxiety reduction. Furthermore, the homework patients usually have to carry out between treatment sessions results in a further exposure to real life situations.

It is important to note that the effects of treatment for social anxiety are rather modest. Several authors point to the limited clinical improvements achieved. Falloon *et al.* (1977) state that "many patients were left with residual deficits. Social skills training is a useful therapeutic advance, but more work is needed to facilitate the transfer of gains from the group to real-life situations, and the maintenance of these gains" (p. 609). Shaw (1978) reported that only a few patients appeared to be completely cured at 6-month follow-up. In the study by Marzillier *et al.* (1976) patients improved in one-to-one interactions at the posttest, but had not progressed in group situations. Marzillier *et al.* concluded that "social skills treatment had a beneficial effect on the patients' social lives, but had less effects in terms of all round clinical improvement" (p. 236).

Hall and Goldberg (1977) compared the results of their patients at the posttest with those of a volunteer nonpatient group, which was matched for age, sex, and social class. Patients in both desensitization and social skills training conditions showed, at the end of treatment, more pathology than the nonpatient group.

Most research in this area has been plagued by the uniformity myth that all social-anxious patients are similar. Generally, researchers do not distinguish between various categories of social-anxious patients: A functional analysis is not made, but patients are randomly assigned to treatment conditions. It is too easy, however, to conceptualize social anxiety in terms of a single theory. Cognitive restructuring, social skills training, and exposure procedures surely can be critical elements in treatment, but no method is so powerful that it can be applied universally across social-anxious patients. For patients who lack adequate social skills, the training of such skills seems essential. On the other hand, for those patients who do have the necessary social skills but whose anxiety is mediated by faulty thinking, cognitive therapy combined with exposure *in vivo* to test the newly acquired cognitions may be the treatment of choice.

4. BEHAVORIAL TREATMENT OF SEXUAL ANXIETY

Anxiety often plays a part in the genesis of sexual dysfunctions. The purpose of this chapter is not to discuss all methods that have proved effective in overcoming sexual inadequacies. Rather the emphasis will be on the role played by anxiety in causing and maintaining sexual dysfunctions and on treatments that explicitly focus on a modification of anxiety. For a more detailed discussion of sex therapy the reader is referred to Masters and Johnson (1970), Kaplan (1974), and Lo Piccolo and Lo Piccolo (1978).

Both male and female dysfunctions may result from many diverse etiological factors. Unfortunately, discussions of the etiology of sexual dysfunctions are based almost entirely on uncontrolled patients' self-reports. Owing to the lack of controlled research in the area, there is little definitive knowledge concerning the etiology of sexual dysfunctions. However, most authors stress the importance of anxiety in the development of the problem. For example, Wolpe (1973) holds that anxiety plays a major role in the genesis of most sexual dysfunctions. In his view, anxiety inhibits sexual arousal. Although there is generally consensus among theorists concerning the relationship between anxiety and erectile failure, there is less consensus about the role played by anxiety in the genesis of orgasmic dysfunction in women and retarded ejaculation in men (Hogan, 1978).

Generally, "fear of failure" or "performance anxiety" (Masters & Johnson, 1970) plays a prominent part in theories concerning the relationship between anxiety and sexual dysfunctions. According to Masters and Johnson (1970), the basis of sexual dysfunctions lies in anxiety related to performance concerns. The dysfunctional person is concerned about his sexual performance, which is assumed to lead to sexual failure. It is important to note that anxiety might be related to other factors besides the performance. The necessity of a detailed analysis into the nature of the anxiety related to the sexual situation may be illustrated by the following case. A female patient was referred for treatment of orgasmic dysfunction after treatment in a group for nonorgasmic women. Previous treatment focused exclusively on the woman's sexual response, including relaxation practice and masturbation exercises. Although treatment had led to the experience of orgasm during self-masturbation, this did not generalize to sexual intercourse. In the initial interviews it became clear that this woman was regularly threatened with death by her husband. During arguments, her husband had several times laid his hands around her neck in an attempt to strangle her. When the couple had intercourse, the patient was terrified to death because of having no control when her husband would attempt to strangle her. Clearly, in this case anxiety during intercourse was caused by the aggressive husband rather than by performance anxiety. Of course, the anxiety-arousing situation in this case is exceptional; the case is cited to stress the importance of looking beyond the concept of performance anxiety. Other anxieties inhibiting sexual functioning may result from fear of venereal disease, fear of blood, fear of discovery (children coming into the bedroom), fear of pregnancy, fear of ridicule, fear of physical disease, anxiety over size or form of genitals, etc. Further, in some cases at least, sexual anxiety appears to stem from social anxiety.

As already mentioned, only a few studies have investigated the role of anxiety in sexual dysfunctions. Cooper (1969) investigated whether male patients with sexual dysfunctions experienced anxiety during co-itus. He had his patients (erectile failure and ejaculatory incompetence cases) rate their anxiety related to coitus. Coital anxiety was defined as anxiety related temporarily to the act of coitus or sexual overtures and stimulations short of intercourse that could culminate in a coital attempt. Of the dysfunctional men, 94% experienced recognizable anxiety during intercourse. The results of this study suggest that anxiety is associated with male sexual dysfunction in the majority of cases. A study by Kockott, Feil, Revenstorf, Aldenhoff, and Besinger (1980) also has some bearing on this issue. In this study psychogenic sexual dysfunctional men were compared with "organic" dysfunctional men and normal controls. Patients with psychogenic dysfunctions formed two groups: (1) erectile impotence ($n = 16$) and (2) premature ejaculation ($n = 16$). The group of "organic" impotent men consisted of patients with diabetes-related erectile impotence ($n = 10$). The results revealed that on the sexual anxiety scale the psychogenic dysfunctional men were more anxious than the diabetics and controls. Interestingly, two types of premature ejaculators could be identified. In only one of these was the premature ejaculation related to anxiety.

In summary, anxiety appears to play a role in some types of cases but not in others. The results of the study by Kockott et al. (1980) suggest that for some premature ejaculators, sexual anxiety does not have the central role as in cases with psychogenic impotence, which might have important implications for treatment.

4.1. The Assessment of Sexual Anxiety

Having acknowledged the important part played by anxiety and fear in sexual dysfunctions, it is surprising to see how little attention is devoted to the assessment of sexual anxiety in studies that investigated treatment effects on sexual dysfunctional patients (Meursing, 1980). Although sexual anxiety is usually not assessed in these studies, most treatment procedures or packages involve elements that aim at anxiety reduction. For example, the now widely used Masters and Johnson program for the treatment of sexual dysfunctions is primarily designed to reduce performance anxiety related to the sexual situation. As already pointed out by several authors (e.g., Ascher & Clifford, 1976; Murphy & Mikulas, 1974) the Masters and Johnson program is essentially behavioral in nature and can be conceived of as graded exposure *in vivo*. Similarly, a number of behavioral procedures currently used in the treatment of sexual dysfunctions can be conceptualized as exposure procedures. Exposure to sexual situations and experiences can be accomplished along several lines: (1) *imaginal* (e.g., systematic desensitization), (2) *in vivo* (e.g., graded homework assignments along the lines of Masters and Johnson), and (3) *vicarious* (e.g., videotapes).

Although there is general agreement that there is a complex relationship between desire, anxiety, and performance in sexual dysfunctions, in most studies dysfunctions are defined as performance problems. Typically, criteria for success of treatment are frequency of orgasm during intercourse, restoration of erectile functioning, and so on. However, the relationship between desire, anxiety, and performance makes assessment that is primarily based on performance difficult to interpret. Therapy may, for example, improve performance without improving anxiety. Levine and Agle (1978) also devoted attention to this issue and argued that figures based on performance only may be very misleading: "Most of the men, despite improvement, continued to have profound disturbances in their sexual lives" (p. 246).

4.2. Controlled Studies

The next section involves a review of studies on treatment of sexual dysfunctions with a special emphasis on the reduction of anxiety. Generally, investigations have been on a very primitive level. Only a handful of researchers employed objective assessment instruments to assess sexual anxiety. The lack of well-controlled research in this area precludes drawing definitive conclusions about the effectiveness of many of the sex therapies currently used with respect to anxiety reduction. In this section only controlled studies will be discussed.

4.2.1. Mixed Populations

Two studies included males and females with sexual dysfunctions. The first controlled study on the effects of systematic desensitization was conducted by Obler (1973). The subjects (volunteering students) were assigned to three conditions: (1) systematic desensitization, (2) group therapy, and (3) no-treatment. Systematic desensitization also included assertiveness training. The group therapy was psychoanalytically oriented. Results indicated that the modified systematic desensitization program was more effective than the other two conditions. An interesting feature of this study was the assessment of sexual anxiety both subjectively and psychophysiologically. The assessment included the Sexual Anxiety Scale (SAS), measuring social and sexual anxieties, and the Anxiety Differential Scale, which was administered after subjects were exposed to a sexual film. Systematic desensitization was found to reduce sexual anxiety both on the self-report anxiety measures and psychophysiologically. A problem in interpreting results of this study is that systematic desensitization and assertiveness training were mixed. In addition, the use of volunteers limits further conclusions from being drawn.

Mathews, Bancroft, Whitehead, Hackmann, Julier, Bancroft, Gath, and Shaw (1976) compared three methods: (1) systematic desensitization plus counseling, (2) Masters and Johnson program plus counseling, and (3) Masters and Johnson program with minimal contact. Thirty-six couples complaining of sexual difficulties were treated, of which 18 were classified as primarily male problems, and 18 as female. The Masters and Johnson program, consisting of directed practice plus counseling was found to be more effective than desensitization and the minimal contact treatment. However, conclusions with respect to anxiety reduction are precluded since anxiety was not assessed. Furthermore, the inclusion of a variety of male and female dysfunctions makes the results of the studies of Mathews *et al.* and Obler (1973) difficult to interpret.

4.2.2. Male Dysfunctions

Everaerd, Stufkens-Veerman, Van der Bout, Hofman, Syben-Schrier, and Schacht (1977) compared the effectiveness of systematic desensitization with a Masters and Johnson program in the treatment of erectile impotence and premature ejaculation. Systematic desensitization was found to be less effective than the Masters and Johnson program.

Kockott, Dittmar, and Nusselt (1975) also attempted to evaluate the effectiveness of systematic desensitization in the treatment of male sexual dysfunctions (impotence). Patients were randomly distributed across three conditions: (1) systematic desensitization, (2) routine therapy, and

(3) no-treatment. Routine therapy consisted of standardized advice and medication. Results were generally poor as far as performance was concerned. However, systematic desensitization resulted in less subjective anxiety during imagination of sexual intercourse as compared with the other two groups. The results are difficult to interpret, since the systematic desensitization subjects were seen much more frequently (14 sessions) than the subjects who received routine therapy (4 sessions).

In sum, although there is some evidence that systematic desensitization leads to anxiety reduction, a gradual exposure *in vivo* program along the lines of Masters and Johnson looks more promising. Unfortunately, conclusions are tempered by the heterogeneous patient populations used and the failure to assess anxiety in some studies.

4.2.3. Female Sexual Dysfunctions

According to Masters and Johnson (1970), female orgasmic dysfunctions are usually classified as either primary or secondary. Primary orgasmic dysfunction is usually defined as the condition in which a female has never experienced orgasm. Secondary orgasmic dysfunction refers to women who achieve orgasm only in response to restricted types of stimulation, or women who in the past were orgasmic, but who are currently unable to experience orgasm. Unfortunately, some studies did not differentiate between primary and secondary dysfunctions, thus precluding conclusions about the differential treatment outcomes of primary and secondary dysfunctional women. Further, some studies also included women with other sexual dysfunctions (e.g., vaginismus) or women whose partners were also dysfunctional. The failure of researchers to identify these differences inhibits the generalizability of the findings.

Many articles have reported systematic desensitization in the treatment of female sexual dysfunctions, but we will limit our scope to controlled studies. Munjack, Cristol, Goldstein, Phillips, Goldberg, Whipple, Staples, and Kanno (1976) found behavior treatment including systematic desensitization and modeling more effective than no-treatment both in terms of orgasmic capacity and decrease in negative feelings. Although their treatment package appeared to be an effective therapy, it is impossible to evaluate the effective ingredients, since Munjack *et al.* included assertiveness training, behavior rehearsal, masturbation training, and the use of mechanical devices as part of their treatment program.

Sotile and Kilmann (1978) investigated the effects of systematic desensitization with 8 primary and 14 secondary nonorgasmic women.

The clients served as their own control. In the control period that preceded actual treatment subjects were asked to read a handout containing general information on female sexual responsivity. Systematic desensitization led to improvements on both sexual anxiety measures and sexual functioning, including percentage of times that orgasm was achieved during extracoital stimulation. When treatment and control periods were contrasted statistically, systematic desensitization was found to be significantly superior. Further, Sotile and Kilmann (1978) found that secondary subjects showed greater positive changes in orgasmic responsivity to extracoital stimulation than did primary subjects. This finding suggests that anxiety toward sexual functioning may be a more important prohibitive factor in secondary anorgasm than in primary cases.

Sotile, Kilmann, and Follingstad (1977) investigated the impact of a sexual enhancement workshop with six of the women who had been treated with systematic desensitization in the Sotile and Kilmann (1978) study. The workshop included various procedures including masturbation retraining, fantasy exercises, sensate focus homework, etc. Results indicated that the workshop facilitated an even greater reduction in reported sexual anxiety than systematic desensitization. However, the workshop did not lead to enhanced orgasmic responsivity for most women. It should be noted that the women who participated in the workshop represented a biased sample, since a number of couples did not wish to participate.

Wincze and Caird (1976) treated 21 women complaining of "essential sexual dysfunction" by either systematic desensitization or video desensitization (modeling). In the modeling condition the hierarchy scenes were presented via videotapes, depicting couples involved in programs on orgasmic dysfunctions. Ershner-Hershfield and Kopel (1979) found this program significantly more effective than no-treatment, both with and without the inclusion of partners: 91% of 24 primary nonorgasmic women achieved orgasm via self-stimulation.

McMullen and Rosen (1979) investigated the effects of a self-administered masturbation-training program under two different conditions: (a) videotape modeling and (b) written instructions. In addition, a waiting-list control group was included. In the modeling condition subjects viewed an actress portraying a nonorgasmic woman who learns to stimulate herself to orgasm and, finally, reached orgasm through intercourse. Subjects in the other treatment condition had to read booklets whose content was equivalent to the videotapes. In addition, subjects in both treatment groups were supplied with an electric vibrator to be used at home. Each condition contained 20 women who had never previously experienced orgasm. Both treatment conditions led to orgasmic capacity in about 60% of the subjects. None of the subjects in the control group became orgasmic during this time. Modeling did not enhance treatment efficacy.

Unfortunately, both Ershner-Hershfield and Kopel (1979) and Mc-Mullen and Rosen (1979) did not assess sexual anxiety. Thus, it is unclear (1) whether anxiety was related to the sexual dysfunction of the subjects and (2) whether the treatment program affected anxiety.

To date, only one study (Andersen, 1981) compared the relative efficacy of masturbation training and systematic desensitization. Assessment included heterosexual anxiety. Subjects were 30 primary nonorgasmic females. Systematic desensitization included *in vivo* exercise. Surprisingly, neither treatment led to anxiety reduction. Generally, masturbation training was more effective in increasing sexual arousal than systematic desensitization.

Summarizing the results of the studies on female dysfunction, there is some evidence that exposure to videotapes portraying sexual scenes leads to anxiety reduction. This treatment proved to be more effective than systematic desensitization. However, anxiety reduction hardly affected orgasmic capacity. Other methods that focus more directly on reaching orgasm (e.g., masturbation training) seem to be more effective in dealing with this target, at least with primary anorgasmic cases. Unfortunately, most studies investigating the effects of masturbation training did not assess sexual anxiety, so that conclusions with respect to anxiety reduction are precluded. The only study that did assess sexual anxiety (Andersen, 1981) found changes in anxiety to be negligible. Finally, there is some evidence that anxiety is more important in secondary cases than in primary cases. This suggests that with secondary anorgasmic women treatment may need to be directed to anxiety reduction, while this may be less necessary with primary anorgasmic women.

4.3. Concluding Comment

The role played by anxiety in sexual dysfunctions is a neglected area. It is felt that sexual dysfunctions often can be conceptualized as phobic reactions. It may be therapeutically wise to assess the role of anxiety in sexual dysfunctional patients. When the analyses reveal that anxiety plays an important part, treatment should focus on this anxiety more directly instead of using a standardized sex-therapy program. Unfortunately, no particular treatment approach to deal with sexual anxiety can be recommended, due to the failure to assess anxiety in most studies.

5. PSYCHOPHARMACA

The subject of this section is the effect of drugs on phobias. Both anxiolytics and antidepressants will be discussed. The emphasis will be on controlled studies. The psychopharmacological treatment of obsessive-compulsive disorders will be dealt with in Chapter 9.

5.1. Anxiolytics

5.1.1. Benzodiazepines

Benzodiazepines are the most prescribed drugs for phobias although there is hardly any evidence that they lead to lasting benefits. Solomon and Hart (1978) reviewed 78 double-blind studies comparing benzodiazepines and placebos in treating neurotic anxiety and found that almost all studies have major flaws in design and execution, which led them to seriously question the efficacy of benzodiazepines:

> it is important to remember that bleeding, leeching, and purgatives were standard treatments for many diseases for hundreds of years, based on hearsay evidence, uncontrolled observation, poor quantification of symptomatology and poor subject choice, essentially the same problems discussed in this paper. (Solomon and Hart, p. 828)

In order to recommend the concomitant use of a drug and behavior therapy it is necessary to show that the combination confers an advantage over behavior therapy alone. Several studies have investigated whether diazepam (valium) enhances the effects of exposure *in vivo*. In a study with specific phobics, Marks *et al.* (1972) compared (1) exposure starting 4 hours after oral diazepam ("waning" group), (2) exposure starting one hour after oral diazepam ("peak" group), and (3) exposure starting after oral placebo. The "waning" condition was superior to placebo, whereas the "peak" group was in between. Diazepam did not increase pleasantness during exposure *in vivo*.

In the study by Johnston and Gath (1973) with agoraphobics, diazepam was found to facilitate exposure. However, this study concerned *only four* patients; with such small numbers, the characteristics of the individual overshadow any treatment comparisons. The only methodologically sound study with agoraphobics as subjects (Hafner & Marks, 1976) found *no* significant differences between diazepam and placebo in phobia reduction at the end of treatment or at follow-ups. However, there was some difference in anxiety or unpleasantness of sessions in diazepam and placebo conditions; diazepam patients showed less anxiety and discomfort during the sessions.

Bernardt, Silverstone, and Singleton (1980) compared the effects of diazepam, placebo, and a beta-blocker (tolamolol) on fear and avoidance, using as subjects 22 female volunteers with spider or snake phobias. Subjects were exposed to the spider or snake on three occasions under the three drug conditions. The order of drug administration was randomly determined. Each exposure lasted only 10 minutes. Diazepam and placebo were significantly better on approach behavior than tolamolol but there was no significant difference between diazepam and placebo. Tolamolol did abolish the stress-induced tachycardia, but this did not generalize to other components of the fear response. Another analog study on volunteers with small animal phobias found diazepam not to enhance the effects of exposure *in vivo* (Whitehead, Robinson, Blackwell, & Stutz, 1978).

Finally, Waxman (1977) compared diazepam and clomipramine with 41 patients. Patients responded better to clomipramine than to diazepam. In sum, controlled studies of diazepam show that this drug is of little value in the treatment of phobias.

5.1.2. Beta-Blockers

It has been suggested that beta-adrenergic receptor blocking agents are useful in the treatment of anxiety disorders and phobias especially when somatic manifestations of anxiety are prominent (Kelly, 1980; Noyes, Kathol, Clancy, & Crowe, 1981). Most studies in this area have involved brief periods of drug administration and small number of patients. Only one study (Noyes *et al.*, 1981) found a significant response on the part of psychological as well as somatic symptoms. However, only five out of 26 patients were agoraphobics and it is unclear from the analysis of data whether these responded to drug or placebo.

Beta-blockers are of particular interest as adjuncts in the behavioral treatment of agoraphobia, because of the presumed reduction of somatic manifestations during exposure *in vivo*. Exposure *in vivo* leads to anxiety which is manifested in such somatic symptoms as palpitations, tremor, and sweating. These physiologic changes that accompany anxiety may in themselves be anxiety provoking. Thus, if beta-blockers could reduce these somatic symptoms during exposure *in vivo* the efficacy of this procedure could be enhanced.

Unfortunately, this was not the case in the studies that investigated this particular issue. The beta-blockers alprenelol (Ullrich, Ullrich, Crombach, & Peikert, 1972), propranolol (Hafner & Milton, 1977), and

bupranolol (Butollo, Burkhardt, Himmler, & Müller, 1978) do not seem
to enhance the effects of exposure *in vivo* and might even have adverse
effects. For example, in the Hafner and Milton study with agoraphobics,
panic attacks during drug assisted exposure were more severe than in the
placebo group. Moreover, patients in the drug conditions spent significantly less time outside than the placebo group when treatment had
ended.

In the study by Butollo *et al.* (1978), drug assisted exposure had an
anxiety reducing effect during treatment with some patients, but less so
with others. During drug-assisted exposure *in vivo* patients with cardiac
neurosis experienced less anxiety than did agoraphobics and social phobics; with the latter categories, the drug even led to more anxiety during
treatment in comparison with placebo. However, neither for patients
with cardiac neurosis nor for agoraphobics or social phobics did the
drug-assisted treatment prove to be superior to exposure *in vivo* alone at
the end of treatment.

Another example of negative results of beta-blockers was provided
in an analog study by Bernardt *et al.* (1980) which was discussed in the
section above on benzodiazepines.

In brief, there is little or no evidence that beta-blockers enhance or
potentiate the effects of exposure *in vivo*. Clinically, these drugs may be
of some value for patients with mitral valve prolapse syndrome although
research in this area is lacking.

5.2. Antidepressants

5.2.1. Tricyclic Drugs

Imipramine has been recommended as treatment of choice for agoraphobics (e.g., Freedman, 1980). Since the early work of Klein and Fink
(1962) and Klein (1964) who suggested that imipramine was effective in
blocking the panic attacks of agoraphobic patients, a number of studies
have tested imipramine on phobic patients. Clomipramine, a tricyclic
antidepressant closely related to imipramine (e.g., Carey, Hawkinson,
Kornhaber, & Wellish, 1975; Colgan, 1975; de Silva & de Wijewickrama,
1976), and zimelidine, a new antidepressant structurally different from
the tricyclics, have also been reported to have beneficial effects on phobic
patients, but these studies were uncontrolled (Evans & Moore, 1980;
Koczkas, Holmberg, & Wedin, 1980).

Eight controlled studies examined the effects of tricyclics on phobias, two on mixed phobics, four on agoraphobics, and two on school-
phobic children. These studies are summarized in Table 7.

Table 7. Summary of Studies on Tricyclics with Phobias

Study	Population	N	Drug[a]	Other treatment	Outcome[a]	Comment
Berney et al. (1981)	School-phobic children	46	Clom.	Individual psychotherapy + family counseling Exposure encouraged	Clom. = Plac.	
Escobar & Landbloom (1976)	Phobics	6	Clom.	Behavior therapy	Clom. = Plac.	
Gittelman-Klein and Klein (1971)	School-phobic children	35	Imip.	Supportive counseling Exposure encouraged	Imip. > Plac.	No blind assessor
Marks et al. (1982)	Agoraphobics	45	Imip.	Behavior therapy + self-exposure homework	Imip. = Plac.	
Sheehen, Ballenger, & Jacobson (1981)	Agoraphobics Anxiety disorders	66	Imip. vs. Phen.	Supportive group therapy: exposure encouraged	Phen. > Imip. Phen. > Plac. Imip. > Plac. (global meas.) Imip. = Plac. (Fears)	Volunteers No blind assessor
Waxman (1977)	Phobics	41	Clom. vs. Diaz.	?	Clom. > Diaz.	No blind assessor No placebo group High drop-out rate Most patients depressed
Zitrin, Klein, & Woerner (1980)	Agoraphobics	76	Imip.	Group exposure in vivo	Imip. > Plac.	Volunteers High relapse
Zitrin, Woerner, & Klein (1978;1981)	Agoraphobics	77	Imip.	Systematic desensitization in fantasy	A: Imip. > Plac.	Volunteers High relapse
	Mixed phobics Simple phobics	60 81		Supportive counseling Exposure encouraged	M: Imip. > Plac. S: Imip. = Plac.	

[a] Imip. = imipramine; Clom. = clomipramine; Phen. = phenelzine; Diaz. = diazepam; Plac. = placebo.
[a] $a > b$ = treatment a superior to treatment b.

5.2.1.1. School Phobics. Gittelman-Klein and Klein (1971) administered 100 to 200 mg imipramine (mean 152 mg) a day to 6 to 14-year-old children, a dose that is much higher than that recommended by the manufacturers for use in children. In addition, the usual psychotherapeutic measures in the treatment of school refusal were employed. Both the patient and the family were seen weekly and the family was instructed to maintain a firm attitude in promoting school attendance. Children accepted for study were randomly assigned to imipramine or placebo. Five children on imipramine dropped out, while only two of the placebo children did so. No independent assessor was used. In measures of global improvement drug and placebo were indistinguishable after a 3-week period, but the imipramine condition was superior to placebo after 6 weeks.

Theoretically, it is puzzling why imipramine should affect the anxiety of school phobic children. It should be remembered that tricyclics were recommended for agoraphobics and patients with spontaneous panic attacks since this class of drugs was assumed to have a specific effect in blocking the spontaneous panics. However, school phobic children do not have panic attacks. Methodologically, there are other issues that limit the conclusions which can be drawn. It is quite possible that the raters were able to guess what drug the subject was using since significantly more side effects were recorded for the imipramine group as compared with the placebo group. The awareness of what drug is being used might have colored the judgement. In addition, this might have affected the parental pressure to attend school. Finally, there is the question of whether the amount and nature of counseling differed for the drug and placebo groups.

Berney, Kolvin, Bhate, Garside, Jeans, Kay, and Scarth (1981) failed to demonstrate any effects of clomipramine in the treatment of children with school refusal. The trial lasted 12 weeks. Subjects were allocated to clomipramine and placebo randomly. The dose was prescribed according to age. Concurrent treatment was tailored to each patient and consisted of case work with parents and individual psychotherapy. All children were encouraged to attend school. An independent assessor was used. Only the placebo condition resulted in a significant improved ability to attend school. No significant between-group differences were found. Further, no evidence was found that clomipramine reduced separation anxiety or that it is specific for depression, although the dose levels used were adequate.

Taken together the findings of Gittelman *et al.* and the better controlled study by Berney *et al.*, tricyclics appear to be of little use in treating school phobia. Even if the positive results of Gittelman *et al.* would be replicated, there are serious questions about the propriety of using such high doses for children.

5.2.1.2. Adult Phobics. Six studies examined the effects of tricyclics on adult phobics. Zitrin, Woerner, and Klein (1978; 1981) compared imipramine and placebo with patients who concurrently received behavior therapy (systematic desensitization). Patients were divided into three groups: agoraphobic patients, simple phobics, and mixed phobics. Simple phobics consisted of patients with discrete phobias, such as claustrophobia, acrophobia, or animal phobias. Simple phobic patients did not experience "spontaneous" panics. Mixed phobics had circumscribed phobias and experienced "inexplicable" panic attacks. A number of patients dropped out of the program, the majority of drop-outs refused to take medication. Imipramine was found to be more effective than placebo for agoraphobics and mixed phobias, but there was no drug effect for the simple phobics. There was a strong tendency to relapse on the stopping of imipramine.

Zitrin *et al.* (1981) argued that imipramine has a beneficial effect on "spontaneous" panic, with secondary effects on overall improvement in related areas: "We believe the sequence to be as follows: imipramine blocks the spontaneous panic. When the patients become increasingly confident that they will not experience these panic attacks, they begin to approach phobic situations. . . . Anticipatory anxiety in relation to phobic situations is reduced because of the patients' changed expectations of these situations" (p. 41).

With 218 patients involved in the study, it is not surprising to find statistically significant differences between groups. However, these differences might be clinically unimpressive, as is the case with the differences found in the Zitrin study. Figure 22 which was derived from the data of their study shows that both placebo and imipramine groups improve along the same line and that the statistical difference found between both conditions is far from clinically significant.

Another difficulty is that on most measures improvement ratings were used rather than pre- and posttest assessment on the same scale, a method known to be particularly susceptible to distortions. Finally, no objective behavioral measure was used, which was also lacking in the other studies reviewed in this section.

In a second study by the same research group (Zitrin, Klein, & Woerner, 1980) 76 agoraphobic patients were randomly assigned to imipramine or placebo therapy. After 4 weeks of medication all patients received exposure *in vivo* therapy, conducted in groups. Exposure *in vivo* consisted of ten weekly sessions, each lasting 3 to 4 hours. Imipramine therapy was significantly better than placebo therapy, although the vast majority of placebo-group patients (72%) were moderately to markedly

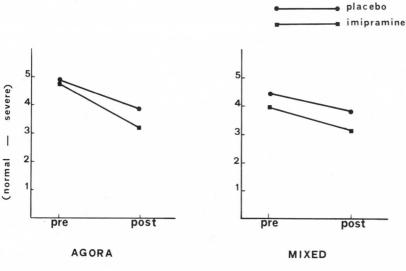

Figure 22. Statistically significant but clinically irrelevant differences between placebo and imipramine for agoraphobics and mixed phobics. (Based on data from Zitrin *et al.*, 1981.)

improved on all variables. Twenty-seven percent of the imipramine-treated patients and 6% of the placebo-treated patients relapsed at 6-month follow-up.

Since the authors reported the results in terms of improvement, it remains unclear what the clinical significance of their findings is. It should be noted that most patients who received placebo were rated as moderately or markedly improved. Further, a high proportion of patients relapsed at follow-up in the imipramine condition, which suggests that the effects of imipramine are short-lived. Another issue is related to the external validity of the studies by Zitrin *et al.* (1980, 1981). Subjects were not patients but volunteers who applied after announcements in the local press (Zitrin, personal communication). Since no behavioral measure was employed, it is unclear whether the population is comparable to a clinical population.

The third controlled study of imipramine was reported by Marks, Gray, Cohen, Hill, Mawson, Ramm, and Stern (1982). Forty-five patients were randomly assigned to treatment by placebo or imipramine. All patients received behavioral treatment (relaxation or exposure *in vivo*) and had systematic self-exposure homework. Results indicated that imipramine had no therapeutic value. It is very unlikely that the lack of a drug-effect could be attributed to the dose used. Their mean dose of 158 mg was comparable to that used in other studies. In addition, imipramine produced significant side effects and a mean plasma level re-

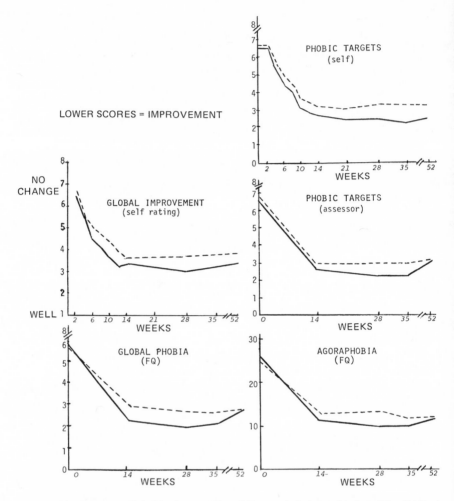

Figure 23. Outcome of phobias in a one-year follow-up in imipramine ($n = 23$, solid line) and placebo ($n = 22$, dashed line) groups. Lower scores indicate improvement. (From Marks *et al.*, 1982. Reprinted by permission of the authors.)

garded as therapeutic in depressed patients. No clear relationship was found between plasma level and outcome, which provides further evidence that imipramine did not affect outcome. Figure 23 shows the results on the Fear Questionnaire (Marks & Mathews, 1979) for agoraphobia and global phobia, and the rating for phobic targets by the independent assessor.

The acid test of the effect of imipramine is a comparison of anxiety attacks in the placebo and drug group, since imipramine is assumed to reduce panic attacks. No significant differences between groups were found. Both imipramine and placebo patients reported a reduction in spontaneous panics over the course of therapy (see Figure 24).

Phenelzine versus imipramine was examined by Sheehan, Ballenger, and Jacobson (1981) in a study with 57 agoraphobic volunteers. Subjects were recruited through news media advertising. No independent assessor was used. The phenelzine group improved more than the imipramine patients on almost all outcome measures, but this trend achieved statistical significance on only two measures. Interestingly, on the two Fear Survey Schedules used, no significant difference between imipramine and placebo groups was found after 12 weeks. The conclusion of the authors that "it is clear that the bulk of the improvement results directly from neurochemical change following specific drug administration rather than from psychological intervention" (p. 57) seems unwarranted. First, all patients attended supportive group therapy sessions, during which they were encouraged to reapproach phobic situations gradually. Thus, if anything, the study demonstrates an interaction between drug and psychological intervention, rather than a drug effect *per se*. Second, the imipramine effect was absent or small on phobic measures. Third, the population used and the lack of behavioral measures and independent assessor preclude the drawing of any firm conclusion.

Escobar and Landbloom (1976) reported another double-blind trial comparing clomipramine and placebo. Generally, no significant differ-

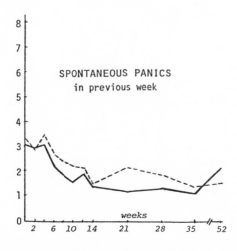

Figure 24. Improvement in spontaneous panic attacks in imipramine and placebo groups. (From Marks *et al.*, 1982. Reprinted by permission of the authors.)

ences between groups were found. Finally, Waxman (1977) found clomipramine superior to diazepam in the treatment of phobic patients. However, results are difficult to interpret. No placebo-control group was included and there was a high drop-out rate (30%), most of the withdrawals being on clomipramine. In addition, most of the clomipramine patients (11 out of 14) had depression rather than phobia as the primary symptom. Thus, the improvement in the phobias of the clomipramine patients may be due to improvement in depression.

5.2.1.3. Concluding Comment. A number of reports appearing in the literature have claimed excellent results in the treatment of phobic patients with tricyclics. The present review tempers this optimism because of several reasons. First, although most studies were double-blind, it is questionable whether patient and assessor were really unaware which drug the patient received. The side effects associated with this drug were more often reported in the drug condition as compared with the placebo condition. Several studies demonstrate that "blind" raters could correctly guess which drug the subject received 63–100% of the time (Solomon & Hart, 1978). The only study that checked whether the assessor was truly "blind" found *no* significant difference between tricyclic and placebo (Marks *et al.*, 1982). Second, when a significant drug effect was found, it was usually small and clinically insignificant. Third, if anything, the studies, supposedly showing a drug effect, actually demonstrate a possible interaction between tricyclic and psychological intervention. In all studies reported here patients received psychological treatment concurrently. Fourth, there is no evidence that tricyclics have a specific effect in reducing panic attacks as originally proposed. In the studies that found a drug-effect, this effect appeared to be more global, also improving anxiety, depression and related "pathology." Finally, a high relapse rate on stopping tricyclics has been noted and side effects are common that may lead to drop-out of treatment.

In sum, the controlled studies have not yet demonstrated a major clinical effect in alleviating anxiety and avoidance of phobic patients. It might be that these drugs may have beneficial effects with phobic patients with depressed mood, but the studies reviewed in this section did not investigate that particular issue.

5.2.2. Monoamine Oxidase Inhibitors

Several controlled studies into the effectiveness of monoamine oxidase inhibitors (MAOIs) have been conducted. Tyrer, Candy, and Kelly (1973) found phenelzine more effective when compared with a placebo after 8 weeks, but the clinical improvement was not very impressive.

Solyom, Heseltine, McClure, Solyom, Ledwidge, and Steinberg (1973) compared phenelzine with various behavioral treatments (systematic desensitization, aversion relief, and flooding, all in imagination). Although the effect of phenelzine was the most rapid, 2 years after the termination of treatment all six (out of ten) patients who stopped taking the drug relapsed, as compared with only 10% of the patients who had been treated by behavior therapy.

Lipsedge, Hajioff, Huggins, Napier, Pearce, Pike, and Rich (1973) compared iproniazid with systematic desensitization (in imagination) and placebo. Although both treatments proved to be more effective than placebo, no significant differences between systematic desensitization and iproniazid were found. Solyom, Solyom, La Pierre, Pecknold, and Morton (1981) compared phenelzine and placebo and could not find any differences between them. In contrast, Sheehan *et al.* (1981) found phenelzine to be superior to placebo. However, no blind assessor or behavioral measures were used, which makes it difficult to evaluate their findings. Improvements were more global rather than specifically related to fears.

Thus, there is some evidence that MAO inhibitors may have beneficial effects on phobic cases, but the effects found were rather small. This conclusion needs to be qualified in several ways. First, most studies instructed patients to expose themselves *in vivo* between treatment sessions. Thus, the effects of MAO inhibitors have not been assessed independently of the effects of exposure *in vivo*. In the only study that attempted to separate these effects (Solyom *et al.*, 1979) phenelzine proved to be no more effective than placebo. Second, discontinuation of medication generally leads to relapse (Lipsedge *et al.*, 1973; Solyom *et al.*, 1973; Tyrer *et al.*, 1973). Third, side effects have often been reported using this class of drugs, including difficulty with micturition, inhibition of ejaculation and anorgasmia, fatigue, dry mouth and blurred vision, edema, and insomnia (e.g., Kelly *et al.*, 1973). Fourth, severe interaction with some foods containing high concentration of amines (Blackwell, 1963) and other drugs (Sjöqvist, 1963) and hepatoxicity (Pare, 1964) have been reported. Finally, as far as comparisons with behavioral treatments are concerned, only "weak" forms of behavioral treatment have been involved. No study has directly compared MAO inhibitors with prolonged exposure *in vivo*, which is far more effective than systematic desensitization, especially with agoraphobics. Briefly, MAO inhibitors have little to recommend in the treatment of phobias and anxiety states.

II

OBSESSIVE-COMPULSIVE DISORDERS

Etiology of Obsessive-Compulsive Behavior

1. LEARNING THEORIES

Numerous studies have been conducted within a learning theory framework that are more or less relevant with respect to the etiology and persistence of obsessive-compulsive behavior. These could be discussed at length (e.g., Teasdale, 1974), but the discussion here must necessarily be brief. Generally, the two-stage theory of Mowrer (1960) plays a prominent role in the behavioral formulations in accounting for the development and the maintenance of obsessive-compulsive behavior. As was discussed in the section on the etiology of phobias (see Chapter 2), Mowrer held two learning paradigms responsible for fear acquisition: classical and operant conditioning. In Mowrer's view classically conditioned fear motivates avoidance behavior, which leads to a reduction of fear and a strengthening of the avoidance behavior. Most of the research supporting Mowrer's view comes from the animal laboratory.

For present purposes it might be useful to differentiate between active and passive avoidance (Teasdale, 1974). With *passive avoidance* the individual avoids stimuli, situations, etc., that might provoke anxiety and discomfort. *Active avoidance* usually refers to the motor component of obsessive-compulsive behavior, for example, checking and cleaning. Let me illustrate the difference between active and passive avoidance with the help of a clinical example. Mrs. X is an obsessive-compulsive patient who fears being contaminated by germs and dust. Whenever possible she avoids going outdoors in order to prevent contamination. For the same reason windows are always kept closed. When objects from the outside are brought into her home (e.g., food, letters), she cleans these for a long time. Touching any of these objects evokes excessive hand washing. Obviously, this case demonstrates both types of avoidance behavior, as is usually the case with obsessive-compulsive patients. The washing and cleaning might be described as active avoidance, while the avoidance of any contamination by staying at home and keeping the windows closed would be classified as passive avoidance behavior. It is important to note that both forms of avoidance behavior usually occur together in the same person. Thus, classifying behavior in these two categories does not refer to patient categories. Active avoidance resembles the escape learning paradigm, whereas passive avoidance looks like the avoidance paradigm. The washing and cleaning in our example can be regarded as escape responses, that is, performance of the washing ritual terminates anxiety. Staying at home and keeping the windows closed can be considered avoidance responses. To help the reader translate the obsessive-compulsive behavior in learning terms, a schematic picture of our patient is presented in Figure 25.

The criticism of the process learning theory of fear acquisition applies equally well in the case of explaining obsessive-compulsive behavior. These criticisms have been discussed in detail in Chapter 2. The discussion here will focus on points that are relevant to obsessive-compulsive disorders.

1.1. Classical Conditioning

As to the classical conditioning component of the two-stage theory, there is little evidence that this type of learning plays a crucial role in the development of obsessive-compulsive behavior. According to a classical conditioning interpretation a traumatic event should mark the beginning

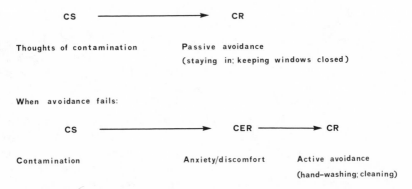

Figure 25. Learning paradigm for obsessive-compulsive behavior.

of the obsessive-compulsive disorder. An analysis of the history of our obsessive-compulsive cases revealed that in a significant number of cases the onset of the obsessive-compulsive behavior was gradual. Generally speaking, patients related the onset of their problems to life stress in general rather than to one or more traumatic events.

The idea that seems to us to come closest to matching the patients' accounts of the course of the problem is that in a stressful period ritualistic activities prove to have powerful anxiety-reducing effects. The view reached on the basis of our clinical observations is that it is not always an actual trauma that gives rise to the obsessive-compulsive problem. Although patients sometimes give a detailed account of one or more traumatic experiences associated with the development of the obsessive-compulsive behavior, the traumatic situation by itself rarely leads to the obsessive-compulsive behavior directly. Let me illustrate this with a description of a few cases. A 22-year-old woman complained of obsessive thoughts concerning being choked to death. These thoughts led to extensive checking rituals involving objects that she might swallow. She related her problem to an accident that had occurred when she was 11 years old, when she almost choked on a piece of candy. However, her obsessive thoughts and checking behavior started some 5 years later. No new accident had occurred but at that time the patient had some serious difficulties in her work. Thus, at the time her obsessive-compulsive problem started there was no direct link between a traumatic experience and the checking behavior. Rather, it appears that the stressful event (associated with the problems at work) preceded the onset of the obsessive-compulsive problem.

The next example involves a 55-year-old man whose primary problem was obsessional ruminating. Five years before the start of his obsessions he reported having had a vision of God, who ordered him to rear his children in a more religious way. Shortly after, his wife had a heart attack, followed a few months later by cancer that was said to be terminal within one year. At this time a second vision of the Lord occurred, now giving him "the last warning." Although he was afraid that his wife might die of cancer, he was not unduly concerned about harm befalling his family. His wife recovered and stayed alive and the following years he had no obsessions whatever. Five years later the obsessions started after he was hospitalized for an infectious disease. The content of the obsessions consisted of thoughts that God would punish him by taking away his wife and children. These obsessions occurred whenever his wife or children were away from home. These thoughts were "neutralized" by prayers, which had an anxiety-reducing effect. This case demonstrates traumatic events that are related to the content of the obsessions. Two sorts of traumatic events can be associated with the development of the obsessions: First, the vision of the Lord (if one may call this "traumatic") and second, the diseases of his wife. A schematic representation in terms of classical conditioning is depicted in Figure 26. It should be noted, however, that 5 years passed before the obsessions started, which makes an explanation in terms of classical conditioning rather difficult. Rather than an association between a traumatic event and anxiety, stress associated with the hospitalization marked the inception of the obsessional problem. According to classical conditioning theory one would have expected the obsessions to occur 5 years earlier, immediately after the occurrence of the visions and the serious diseases of his wife. Nevertheless, this patient functioned quite well all the time until his hospitalization, which poses serious problems for an interpretation in terms of classical conditioning. Taking together the two cases discussed so far, there is no evidence that traumatic learning played a crucial role in the development of the obsessive-compulsive disorders. The precipitating factors preceding the onset of the symptomatology (problems at work, hospitalization) can better be regarded as more generalized stress factors than as unconditioned stimuli. It is hypothesized than in the two cases just described the stored representation of past events could be activated at the time of stressful life experiences.

Other clinical observations pose further insoluble problems for the classical conditioning theory. In a number of obsessional patients, several different obsessions and rituals occur simultaneously. Theoretically, one should find several traumatic episodes to account for the onset of the various obsessions. Of course, one could hypothesize that secondary obsessions might develop as a result of generalization. An explanation like this would mean that the different obsessions are in some way related. However, it is a common finding that different obsessions in the

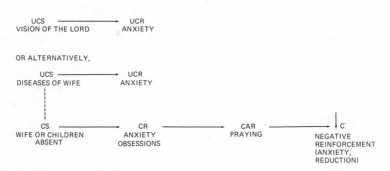

Figure 26. Schematic representation in terms of classical conditioning.

same individual are totally unrelated to each other. Similarly, with some patients the content of obsessions regularly changes, without accompanying traumatic learning experiences. This point is well illustrated by the following two cases. One patient had the obsession that her baby might be possessed by the devil. After some time this obsession disappeared but a new obsession appeared shortly after. The content of this obsession concerned pictures in which the patient imagined being a horse. Another patient started her obsessional career with obsessions of being a lesbian; later the content of her obsessions changed spontaneously to consist of thoughts about killing her children. In both patients, the content of the obsessions changed without any environmental event occurring that would fit into a classical conditioning interpretation.

To summarize this discussion, there is no evidence to support a classical conditioning interpretation to account for the development of obsessional phenomena. First of all, many patients do not relate traumatic experiences associated with the onset of the symptoms. In addition, when such traumatic events are reported, they often took place much earlier than the onset of the obsessive-compulsive problems, thus making an explanation in terms of classical conditioning less credible. Finally, clinical observations clearly demonstrate the occurrence of several obsessions together as well as the regular change of obsessions, in some patients, unrelated to new traumatic learning experiences. In conclusion, there is little or no evidence that classical conditioning provides an adequate account of the development of obsessional problems.

1.2. Anxiety Reduction

Although there is little evidence that classical conditioning plays an important role in the development of obsessive-compulsive behavior, there is some evidence that the rituals may serve to reduce anxiety. Let us now consider research into the second stage of the process learning theory conducted on obsessive-compulsive patients. According to the two-stage theory, it is assumed that performance of rituals will lead to anxiety reduction.

Rachman and his colleagues studied the provocation of compulsive acts and the effects of performance of the rituals under controlled laboratory conditions. One of the aims of these studies was to test the anxiety-reduction theory of obsessive-compulsive behavior. Before embarking on the task of reviewing their research, some preparatory comments may be helpful. First, if studies would demonstrate the occurrence of anxiety reduction after the execution of a ritual, this would not prove the superiority of the behavioral model. It should be noted that psychoanalytic theory and behavioral theory are in agreement on the anxiety-reducing character of rituals. The psychoanalytic position as well as most other nonbehavioral theories differ from the behavioral theory with respect to the consequence of preventing a person from performing the rituals: In the former nonperformance is supposed to lead to displacement. In addition, the experiments studying the anxiety-reducing mechanisms of rituals do not elucidate the processes involved in the development of obsessive-compulsive disorders. Rather, they might give us some clues with respect to factors involved in the maintenance of these behaviors. Thus, studies into anxiety-reducing mechanisms of rituals should not be regarded as tests of the validity of the behavioral model itself concerning the etiology of obsessive-compulsive disorders. Let us postpone any further discussion of this for the time being and turn to a discussion of the studies of Rachman and his colleagues (Hodgson & Rachman, 1972; Röper, Rachman, & Hodgson, 1973: Röper & Rachman, 1976; Rachman, de Silva, & Röper, 1976; Rachman & Hodgson, 1980).

The design of these studies was usually as follows. Obsessive-compulsive behavior was provoked and measurements of subjective anxiety were taken before and after provocation, and after performance of the (checking or cleaning) ritual. In addition, patients' reactions were tested when the performance of the ritual was interrupted and when it was delayed. Two studies (Hodgson & Rachman, 1972; Röper, Rachman, & Hodgson, 1973) also used psychophysiological assessment (pulse rate variability) during the course of the experiment. The results of these studies can be summarized as follows. With patients whose primary problem was obsessive-compulsive washing arising out of fears of contamination or dirt, contamination led to an increase of subjective anxiety/discomfort, while the completion of a washing ritual had the opposite effect. Spontaneous decrease in discomfort occurred when the performance of the hand-washing ritual was postponed for half an hour. The interruption of the ritual produced neither an increase nor a decrease in subjective anxiety/discomfort. (Hodgson & Rachman, 1972; Rachman & Hodgson, 1980). For pulse rate variability, the same trends occurred, but the differences between occasions were not significant (Hodgson & Rachman, 1972).

The results of studies on checkers are less clear cut. In their first study (Röper, Rachman, & Hodgson, 1973), which followed the same basic design results, the pattern was comparable to that observed among washers. However, three qualifications should be made. First, contrary to expectations, several patients reported an increase in anxiety/discomfort after the performance of the checking ritual rather than a decrease. Second, pulse rate variability did not covary with subjective anxiety:

There was very little change in pulse rate. Finally, comparison of data on washers and checkers revealed that patients with a washing compulsion reported more anxiety/discomfort when provoked than patients with checking rituals. The low level of arousal of checkers might be due to a serious distortion introduced by the experimental situation. During the experiment, the experimenter was present, which might have inhibited the arousal of anxiety, since checkers could allocate responsibility to the experimenter. To test this proposition, Röper and Rachman (1976) replicated this experiment with another series of checkers. In order to reduce the potentially distorting effects of experimental artificiality, testing was conducted in the patient's natural environment (home or therapeutic community) rather than in the laboratory. Patients were tested under two conditions: (1) therapist present, and (2) therapist absent. These two conditions were given in a balanced order. Compulsive urges were successfully provoked in both conditions, but they were stronger when the experimenter was absent. As found in the earlier studies, carrying out the provocative act produced discomfort and performing the checking ritual reduced it. Only a minority of patients showed an increase of anxiety/discomfort after performance of the ritual.

To investigate whether the differences between natural environment and laboratory also had a significant influence on washers, Rachman and Hodgson (1980) conducted the following study. Contamination and washing were compared on two occasions: (1) at home and (2) in the laboratory. Patients were obsessive-compulsive washers. Although contamination in the natural environment produced slightly more anxiety than in the laboratory, the overall results in both situations were comparable.

Finally, the findings of a study by Hornsveld, Kraaymaat, and van Dam-Baggen (1979) are of interest for the present discussion. In their study, both obsessional patients and psychiatric control patients were contaminated and allowed to wash their hands after the provocation. Interestingly, anticipation of contamination produced an increase in subjective anxiety in both groups. Similarly, performance of handwashing led to a decrease of subjective anxiety in both groups.

Taken together, the findings of studies reviewed so far support the anxiety-reduction theory, as far as the maintenance of obsessive-compulsive behavior is concerned. With only a few exceptions among checkers, provocation of rituals led to an increase in subjective anxiety/discomfort and performance of rituals reduced discomfort. The Hornsveld *et al.* (1979) study provides evidence that this finding is not specific for obsessionals, since essentially similar results were found on nonobsessional psychiatric patients. However, the latter finding also poses some interesting theoretical questions. Since the Hornsveld *et al.* (1979) study did not include a normal control group, it cannot be concluded that washing does reduce anxiety/discomfort in normals when contaminated by dirt to the same extent as it does in patients. If it can be demonstrated in future studies that neurotics react more emotionally to dust and contamination and show a more marked anxiety reduction after hand washing than normals, this would provide important information concerning the etiology of obsessive-compulsive behavior. If the finding of Hornsveld *et al.* (1979) is repeated, and particularly if the effects after contamination and washing are shown to be more marked for obsessionals and neurotics than for normals, it will require incorporation into a comprehensive explanation of compulsive behavior.

Generally, patients' performances of rituals led to anxiety reduction. Nevertheless, on some occasions performance of rituals had an anxiety-augmenting effect. Although this occurrence was rather rare and was only found in a minority of checkers, a comprehensive account of the functioning of obsessive-compulsive behavior should take full account of the exceptions to the rule.

One alternative to the two-stage theory (Herrnstein, 1969) holds that anxiety reduction *per se* is not the reinforcing agent; rather it predicts that subjects should experience less anxiety after the performance of a ritual than they would have experienced if they had not performed the ritual. It is quite reasonable to assume that this is exactly what happens with some obsessional checkers.Take, for example, a patient who performed a lot of stereotyped rituals in order to prevent family members from getting cancer. When going upstairs or downstairs, this patient had to count to ten before he could proceed to the next step. When he was not sure that he had counted to ten he had to start all over again. This ritual was anxiety inducing rather than anxiety reducing according to the patient's own account. Nevertheless, he continued to do this, because in this way he could prevent the occurrence of even greater anxiety and guilt feelings associated with the nonperformance of the ritual. Thus, when he had the option of moderate anxiety associated with the performance of the ritual or maximal anxiety and guilt feeling associated with the nonperformance of the ritual, he chose the former. His behavior in this situation is quite comparable to that of the animals in the Herrnstein and Hineline (1966) experiment, discussed on page 16. These animals learned avoidance responses to reduce the frequency of shocks, when given the option of low-shock frequency or high-shock frequency. In conclusion, whereas the two-stage theory cannot account for the few exceptions found in which performance of rituals has an anxiety-augmenting effect, Herrnstein's (1969) alternative version is quite able to do so.

Herrnstein's theory might also apply to obsessional patients with nonsensical obsessions. Such obsessions may involve thoughts like "Why is grass green" or "Why is a table made of wood," etc. Usually, such obsessions have the function to ward off other anxiety-arousing thoughts. In these cases the discomfort experienced as a result of the "nonsense" obsessions is presumably to be preferred to other more anxiety arousing thoughts. Similarly, in several of our obsessive-compulsive patients the rituals appeared to serve the function of avoiding such painful emotions as depression and guilt feelings. The development of obsessive-compulsive behavior in these individuals can also be explained in terms of Herrnstein's theory.

1.3. Genesis of Checking and Washing

Rachman (1976) postulated that the genesis of cleaning and checking compulsions differ in the nature of parental control. According to Rachman, cleaning rituals are most likely to develop in families where the parents are overprotective, while checking rituals emerge in families where the parents set high standards and are overcritical. Due to such an overcritical, meticulous upbringing, guilt feelings are easily aroused in checkers which make them oversensitive to criticism. Rachman suggested that checking is guilt motivated and washing fear motivated.

Turner, Steketee, and Foa (1979) investigated whether checkers are more sensitive to criticism than washers. No difference in fear of criticism was found between washers and checkers on items of the Fear Survey Schedule which had been selected to measure fear of criticism. However, both groups of obsessionals were found to be more sensitive to criticism than a control group of phobic patients. Thus, Rachman's hypothesis that checkers are more fearful of criticism than washers was not supported.

Emmelkamp and Rabbie (1982) suggested that the predominant phenomenon of a given obsessional patient depends primarily on the areas for which the patient is responsible. They hypothesized that there are sex differences in the development of obsessive-compulsive behavior which are linked to sex-role related differences in work areas. In our culture most women are responsible for running the household (i.e., cleaning). According to the sex-role theory we might expect a preponderance of washing rituals among women as compared with men. If this argument is correct then "washing" should be more typical for women and "checking" more typical for men. In addition, no differences in parental rearing style should be found with respect to overprotection and criticism. Alternatively, if Rachman's theory is correct, no sex differences in the prevalence of "checking" and "washing" are to be expected but differences in parental rearing practices are expected.

To test between these conflicting predictions, we investigated the parental characteristics perceived by obsessional patients and the prevalence of washing and checking among male and female patients. The perceived parental characteristics were assessed by the EMBU (Perris, Jacobsson, Lindströnn, von Knorring, & Perris, 1980). Obsessive-compulsives (checkers and washers) of whom we had conpleted questionnaires and who did not have overlapping washing and checking rituals participated in this study. No significant differences in parental rearing practices were found. Neither was "overprotection" related to washing nor "controlling" and "rejecting" parental characteristics associated with checking. As to the hypothesized relationship between sex and type of complaint, results supported the sex-role theory. Sixteen out of 24 checkers were men and 11 out of 12 washers were women.

The present findings require cautious interpretation. While the sex-role theory was supported by our data, the results must be qualified. The rearing practices were not directly assessed but rated by the patient which might have influenced the results. Further, cross-validation of this theory on a different sample of obsessionals is required. A final test of the developmental model awaits a direct, prospective investigation, which will be difficult to realize.

2. COGNITIVE THEORIES

2.1. Decision-Making Difficulties

Clinically, one is often impressed by the difficulties obsessional patients have in reaching decisions. Several authors (e.g., Beech, 1971; Reed, 1968, 1976) have suggested that the difficulty in making decisions is a central feature of obsessive-compulsive neurosis. In this section studies concerning decision making of obsessional patients will be reviewed.

Earlier work in this area focused on the tolerance of ambiguity and rigidity of obsessional patients. Hamilton (1957) held that avoidance of ambiguity serves to minimize conflict and anxiety. To test the hypothesis that obsessional patients need to make decisions in order to prevent anxiety he set up the following experiment. He had his subjects perform a number of tasks (discrimination tasks, ambiguous drawings, block sorting, etc.) and found that obsessionals tended to avoid ambiguity more than normal controls and anxiety states. In attempting to explain the differences in tolerance of ambiguity found among his groups Hamilton (1957) proposed that

> limitations placed upon behavior such as obsessive-compulsive symptoms, avoidance of difficulties, rigid classifications of the environment, scotomization and physical conversion symptoms, which appear in the process of controlling anxiety, would all seem to be designed to reduce the chances of further conflicts and anxiety having to be faced by the subject. (pp. 212–213)

Other studies (reviewed by Fransella, 1974) generally support the notion that obsessionals have considerable difficulty in tolerating ambiguity.

Several studies investigated if obsessionals needed more information before making a decision than controls. In these experiments, the experimental tasks usually consisted of discrimination tests (expanded judgment tasks). Subjects had to discriminate shapes (Walker) or photographs (Beech & Liddell) or to detect auditory tones (Millner, Beech, & Walker, 1971). In an experiment by Walker (1967, cited in Beech & Liddell, 1974) subjects could choose to make additional observations before reaching a decision. Patients with obsessional symptoms needed to make more observations than controls. In a subsequent study, however, no tendency was found for obsessionals to ask for more information before reaching a decision as compared with controls. Other studies (Millner, Beech, & Walker, 1971; Beech & Liddell, 1974; Volans, 1976) found that obsessionals requested more trials before reaching a decision than controls. Moreover, the obsessional patients in the Beech and Liddell study complained significantly more frequently of decision-making problems than the control groups as measured by items on the Sandler-Hazari Scale.

Taken together, the results of studies into tolerance of ambiguity and studies involving expanded judgment tasks indicate that (some) obsessionals have considerable difficulty in tolerating uncertainty. Apparently, obsessionals need to reach decisions more frequently than controls, but given the opportunity to delay the decision, they are inclined to postpone the final decision in order to get more information.

Reed (1968) has argued that the decision difficulties of obsessionals reflect a basic cognitive characteristic. In a series of experiments, Reed attempted to test the hypothesis that obsessionals are characterized by a failure to structure and organize experiences that would express itself in an overstructuring of input and in maladaptive overdefining of categories and boundaries (Reed, 1968). In his first study (Reed, 1969a) obsessionals were found to be overspecific when they had to categorize words that belonged to the same class as compared with the controls. In a subsequent study Reed (1969b) found some evidence that obsessionals needed more categories to classify items in an experimental task than did controls. More recently, evidence was provided indicating that the less structured the task, the more indecision was experienced by the obsessional (Reed, 1977). The finding of the research program of Reed provides further support for the impairment in decision making as characteristic of this group. As an aside, it might be mentioned that the results of these studies agree with predictions from a psychoanalytic point of view, although Reed does not discuss his findings in this way. Fenichel (1977) relates the defense mechanism isolation of affect (see page 180) with the obsessional's tendency to classify events, objects, and ideas into mutually exclusive categories.

Carr (1974) suggested that obsessionals have an abnormally highly subjective estimate of the probability of an unfavorable outcome in decision making. Results of his study indicate that obsessionals and normals made the same threat appraisal under high cost conditions. However, as predicted, under low cost conditions obsessionals reacted differently from normals, showing similar responses as under high cost conditions. Walker (1967, cited in Beech & Liddell, 1974) examined the extent to which obsessionals viewed everyday mistakes with greater seriousness and with greater feelings of unpleasantness than anxiety neurotics and normal controls. Although no abnormality specific to the obsessional group was observed in estimates of the *probability* of everyday mistakes occurring, some obsessionals did offer abnormally high estimates of the *unpleasantness* of mistakes occurring. Her results suggested that obsessionals may react strongly only to those mistakes that occur in certain areas of life. This abnormally high estimate of the unpleasantness of making mistakes seems related to the finding that obsessionals are highly reluctant to take risks (Beech & Liddell, 1974; Steiner, 1972).

To summarize, obsessionals have been shown to have considerable difficulty in reaching a decision, which seems to be related to the anticipated unpleasantness of decision-making consequences.

It seems reasonable to assume that environmental factors account for the observed differences in decision making between obsessive-compulsives and others. Several authors have suggested that obsessionals have an exaggerated fear of criticism as a result of their upbringing (e.g., Rachman, 1976). However, several findings (Beech & Liddell, 1974) make an explanation in terms of environmental circumstances producing a predisposition to avoid painful consequences or make punishment less likely. In their study, patients were asked to recall unpleasant happenings that had occurred during their life. Interestingly, when compared with a group of mixed neurotics and a group of normals, obsessionals

> tend to remember worrying a great deal more about events that *had not happened but could possibly happen,* while they appeared to recall fewer events of an unpleasant character that had actually happened to them. (p. 158)

In addition, the analysis of responses to questions relating to punishment which had occurred at home or at school and to quarrels with friends revealed a difference between both patient groups and the normal controls, obsessionals and other neurotic patients reporting far less punishment or disagreement. However, both patient groups were much more affected by such noxious events than the normal controls. Beech and Liddell suggest that "obsessionals perhaps throughout their lives, have been especially alert to the possible harmful consequences of interacting with their environment, and have shown an exaggerated sensitivity to aversive circumstances" and they go on to suggest that "the two neurotic groups feared the possibility of punishment so much that they went to extreme lengths to avoid this kind of occurrence" (p. 159). An alternative explanation for the observed differences between both patient groups and normal controls might be that patients reported less punishment and fewer quarrels because these had been very traumatic. During the treatment of obsessional patients we found a lot of "childhood traumas" that were not reported in the first interview. Not uncommonly, when questioned in this area, obsessionals at first cannot remember such noxious events or they relate them without any apparent affect. Thus, obsessional patients are not likely to bring up these topics unless the therapist has established rapport with them. With ensuing interviews, however, many new facts emerge. It is argued that obsessionals manifest difficulties in remembering the occurrences of punishments and quarrels, because this would be too threatening. Of course, this suggestion is highly speculative and needs to be tested experimentally.

On the whole, there is ample evidence that decision-making difficulties are characteristic of obsessionals. This may mean that the impairment in decision making and the obsessive-compulsive behavior are parallel coeffects or that there is a causal relationship between the two. A likely interpretation is that the indecision gives rise to the obsessive-compulsive behavior: for instance, when washing one's hands one has to decide whether the hands are sufficiently clean or not. A person who has considerable difficulty in making decisions will need a long period to be sure that the hands are indeed clean. Thus, it is not surprising to find that many patients have difficulty in deciding when to stop. Similarly, the indecisiveness of patients may give rise to the doubt and uncertainty as to whether a ritual should be performed, which is seen in a considerable number of obsessional patients. But, given that the obsessional behavior does, in fact, reflect a failure in decision making, this failure itself has yet to be explained. Alternatively, the causal relationship (if any) may be the other way around. It may well be that the impairments in decision making are a consequence rather than the cause of the obsessive-compulsive symptoms. Further studies are needed to determine whether there is a causal link between indecisiveness and obsessive-compulsive behavior.

2.2. Personal Constructs of Obsessional Patients

A different line of research into cognitive impairments of obsessional patients involved Kelly's (1955) personal construct theory. A detailed account of Kelly's personal construct theory is not possible here; the reader is referred to Kelly (1955). To put it rather simply, Kelly used the term "construct" to refer to the basis upon which a person sorts the events, objects, or people in his environment. The Repertory Grid Technique was developed to assess the constructs particularly relevant for a person.

Makhlouf-Norris, Jones, and Norris (1970) administered the Repertory Grid to 11 obsessive-compulsive patients and to an equal number of normal controls. A differentiation was made between different types of clusters of constructs. A primary cluster was defined as a group of constructs that all correlated significantly together. They considered clusters that were significantly related to one or more constructs in a primary cluster as "secondary." Two main classes of organization were described: (1) a monolithic construct system and (2) articulated systems. A monolithic construct system consisted of a single primary cluster, whereas an articulated system contained two or more primary clusters, joined together by linking constructs. Results of the study revealed that obsessional patients demonstrated significantly more monolithic construct organization than controls. In discussing the theoretical implication of this finding, Makhlouf-Norris *et al.* (1970) argue that in a monolithic structure, independent judgments with opposing implications cannot be made. Obsessional patients seem to avoid the use of constructs that could set up opposing implications. In summarizing their main findings, Makhlouf-Norris *et al.* (1970) state:

> Thus the obsessional narrows the range of his constructs, and reiterates judgements on the same theme: unfriendly, outcasts, hated, lost, isolated, troubled, etc. The theme appears to be one of blanket condemnation to be imposed upon the world as he sees it. (p. 273)

Millar (1980) attempted to replicate the findings of Makhlouf-Norris *et al.* (1970). In his study 15 obsessive-compulsive patients and an equal number of nonneurotic controls were tested with the Repertory Grid Technique. Unlike the results of Makhlouf-Norris and Norris, the obsessional group was not more monolithic than normals in cognitive structure. Thus this study failed to replicate the finding of construct organization typical of obsessional patients. Further analysis of the data revealed that the grid profile of the obsessive-compulsives was very similar to that of neurotic patients in general. On the other hand, the content of thinking did differentiate obsessive-compulsive patients from other neurotics. The distinctiveness exhibited by the obsessionals on the grid profile shows a very negative, isolated, and extreme view of the self.

To summarize the findings of studies into the cognitive structure of obsessional patients, there is little evidence to support the view that obsessionals are differentiated as a group by the clustering of constructs: obsessionals were not more monolithic than normals. However, some evidence is provided that obsessionals have a more negative, isolated, and extreme view of the self as compared with other neurotics.

3. BIOLOGICAL THEORIES

3.1. Arousal

Beech and his colleagues attribute an important role to adverse mood states in obsessional patients:

> it became apparent that mood state was of paramount importance as a determinant of ritualistic behavior and that depression and hostility, rather than anxiety, were the adverse mood states which most affected our patients. (Beech & Liddell, 1974, p. 147)

According to their view, obsessionals are characterized by an elevated level of physiological arousal that is assumed to be related to the indecisiveness of these patients. On the one hand it is suggested that indecisiveness leads to heightened arousal: "The result of this is a state of unpleasant high arousal which is reflected in the measures of mood states of hostility, depression and anxiety" (Beech & Liddell, p. 149). However, elsewhere it is argued that a pathological state of overarousal is primary in causing the decision-making deficits: "the obsessional patient's estimate of the probability of making a mistake will deviate from the normal as a function of the abnormality of mood state" (p. 150). Thus, mood state is seen as both cause and effect of decision making difficulties.

Another important proposition of their theory postulates that pathological arousal leads to obsessional thoughts through attributional processes:

> the cognitions which appear as part of the obsessional complex might be seen as *post hoc* accounts offered by the patients as means of explaining the subjective experience of disturbance. In other words the individual who is subject to massive unsolicited mood changes is prompted to explain these experiences and, in the absence of any "real" external cause, will create a fiction or pathological idea (such as that concerning some source of contamination) and abnormalities of overt behaviour (e.g., rituals or avoidance behaviour) which are consistent with these ideas. (Beech & Perigault, 1974, pp. 114–115)

It is argued that obsessionals are susceptible to high arousal and slow recovery from stimulation, "thus creating more opportunities for special conditioning effects of the kind where the exceptional state of the organism becomes attached to discriminable environmental cues" (Beech & Perigault, 1974, p. 116). To summarize the main points of the theory of Beech and his colleagues: obsessionals are characterized by a pathological state of overarousal that leads them to search for environmental cues to explain the feelings of disturbance experienced. The arousal is further assumed to be related to indecisiveness.

What evidence is provided in support of the idea that obsessionals show heightened arousal? Beech and Perigault (1974) and Beech and Liddell (1974) reported some "exploratory studies" that are cited in support of this proposition. However, a closer reading of their data reveals that the evidence is far from conclusive. The evidence provided by Beech and Perigault consists of case studies. Since no controls were included, it is difficult to see how this can lead to their impression that "obsessionals, more than any other group, experience difficulty in habituation and, instead, show a continued tendency to GSR responsivity to repeated stimulation" (p. 138). In the Beech and Liddell study the general level of spontaneous fluctuations among obsessionals was found to be lower rather than higher as compared with mixed neurotics and controls, which outcome was directly contrary to expectations.

Finally, a study by Rabavilas, Boulougouris, Stefanis, and Vaidakis (1977) is of some importance. Rabavilas *et al.* hypothesized that obsessionals have greater anticipatory fear responses than normals. Eight obsessive-compulsive patients and eight controls took part in the experiment. To begin with, no significant differences were found between groups for heart rate and skin conductance during base line. However, on shock anticipation, obsessionals were more aroused (heart rate and maximum deflection of skin conductance) when compared to controls. Thus, while the findings of this study did not support the idea that obsessionals have an abnormal state of arousal, evidence was provided that obsessionals show higher autonomic arousal during anticipation of threatening situations as compared with controls.

In conclusion, little or no evidence is provided that obsessionals show an abnormality of arousal. Further, even if there was more confirmatory evidence than available at present, it still has to be demonstrated that this unusual state of arousal is characteristic of obsessionals. It should be remembered that overarousal has been found among other neurotic conditions such as anxiety states, agoraphobia, and social anxiety (see p. 31). Thus, there is no reason for assigning primary importance to physiological arousal causing obsessive-compulsive disorders, until new evidence indicative of a causal link is presented.

3.2. Displacement Activity

In a provocative paper, Holland (1974) suggested that obsessional behavior could be regarded as a form of "displacement activity." *Displacement activity* is inappropriate "out of context" behavior that has been observed in a wide variety of species "ranging from invertebrates to apes and encompassing a considerable proportion of the phylogenetic scale" (Holland, p. 164). For example, male sticklebacks may dig nests rather than attack or flee when another male stickleback crosses the boundary of their territory. Bindra (1959) lists the following stimulus situations that give rise to displacement activity: motivational conflict, frustration, and thwarting. The displacement activity usually consists of feeding, grooming, or cleaning and nestbuilding.

The observed forms of displacement activity suggest that obsessional washing and cleaning may be explicable in terms of displacement, since there is some resemblance to the grooming behavior of animals. At first glance, checking rituals seem to be more difficult to accommodate in a displacement theory. However, Holland provides some evidence that checking can also be regarded as a form of displacement.

Holland assumes that obsessionals experience an internal state that is equivalent to that found in animals in displacement situations. He cites Delius (1970) who argued that displacement activity occurs when information can no longer be adequately processed, which leads to a state of overarousal. According to Delius, there is an upper limit to the amount of information the organism is able to process efficiently; when the "channel capacity" is exceeded, the sleep system may be set in action which is postulated to affect the afference of the sensory information. Displacement activities are assumed to be activated by the sleep system.

Holland (1974) argues that "the obsessional is not being bombarded with input, but is simply unable to deal effectively with amounts of information which other people process with ease" (p. 171). He holds that obsessionals are more susceptible to overload and hence to the automatic activation of the sleep system: "He, therefore, exhibits ritualistic displacement activity in situations in which most other people are functioning efficiently" (p. 171).

The idea of an overload of information that sets into action obsessive-compulsive behavior has some appeal. The quantity of information might exceed the "channel capacity" of an individual and thus may give rise to displacement activity, that is, obsessive-compulsive behavior. Alternatively, the emotional value of the information might also be of importance. It is conceivable that unsatisfactory emotional processing is involved. The sleep system may be set into action as a direct consequence of high arousal related to traumatic experiences.

Of course, the "displacement model" of Holland is highly speculative. While we may say that the interpretation of many of the findings are open to doubt, there may be some resemblance of displacement activity to ritual behavior of obsessionals that deserves further study. However, it is very unlikely that displacement activity might have relevance for most forms of obsessive-compulsive behavior. The mere recognition that displacement activity resembles (some) obsessional behavior does little to clarify the nature of the latter. Moreover, it is difficult to see how obsessional ruminations that often accompany ritualistic acts are related to displacement activities.

In conclusion, extrapolation from animals to human beings is unwarranted: The analogy drawn between obsessive-compulsive behavior and displacement activity is far from perfect.

3.3. Genetic versus Environmental Contribution

Several studies investigated whether a genetic component plays a part in obsessive-compulsive disorders (see review by Black, 1974). While several instances of monozygotic twins, who were concordant for obsessionality, have been reported in the literature, the value of these studies are vitiated by the dubious quality of the diagnosis and failure to provide evidence of zygosity. Black found only three reports of identical twins with obsessional neurosis in which both zygosity and diagnosis had been reliably determined (Woodruft & Pitts, 1964; Parker, 1964; Marks, Crowe, Drewe, Young, & Dewhurst, 1969). Further, there is some evidence provided that there is a roused incidence of obsessionality among relatives of obsessional patients. However, neither the reports of monozygotic twins, who are concordant for obsessionality, nor elevated rate of obsessional disorders in close relatives prove a genetic contribution. Just as easily as genetic factors, environmental factors could explain these findings. Moreover, it should be noted that the incidence of obsessive-compulsive *symptoms* in the parents of obsessional patients is far from impressive, ranging from 0.1% to 8% (Rachman & Hodgson, 1980). A recent study by Rapoport, Elkins, Langer, Sceery, Buchsbaum, Gillin, Murphy, Zahn, Lake, Ludlow, and Mendelson (1982) also found an absence of obsessive-compulsive disorders in the parents and siblings of obsessional children.

Very few studies have been conducted on the children of obsessive-compulsive patients. Rachman and Hodgson (1980) reviewed these studies and found that most studies failed to show an increased incidence of obsessional patients. However, a significant number of children were found to have psychological difficulties. Rachman and Hodgson hypothesized that a general neurotic predisposition is transmitted socially: "a high percentage of obsessional parents transmit behavior that emerges as a general maladjustment rather than as a specific problem with an obsessional character" (p. 46).

Considering the limited data available at present, we concur with Black (1974) that "the information available is still quite insufficient to assess the contribution of genetic factors to the development of obsessional neurosis in identical twins" (p. 25).

3.4. Brain Pathology

Some authors have argued that brain pathology is related to obsessive-compulsive disorders (e.g., Alsen, 1970; Flor-Henry, Yeudall, Koles, & Howarth, 1979; Schilder, 1938). Pacella, Polatin, and Nagler (1944) found that two-thirds of patients with obsessive symptoms had abnormal EEG recordings. Assessment of the results of this study is fraught with difficulties, largely because of unreliable EEG recordings and loose diagnostic criteria. In sharp contrast, both Ingram and McAdam (1960) and Rockwell and Simons (1947) found very few abnormal EEG recordings as far as pure obsessionals were concerned. In a more recent study (Flor-Henry *et al.*, 1979), EEG recordings from 10 obsessionals and 23 normal subjects were compared. Only on two variables was a significant between-group difference found, which is difficult to interpret since an unspecified number of statistical comparisons was conducted. In addition, the subjects and patients were administered a neuropsychological test battery. On a number of these tests significant differences between groups were found suggesting a predominantly left frontal dysfunction in the obsessional patients. However, most of these findings could not be replicated in a study on nine obsessional children (Rapoport *et al.*, 1982).

Finally, a study of Capstick and Seldrup (1977) may have a bearing on this issue. These investigators found a history of abnormal birth events in one-third of their obsessional patients, which was significantly more frequent than in a control group. Although this finding is interesting, it does not necessarily indicate that birth complications led to an organic pathology that was in some way related to the obsessive-compulsive disorders of these patients.

Although the evidence is far from conclusive, the findings of the studies by Capstick and Seldrup (1977) and Flor-Henry and his colleagues (1979) warrant further studies in this area. If a causal connection between cerebral pathology and obsessive-compulsive disorders could be demonstrated in some patients (which in the opinion of the author has not yet been done) this could have important implications for the treatment of patients.

Finally, obsessive-compulsive symptomatology is sometimes observed in brain-injured individuals (Brickner, Rosner, & Munro, 1940; Schilder, 1938). According to Rachman and Hodgson (1980) these "organic obsessional-compulsive disorders" are psychologically and phenomenologically distinct from obsessional-compulsive disorders and will not be discussed here.

4. PSYCHOANALYTIC THEORY

Only the theoretical contribution concerning the etiology of obsessive-compulsive disorders will be discussed in this section.

No attempt is made to give a full account of the psychoanalytic point of view. For a more detailed review of this subject the interested reader is referred to the original writings of Freud as cited in this text, to Nagera (1976), and to the proceedings of the 24th International Psychoanalytical Congress, which was devoted to obsessive-compulsive neurosis (published in the *International Journal of Psychoanalysis*, 1966).

Freud had a special interest in obsessive-compulsive neurosis. Two out of 12 of his major cases and 32 out ʳ ᶜ 133 of his minor cases were diagnosed as obsessional neurosis (Bro ₁y, 1970). In 1926 Freud remarked: "Obsessional neurosis is unquestionably the most interesting and repaying subject of analytic research. But as a problem it has not yet been mastered" (p. 113).

4.1. Theoretical Developments

Freud's theory concerning the psychodynamics of obsessive-compulsive disorders underwent major changes throughout his life. In his earlier writing on this subject Freud (1896) held that sexual experiences in the period of "childhood immorality" had the same significance in the etiology of obsessional neurosis as in hysteria. The major difference between these precocious sexual experiences was that in the case of hysteria an event of passive sexuality was found whereas in obsessional cases the sexual experience had given pleasure. The obsessional ideas were viewed to be the result of repression:

> *Obsessional ideas* are invariably transformed *self-reproaches* which have re-emerged from *repression* and which always relate to some *sexual* act that was performed with pleasure in childhood. (Freud, 1896, p. 169)

When eventually the defense failed, the obsessive-compulsive disorder started. However, the repressed memories were changed before coming into consciousness:

> what becomes conscious as obsessional ideas and affects, and take the place of pathogenic memories so far as conscious life is concerned, are structures in the nature of a compromise between the repressed ideas and the repressing ones. (Freud, 1896, p. 170)

In later years Freud abandoned both the notion of the precocious sexual experience and the part played by repression in obsessional neurosis.

Freud discussed the relationship between obsessive-compulsive *neurosis* and the anal phase for the first time in 1913, although he had already suggested a link between the obsessional *personality* and anal erotic instincts in earlier writings (Freud, 1908). This personality type is characterized by traits of orderliness, parsimony, and obstinacy. The anal character traits are supposed to be the results of conflict aroused in the child during toilet training in early life. Thus, problems concerning bowel training were thought to lay the basis for anal fixations.

It is important to note that a distinction is made between obsessional personality (sometimes referred to as anal character) and obsessive-compulsive neurosis or disorder. Individuals with an obsessional personality are normal functioning persons, who are not considered to be psychiatric cases; in other words, the traits are an integral part of their personality. On the other hand, the person with an obsessional neurosis really suffers from obsessions and compulsions.

The Oedipus complex plays a crucial part in the development of the obsessive-compulsive disorders. The warding off of the libidinal demands of the Oedipus complex leads to regression of the libido to the anal phase. This process is perhaps best explained in the following quotation:

> In obsessional neuroses these processes are carried further than is normal. In addition to the destruction of the Oedipus complex, a regressive degradation of the libido takes place, the super-ego becomes exceptionally severe and unkind, and the ego, in obedience to the super-ego, produces strong reaction formations in the shape of the conscientiousness, pity and cleanliness. (Freud, 1926, pp. 114–115)

The regression of the libido to the anal phase leads to "anal sadism" and aggressive tendencies. Actually, the love impulses transformed themselves into aggressive impulses (Nagera, 1976). The obsessive-compulsive patients are characterized by ambivalent feelings (love and hatred) directed towards the same person. These ambivalent feelings are one of the main characteristics of obsessional neurosis (Freud, 1909b, p. 239).

Finally, the part defense mechanisms play in the symptom formation should be explained. As contrasted with hysteria, where repression leads to amnesia, other defense mechanisms are said to be more typical of the obsessional neurosis. Although repression may take place in obsessional neurosis, this is often incomplete (Freud, 1909b, pp. 195–196). A common characteristic of the defense mechanisms of obsessional patients is that the significant experience has not necessarily been forgotten, but instead, has been deprived of its affect. The most important defense mechanisms in obsessional neurosis are: undoing, displacement, reaction formation, and isolation of content and affect (Nagera, 1976). However, these defense mechanisms are never totally successful. The obsessive-compulsive symptoms are the compromise between instinctual drives and defenses against them. In Freud's words:

> The symptoms belonging to this neurosis fall, in general, into two groups, each having an opposite trend. They are either prohibitions, precautions, and expiations—that is, they are negative in character—or they are, on the contrary, substitutive satisfactions which often appear in symbolic disguise. . . . [and] the symptom-formation scores a triumph if it succeeds in combining the prohibition with satisfaction so that what was originally a defensive command or prohibition acquires the significance of satisfaction as well. (1926, p. 112)

In Freud's view the satisfaction component predominates the prohibition component later on in the illness:

> The result of this process, which approximates more and more to a complete failure of the original purpose of defence, is an extremely restricted ego which is reduced to seeking satisfaction in the symptoms. (Freud, 1926, p. 118)

Other psychoanalysts have contributed little to the psychoanalytic theory of obsessional neuroses. Most of the contributions consist of repetitions, elaborations, or confirmations of Freud's point of view (Nagera, 1976). Thus, the clinical experience and the theoretical formulations of Freud are still the cornerstones of psychoanalysis as currently practiced. Therefore, it is important to note that Freud's case load of obsessive-compulsive patients was highly atypical. Each of these patients was a member of the upper class (Brody, 1970). In addition, most obsessive-compulsive patients were seen before 1900. It should be remembered that several years later Freud started to revise his theory dramatically. Thus, during the period of his major revisions when he developed the libido theory Freud had relatively little contact with obsessive-compulsive patients.

Although there is little empirical support for the psychoanalytic point of view, which will be discussed later on, one cannot help but being impressed by some of the clinical observations of obsessional patients made by psychoanalysts, especially by Freud and Fenichel. For instance, Fenichel (1977) describes a patient who had to rearrange books on the shelf in order to avoid hurting someone with the books. However, by continuously replacing the books the actual danger of falling books and hence hurting someone was much greater than if the patient had not touched the books (p. 271). This observation is entirely in keeping with the psychoanalytic notion of the compromise between defense and impulse. What are we to think of the following quotations from behavior therapists Rachman and Hodgson (1980)?

> We learned to expect that the homes of compulsive cleaners would contain a bizarre mixture of excessively clean areas and indescribably dirty parts as well. In the same home, the lavatory might be brightly clean and strongly disinfected while parts of the kitchen were caked with month-old food remains. (Incidentally this peculiar contrast is often encountered in the patients themselves—a compulsive cleaner who washes her hands 200 times per day may leave her legs and feet unwashed for months and wear the same dirty underwear for weeks on end.) . . . [and] In one extreme case the patient had been trying to complete the cleaning of the motor of his second automobile for almost three years. He had succeeded in taking out some of the parts and cleaning them, but had gotten no further. This immobilized car was kept in the well-protected garage, while the more valuable vehicle that was in daily use was left unsheltered in the street outside. (p. 65)

Rachman and Hodgson do not mention the analytic meaning of these behaviors. Obviously, the theoretical models put forward by behavior therapists do not offer a ready explanation for these seemingly contradictory behaviors. Although psychoanalytic theory offers a possible basis for explaining these behaviors, scientific evidence to support their theory is lacking. Thus, there is no reason at all to assume that the analytic model concerning symptom formation of obsessional patients is correct. However, despite the serious weakness of the psychoanalytic point of view, behavior therapists need to take into account observations that cannot easily be fit in their own theories.

4.2. The Scientific Evaluation of the Psychoanalytic Theory

According to Freud, the anal character type consists of a cluster of three traits, namely, obstinacy, parsimony, and orderliness. A number of studies have attempted to test the psychoanalytic theory of the anal personality. In this section we are particularly concerned with the evidence (if any) that is provided pertinent to three questions:

1. Is there a relationship among obstinacy, parsimony, and orderliness that would justify the concept of the obsessive-compulsive personality?
2. Is there a relationship between toilet training and the development of the obsessive-compulsive personality?
3. Is there a relationship between the obsessive-compulsive personality and obsessive-compulsive neurosis?

4.2.1. The Obsessive-Compulsive Personality

Many studies sought to show, through correlational and factor analytic methods, that the "anal" traits (obstinacy, parsimony, and orderliness) are related to each other. After a thorough review of most of these studies Pollak (1979) concludes:

> Obsessive-compulsive personality, as a cluster of traits appears to possess considerable empirical validity and to fairly closely adhere to clinical descriptions and predictions. This is true despite the fact that an array of measurement approaches and specific measurement instruments have been employed in an attempt to correlate measures of anality with various behavioral indices. (p. 238)

In another recent review, Fisher and Greenberg (1977) come to almost similar conclusions. However, Rachman and Hodgson (1980) hold that the psychometric studies do not confirm a strong relationship among orderliness, parsimony, and obstinacy. However, as they themselves point out, the obsessional factors that emerge from a study will depend on the range of obsessional traits that are included and on the type of analysis conducted. Thus, studies that use obsessional items only are more likely to find several obsessional factors, whereas studies that include other factors as well may find one obsessional factor only.

In order to clarify the different conclusions of the reviews in this

Table 8. Trait Definitions of the Obsessive, Oral, and Hysterical Personality Patterns from the Literature Review [a]

Oral	Obsessive	Hysterical
Aggression	Emotional constriction	Dependence
Dependence	Obstinacy	Egocentricity
Oral aggression	Orderliness	Emotionality
Parsimony	Parsimony	Exhibitionism
Passivity	Perseverance	Fear of sexuality
Pessimism	Rejection of others	Sexual provocativeness
Rejection of others	Rigidity	Suggestibility
	Self-doubt	
	Superego	

[a] From "Oral, Obsessive and Hysterical Personality Patterns: Replication of Factor Analysis in an Independent Sample" by A. Lazarre, G. L. Klerman, and D. J. Armor in *Journal of Psychiatric Research*, 1970, 7, 275–290. Copyright 1970, Pergamon Press. Reprinted by permission.

area, one series of studies that used the same questionnaire will be discussed in some detail. After a review of the clinical literature Lazare, Klerman, and Armor (1966) constructed a questionnaire to verify the existence of three personality patterns derived from psychoanalytic theory: (1) obsessive, (2) oral, and (3) hysterical personality. In two studies (Lazare *et al.*, 1966; Lazare, Klerman, & Armor, 1970) the Lazare-Klerman questionnaire was applied to samples of female psychiatric patients and the responses of these subjects were factor analyzed. Other research groups have subsequently replicated these studies, also using the Lazare-Klerman questionnaire (Paykel & Prusoff, 1973; Torgesen, 1980; Van den Berg & Helstone, 1975).

The Lazare-Klerman scale measures 20 traits, each consisting of 7 items. The trait definitions were based on psychoanalytic writings. Table 8 provides the *a priori* clusters of traits according to psychoanalytic theory (Lazare *et al.*, 1966). Comparing the various factor analyses that have been conducted on the results of these questionnaires, we see a close resemblance among the factors found. All studies found three main factors, roughly comparable to the obsessive, oral, and hysterical personality patterns. Table 9 shows the percentage of variance explained by the

Table 9. Comparison of Five Studies: Percentage of Variance of Three Rotated Factors

	Lazare (1966)	Lazare (1970)	Van den Berg (1975)	Torgersen (1980) females	Torgersen (1980) males
Obsessional factor	13	14	20	14	15
Hysterical factor	16	15	15	19	9
Oral factor	12	15	17	17	22
Total	41	44	52	50	46

three first extracted factors in the studies by Lazare *et al.* (1966, 1970), Van den Berg and Helstone (1975), and Torgersen (1980). Inspection of this table reveals that much of the variance is explained by these three factors.

The hysterical and the oral factors bear only a very moderate resemblance to the classical clinical description of the hysterical and oral personality as listed in the table. However, the obsessive factor contains defining traits that were all predicted from psychoanalytic theory. Table 10 presents a summary of the results of these studies with respect to the obsessive trait. The data of the Paykel and Prusoff (1973) study could not be included, since factor loadings were not reported. Five traits are consistently reported to have high loadings on the obsessive factor: "orderliness," "severe superego," "rigidity," "emotional constriction," and "parsimony," whereas "obstinacy" and "perseverance" have moderate to high loadings on this factor. However, there is less evidence that "rejection of others" and "self-doubt" belong to this cluster.

In summary, factor analytic studies conducted in various countries (the United States, Norway, and the Netherlands) clearly demonstrate a relationship among orderliness, parsimony, and obstinacy as originally predicted from psychoanalytic theory. The obsessive personality pattern as derived from the factor analytic studies using the Lazare-Klerman scale is depicted in Table 11.

4.2.2. Etiological Considerations

Although the trait constellation of the obsessive personality matches the psychoanalytic notion of the anal personality, the fact that such traits as orderliness, parsimony, and obstinacy hang together is by itself no proof of the psychoanalytic theory of the anal phase. The present section

Table 10. Comparison of the Obsessive Factor of the Lazare and Klerman Scale

Psychoanalytic description	Lazare et al. (1966)	Lazare et al. (1970)	Van den Berg & Helstone (1975)	Torgersen (1980) Females	Torgersen (1980) Males
Orderliness	.74	.66	.81	.80	.68
Severe superego	.62	.55	.54	.65	.67
Perseverance	.54	.50	.59	.38	.30
Rigidity	.50	.61	.74	.71	.61
Parsimony	.37	.63	.59	.65	.71
Emotional constriction	.35	.67	.70	.53	.75
Obstinacy	.54	.37	.59	.42	.38
Rejection of others	.38	.04	.47	.16	.55
Self-doubt	.12	.06		.19	.35

Table 11. The Obsessive Personality Pattern[a]

Orderliness: Love of order which develops to pedantry, pleasure in details of work, compulsive listing, pleasure in indexing and cataloguing, thorough, accurate, meticulous, fastidious, perfectionistic, organized, precise, excessive and inappropriate orderliness, punctilious.

Obstinacy: Obstinacy which may become defiance, stubborn, stands on rights, self-righteous, highly opinionated, one way of doing things.

Parsimony: Avarice, parsimony which develops to miserliness, thriftiness, tendency to collect things, fondness for collecting or hoarding, all object relations are like possessions, take pleasure in possessing things nobody else has, impulse to collect and look at possessions.

Emotional constriction: Narrow range of affective reactions, warm outgoing contacts difficult, cold, abstract, emotionless, morose expression, lacks charm and grace, interest in fine arts is slight or pretended, keen sense of reality, avowed rationality.

Severe superego: Exaggerated sense of duty, scrupulous, conscientious, oversevere superego, love of discipline, dependable, reliable, punctual, ascetic, overconscientious, compliant and correct behavior, tendency to literal obedience, superego functions are severe, addicted to rules of conduct, overidealistic, unswerving integrity.

Rigidity: Rigid, lack of adaptability, not imaginative or creative, conservative, propriety, formal, unable to carry on under pressure, reserved, guarded, inflexible.

Perseverance: Persistence and endurance, lacks normal capacity for relaxation, great perseverance with tendency to put things off till last minute, nonproductive perseverance, tremendous capacity for work.

[a] From "Oral, Obsessive, and Hysterical Personality Patterns: An Investigation of Psychoanalytic Concepts by Means of Factor Analysis" by A. Lazarre, G. L. Klerman, and D. J. Armor in *Archives of General Psychiatry*, 1966, *14*, 624–630. Copyright 1966 by the American Medical Association. Reprinted by permission.

deals with a question that is a more direct test of the Freudian theory: What evidence is available demonstrating a relationship between toilet training and the development of the obsessive personality pattern?

Freud's developmental theory implied that both biological and social factors contribute to an anal orientation. The constitutional influence consists of a special sensitivity to anal sensations. Unfortunately Freud was not very specific about what environmental factors during toilet training would lead to "anal fixations." "The training may be too early, too late, too strict or too libidinous" (cited by Fenichel, 1977, p. 305). Thus, almost any deviation from "normal" toilet training could lead to anal fixation.

Several studies have attempted to show a relationship between toilet training and anal orientation of the child. The anal orientation was measured by questionnaires or rated by parents or teachers of the child or adolescent. The information over the toilet training period was gathered through interviewing the mothers. Thus, these reports were retrospective in nature: No prospective studies have been carried out. Generally, little or no evidence was found to support the psychoanalytic theory, that is, no relationship was found between a child's toilet training and the traits constituting the obsessive personality (Fisher & Greenberg, 1977; Pollak, 1979).

Interestingly, several studies found a relationship between obsessive traits of mothers on the one hand and similar traits of her children on the other (Beloff, 1957; Hetherington & Brackbill, 1963). In the Hetherington and Brackbill study significant positive correlations were found between a mother's degree of obsessive traits and her daughter's. In a study by Finney (1963) a clear relationship was found between the rigidity of the mother (as rated by clinicians) and the obsessive-compulsive traits of her child. Thus, there is some evidence that the personality style of the mother influences the personality style of the child. However, it is important to point out that this does not prove the classical psychoanalytic position that toilet training *per se* is responsible for the development of an obsessive-compulsive personality makeup. Rather, it suggests that social learning factors may account for the development of the obsessive-compulsive personality. Thus, children who are reared by parents who are unusually strict and controlling may learn these behaviors by imitation during childhood.

4.2.3. Relationship between Obsessive-Compulsive Personality and Obsessive-Compulsive Neurosis

Freud held that anally fixated persons have a predisposition to the development of obsessive-compulsive neurosis. It should be remembered that psychoanalysts make a clear distinction between obsessive-compulsive traits and symptoms. Obsessive traits are said to be sublimations of the libido in a normal functioning individual, whereas the obsessional symptoms develop after a breakdown in the defense mechanisms.

Several studies have addressed the issue of whether the obsessive personality can be differentiated from obsessional neurosis. For instance, Sandler and Hazari (1960) identified a cluster of obsessional traits and obsessional symptoms that were relatively independent. The items that loaded on the *trait* dimension refer to people who are exceedingly punctual, methodical, and systematic, and who are meticulous in their use of words. The obsessive-compulsive *complaint* dimension consists of items that reflect the symptomatology of obsessive-compulsive patients. Slade

(1974) reviewing subsequent studies concluded that the obsessive-compulsive personality can be statistically differentiated from obsessive-compulsive symptomatology through factor analysis. However, a more recent study (Fontana, 1980) using the Sandler-Hazari Inventory found a low-level correlation between traits and symptoms in both clinical and nonclinical populations. In addition, Dijkema (1978) found a high correlation between traits and symptoms using the Leyton Obsessional Inventory (Cooper, 1970) in two samples of psychiatric patients ($r = .61$ and $r = .76$ respectively). Similar high correlations between the two measures were found by Kendell and diScipio (1970) on depressed patients and by Cooper (1970) on normals.

It is difficult to interpret the conflicting results of the psychometric studies reviewed above. Even if we assume that obsessional traits and symptoms are statistically unrelated, it is difficult to see how this finding could prove or disprove the psychoanalytic theory. Of more importance to the present question is the premorbid personality of obsessional patients. According to the psychoanalytic notion, obsessive-compulsive patients should have a premorbid obsessional personality. Black (1974) reviewing the literature in this area found that 71% of obsessional patients had marked or moderate premorbid obsessive traits. However, the studies listed in this review were retrospective and few of the studies were adequately controlled. Kringlen (1965) compared the premorbid personality traits of obsessional patients with those of nonobsessional control patients. Seventy-two percent of the obsessional patients and 53% of the control patients were rated to have premorbid obsessional traits. Although significantly more obsessional patients than control patients showed obsessional traits, the finding of his study suggests that a premorbid obsessional personality may also be associated with the development of other disorders. Similarly, Rachman and Hodgson (1980) found that one of the obsessional traits (orderliness) was not specifically associated with obsessional complaints. Items that were included in their questionnaire to cover the concept of orderliness did not discriminate between obsessional and nonobsessional traits but traits of introverted neurotics.

Taken together, these data indicate that there is a strong relationship between premorbid obsessional personality traits and the development of obsessional neurosis. However, the data of Kringlen's (1965) and Rachman and Hodgson's (1980) nonobsessional control patients bring the clinical significance of this finding into a different perspective. Moreover, the finding that a small but still substantial number of obsessive-compulsive neuroses develop without any evidence of a premorbid obsessional personality shows that there is no one-to-one relationship between obsessional traits and obsessive-compulsive neurosis. Thus the psychoanalytic hypothesis that obsessive-compulsive neurosis can only develop in persons with an "anal" character has to be rejected.

4.2.4. Summary

In conclusion, the answers to the three questions pertinent to the psychoanalytic theory of anal fixations can be summarized as follows:

1. There is strong evidence that orderliness, parsimony and obstinacy hang together, which justifies the concept of the obsessive-compulsive personality.
2. No relationship has been found between toilet training and the development of the obsessive-compulsive personality.
3. The results of psychometric studies investigating the relationship between obsessive-compulsive traits and symptoms are inconclusive and difficult to interpret. Retrospective studies indicate a strong relationship between premorbid obsessional traits and the development of obsessional disorders. Conclusions, however, are tempered by the finding that neurotic patients in general might have premorbid obsessional traits.

In summary, there is no evidence whatever to support the psychoanalytic theory that relates anal eroticism to the obsessive personality and to the development of obsessional neurosis.

7

Assessment of Obsessive-Compulsive Disorders

1. QUESTIONNAIRES

Several questionnaires have been developed to assess obsessive traits and obsessive-compulsive neurosis or complaints. Although several personality questionnaires contain subscales to measure this dimension (e.g., MMPI and HOQ; Foulds, 1965), these will not be dealt with in this chapter. Similarly, scales that have been devised to measure obsessive traits only (e.g., Beloff, 1957; Kline, 1967; Lazare *et al.*, 1970) will also be omitted in this review.

There are two questionnaires that are generally used to measure symptoms and traits; namely, the Sandler-Hazari Obsessionality Inventory and the Leyton Obsessional Inventory. More recently another questionnaire has been developed to measure obsessional complaints: the Maudsley Obsessional-Compulsive Questionnaire. These questionnaires will be discussed in some detail.

1.1. The Sandler-Hazari Obsessionality Inventory

This inventory consists of 40 items relating to obsessive-compulsive traits and symptoms. Sandler and Hazari (1960) factor-analyzed the responses of 100 unselected neurotic patients and found two orthogonal factors (traits and symptoms). They suggest that the trait factor is quite independent of obsessional illness, whereas the second factor is said to represent a continuum from mild to severe (neurotic) symptoms. Although Sandler and Hazari did not devise a standard obsessionality inventory, others have attempted to use this inventory for clinical purposes. Most of the studies failed to validate the Sandler-Hazari scale.

Both Reed (1969c) and Orme (1965) administered the inventory to obsessional and control patients. However, the scores on the Sandler-Hazari scale did not differentiate obsessional patients from controls. Contrary to these studies, Fontana (1980) found this inventory to be a useful tool for discriminating between normal and clinical populations. Therefore, he suggested that this instrument might be used more widely in the future as a diagnostic instrument. This conclusion, however, needs some qualification. The clinical group used in his study consisted of patients at the day unit of a psychiatric hospital. None was diagnosed as exclusively obsessional. In addition, the normal controls were not matched with the patients but consisted of teachers and lecturers.

Several studies investigated the relationship between the Sandler-Hazari trait and symptoms scales vis à vis measures of neuroticism and introversion. Generally, a significant positive relationship was found between the obsessional symptom scale on the one hand and emotional instability (Kline, 1967, 1968; Meares, 1971) and introversion (Kline, 1967) on the other.

In summary, the Sandler-Hazari scale is of little use for clinical purposes.

1.2. The Leyton Obsessional Inventory

The Leyton Obsessional Inventory (LOI) (Cooper, 1970) consists of 69 questions printed on separate cards, which a respondent puts into either the "Yes" or "No" slots of an answer box. Forty-six of the questions are concerned with obsessional symptoms and the other 23 with obsessive traits, thus giving *symptom* and *trait* scores. Further questions regarding 35 of the cards provide a *resistance* score (measuring the severity rather than extent of the symptoms) and an *interference* score (measuring the disability caused by the symptoms).

A major disadvantage of this inventory is the time taken to administer it. For obsessional patients the time taken may be over one hour. Snowdon (1980) compared results on the postbox form with results when the LOI was administered as a questionnaire. Correlations between both versions of the LOI were reasonably good ($r = .72-.77$), which suggests that the LOI might be used in written questionnaire form. Another disadvantage of the LOI concerns the interdependence of the subscales. All items that might involve resistance and interference and that have been put in the "Yes" box the first time have to be rated a second and a third time for resistance and interference, respectively. Thus, the scores on the latter scales are not independent from the scores on the symptom and trait scales. Finally, the LOI contains items concerning neither unpleasant nor abhorrent thoughts nor items concerning excessive hand-washing (Beech & Vaughan, 1978).

Cooper (1970) demonstrated that the scales of the LOI could discriminate among obsessional patients, house-proud housewives, and normal women. The obsessional patients received the highest scores, normal women the lowest, and the house-proud housewives scored between the other groups. Both Millar (1980) and Murray, Cooper, and Smith (1979) found the four subscales discriminated between obsessional patients and normals. In addition, Kendel and diScipio (1970) found that depressed patients with obsessional symptoms and traits gave raised symptom and trait scores on the LOI, but scored much lower than obsessional neurotics on resistance and interference. Thus, the latter scales distinguish primary obsessional patients from primary depressives. Figure 27 demonstrates the distribution of the scores of obsessionals and

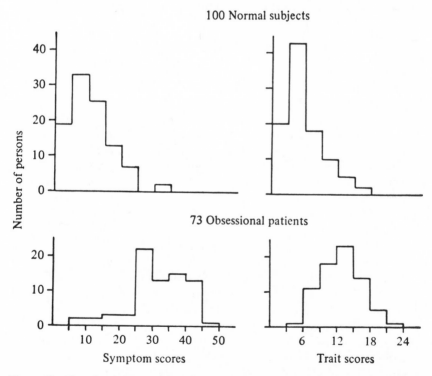

Figure 27. Obsessional "symptom" and "trait" scores in normal subjects and obsessional patients (Leyton Obsessional Inventory). (From "The Leyton Obsessional Inventory: An Analysis of the Responses of 73 Obsessional Patients" by R. M. Murray *et al.*, *Psychological Medicine*, 1979, *9*, Fig. 1. Reprinted by permission.)

normals in the study of Murray *et al.* (1979). The scores are widely separated between groups. There is almost no overlapping on symptom, resistance, and interference scores, while there was considerable overlap in trait scores. Similar results were reported by Millar (1980).

Several studies have addressed themselves to the issue of reliability of the LOI. Test-retest reliability is satisfactory for both the symptom and trait scale (Cooper, 1970; Dijkema, 1978).

Finally, Murray *et al.* (1979) performed a principal component analysis on the correlation matrix formed from the responses of 73 obsessional patients on the LOI. The first 5 components that emerged from the analysis accounted for 30% of the variance. Three of the components were unipolar and were labeled (1) household order, (2) personal contamination, and (3) doubting. The other two components were bipolar and concerned (4) checking/parsimony and (5) desire for closure/unpleasant ruminations. Earlier analysis on normal subjects had provided an almost similar picture (Cooper & Kelleher, 1973).

1.3. The Maudsley Obsessional-Compulsive Inventory

Hodgson and Rachman (1977) developed the Maudsley Obsessional-Compulsive Inventory (MOCI) to investigate types of obsessive-compulsive complaints. The MOCI consists of 30 items that differentiated between obsessional patients and matched nonobsessional neurotic patients. A principal-component analysis performed on the responses of 100 obsessionals revealed 5 components, namely checking, cleaning, slowness, doubting-conscientiousness, and ruminating. Since the ruminating component consisted of two items only, the authors ignored it. The questionnaire provides 5 scores: Total obsessional score, checking, washing, slowness-repetition, and doubting-conscientious. The description of the four components is provided in Table 12.

In order to validate the MOCI, Hodgson and Rachman (1977) compared the scores on two of the subscales (checking and washing) with retrospective therapist ratings of 42 obsessional patients. A satisfactory relationship between therapist rating and questionnaire score was found. Thus, patients who were categorized as checkers or cleaners on the basis of their questionnaire score were usually assigned to the respective category by the therapist. To date, two studies found this questionnaire to discriminate reliably between groups of phobic and obsessional patients (Volans, 1976; Hodgson, Rankin, & Stockwell, 1980). In addition, concurrent validity was assessed by comparing total MOCI scores with Leyton Obsessional Inventory scores. For 30 obsessional patients the correlation was found to be .60 (Rachman & Hodgson, 1980) which is

Table 12. Description of Components of MOCI[a]

1. Obsessional checking. Repeated checking is a major problem, and a great deal of time is spent every day checking things over and over again (e.g., gas or water taps, doors, letters, etc.) The morning wash takes a long time to complete (possibly because checking is involved). Some numbers are considered to be extremely unlucky, and there is a tendency to suffer from obsessional ruminations.
2. Obsessional cleaning. Obsessional cleaning involves excessive concern about germs, diseases, and cleanliness, and worries about contamination from money, public telephones, toilets, and animals. Soap and antiseptics are used excessively, and washing takes up a lot of time.
3. Obsessional slowness. Dressing and hanging/folding clothes take up a lot of time. A person suffering from this problem is often late because he or she cannot get through everything on time. The person adheres to a strict routine and often counts when doing a routine task. He or she tends not to suffer from obsessional ruminations.
4. Obsessional doubting-conscientiousness. A person suffering from this problem often feels that a job has not been completed correctly even when it was performed very carefully. The person usually has serious doubts about simple everyday events. He or she gets behind with work because things are repeated over and over again and too much attention is paid to detail. The person has a strict conscience and is more concerned than most people about honesty (and probably had strict parents).

[a] From *Obsessions and Compulsions* by S. Rachman and R. J. Hodgson. Copyright 1980 by Prentice-Hall. Reprinted by permission.

rather low for inventories that purport to measure the same dimension. Finally test–retest reliability is satisfactory.

Obvious advantages of the MOCI are its easy administration, its discrimination of obsessionals from other neurotic patients, and the validation of two of the subscales (checking and washing). However, evidence with respect to the usefulness of the slowness and doubting subscales is lacking. Rachman and Hodgson (1980) reported a principal component analysis performed on 100 nonobsessionals (50 neurotic patients and 50 nightschool attenders). The components that emerged were very similar to the checking, cleaning, and doubting components identified in the earlier analysis on obsessional patients. However, no slowness component emerged. Moreover, items that loaded highly on the doubting component tended also to have high loadings on the checking component.

2. PSYCHOPHYSIOLOGICAL ASSESSMENT

Psychophysiological measures have been employed to investigate the nature of the obsessive-compulsive disorders and the mechanisms through which behavioral treatments achieve their results. In addition, psychophysiological assessment has been utilized as the outcome measure and as the predictor of treatment response.

Studies in this area employed heart rate, pulse rate variability, and skin conductance (both spontaneous fluctuations and maximal deflection). Most of the work in this area has been conducted by Boulougouris and his colleagues. In their investigations multiple psychophysiological measures were taken. Each of the separate measures is thought to be a reflection of the same single underlying state of arousal.

Several studies provide evidence that provocation of rituals through exposure *in vivo* leads to an increase in arousal as measured psychophysiologically. In these studies patients are assessed psychophysiologically during different phases of the experiment. After a neutral baseline period, washers were asked to touch a contaminated object and checkers were brought into a situation that provoked the urge to check. For instance, a patient who repetitively checked to ensure that no knives or other sharp instruments were left lying around in vulnerable positions was asked to use such objects and then return them immediately to the correct drawer (Röper & Rachman, 1976). Provocation of urges by exposure *in vivo* to distressing stimuli produced significantly more autonomic activity than neutral stimulation (Boulougouris & Bassiakos, 1973; Boulougouris, Rabavilas, & Stefanis, 1977; Hornsveld, Kraaymaat, & van Dam-Baggen, 1979; Rabavilas & Boulougouris, 1974). However, the evidence with respect to pulse rate variability is less clearcut. Although in a study by Röper, Rachman, and Hodgson (1973) on checkers' provocation of urges to check led to an increase of subjective anxiety, this was not reflected on pulse rate variability scores. In fact, there was very little change in pulse rate throughout the experiment. In an earlier study by the same research group on obsessional washers (Hodgson & Rachman, 1972) pulse rate measures did not significantly increase after touching a contaminated object, while subjective anxiety did so. However, here the results of the pulse rate measure showed a trend along the same lines as subjective anxiety. In summary, provocation of rituals by exposure *in vivo* leads to increase in heart rate and skin conductance. The data with respect to pulse rate variability are inconclusive.

So far the results of studies that made use of external stimuli to provoke urges to wash or check have been discussed. Let us now turn our attention to psychophysiological responsiveness in response to imagined stimuli. Rabavilas and Boulougouris (1974) sought to investigate whether psychophysiological measures could be used with obsessional ruminations. Eight patients suffering from obsessional ruminations took part in this experiment. During 60 second periods the experimenter presented neutral and obsessional material to the patients by verbal instruction. The experimenter did not describe the obsessional scene to be imagined but waited until the patient signalled that he held his main obsession in fantasy. Significant differences were found on heart rate and skin conductance deflection between obsessive and neutral fantasy. No significant difference was found on spontaneous fluctuations of skin conductance. It should be noted that the intra-individual correlation between physiological measures was minimal. In a related study, Stern, Lipsedge, and Marks (1973) could not find any difference between obsessional imagery and neutral imagery on physiological measures (heart rate and spontaneous fluctuations of skin conductance) although there was higher subjective anxiety during obsessional imagery. The different results of both studies can possibly be explained by the fact that in the Stern *et al.* study obsessional imagery was recorded on tape rather than self-induced as was the case in the Rabavilas and Boulougouris (1974) study.

Although psychophysiological measures might be fruitfully employed to investigate the nature of obsessive-compulsive disorders, to date there is insufficient evidence provided that supports the use of these measures to assess the outcome of treatment. Further studies are needed before recommendations can be made with respect to the utility of psychophysiological assessment in this area.

3. BEHAVIORAL ASSESSMENT AND RATING SCALES

Rachman, Hodgson, and Marks (1971) developed a behavioral test to observe the obsessional patient's behavior directly. Patients had to perform a number of difficult tasks (e.g., touching contaminated material) in the laboratory. They provided no data with respect to the validity and reliability of this measure.

In our studies (Boersma, Den Hengst, Dekker, & Emmelkamp, 1976; Emmelkamp & Kraanen, 1977) the occurrence and duration of rituals was recorded by the patient in the natural environment. Patients had to record two to three compulsive rituals during one week baseline before and at the end of treatment. The patients had to note down the frequency and/or duration of these actions on observation forms. For instance, patients with a relatively low frequency of washing rituals (e.g., 10 items a day) but with a long duration had to record the duration of the rituals. On the other hand, patients with a high frequency of washing rituals of a relatively short duration had to record the frequency of the rituals.

The behavioral measure was omitted in subsequent studies for various reasons. First, the assessment procedure proved to be difficult to conduct. Second, results are not comparable across patients, due to the idiosyncrasy of the target behaviors which are assessed. Finally, the behavioral measure in our previous studies seemed to offer little or no more information than already gathered by the clinical ratings for anxiety and avoidance.

Adapted versions of the Watson and Marks (1971) scales, which were originally devised to assess phobic anxiety and avoidance, are quite useful to assess obsessive-compulsive behavior. In our studies patient, therapist, and independent assessor rate five main obsessions for anxiety/discomfort and avoidance. Thus, the situations that are rated differ from patient to patient. The interrater reliability is satisfactory. Furthermore, these scales are sensitive to changes in obsessive-compulsive behavior after treatment. Concurrent validity was evaluated through correlation with the MOCI. We found correlation coefficients ranging from .57 to .80 between anxiety and avoidance ratings on the one hand and MOCI on the other.

Obviously, direct behavioral assessment of obsessional ruminations is impossible and we have to rely on the patient's report on his obsessional thoughts. Usually, the frequency of obsessional thoughts is recorded by the patient (with the aid of a counter). However, the interpretation of the frequency measurement of obsessions involves certain problems. First, it is not always possible to make a straightforward comparison between the frequency measurement of different patients because of the nature of their obsessions. Some patients can make a clear distinction between different obsessional thoughts, although these thoughts occur as a sequence; others score a sequence of this kind as one single obsession. Further, the duration and intensity of an obsession can differ markedly. Thus obsessions can become less protracted, less concrete, and less anxiety-arousing in the course of treatment, and this would not find expression in the frequency measurement. Although reliability and validity of the frequency measurement is unknown, there is some evidence that frequency and distress are not always correlated (Emmelkamp & Giesselbach, 1981).

8

Behavioral Treatment of Obsessive-Compulsive Disorders

In this chapter the variety of behavioral procedures that have emerged for the treatment of obsessive-compulsive behavior will be reviewed and evaluated. A detailed analysis of the treatment process is provided in Chapters 10 and 12. Compulsions and obsessions will be treated in separate sections.

1. TREATMENT OF COMPULSIONS

There is little evidence that systematic desensitization is of any value with obsessive-compulsive disorders. Although controlled studies are lacking, the published case studies on systematic desensitization give little reason to recommend this approach. Beech and Vaughan (1978) reviewed most of the published case studies and found that the reported success rate is slightly over 50%. If one takes into account the bias in selection of cases for publication, it is reasonable to assume that the actual success rate is even lower. A closer analysis of the successful cases reveals that the improvement may be due to gradual exposure *in vivo* plus self-imposed response prevention rather than to systematic desensitization *per se* (Hersen, 1970; Lautch, 1970; Marks, Crowe, Drewe, Young, & Dewhurst, 1969; Walton & Mather, 1963; Wolpe, 1964; Worsley, 1968, 1970). Other therapists also reported on the positive results of exposure *in vivo* procedures with or without response prevention (Fine, 1973; Gentry, 1970; Heyse, 1973; Mills, Agras, Barlow, & Mills, 1973; Petrie & Haans, 1969; Rainey, 1972; Walton, 1960). Most of the studies using these techniques, however, are based on uncontrolled case reports, and do not provide adequate follow-up data. A variety of other behavioral treatments have been proposed, including aversion therapy (Le Boeuf, 1974), aversion relief (Solyom, Zamanzadeh, Ledwidge, & Kenny, 1971) and covert sensitization (Wisocki, 1970), but due to the recent developments in exposure *in vivo* and response prevention methods, little interest seems to have been shown in evaluating the efficacy of these procedures. The only controlled study into the effectiveness of aversion relief with obsessive-compulsives found this treatment to be ineffective (Sookman & Solyom, 1977).

The value of prolonged exposure *in vivo* and response prevention was suggested by uncontrolled studies of Meyer and his colleagues' (Meyer, 1966; Meyer & Levy, 1970; Meyer, Levy, & Schnurer, 1974). The essence of their treatment approach which at that time was called "apotrepic therapy" consists of response prevention, modeling, and exposure *in vivo*. The treatment involves several stages. After a behavioral analysis, nurses were instructed to *prevent* the patient from carrying out his rituals. *Exposure in vivo* was introduced as soon as the total elimination of rituals under supervision was achieved. The therapist increased the stress by confronting the patient with situations that normally triggered obsessive rituals. During this stage of treatment *modeling* was employed. With modeling the therapist first demonstrated what the patient had to do afterward. For example, the therapist touched contaminated objects such as underwear and he encouraged the patient to imitate it. When patients could tolerate the most difficult situations, supervision was gradually diminished.

Meyer *et al.* (1974) reported the results of this program with 15 obsessionals. Most patients showed a marked reduction of compulsive behavior. The positive results of this approach have now been replicated in several uncontrolled studies (Catts & McConaghy, 1975; Foa & Goldstein, 1978; Marks, Hallam, Connolly, & Philpot, 1977; Ramsay & Sikkel, 1973).

1.1. Controlled Studies

A first attempt into unraveling essential treatment components was carried out by the Maudsley group (Rachman, Hodgson, & Marks, 1971; Hodgson, Rachman, & Marks, 1972). They compared (1) modeling, (2) flooding, and (3) flooding plus modeling in a between-group design. Each treatment condition contained five patients. Modeling consisted of gradual exposure *in vivo* plus modeling through the therapist. Flooding consisted of rapid exposure *in vivo* to the most difficult stimuli. Patients in the combined condition received treatment by rapid exposure *in vivo* plus modeling by the therapist. All patients received relaxation treatment before the start of the exposure treatments. Results revealed that all exposure treatments were far more effective than the relaxation–control treatment and that the combined treatment procedure was superior to modeling or flooding alone. However, the superiority of the combined procedure was not replicated with another five patients (Rachman, Marks, & Hodgson, 1973).

This study has several methodological confounds that limit the conclusion which can be drawn. First, patients were not randomly divided across conditions. Second, the design was not counterbalanced: Patients received the control treatment before the exposure treatment. Thus, it is reasonable to assume that an interaction between relaxation and the various exposure procedures was measured. It should be noted that the results with the second series of five patients, who were treated by modeling/flooding treatment without the preceding relaxation phase, were less positive as compared with the first series of patients who all had received relaxation training (Rachman *et al.*, 1973). Third, no "blind" assessor was used, which might have colored the clinical judgment. Finally, modeling and gradual exposure were confounded in the design, since the study did not contain a gradual exposure only condition.

1.1.1. Rapid versus Slow Exposure

In our first study (Boersma, Den Hengst, Dekker, & Emmelkamp, 1976) we attempted to separate the effects of gradual exposure *in vivo* and modeling. On the basis of our research with agoraphobics from which it appeared that gradual exposure *in vivo* alone can be an effective treatment, we hypothesized that gradual exposure *in vivo* by itself would also have beneficial results in the treatment of compulsive behavior.

Four experimental conditions were obtained through a 2 × 2 factorial design, in which two main variables were rotated: (1) gradual exposure versus flooding and (2) modeling versus no-modeling. Thus, group A was treated with the gradual method plus modeling; group B with the gradual method without modeling; group C was treated with flooding plus modeling; and group D with flooding without modeling.

Thirteen patients completed the project. In this study and in subsequent ones discussed in this chapter, we included only patients who displayed overt rituals. Patients with pure obsessions were excluded from the study and they were investigated in separate studies. Care was taken that only severe cases were included in our trials. A number of patients with mild problems were excluded from participation and treated outside the experimental trial. Most patients were washers or checkers and a number of patients suffered from both washing and checking rituals. Some patients referred themselves for treatment after a publication in the local press. No differences were found between volunteers and patients who were referred by psychiatrists. If anything, the volunteers were more severe, most of them having received previous psychiatric treatment including hospitalization without any benefit. All patients had been handicapped for several years before entering the trial. Patients as a group were moderately depressed. The patients in this study appear to have been at least as severely disturbed as the patients in the Maudsley studies (Rachman & Hodgson, 1980, p. 339) and more chronic. The mean duration of the obsessive-compulsive disorder was 15 years (range 2–50 years) as compared with 10 years in the Maudsley studies.

The Boersma *et al.* study was the only one in which patients who referred themselves for treatment were used. Patients in our other studies were referred by mental health agencies and general practitioners.

Assessments were held at pretest, posttest, one month and three months after treatment. Assessment included self-report (Leyton Obsessional Inventory, Self-Rating Depression Scale of Zung, phobic anxiety, and avoidance scales), therapist ratings of target symptoms, depression, and social adjustment and behavioral assessment. In addition, an independent assessor who was "blind" with respect to the treatment conditions evaluated the patients.

Treatment consisted of 15 treatment sessions, each lasting two hours. With *flooding*, only the most difficult situations were practiced *in vivo*. Only those situations that had a score of 80 or higher on a fear thermometer (range 0–100) were used during practice. The clients were not allowed to perform any compulsive ritual during the therapy sessions. Also, they were instructed to relinguish *all* avoidance behavior and rituals outside the therapy sessions (self-imposed response prevention). If necessary, patients were pressed verbally during therapy not to evade practicing. However, no patient was exposed to situations against his or her will.

With *gradual exposure*, all items in the hierarchy were practiced *in vivo*, starting with the easiest. As a rule, clients themselves determined the speed at which they worked through the hierarchy. If a patient tried to avoid exposure by not choosing new items for practice, some pressure was exerted to induce the client to carry on practicing. If the whole hierarchy had been worked through before the end of treatment, practice of the most difficult items was repeated during the last session. During the therapy sessions, the patients were not allowed to perform compulsive rituals which had been dealt with in previous sessions. Also, they were instructed not to avoid situations that had been practiced and not to perform the associated compulsive rituals between treatment sessions (self-imposed response prevention). All treatment sessions were conducted in the home and natural environment of the patient.

The main treatment effects revealed that treatment resulted in statistically and clinically significant improvements. On the behavioral measure, the main compulsion improved on an average of 78%. All raters agreed that treatment resulted in marked reductions in anxiety and avoidance. The Leyton Obsessional Inventory revealed significant reductions for symptoms, trait, interference, and resistance. In addition it was found that patients had become less depressed at the end of the trial (see Figures 28A and 28B). Results of treatment generalized to improvements in social adjustment.

Results showed that gradual exposure was about equally effective as flooding (see Figure 29). On only one variable (anxiety-main compulsion, as rated by patient) had the gradual method been superior to

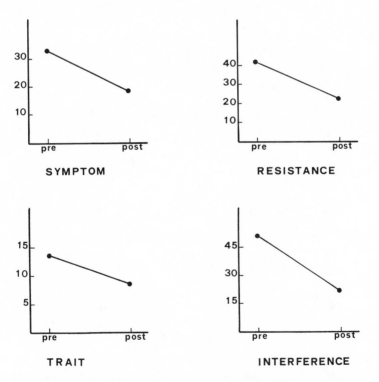

Figure 28A. Improvement on Leyton Obsessional Inventory.

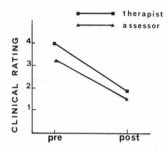 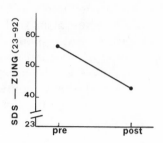

Figure 28B. Improvement on clinical rating of depression (0–8) and Self-rating Depression Scale (SDS-Zung).

flooding. This suggests that gradual treatment is at least as effective as flooding. As this method evokes less tension and is easier for the patient to carry out by himself, it is to be preferred to flooding. The results of this study are in accord with results of studies with phobic patients (Everaerd, Rijken, & Emmelkamp, 1973; Emmelkamp, 1974). Here flooding was also found to be about equally effective as gradual exposure *in vivo.*

The second aim of the study discussed above was to separate the effects of modeling and exposure. Therefore, half the patients received modeling by the therapist before actual exposure *in vivo.* In the modeling conditions, at each stage the therapist exposed himself to the anxiety-

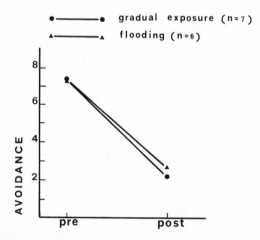

Figure 29. Improvement in avoidance obtained with gradual exposure *in vivo* was very similar to that obtained with flooding.

arousing situations without performing compulsive behavior. For example, the patient had to observe his therapist exposing himself deliberately to "contaminated" material by stepping in dog droppings or cooking meals without checking. After each demonstration the patient had to follow suit. The other half of the patients received plain exposure *in vivo*.

Hardly any differences between the two conditions were found (see Figure 30). The results of this study suggest that the effects of the modeling condition in the studies in London (Rachman *et al.*, 1971) should not be attributed to the modeling component but to the gradual exposure *in vivo* that patients received.

Another controlled study, investigating the value of modeling was reported by Röper, Rachman, and Marks (1975). Two conditions were compared: (1) 15 sessions of relaxation followed by 15 sessions of gradual exposure *in vivo* preceded by modeling, and (2) 15 sessions of passive modeling followed by 15 sessions of gradual exposure *in vivo* preceded by modeling. Passive modeling had weak effects when compared with the second block of treatment consisting of gradual exposure *in vivo*. Design flaws confound interpretation of the findings, the major flaw being the lack of a pure exposure condition in the first phase of the experiment. Further, numbers were small, five patients in each condition.

The results of the studies reviewed so far strongly suggest that all treatments (floodings, modeling and gradual exposure) act through common factors, which are real-life exposure to provoking situations and (self-imposed) response prevention.

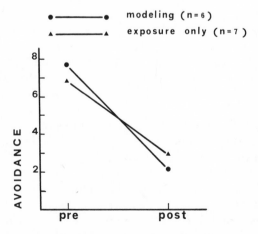

Figure 30. Modeling does not enhance the effects of exposure *in vivo*.

1.1.2. Self-Controlled Exposure

After having established the usefullness of gradual exposure *in vivo* without modeling, our next question was whether it would be possible to reduce the intervention of the therapist. At the time we had already conducted some studies on agoraphobics that supported the value of self-exposure homework. The aim of our second study (Emmelkamp & Kraanen, 1977) was to determine whether self-controlled exposure would be an effective treatment for obsessive-compulsive patients.

Fourteen patients who were referred for treatment were randomly assigned to two conditions: (1) therapist-controlled exposure, and (2) self-controlled exposure. Both treatment variants consisted of gradual exposure *in vivo*. With the therapist controlled condition, treatment was conducted along the lines of treatment in our earlier study. Thus, treatment was conducted in the homes and natural environment of the patients and consisted of gradual exposure and gradual response prevention in the company of the therapist. Each treatment session lasted 2 hr. With the self-controlled exposure condition, patients were treated as outpatients at the University Hospital. Each treatment session lasted only an hour. At each session the patient was given a number of tasks that consisted of items from the hierarchy. These tasks had to be performed by the patient himself at home. These tasks were described clearly, written down, and discussed with the patient at length. Treatment consisted of two components: self-controlled exposure *in vivo* and self-imposed response prevention. During the treatment sessions these tasks were *not* practiced. An example might illustrate this procedure. Patients could be instructed to touch the ground, shake hands, touch the toilet, or "contaminate" their houses without washing their hands or using other cleaning rituals afterwards. Or, in the case of checking rituals, patients could be instructed to leave the house without checking light, gas, doors, visit cemeteries or funerals without rituals, and so on. Treatment tasks followed the hierarchy closely; thus, more difficult tasks were given only if tasks lower in the hierarchy had been performed successfully.

On almost all variables treatment resulted in significant improvements at the posttest. Although no significant differences were found between the two conditions, self-controlled exposure was consistently superior to therapist-controlled exposure at one-month follow-up (see Figure 31). Between the posttest and follow-up patients received no treatment. The results show a slight relapse in the therapist-controlled condition, while the self-controlled patients continued to improve.

The advantages of self-controlled exposure are obvious. Treatment

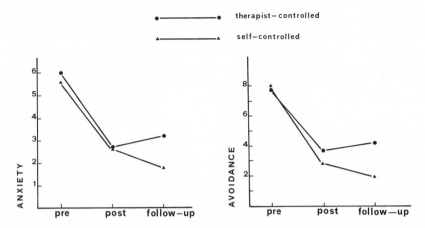

Figure 31. A comparison of self-controlled exposure *in vivo* and therapist-controlled exposure. Treatments result in similar effects at the posttest, but at a 1-month follow-up self-controlled exposure tends to be superior.

costs the therapist much less time than therapist-controlled exposure. The total treatment time spent by the therapist with the patient amounted to 30 hr, including travelling time to visit the patient. This is much more therapist time than the self-controlled exposure patients received (10 hr). Thus, this study shows that self-controlled exposure is an economic way to treat obsessional patients.

Aside from the costs-benefits issue, another advantage of self-controlled exposure is the patient's independence from the therapist. In addition, self-controlled exposure *in vivo* abolishes the problem of generalizing the effects of the therapy from the treatment sessions to the patient's normal environment. Especially with checkers, self-controlled exposure seems to be superior to therapist-controlled exposure. Checkers often have fewer difficulties when accompanied by a trusted person, including the therapist. The therapist's presence during exposure often prevents an adequate exposure for checkers, since they may attribute the responsibility of possible harm to the therapist. Our clinical experience suggests that checkers are often quite able to resist their urges to check when the therapist is present; however, in the periods between the treatment sessions they are often unable to do so. There is some experimental evidence that lends support to our clinical observations. Röper and Rachman (1976) showed that when checking rituals were provoked, increases in discomfort were much more pronounced when the experimenter was absent than when he was present.

With self-controlled exposure *in vivo*, as carried out in this study, the therapist was never present during practice. However, for some patients it might be therapeutically wise to use a fading procedure. In the first few sessions the therapist actively assists with the exercises, but as soon as possible the therapist fades out. Research with agoraphobics demonstrates that such therapist controlled exposure followed by self-controlled exposure may be highly effective (see Chapter 5).

1.1.3. Family Involvement

Family members of obsessive-compulsives are often involved in the rituals of these patients. Family members often have to carry out the same washing rituals as the patient in order to reduce patient's anxiety. In the cases of checking rituals, patients can avoid the provocation of some of their rituals by trusting their partner to do these activities. Some patients seek constant reassurance from their partners by questions such as: "Are you sure I didn't cause an accident?" "Is that non-poisonous?" or "Did you wash your hands?" Partners often accommodate the wishes of the patients and hence reinforce the obsessive-compulsive behavior.

We were interested in whether the involvement of the partner in the treatment would enhance the effectiveness of treatment by self-controlled exposure *in vivo*. Therefore, we designed a study in which two conditions were compared: (1) self-controlled exposure by the patient alone, and (2) self-controlled exposure with assistance of the patient's partner. Twelve obsessive-compulsives who had a relationship of at least one year's duration were randomly assigned across these two conditions. Owing to the high celibacy rate among obsessionals, no more couples were available to participate in this study.

In the patient alone condition, treatment consisted of self-controlled exposure *in vivo*. Each session patients received instructions from the therapist how he should practice therapeutic tasks in his natural environment. In this condition the patient's partner was neither involved in the discussions with the therapist, nor in the execution of the homework assignments. Family members were instructed to be absent during the practice hours.

In the couple condition the partner had to accompany the patient to each treatment session. After the rationale was explained to the couple, the patient received instructions for self-controlled exposure: He had to carry out his homework assignments with his partner present. The task of the partner was to encourage the patient and to have him confront the stimuli that distressed him until the patient got used to them. In addition, when the patient constantly asked for reassurance, the partner was instructed to withold reassurance. As in the patient alone condition, the

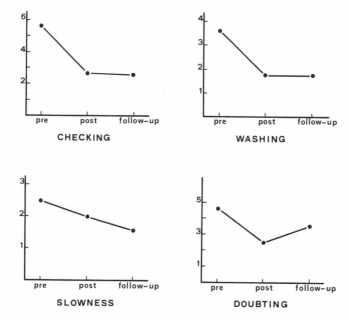

Figure 32. Treatment effects on the Maudsley Obsessional-Compulsive Inventory.

patient was not allowed to perform his rituals. Treatment in both conditions consisted of 4 information sessions and 10 treatment sessions. There was not any practicing of the tasks during treatment sessions. Treatment led to significant improvements on MOCI (Hodgson & Rachman, 1980), anxiety, and frequency of obsessive-compulsive behavior. Further improvements were found in depression as measured by the Zung-Self-Rating Depression Scale and therapist rating. The results are presented in Figure 32 and Figure 33.

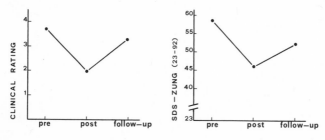

Figure 33. Successful treatment led to concomitant improvement on depression, but a relapse occurred at 1-month follow-up.

Turning to the differences between both groups, there was a consistent trend for the partner-assisted group to improve more, but this difference failed to reach statistical significance on most measures due to the small number of patients in each condition. In Figure 34 the results of the anxiety-main compulsion are given for both groups. The partner-assisted group improved more at the post-test, but at one month follow-up the difference between both groups disappeared.

Most partners were enthusiastic about the opportunity to be involved in the treatment. In only one couple did the involvement of the partner lead to conflicts, and this patient did not improve during the treatment. After the experimental trial, this patient was treated individually with beneficial effects. During this phase of the treatment the patient could determine her own pace, without provoking remarks of her husband. This couple was the most severely maritally distressed couple of the sample.

In brief, partner-assisted treatment may result in beneficial effects for most obsessional patients, but in cases involving clear marital discord an individual program of exposure is to be preferred.

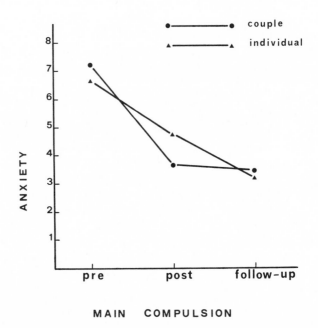

Figure 34. Self-rating of anxiety (main obsessive-compulsive problem).

1.1.4. Cognitive Modification

Cognitions are presumably of paramount importance in mediating overt compulsive behavior. For example, most washing rituals are mediated by unrealistic beliefs about the possibility of contamination and checking rituals are often provoked by ideas of harm befalling oneself or others. Although treatment by exposure *in vivo* and response prevention is not directly aimed at treating obsessive thoughts that trigger or accompany overt rituals, such obsessive thoughts often decrease spontaneously as a result of treatment. In general, however, treatment affects compulsions more than obsessions. The aim of our following study (Emmelkamp, van de Helm, van Zanten, & Plochg, 1980) was to investigate whether a modification of cognitions would enhance the effectiveness of gradual exposure *in vivo*.

Fifteen obsessive-compulsive patients who were referred to our department were assigned at random to two conditions: (1) exposure *in vivo*, and (2) self-instructional training and exposure *in vivo*. The design of this study is presented in Figure 35. Treatment took place at the patients' home. The first two treatment sessions in both conditions were in relaxation training. Since relaxation training was a component of the

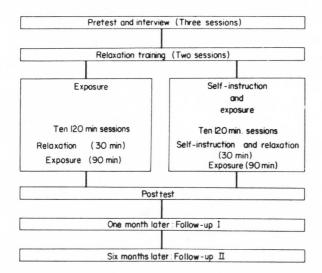

Figure 35. Design. (From "Contributions of Self-Instructional Training to the Effectiveness of Exposure *in Vivo*: A Comparison with Obsessive-Compulsive Patients" by P. M. G. Emmelkamp *et al.*, *Behaviour Research and Therapy*, 1980, *18*, Fig. 1. Copyright 1980 by Pergamon Press. Reprinted by permission.)

self-instructional training of Meichenbaum (1975), we decided to give an equal amount of relaxation to the exposure only subjects in order to keep both conditions identical apart from cognitive modification.

After two relaxation sessions, ten treatment sessions followed. Follow-ups were conducted 1 month and 6 months after treatment. Between posttest and one-month follow-up no treatment was provided. After this follow-up treatment was continued with a number of patients.

Treatment session in the exposure only condition consisted of 90 min gradual exposure *in vivo* in the company of the therapist, preceded by 30 min relaxation. With self-instructional training and exposure, the first half hour of each session was devoted to self-instructional training: Patients were trained to emit more productive self-statements. After a short relaxation period the patients cognitively rehearsed self-instructional ways (including relaxation) of handling anxiety by means of an imagination procedure. The patient had to imagine the situations, which had to be dealt with *in vivo* afterwards, to ascertain how anxious he felt, to become conscious of his negative self-statements, and then to replace them by more productive self-statements and relaxation. The self-instructional phase was followed by 90 min of gradual exposure *in vivo* to the same situations that were rehearsed. Patients were instructed to use their productive self-statements during the practice *in vivo*. Results on anxiety and avoidance scales are shown in Figure 36.

Self-instructional training did not enhance the effectiveness of exposure *in vivo*. If anything, exposure *in vivo* appeared to be superior to the combined approach, although this difference failed to reach statistical significance on most measures. Presumably, time devoted to self-instructional practice during the exposure *in vivo* phase had slowed down the tempo in which exposure *in vivo* had been carried out. The meager results are in accord with the results of our studies with agoraphobics (Emmelkamp *et al.,* 1978; Emmelkamp & Mersch, 1982). In the present study several patients questioned the usefulness of the self-instructional training, since they did not experience that the positive self-statements were helpful during exposure *in vivo*. In spite of their attempts at controlling their anxiety, they became as anxious as before.

Although exposure *in vivo* does not directly focus on a modification of anxiety inducing cognitions, treatment leads to cognitive changes with some patients. Similar cognitive changes are found with phobic patients treated by exposure *in vivo*. However, while for phobics anxiety reduction during exposure sessions is often sufficient to let them change their unproductive thoughts, this proves to be insufficient for a number of obsessional patients. Obviously, one can hardly expect that a patient who

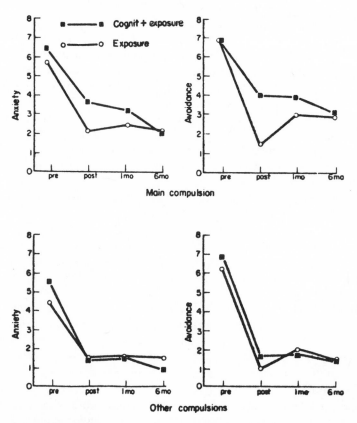

Figure 36. Contributions of self-instructional training. (From "Contributions of Self-Instructional Training to the Effectiveness of Exposure *in Vivo:* A Comparison with Obsessive-Compulsive Patients" by P. M. G. Emmelkamp *et al., Behaviour Research and Therapy,* 1980, *18*, Fig. 2. Copyright 1980 by Pergamon Press. Reprinted by permission.)

believes that someone unknown to him may die unless he carries out checking rituals will change these irrational beliefs after the experiencing of anxiety reduction during treatment by exposure *in vivo.*

Although the results of this study are negative with respect to the usefulness of self-instructional training with obsessional patients, no conclusions can be drawn with respect to the effects of other cognitive procedures. Bleijenberg (1981) attempted to study the relative contribution of behavior therapy and rational therapy with a series of ten obsessionals. Most of his subjects were not patients but volunteers; the sample appears to have been less chronic and less incapacitated than

Emmelkamp *et al.*'s (1980) patients (both on Leyton's Interference and Resistance Scales and Zung's Self-Rating Depression Scale).

Treatment involved 20 sessions (10 cognitive and 10 behavioral). Half of the patients started with cognitive therapy followed by behavior therapy. The order of treatment was reversed with the other patients. Cognitive therapy consisted of disputing the irrational beliefs and making rational self analyses concerning obsessional situations. In addition, rational emotive imagination exercises were rehearsed. The behavior therapy consisted of imaginal exposure and *in vivo* homework assignments. In some cases exposure *in vivo* was conducted in the therapist's office.

Results revealed that behavior therapy was consistently superior to cognitive therapy. On some measures (including Leyton's Interference Scale) the difference between both conditions reached statistical significance. Cognitive therapy resulted in significant improvement only on 1 out of 19 dependent variables, which obviously can be accounted for by chance. Most interestingly, cognitive therapy did *not* result in cognitive changes. Thus, the conclusion of the author that both cognitive therapy and behavior therapy were effective appears to be unsubstantiated by his data as far as the cognitive therapy is concerned. Further, conclusions seem unwarranted due to serious methodological shortcomings (e.g., treatment not standarized; no blind assessor; author served both as therapist and assessor; small number of subjects).

In summary, at present there is no evidence that cognitive modification (self-instructional training as well as rational therapy) is of any value with respect to the treatment of obsessive-compulsive behavior. Possibly, cognitive therapy may have some beneficial effects on additional problems of these patients, but further studies have to address this issue before cognitive therapy can be recommended for this purpose. Clinically, real obsessional patients are often very insecure concerning the result of their rational self-analyses and constantly seek reassurance from the therapist. If cognitive therapy is of any help, this will presumably be the case with a minority of (less severe) cases only.

1.1.5. Imaginal Exposure

A better way to change the cognitive ruminations of obsessive-compulsives may be to expose them to their obsessional thoughts for a prolonged period (Emmelkamp & Kwee, 1977). When imaginal exposure was contrasted with *in vivo* exposure, actual exposure was superior to imaginal (Rabavilas *et al.*, 1976). Subjects were 15 obsessive-compulsives with checking rituals. However, design characteristics pre-cluded conclusions with respect to long-term outcome.

More recently, Foa, Steketee, Turner, and Fischer (1980c) investi-gated whether imaginal exposure would enhance the effectiveness of *in vivo* exposure. It was hypothesized that checkers who fear disastrous consequences that cannot be produced in reality should improve more when imaginal exposure was added to actual exposure. Fifteen obsessive-compulsive patients with checking rituals and fears of disastrous con-sequences were randomly assigned to two conditions: (1) exposure *in vivo* (2 hr), and (2) exposure in imagination (90 min) followed by exposure *in vivo* (30 min). In both groups treatment involved 10 sessions. For both groups, response prevention was imposed from the first session; patients were not permitted to engage in any ritualistic behavior. Response pre-vention was conducted in the hospital or at home under the supervision of nurses or relatives. Imaginal exposure was to the feared disasters rather than to tangible cues. The results are depicted in Figure 37.

Imaginal exposure did not enhance the effectiveness at the posttest, a finding that is in accord with results of studies on phobias. However, at follow-up (11 months) patients who received both imaginal and *in vivo* exposure showed more improvement than those exposed *in vivo* only, due to relapse in the exposure *in vivo* group. Foa *et al.* (1980c) wondered whether the slightly greater long-term improvement of the combined treatment group might be attributable to their having achieved long-term habituation as compared to those who had exposure *in vivo* alone. Patients received additional treatment during the follow-up period, which might have confounded results at follow-up. Nevertheless, the results are intriguing and—when replicated—could have important consequences for the treatment of obsessive-compulsive patients who manifest thoughts of possible disaster.

1.1.6 Response Prevention

Response prevention was assumed to be the most essential com-ponent of the "apotrepic therapy" of Meyer and his colleagues. Patients were supervised by staff members 24 hr daily in order to prevent them from performing their rituals. Walton and Mather (1963) suggested that exposure to distressing stimuli was essential when anxiety evoked the ritual. Conversely, they assumed that with some obsessive-compulsives the rituals had been functionally autonomous. "Functional autonomy" meant therefore that the rituals would now be evoked by a wide range of stimuli in addition to the anxiety that originally controlled them. With

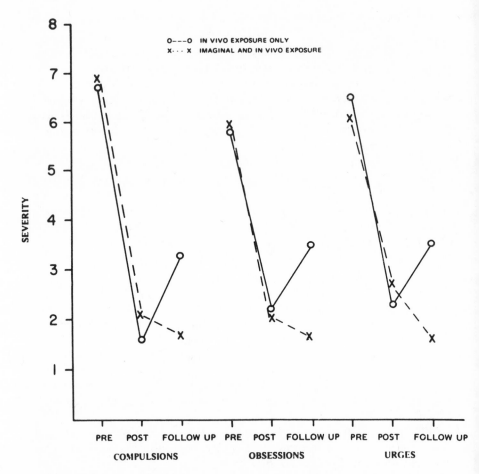

Figure 37. Mean severity of compulsions, obsessions, and urges for the two experimental groups at pre- and posttreatment and at follow-up (mean 11 months). A number of patients received additional treatment. (From "Effects of Imaginal Exposure to Feared Disasters in Obsessive-Compulsive Checkers" by E. B. Foa *et al.*, *Behaviour Research and Therapy*, 1980, *18*, Fig. 1. Copyright 1980 by Pergamon Press. Reprinted by permission.)

the latter (long-standing) cases response prevention was recommended. Although Walton and Mather describe several cases to support their hypothesis, it is clear from the description of their long-standing cases that in addition to response prevention patients were exposed to distressing stimuli.

Although most behavioral treatment programs include response prevention, few studies investigated the contribution of response prevention directly. The first study to investigate this particular issue was reported by Mills, Agras, Barlow, and Mills (1973). Five obsessive-compulsive patients were studied in single-case designs while treatment conditions were systematically varied. Response prevention was found to be more effective than when patients were simply given instructions to stop the rituals. Other series of single-case studies demonstrated again the value of response prevention (Turner, Hersen, Bellack, & Wells, 1979; Turner, Hersen, Bellack, Andrasik, & Capparrell, 1980).

To date, only one controlled between-group study was reported in the literature (Foa, Steketee, & Milby, 1980b). Eight obsessive-compulsive patients served as subjects. Patients were randomly assigned to two treatment conditions: (1) exposure alone followed by exposure and response prevention, and (2) response prevention alone followed by the combined treatment. In total, treatment consisted of 20 sessions. Exposure led to more anxiety reduction but less improvement of rituals, while the reverse was found for response prevention. When the combined treatment was applied at the second period, the differences between the groups on anxiety and ritualistic behavior disappeared. The results of this study are interesting in showing that rituals may persist after anxiety is reduced, thus challenging the two-stage theory of learning. It should be remembered that two-stage theory holds that avoidance behavior is controlled by anxiety. The results of the present study are in accord with our own clinical experience that rituals may be performed without any accompanying anxiety. For example, with some patients exposure to the distressing stimuli does not lead to anxiety or discomfort, especially when the rituals have become a matter of habit. Although the number of patients is small, the Foa et al. (1980b) study suggests that it is therapeutically wise to combine exposure and response prevention in a routine treatment program. Clinically, the emphasis on exposure or response prevention will depend on the behavioral analysis.

1.1.7. Duration of Exposure

The duration of exposure varied from study to study. In our own research program we usually applied exposure for 2 hr continuously, but others found beneficial effects with sessions of shorter duration. For example, exposure sessions in the studies conducted by Rachman and his colleagues usually lasted for 45 min.

Rabavilas et al. (1976) set out to investigate the optimal duration effect of exposure sessions with 12 obsessive-compulsive patients. Prolonged exposure in vivo (2 hr) was found to be significantly superior to short exposure segments. Short exposure consisted of 10-min exposure, followed by 5-min neutral material followed by 10-min exposure, etc., until the 2-hr period elapsed. Short exposure *in vivo* had a deteriorating effect on patient's affective state.

The results of this study have important implications for conducting exposure sessions in clinical practice. First, it might be necessary that the therapist prolong sessions up to 2 hr with obsessional patients. In addition, it is important that during exposure sessions no breaks occur. Thus, drinking coffee, having a friendly chat with the patient, or discussing additional problems during an exposure session may all be counter therapeutic. Therefore, it is important that the therapists explain in advance the details of the treatment and the necessary conditions to achieve optimal therapeutic outcome. As a rule, it is recommended to postpone any discussion of additional problems the patients wants to talk about to the end of the exposure session.

1.2. Related Issues

In this section studies will be discussed dealing with issues that may have important implications for the clinical management of obsessive-compulsive patients. Most of these studies were uncontrolled.

1.2.1. Patients as Cotherapist

There is some limited evidence that (former) patients may be used as cotherapist in the treatment of obsessive-compulsives. To date, two studies (Hand & Tichatzky, 1979; Wonneberger, Henkel, Aventewicz, & Hasse, 1975) used patients as cotherapists. Wonneberger *et al.* treated seven obsessive-compulsives by exposure *in vivo* and response prevention without any therapist contact. Treatment sessions were conducted by a student who simulated an obsessive-compulsive patient. The "model-patient" demonstrated exposure to distressing stimuli and refrained from ritualizing. The "real" patient had to follow suit. Treatment consisted of 14 sessions lasting for 30 min each. Despite the short exposure sessions treatment resulted in beneficial effects on anxiety and avoidance ratings. Improvement hardly generalized to the natural environment of the patient. Patients did not discover that the "model-patients" actually were stooges.

The second study (Hand & Tichatzky, 1979) investigated the efficacy of a package approach for obsessive-compulsives. Their treatment package consisted of a number of ingredients, including family involvement, group therapy and exposure *in vivo*. After a few demonstrations of how exposure sessions should be conducted each patient was assigned to another patient as cotherapist. In general, *in vivo* training took place

in the home setting. The fading out of therapist was not without difficulties: "there was heavy protest that the treatment was much too
short" (p. 287). Preliminary results revealed that patient-assisted exposure failed. Since treatment consisted of so many elements, conclusions with respect to the value of having a patient assist as a cotherapist
were precluded.

In summary, although controlled studies of the use of patients as
cotherapist are lacking, there is some evidence that this approach might
be of value. Apart from the cost-effectiveness of treatment, there may be
other advantages associated with this approach. When exposure *in vivo*
is conducted by former patients, patients might feel better understood
and experience treatment as less harsh than when conducted by a
therapist. Similarly, former patients might be better able to convince
patients of the necessity to deal with *all* obsessions, including those that
do not bother them at the moment. Obviously, not all obsessive-
compulsives will be suitable therapists.

1.2.2. Group Treatment

Although group exposure *in vivo* has been widely studied with
agoraphobics, no controlled studies have been published on group treatment with obsessive-compulsives. Treatment in the study of Hand and
Tichatzky (1979) consisted of group treatment but they did not investigate this particular issue. The group treatment dealt with obsessive-
compulsive problems as well as with additional problems (marital and
social interactions). Since the study was uncontrolled, no conclusions can
be drawn with respect to the value of group treatment. Marks *et al.* (1975)
reported beneficial effects of booster sessions conducted in groups with
patients who had been treated individually with exposure *in vivo* and
response prevention, but no data were provided.

Since very few obsessive-compulsives apply for treatment (1 to 2% of
outpatients), group treatment will be difficult to organize for most treatment agencies. Therefore, studies investigating the value of group
treatment for obsessive-compulsives are difficult to realize. Further,
when such a study would demonstrate group treatment to enhance treatment effectiveness, such a finding would probably be of little clinical
utility, because of the small availability of suitable patients.

1.2.3. Interpersonal Problems

Behavioral research into the treatment of obsessive-compulsives
almost exclusively dealt with the effectiveness of various exposure procedures and with parameters influencing its outcome. Since behavioral

theories about the development and the maintenance of obsessive-compulsive disorders relied heavily on the anxiety reduction hypothesis, it is not surprising that most of the behavioral research in this area focused on exposure procedures. Although the procedures have been found to be effective, it needs to be stressed that not all patients can be helped by these methods. In addition, some of the patients who derive benefit from treatment by exposure need additional treatment for related problems. Thus exposure procedures are not the panacea for all obsessive-compulsive patients.

In a number of obsessive-compulsives the rituals seem to serve another function. This section will deal with the treatment of the interpersonal problems of these patients.

1.2.4. Marital Complication

System theorists hold that neurotic symptoms play a functional role within the family system, but there are little data to support this position. Obviously, a number of obsessive-compulsives have interpersonal problems, but this does not necessarily mean that these conflicts are instrumental in causing the obsessive-compulsive disorder. For a detailed discussion of this issue the reader is referred to Chapter 10. At present, there is little evidence that behavioral treatments that focus on the marital relationship are of much value with respect to improvement of the obsessional problems.

Recently, Cobb et al. (1980) compared the effects of behavioral marriage therapy and exposure in vivo in a cross-over design. Eleven patients (four obsessive-compulsives) who had both marital discord and phobic-obsessive disorders were randomly assigned to two conditions. Marital therapy consisted of reciprocity counseling; communication skills and sexual skills training were added where indicated. With exposure in vivo the spouse acted as cotherapist. During exposure, marital problems were not treated. Results indicated that exposure treatment led to significant improvement in both phobic-obsessive and in marital targets, while marriage therapy led to improvements only in marital targets. It is noteworthy that for marital targets marital therapy was not significantly better than exposure treatment.

The results of this study have to be qualified. There is little evidence that the particular approach of marital therapy as conducted in this study was effective in treating relationship problems. Patients did not improve on the Maudsley Marital Questionnaire, while other studies with maritally distressed couples found highly significant improvements using the same questionnaire (Emmelkamp, van der Helm, van Zanten, &

MacGillavry, 1982). This suggests that behavioral marital therapy may be less appropriate for this population. It remains to be seen if other approaches are more profitable for obsessive-compulsives with marital complications. Several controlled studies found system-theoretic counseling to have beneficial effects with marital distressed couples (Boelens, Emmelkamp, MacGillavry, & Markvoort, 1980; Emmelkamp *et al.*, 1982) and further studies are needed to investigate whether a system-theoretic approach is more appropriate for treating the marital problems of obsessive-compulsives. Furthermore, the finding of Cobb *et al.* that exposure treatment led to improved marital functioning might be attributable to the conjoint treatment format, rather than to exposure *per se.*

Although there is no controlled clinical evidence at the present time for the value of marital therapy for obsessive-compulsive disorders, clinical experience and a few published uncontrolled studies suggest that marital therapy may have beneficial effects for selected patients (e.g., Hand, Spoehring, & Stanik, 1977; Hand &Tichatzky, 1979; Stern & Marks, 1973). To give an example, when obsessive-compulsive behavior is triggered by jealousy, marital therapy may enhance treatment effectiveness (Cobb & Marks, 1979). Whether the marital problems of the patient should be the focus of treatment and if so, which type of intervention has to be used to deal with these problems depends on the functional analysis of the case.

1.2.5. Assertiveness Training

Clinical observations suggest that obsessive-compulsive patients are often social-anxious and unassertive. In some of these cases the obsessive-compulsive problems might serve the function of avoiding people. In such cases exposure and response prevention procedures alone are usually of limited value and need to be supplemented by other therapeutic interventions. Let me illustrate this point by a case report (Emmelkamp, 1982).

The patient was a 32-year-old unmarried woman with extensive obsessive-compulsive problems. As she defined the problem, she was afraid of contaminating other people and, therefore, she had to avoid contact with people: She had no relationships, lived socially isolated, and no one was allowed to visit her home. At the start of treatment, the patient denied having any problems in social relationships. In her view, the lack of acquaintances and friends was not the cause but the result of her obsessive-compulsive problems. Initially, treatment was directed to her obsessive-compulsive problems by means of gradual exposure *in vivo* plus response prevention. Although rather slowly, treatment along these lines progressed as long as direct contact with people was avoided. At that time the therapist discussed with her the possibility that the rituals could serve the function of avoiding people because of her anxiety in social situations. Although the patient was reluctant to accept such a definition of her problem, she finally agreed on treatment of these problems by assertive training. During the course of the assertive training, the patient became aware that her obsessive-compulsive problems were enhanced when she was criticized or when she did not know how to deal with social situations. After having become more assertive, the patient succeeded on her own initiative in shaking hands with people, joining social clubs, taking dancing lessons, and inviting people into her own home without feeling urges to execute compulsive rituals. The evidence in this case is incomplete because delayed effects of the exposure *in vivo* phase cannot be ruled out.

It is astonishing how little controlled work has been carried out on assertive training for obsessive-compulsives, although there has been some suggestion in the literature that obsessive-compulsives could be treated by assertive training (Walton & Mather, 1963; Wolpe, 1958). In the light of our often successful treatment of obsessive-compulsive patients with assertive training after preceding exposure *in vivo* treatment, it became a matter of interest to know whether assertive training on its own would lead to a reduction of the obsessive-compulsive problems. Another case study (Emmelkamp, 1982) may yield some information that is of direct bearing on the present question. The patient was a young man in his early twenties with obsessive-compulsive checking as his main problem. He worked as a motor mechanic and his work took at least four times as long as compared to his colleagues. On the ground of a functional analysis it was hypothesized that his compulsive checking was caused by his social anxiety and unassertiveness. After a base-line period of three weeks, 12 sessions of assertive training followed. Treatment was conducted twice weekly. The patient had to report on social situations in which he was unassertive or he felt uneasy. These situations were discussed and a more adequate handling of these situations was trained through modeling by the therapist and behavioral rehearsal. After each session, the patient received homework assignments in order to use his newly acquired skills in his daily life. These homework assignments followed a hierarchy and involved situations such as looking at people, starting a conversation with strangers, inviting people home, refusing requests, etc. After this phase of treatment, base-line conditions were reintroduced and then treatment focused directly on his obsessive-compulsive problems by means of self-controlled exposure in vivo. Exposure *in vivo* lasted 6 weeks (7 sessions). Then the posttest was applied.

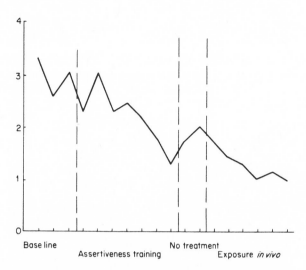

Figure 38. Weekly means of daily ratings of obsessive-compulsive problems (range 0–8). (From "Recent Developments in the Behavioral Treatment of Obsessive-Compulsive Disorders" by P. M. G. Emmelkamp, in J. Boulougouris (ed.), *Learning Theories Approaches in Psychiatry*. Copyright 1982 by Wiley. Reprinted by permission.)

Figure 38 presents patient's daily ratings of his obsessive-compulsive problems during the course of treatment. Clearly, assertive training led to a clinically significant reduction of his obsessive-compulsive problems. During the second phase of treatment (exposure *in vivo*), the improvement continues. Treatment by assertive training led not only to less anxiety experienced in social situations, but the improvement generalized to the obsessive-compulsive problems and depression. Exposure *in vivo* could add little to the improvements already achieved (see Figure 39).

Further positive results of assertive training with another series of obsessional patients were found in the study of Emmelkamp and van de Heyden (1980) which will be discussed later on. The positive results of assertiveness training indicate that obsessive-compulsives may benefit from other approaches other than exposure *in vivo* and emphasize the value of a functional analysis.

1.3. Follow-up

Most studies reviewed in the preceding sections involved short-term outcome, with follow-up usually taking place 1 to 6 months after

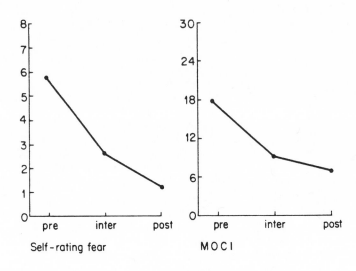

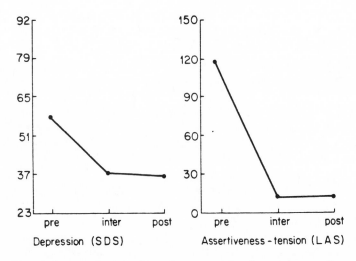

Figure 39. Relative contribution of assertiveness training (pretest-intermediate test) and exposure *in vivo* (intermediate test–posttest). (From "Recent Developments in the Behavioral Treatment of Obsessive-Compulsive Disorders" by P. M. G. Emmelkamp, in J. Boulougouris (ed.), *Learning Theories Approaches in Psychiatry*. Copyright 1982 by Wiley. Reprinted by permission.)

treatment. Several studies provided follow-up data 2 to 6 years after treatment which will be discussed in detail below.

The first follow-up study on the behavioral treatment of obsessive-compulsives was reported by Marks, Hodgson, and Rachman (1975). Twenty patients were reassessed 2 years after completion of treatment. Unfortunately, only half of the patients were interviewed, thus most data consisted of self-ratings. At 2-year follow-up, 14 of the patients were classified as "much improved," 1 as "improved," and 5 as "unchanged." Improvement indicates a reduction on pooled anxiety and avoidance ratings by 2–3 points on an 0–8 scale. "Much improved" indicates a reduction by 4 or more points. The mean number of treatment sessions was 23, including further domiciliary treatment after the actual experimental period.

Another follow-up study was reported by Boulougouris (1977). Fifteen obsessive-compulsives underwent follow-up 2.8 years after treatment (range 2–5 years). Treatment involved both imaginal and *in vivo* exposure. Most of the sessions consisted of exposure *in vivo*. Nine patients were rated as improved at follow-up. The most improved patients were washers. Treatment was least effective with patients who had ruminative thoughts and checking rituals. More recently, Rabavilas and Boulougouris (1979) reported on mood changes in the same sample and found that patients with significant mood changes showed significant relapse at follow-up.

Foa and Goldstein (1978) reported follow-up data of 21 obsessive-compulsives. Follow-up ranged from 3 months to 3 years (mean of 1 year). Treatment consisted of imaginal and *in vivo* exposure. On the average patients received 20 sessions. Two-thirds of patients were classified as improved at follow-up. In contrast to Boulougouris's data, patients who relapsed at follow-up ($n = 3$) were all washers. Conversely, three checkers who were mildly or moderately symptomatic at the end of treatment continued to improve after therapy.

Emmelkamp and Rabbie (1981) reassessed 23 patients who were treated in the experimental trials of Emmelkamp and Kraanen (1977) and Emmelkamp et al. (1980). After the experiment which consisted of 10 treatment sessions of gradual exposure *in vivo*, two-thirds ($n = 14$) of the patients received additional treatment sessions, which were adapted to the individual needs of the patients (including assertive training, marital therapy, and cognitive restructuring). When we exclude one patient who received 150 sessions, the mean number of treatment sessions (clinical trial plus further treatment) averaged 21 sessions. Follow-up ranged from 3–6 years (mean of 4.5 years). Results are presented in Figure 40.

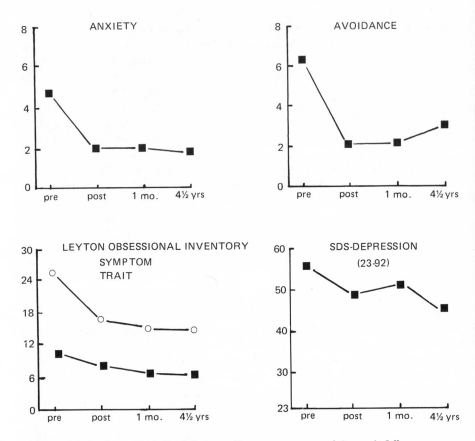

Figure 40. Results to 4.5 years follow-up. Between posttest and 1-month follow-up, no treatment was provided. After 1-month follow-up a number of patients received additional treatment. (From "Psychological Treatment of Obsessive-Compulsive Disorders: A Follow-Up 4 Years after Treatment" by P. M. G. Emmelkamp and D. Rabbie in B. Janson *et al.* (eds.), *Biological Psychiatry.* Copyright 1982 by Elsevier. Reprinted by permission.)

At follow-up, 17 of 23 patients were found to have improved on the pooled self-ratings on the anxiety and avoidance scales. Improvement was maintained on anxiety and avoidance ratings, Leyton Obsessional Inventory and depression (Zung-SDS). Further analyses of the data revealed significant improvement on depression and Leyton-Trait between posttest and follow-up.

Interestingly, depression predicted success of treatment at posttest (LOI-symptom, $r = .53$; LOI-trait, $r = .41$; Avoidance Scale, $r = .44$), but not at follow-up. Thus, there is no relationship between initial depression and success of treatment at follow-up (4.5 years after treatment). Presumably, the finding that initial depression was unrelated to long-term outcome is due to the fact that depressed patients received further behavioral treatment after the experimental trial. Depressed patients received more additional treatment sessions as compared with nonde-pressed patients. Thus, the findings suggest that high-depressed patients may benefit equally from behavioral treatment as do low-depressed patients if they receive additional treatment sessions. The results indicate that for the majority of patients, hospitalization is unnecessary since treatment was conducted in the patients' homes and natural environment. Although no formal control group was included, the results at 4.5 years follow-up are impressive as the patient group was chronic and severely incapacitated at the start of treatment. Further, Figure 40 shows that the major changes took place within the remarkably short space of one month of intensive behavioral treatment. The improvements achieved were consolidated in the years following active behavioral treatment. Thus, it is logical to assume that the improvements found can be ascribed to the specific treatment, rather than to spontaneous remission.

It is unlikely that the improvement should be attributed to the use of tricyclic antidepressants. Only a minority ($n = 4$) of patients used these drugs and two of these patients were *failures* at follow-up. Further, with the other two patients previous use of antidepressants did not lead to improvement of the obsessive-compulsive behavior: Improvement commenced during the intensive behavioral treatment.

Finally, the improvement of depression is interesting. There are some indications that the amelioration of depression should be attributed to the improvement of the obsessive-compulsive problems. It should be noted that only during the active phase of treatment, a decrease in depression took place: first, during the month of intensive treatment and second, during the treatment period immediately following the 1 month follow-up. In the period between the posttest and the 1 month follow-up no treatment was provided and during this period depression remained stable.

Recently, we followed up another sample of obsessive-compulsives. Patients investigated had been treated in the experimental trial comparing conjoint therapy with individual treatment. All patients were treated with self-controlled exposure *in vivo*. The partner of the patient was involved in the treatment of half of the sample. As in the Emmelkamp and Rabbie study, patients were visited by a member of our research team, with whom the patient had had no contact previously. One patient could not be reassessed since she moved to another country. The data of another patient, who was classified as much improved at follow-up, were

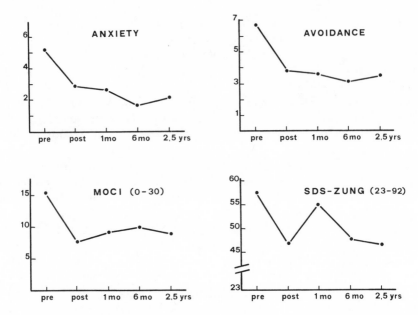

Figure 41. Results to 2.5 years follow-up. Between posttest and 1-month follow-up, no treatment was provided. After 1-month follow-up a number of patients received additional treatment.

not processed in the data analysis because of the relatively short follow-up period (less than 2 years). The data of the remaining ten patients will be discussed. Follow-up ranged from 2 to 3 years (mean of 2.5 years). Figure 41 shows the results on anxiety, avoidance, Maudsley Obsessional-Compulsive Inventory (MOCI) and Zung-Depression. Multivariate analysis of variance revealed a significant time effect which was also reflected in the univariate F-ratios (Anxiety, $F = 14.13$; Avoidance, $F = 6.38$; MOCI, $F = 7.57$, and SDS, $F = 3.57$). Further analyses revealed that improvement was maintained after the posttest up to 2.5 years follow-up. Interestingly, depression showed a slightly different picture. Depressed mood improved at the posttest, but a relapse was noted at one-month follow-up. However, further improvement occurred between 1 month and 6 months follow-up, during which period most patients received additional treatment for related problems. No relapse occurred at 2.5 years follow-up. This pattern clearly suggests that improvement in depression is related to treatment. It should be remembered that during the period between posttest and one month follow-up no treatment was provided. Figure 42 presents the classification in terms of improvement of the patients who were followed up in our studies

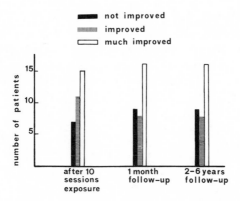

Figure 42. Number of patients rated as improved on pooled rating for obsessive anxiety and avoidance.

(n = 33). At follow-up (range 2–6 years), 16 patients were rated as "much improved," 8 patients were rated as "improved,"and 9 patients as "not improved." Only 3 patients who were classified as "improved" at posttest relapsed at follow-up, while one patient who was classified as "un-improved" at posttest was rated as "improved" at follow-up. Thus improvement after five weeks exposure predicted good outcome at long-term follow-up. Finally, there was no evidence of symptom substitution. Generally, improvement generalized to other areas of functioning as manifested in the improvement of depressed mood.

A summary of the follow-up studies is provided in Table 13. In conclusion, behavioral treatment of obsessive-compulsives is highly effective with about 70% of the patients and the effects are maintained up to 4.5 years follow-up.

Table 13. Summary of Long-Term Follow-up Studies

	N	Duration of symptoms (years)	Treatment	Follow-up (years)	Outcome at follow-up
Marks *et al.* (1975)	20	10	Exposure *in vivo*	2	75% improved
Boulougouris (1977)	15	8	Exposure in imag. + Exposure *in vivo*	2.8	60% improved
Emmelkamp & Rabbie (1981)	23	12	Exposure *in vivo*	4.5	73% improved
Emmelkamp (present data)	11	8	Exposure *in vivo*	2.5	

2. TREATMENT OF OBSESSIONS

Research into the treatment of obsessions has lagged significantly behind that into the treatment of compulsions, probably due to the small prevalence of patients with obsessional ruminations unaccompanied by rituals.

Behavioral treatments for obsessions can be grouped into three categories. The first approach involves procedures that focus on a removal of the obsessions (e.g., thought-stopping and aversion therapy). The second series of treatments is directed at habituation to the distressing thoughts. Examples of this strategy are prolonged exposure in imagination and satiation training. The third approach does not deal directly with the obsessions but attempts to treat other problems, presumed to underlie the obsessions. Treating obsessional patients by assertiveness training is an example of the latter strategy.

2.1. Dismissal Training

In thought-stopping, patients are requested to imagine one of their obsessions, and then to stop them at the therapist's command. In our studies the following procedure was used. Patients are asked to reproduce an obsession in their minds and to raise their finger when the obsession is obtained clearly. This is immediately followed by a stop stimulus. The following fading procedure is used:

1. Therapist makes a sudden noise (loud hooter).
2. Therapist shouts "stop."
3. Therapist says "stop."
4. Patient shouts "stop."
5. Patient says "stop."
6. Patient whispers "stop."
7. Patient subvocally says "stop."

If the "stop" stimulus is effective in blocking the obsession, the patient is instructed to think pleasant or neutral thoughts. Usually, the obsessions that troubled the patient most in the preceding few days are dealt with.

Following Wolpe's (1958) introduction of thought-stopping, a number of case studies were reported that demonstrated the value of this procedure in reducing unwanted thoughts. With respect to obsessional patients, a number of authors reported this procedure to have some beneficial effects (Leger, 1978, 1979; Lombardo & Turner, 1979; Samaan, 1975; Stern, 1970; Yamagami, 1971), although others were more negative about the effects achieved (Stern, 1978; Teasdale & Resin, 1978).

Only four controlled studies have been conducted in each of which thought-stopping was compared with an alternative approach. Stern *et al.* (1973) compared thought-stopping with a placebo condition (stopping neutral thoughts). Treatment was tape recorded. Eleven patients participated in the trial. Treatment had a weak effect: Stopping of obsessional thoughts proved to be no more effective than stopping of neutral thoughts.

Another controlled study was reported by Hackman and McLean (1975), who treated 10 patients in a cross-over design. Treatment involved four sessions of flooding *in vivo* followed by thought-stopping or vice versa. It was found that thought-stopping was practically as effective as flooding. It is not clear whether thought-stopping was effective in dealing with the obsessive ideation *per se*. Their sample included a number of patients in whom rituals were prominent, and the effect on obsessions was not given separately from that on rituals.

Emmelkamp and Kwee (1977) treated obsessional patients by thought-stopping and prolonged exposure in imagination and found no differences between both procedures. In a following study (Emmelkamp & van de Heyden, 1980) thought-stopping was compared with assertive training. Most patients seemed to have benefitted more from assertive training than from thought-stopping. These studies will be discussed in more detail below.

Another form of dismissal training is aversion therapy. Several authors claimed that obsessional thoughts can be changed by aversion therapy (Bass, 1973; Kenny, Solyom, & Solyom, 1973; Kushner & Sandler, 1966; Mahoney, 1971) and aversion relief (Solyom & Kingstone, 1973). To date, only one controlled study investigated the efficacy of aversion therapy with obsessional patients. Kenny, Mowbray, and Lalani (1978) compared faradic disruption of obsessive ideation with no-treatment. With faradic disruption an electric shock was given when patients reproduced an obsessive thought in their minds. It was found that patients who were treated by faradic disruption showed more improvement than the waiting list control group.

Taking the controlled studies together, dismissal training leads to variable results. Thought-stopping has no adequate theoretical basis, although some attempts have been made to explain the effects achieved (Beech & Vaughan, 1978). Rachman (1976) speaks of thought-stopping as an *ad hoc* technique that rests on its empirical strength. Unfortunately, as evidenced in the previous review, even its empirical strength is far from convincing.

2.2. Habituation Training

Rachman (1971, 1978) hypothesized that obsessional ruminations may be regarded as noxious stimuli to which patients have difficulty in habituating. Rachman (1976) suggested "satiation training" as method for treating obsessions. In addition, it was proposed to instruct patients to refrain from putting things right both overtly and covertly. Obsessional patients often engage in neutralizing thoughts in order to undo the possible harmful effects of their obsessions. For example, one of our patients with the obsession "God is mad" had to think positive thoughts ("I remain Catholic") each time when the obsession occurred, which led to temporary relief of anxiety provoked by the blasphemous thought. The neutralizing behavior engaged in by obsessional patients presumably serves the same function as the checking or washing rituals of obsessive-compulsives (i.e., to produce anxiety reduction).

With satiation training patients are requested to evoke and maintain the obsessions for prolonged periods up to fifteen minutes. Originally (Rachman, 1971) it was proposed to deal with the most disturbing obsessions, but in a later publication hierarchical presentation was preferred: "the troublesome obsessions are subjected to habituation training in ascending order as for desensitization" (Rachman & Hodgson, 1980, p. 282). With patients who engage in "neutralizing activities" response prevention instructions are added.

The efficacy of satiation training has not been evaluated. Both Rachman (1976), Broadhurst (1976), and Stern (1978) provided accounts of patients who had been successfully treated by satiation training, but Beech and Vaughan (1978) reported failure with two cases treated by habituation (p. 96). However, their study may have militated against revealing any improvement, as the ruminations were presented by tape.

Finally, two analog studies have a bearing on this issue. Studies of Rachman and de Silva (1978), and Parkinson and Rachman (1980) suggested that with repeated practice the duration and accompanying discomfort of "normal obsessions" formed to instructions decreased. However, the clinical value of these studies is limited since normal adults rather than obsessional patients participated in these studies. Their "normal obsessions" were of mild intensity.

About the same time Rachman developed his satiation method, we started to study the effects of prolonged exposure to obsessional material on obsessional patients (Emmelkamp & Kwee, 1977). With this procedure the patient is exposed uninterruptedly to his obsessions for 60 min. He is instructed to sit in a relaxed way and to close his eyes. Next, the therapist asks the patient to imagine as vividly as possible the obsessions described by the therapist and not to avoid imagining these scenes in any way. Special attention is given to prevent the patient from neutralizing the effects of their obsessional thoughts during exposure sessions. Again and again the obsessions that arouse the most anxiety are described. If the tension aroused by imagining a certain obsession has dropped considerably, this scene is no longer used. The scenes presented by the therapist consist solely of the obsessional material; no attempt is made to increase the feelings of anxiety. For example, in one patient seeing a child aroused the obsessional thought of hitting out in the child's direction. He "sees" himself making this movement and thinks he has actually hit the child, but the precise nature of the consequences is not clear. During the treatment, the imagining of the scenes stopped at the same moment—the moment at which the patient hits the child—and no attempt was made to put the consequences of this act into the concrete form of the child's being wounded, dying, or being buried.

Prolonged exposure differs from satiation training in several respects. First, the therapist guides the imagining of the patient actively in order to prevent covert avoidance and neutralizing. Second, the sessions are prolonged to facilitate habituation occurrence. Third, the most troublesome obsessions are used from the beginning rather than presenting scenes in ascending order. It is important to note that no breaks occur during the 60-min sessions apart from a few seconds after each scene presentation when the patient has to rate his level of anxiety.

To establish whether the process of treatment by prolonged exposure in imagination could be interpreted in terms of habituation, we had our patients rate the level of subjective anxiety throughout treatment sessions. It would be predicted by a habituation model that continuous presentation of obsessional stimuli would lead to a decrement in response to these stimuli during treatment sessions. As a rule, habituation of subjective anxiety occurs within sessions. Equivalent changes in response to phobic stimuli have been observed by Foa and Chambless (1978). The reduction in subjective distress to ruminative stimuli is illustrated in Figure 43. After a predicted increase in level of subjective anxiety at the beginning of each session, the ratings show a consistent reduction within sessions. The peaks in the graphs are due to the introduction of new obsessional material. However, it has to be said that with a few cases we failed to achieve within-session habituation and subsequent reduction in obsessive thoughts. Let us now turn to two pilot studies in which we attempted to investigate the efficacy and the therapeutic process of prolonged exposure in imagination.

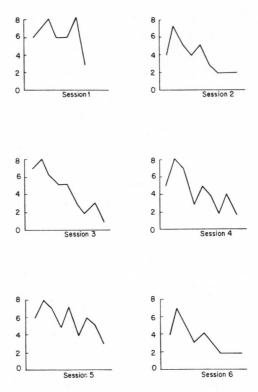

Figure 43. Subjective anxiety ratings of one patient during treatment by prolonged exposure in imagination to obsessions. (From "Recent Developments in the Behavioral Treatment of Obsessive-Compulsive Disorders" by P. M. G. Emmelkamp, in J. Boulougouris (ed.), *Learning Theories Approaches in Psychiatry.* Copyright 1982 by Wiley. Reprinted by permission.)

2.2.1. Prolonged Exposure versus Thought-Stopping

Emmelkamp and Kwee (1977) compared the efficacy of prolonged exposure in imagination with that of thought-stopping. Subjects were five patients whose major problem was obsessional ruminations but who did not suffer from compulsive rituals. A cross-over design was used. Thus, all patients received both treatments.

The first four sessions were used for information gathering and pretest. One week's baseline was carried out before and after the first treatment and again after the second treatment. Then the posttest was carried out. Each treatment consisted of five sessions of 60 min each.

Patients kept count of the number of obsessions (frequency) and had to rate their *distress* on a 0–8 scale each day. In addition, at the pretest and posttest they completed the Leyton Obsession Inventory and the Self-Rating Depression Scale.

After the completion of both treatments, patients showed improvement on the Leyton Obsessional Inventory and on distress ratings. Results in frequency of obsessions are presented in Figure 44. No clear differences were found between both procedures. Patients who responded favorably to the treatment usually derived equal benefit from both procedures. This suggests that a common mechanism in both treatments is responsible for the improvement.

Both with thought-stopping and with prolonged exposure, patients are exposed to their obsessions. However, the way in which this exposure is carried out is different: with thought-stopping short exposure trials are used, while with prolonged exposure the exposure is continuous. We assume that the effects of thought-stopping may also be due to habituation.

2.2.2. Relevant versus Irrelevant Exposure

The aim of our second study (Emmelkamp & Giesselbach, 1981) was two-fold: First, to replicate the therapeutic value of prolonged exposure in imagination with another series of obsessional patients, and second, to investigate whether the effects of prolonged exposure in imagination are due to habituation to the obsessions or, alternatively, could be accounted for by habituation to fear in general. Once more a cross-over design was

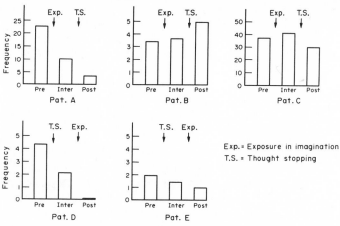

Figure 44. Frequency of obsessions. (From "Obsessional Ruminations: A Comparison between Thought-Stopping and Prolonged Exposure in Imagination" by P. M. G. Emmelkamp and E. G. Kwee in *Behaviour Research and Therapy*, 1977, *15*, Fig. 1. Copyright 1977 by Pergamon Press. Reprinted by permission.)

implemented with six patients with obsessional ruminations unaccompanied by compulsive rituals. Patients whose obsessions involved harming others or harming themselves were excluded from participation, since these patients were treated in another experimental trial (Emmelkamp & van der Heyden, 1980) which was conducted in the same time period. Half of the patients received six sessions of prolonged exposure to relevant cues followed by six sessions of prolonged exposure to irrelevant cues, and the remaining patients had the treatment in the reverse order. The prolonged exposure to relevant cues procedure was similar to that described above. With prolonged exposure to irrelevant cues patients were uninterruptedly exposed to scenes that were made up of situations that anyone would fear. For each patient, the therapist selected situations that were particularly anxiety arousing and were unrelated to the patients' obsessions. These scenes involved situations such as being burnt to death, being strangled, being devoured by a tiger, dying in an aircrash, etc. Patients had to rate their anxiety after each scene presentation. If a scene ceased to arouse anxiety, the scene was no longer used.

Total treatment led to reduction in the number of obsessions and to significant improvements on the Leyton Obsessional Inventory. The results of this study indicate that relevant exposure resulted in more improvement than irrelevant exposure (see Figure 45). Actually, irrelevant exposure even led to a significant deterioration on the distress rating. Taken together, these data indicate that prolonged exposure to the obsessions is a valuable treatment for obsessional ruminations and corroborate the findings of Emmelkamp and Kwee (1977).

The present data are in contrast with the results of a study by Watson and Marks (1971). These investigators studied the role of relevant versus irrelevant fear cues in imaginal flooding using agoraphobic patients as subjects. The two treatments did not differ from each other in their effects although anxiety reduction was probably effected through different mechanisms. On the other hand, McCutcheon and Adams (1975) found that relevant exposure was more effective than irrelevant exposure with subjects who were afraid of surgical operations, which is in line with the findings of the present study.

Prolonged exposure to obsessional material is a valuable treatment but not the panacea for the treatment of obsessional ruminations. While prolonged exposure leads to clinically meaningful improvement for most patients, a number of them need additional treatment for related problems. Of the 11 patients treated by prolonged exposure in the studies by Emmelkamp and Kwee (1977) and Emmelkamp and Giesselbach (1981), seven received additional treatment after completion of the experimental trial. The two cases who did not need further treatment in

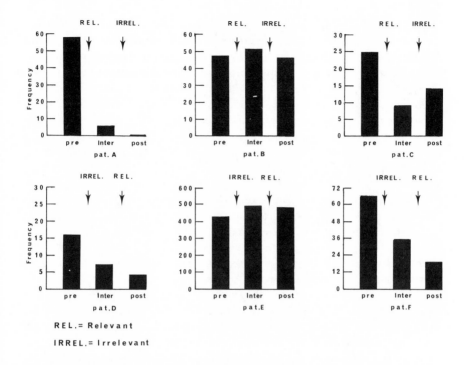

REL.= Relevant

IRREL.= Irrelevant

Figure 45. Frequency of obsessions. (From Emmelkamp & Giesselbach, 1981.)

the study of Emmelkamp and Giesselbach differed from the other patients in that their obsessions started after a traumatic experience. The obsessional ruminations of one patient started just after a bank robbery while the second patient's obsessions started after an operation for breast cancer. The other patients could not recall any traumatic experience relating to the genesis of their obsessions. Treatment by exposure was clearly unsuccessful with a patient whose obsessions consisted of existential doubts, the content of which changed regularly. This patient experienced little anxiety during treatment by relevant exposure, hence habituation could not occur. All other patients showed habituation of subjective anxiety when exposed to their obsessions which might be a good prognostic index for success of relevant exposure. Obviously, further studies are needed before more definitive conclusions can be drawn.

In sum, habituation training by means of prolonged exposure in imagination holds promise for the treatment of obsessional ruminations. The therapeutic mechanism by which this procedure achieves its results, seems to be exposure to obsessional material instead of exposure to irrelevant fear cues. It should be noted that exposure to obsessional stimuli is a common component in such various treatment procedures for obsessions as thought-stopping, aversion therapy, and aversion relief. It is proposed that the effects achieved by these procedures are due to habituation to the obsessional material. It seems worthwhile to investigate further the optimal conditions for such an exposure with obsessional patients.

2.3. Assertiveness Training

One important category of obsessions comprises obsessions concerning harming oneself or harming others. For example, such patients may suffer from obsessions that they might kill or have killed someone or that they might commit suicide. Since we found such patients quite unassertive, we hypothesized that these patients could not handle their aggressive feelings adequately. It was proposed that the harming obsessions were generated by unexpressed aggressive feelings and by the associated guilt feelings. We wondered whether assertiveness training would lead to a more adequate handling of aggression and hence to a reduction of the harming obsessions.

To test this notion, assertiveness training and thought-stopping were compared in a cross-over study (Emmelkamp & van der Heyden, 1980). Subjects were six patients with obsessional ruminations concerning harming others or harming themselves as their major problems.

Each treatment consisted of eight sessions, with each session lasting 60 min. With assertiveness training patients were instructed to report on social situations in which they were unassertive or felt uneasy. These situations were discussed and a more adequate handling of these situations was trained through modeling by the therapist and behavior rehearsal. Thus, no standardized training program was used.

As expected most patients were indeed quite unassertive before the start of treatment as measured by an assertiveness inventory. Interviews revealed that most patients reported an increase of their obsessions during unresolved interpersonal conflicts. The relationship between aggression and obsessions was clearly demonstrated with one patient who felt quite uneasy when she was criticized. Instead of adequately reacting in such situations this patient typically thought: "I may kill you."

After the completion of both treatments, patients showed improvement on Leyton Obsessional Inventory, Distress and Assertiveness.

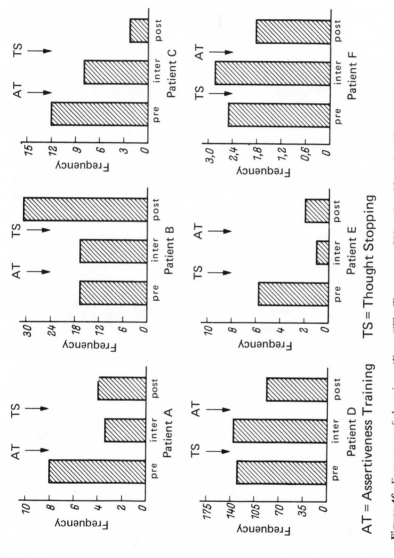

Figure 46. Frequency of obsessions. (From "The Treatment of Harming Obsessions" by P. M. G. Emmelkamp and H. van der Heyden in *Behavioural Analysis and Modification*, 1980, *4*, Fig. 1. Copyright 1980 by Urban and Schwarzenberg. Reprinted by permission.)

The results of this study show assertiveness training to be at least as effective as thought-stopping (see Figure 46). In four of the six cases a considerable decrease in the frequency of obsessions was found after assertiveness training. The results for thought-stopping were less positive: In two patients a decrease was found, but with other patients thought-stopping even led to an increase in the number of obsessions.

Although most patients seem to have benefited more from assertiveness training than from thought-stopping, the cross-over design used precludes the drawing of conclusions about the long-term effectiveness of treatment.

2.4. Concluding Comment

Although no firm conclusions can be drawn on the basis of the results of our studies, because of the small number of subjects, it does seem that prolonged exposure in imagination has beneficial effects, while the results of thought-stopping are more variable. Further, assertiveness training was found to be quite effective in the treatment of harming obsessions. Whether other obsessional patients may also benefit from assertiveness training is a question for further study.

It should be noted that with most obsessional patients, treatment was continued after the experimental trial was finished (including exposure *in vivo*, marital therapy, and assertiveness training). With several patients prolonged exposure *in vivo* to provoking stimuli was successfully applied. Whether this procedure on its own would have led to a decrease in the frequency of obsessions is unknown and deserves further study. However, this procedure is applicable to a limited category of obsessional patients only, that is, to those patients whose obsessions are triggered through external stimuli.

In some cases the obsessions seemed to be related to marital problems. For example, Emmelkamp and Giesselbach (1981) reported that divorce led to a definite improvement of the obsessional ruminations with two patients. In other cases we found marital therapy to result in beneficial effects.

Taking into account the present status of research in this area, there is little reason to recommend one particular approach for the treatment of obsessional ruminations over another. To quote Rachman (1982): "The main obstacle to the successful treatment of obsessions is the absence of effective techniques." Rather than treating obsessionals with canned procedures, it would be better to carry out a detailed analysis of each case referred for treatment and to devise treatments tailored to the individual needs of patients.

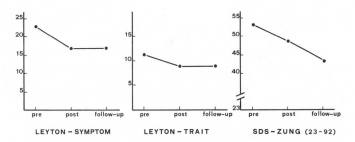

Figure 47. Results at pretest, posttest and follow-up.

2.5. Follow-up

Recently, we conducted a follow-up study on the patients treated in the studies of Emmelkamp and Kwee (1977), Emmelkamp and van der Heyden (1980), and Emmelkamp and Giesselbach (1981). Of the 17 patients who participated in the trials, 15 could be visited by a member of our research team. One patient had moved to another part of the country and the other patient did not reply to our invitation. Of the remaining patients one refused to complete questionnaires thus leaving 14 patients. Patients were seen 4 years (range 3–6 yrs.) after treatment. Patients completed the Leyton Obsessional Inventory and the Self-Rating Depression Scale at follow-up. Results are shown in Figure 47. Multivariate analysis of variance revealed a significant time effect which was also reflected in the univariate F ratios (LOI-symptom, $F = 8.75$; LOI-trait, $F = 4.40$ and SDS, $F = 4.86$). Inspection of Figure 47 shows that the improvements in obsessions (LOI) occurred during the relatively short period of the experimental trial, which makes an interpretation in terms of spontaneous remission less likely.

Interestingly, patients continued to improve in depression after the posttest. It should be remembered that similar results were found at follow-up with our obsessive-compulsive patients. The continuing improvement in depression is presumably due to the additional behavioral treatments that patients received after the completion of the experimental trial.

In sum, results at follow-up indiated that we were moderately successful in modifying the obsessions and related depression of our obsessional patients. Since all patients were treated with more than one method during the experimental trial and a number of them received broad-spectrum behavior therapy in addition, conclusions with respect to the long-term efficacy of particular treatment procedures are precluded.

9

Psychopharmacological Treatment and Psychosurgery

1. PSYCHOPHARMACOLOGICAL TREATMENT

A wide variety of drugs have been employed in the treatment of obsessive-compulsive disorders but most of the studies have thus far been uncontrolled. These drugs have included MAO inhibitors (Annesley, 1969; Jain, Swinson, & Thomas, 1970), L-Tryptophan (Yaryura-Tobias & Bhagavan, 1977), LSD (Brandrup & Vanggaard, 1977), benzodiazepines (Burrell, Culpan, Newton, Ogg, & Short, 1974), chlorpromazine (Trethowan & Scott, 1955), and tricyclic antidepressants (e.g., Ananth, Solyom, Solyom, & Sookman, 1975).

1.1. Major Tranquilizers

Trethowan and Scott (1955) investigated the efficacy of chlorpromazine in the treatment of obsessive-compulsive disorders. All patients received both chlorpromazine and placebo; the order of drugs given was randomly determined. No improvement of compulsive rituals was observed using either drug. Thus, chlorpromazine seems to be of no value with a compulsive population.

1.2. Tricyclic Antidepressants

Most studies examined the effects of tricyclic antidepressants. Some have argued that clomipramine may have a specific antiobsessional effect (e.g., Yaryura-Tobias & Neziroglu, 1975). Several case studies and uncontrolled studies reported good results using clomipramine in obsessional neurosis (Marshall, 1971; Capstick, 1975; Yaryura-Tobias & Neziroglu, 1975; Wyndowe, Solyom, & Ananth, 1975; Ananth & Van den Steen, 1977) but others were more negative about the effects achieved (Rigby, Clarren, & Kelly, 1973). Despite the existence of a considerable literature on clomipramine, it is somewhat difficult to evaluate its effect on the obsessive-compulsive behavior *per se* owing to the existence of methodological inadequacies. Many of the reports provide clinical impressions rather than more objective measures. An alternative interpretation for the improvements found after clomipramine may be that the mood (depression and anxiety) which is often associated with the obsessive-compulsive disorder improves instead of the obsessive-compulsive behavior.

1.2.1. Clomipramine: Controlled Studies

At present four controlled studies which will be discussed in some detail have been carried out. Karabanow (1977) reported a double-blind study comparing clomipramine and placebo. Twenty patients who were clinically depressed and who had, in addition, some obsessive-compulsive traits were randomly allocated to treatment with clomipramine or placebo. Clomipramine was found to be significantly superior to placebo with respect to improvement of obsessions. However, it should be noted that patients were depressed with obsessive-compulsive symptoms as a secondary reaction. When obsessional symptoms appear during depressive episodes, the obsessional symptoms usually resolve when depression improves. Thus, this study does not provide evidence for a specific anti-obsessive effect of clomipramine. Yaryura-Tobias, Neziroglu, and Bergman (1976) treated 18 obsessionals with clomipramine. Placebo was given for two weeks, starting either on the fourth or sixth week. Of the 18 subjects, 5 dropped out. To determine the effect of placebo, the week prior to placebo was compared to the week after placebo. Very few significant differences were found between clomipramine and placebo. The results of this study are difficult to interpret due to methodological confounds and high drop-out rate.

Thorén, Åsberg, Cronholm, Jörnestedt, and Träskman (1980) compared the effects of clomipramine, nortriptyline, and placebo over the course of five weeks with 22 patients. During the treatment period, the patients were encouraged to resist their compulsions, but no formal behavior therapy was given. Clomipramine was found to be superior to placebo, while the effects of nortriptyline were found to fall between those of clomipramine and placebo. No significant differences between clomipramine and nortriptyline were found. It is important to note that the superior effect of clomipramine was only found on the clinical ratings and *not* on patients' self-ratings of symptoms. Further, the improvements achieved were moderate: The mean improvement on the Leyton Obsessional Inventory for the clomipramine patients was 4.4 for Symptom, 1.9 for Trait, 13.0 for Resistance, and 12.3 for Interference, which is much less than usually is achieved with behavior therapy (see Chapter 8).

Thorén *et al.* suggest that clomipramine has a specific antiobsessive effect since "a favorable response was seen in many patients who did not have secondary depression" (p. 1285). However, Marks (1981b) reanalyzed their data and found that clomipramine seemed to act more as an antidepressant than as an antiobsessive drug. On measures both for depression and obsessive-compulsive symptoms, the group of patients who were initially the most depressed showed some improvement, whereas the nondepressed patients did not improve at all.

In addition, the finding that no significant differences were evident between clomipramine and nortriptyline casts further doubts on the presumed antiobsessive effect of clomipramine. It has been suggested that clomipramine has favorable effects in obsessional disorders because of the inhibition of serotonin uptake (Yaryura-Tobias, 1977). Nortriptyline has little effects on serotonin uptake. Thus, the finding that both drugs were about equally effective should be attributed to some other processes.

Another controlled study comparing clomipramine with placebo was reported by Marks, Stern, Mawson, Cobb, and McDonald (1980). Clomipramine produced significantly more improvement than placebo on depression measures and anxiety ratings. A further analysis (Marks, 1981b) revealed that in the least depressed patients clomipramine was about equally effective as placebo. In contrast, the most depressed patients benefited more from clomipramine than from placebo on depression measures and on rituals. This finding is in keeping with that of Thorén *et al.* (1980) and suggests that clomipramine acts as an antidepressant rather than as an antiobsessive agent.

Both Thorén *et al.* and Marks *et al.* (1980) used obsessive-compulsive patients with clear rituals as subjects. A methodological problem is that the drug effect may interact with self-exposure homework which might have confounded the results. It is possible that clomipramine enhances compliance with exposure *in vivo*, be it self-exposure homework or therapist-aided exposure. A better way to study whether clomipramine has a specific antiobsessive effect is to use obsessional patients who do not perform rituals (pure obsessionals). If clomipramine would show therapeutic effects on pure obsessionals, this effect could not be explained in terms of exposure *in vivo*.

In conclusion, in obsessional patients who have a depressed mood, clomipramine may be of some help (and probably other antidepressants as well) but this drug is of little or no value for undepressed patients. Further, even with those patients who have high depression scores at the start, behavioral treatment may result in clinically significant improvement when the course of treatment is prolonged and related problems are also dealt with (Emmelkamp & Rabbie, 1981). It is important to note that most patients who stop taking clomipramine relapse (Thorén *et al.*, 1980; Marks *et al.*, 1980). In addition, adverse effects have been reported (Marks, 1981b) such as toxic cardiovascular effects, hypomania and— when given in combination with MAO inhibitors—fatalities occurred. Thus, at present there is little reason to recommend the use of clomipramine as a routine treatment for obsessive-compulsive disorders.

1.2.2. Behavior Therapy and Antidepressants

Several studies have sought to investigate the relative contribution of pharmacological and behavioral treatments in obsessive-compulsive disorders. In a series of case studies, Turner and his colleagues systematically compared tricyclic antidepressants and behavioral treatment components. In the first study (Turner *et al.*, 1979), imipramine was compared with flooding and response prevention in one patient only. Imipramine did not have an effect on frequency of compulsive behavior. In a second study (Turner *et al.*, 1980), imipramine was again compared with flooding and response prevention in four single case experiments. Since the various treatment components were varied from patient to patient, firm conclusions cannot be drawn. Generally, the behavioral interventions appear to have led to more improvement as compared with imipramine. Imipramine had positive effects only in one patient.

Foa, Steketee, and Groves (1979) reported good results following imipramine in an uncontrolled case study. The patient had been treated with exposure *in vivo* and response prevention, which led to a reduction of ritualistic behavior, but not of obsessions and anxiety. Imipramine resulted in a gradual decrease of discomfort.

The first between-group study comparing clomipramine and behavior therapy was reported by Solyom and Sookman (1977). Patients were *not* randomly allocated to treatment groups. Six patients completed treatment by clomipramine, nine patients received flooding and eight patients received thought-stopping. Most patients in the flooding group received a combination of flooding in imagination and flooding *in vivo*.

No statistical tests were reported. There was a greater reduction in the obsessive symptom score as measured on the Leyton Obsessional Inventory in the behavior therapy groups as compared with clomipramine; improvement of compulsive rituals was clinically insignificant after pharmacological treatment. However, due to serious methodological shortcomings conclusions are unwarranted.

The only double-blind controlled study comparing the effects of a tricyclic antidepressant (clomipramine) with behavioral treatment (exposure plus response prevention) was conducted at the Maudsley Hospital in London (Marks *et al.*, 1980; Rachman *et al.*, 1979). Results were reported to one year follow-up. In a 2 × 2 experimental design behavioral treatment (exposure vs. relaxation) and psychopharmacological treatment (clomipramine vs. placebo) were systematically varied. Exposure produced significant lasting improvement in rituals, but less change in mood. Clomipramine resulted in significant improvement in rituals and mood, but only in those patients who initially had depressed mood. Since all patients received exposure after some time the long-term effects of exposure alone and clomipramine alone could not be established. Although Marks *et al.* concluded that the effects of clomipramine and of exposure were additive, design characteristics limit such conclusions from being drawn from this study.

In brief, the way in which tricyclic antidepressants interact with exposure *in vivo* is still obscure.

1.3. Beta-Blockers

Only one study tested the value of beta-blockers on obsessive-compulsive disorders (Rabavilas, Boulougouris, Perissaki, & Stefanis, 1979). These investigators studied the psychophysiological arousal during internal stimulation before and after beta-blockade with practolol. Twelve patients were treated in a cross-over design. The autonomic arousal responded favorably to beta-blockade, but did not have clinically significant effects. No significant improvements were found on subjective anxiety, depression, or the Leyton Obsessional Inventory. Thus these drugs are of little use for obsessionals, which is in accord with results of studies on phobias.

2. PSYCHOSURGERY

Since psychosurgery is still practiced on obsessive-compulsive patients, it is important to look at the evidence that is provided to support claims made by proponents of this treatment such as "a good response may be obtained by treating selected obsessional patients" (Bridges, Goktepe, & Maratos, 1973, p. 673).

A number of studies have been reported since the early 1940s claiming that psychosurgery provides an effective way of treating obsessional disorders. Unfortunately, these claims are not substantiated since several issues limit conclusions from being drawn. First, there are several types of operations ranging from the standard leukotomy (Freeman & Watts, 1950) to stereotactic limbic surgery (Mitchell-Heggs, Kelly, & Richardson, 1976) that may have different effects. A number of patients receive additional operations, often of a different type (e.g., Bridges *et al.*, 1973). Second, in most studies assessment is poor, often consisting of global ratings of improvement by the therapist who is in charge of the case. Third, prospective controlled trials comparing psychosurgery patients with adequate controls have not been conducted.

2.1. Standard and Modified Leukotomy

Sternberg (1974) reviewed the earlier studies on standard and modified leukotomy conducted on obsessionals and concluded:

> The present situation, therefore, seems to be that while half the patients with obsessional disorders who have some form of leucotomy may be expected to benefit greatly, these are also the patients who have a better prognosis without leucotomy. Those undergoing operation run a 1.5 per cent to 4 per cent risk of dying. Sixteen per cent may be expected to have up to twelve epileptic fits. There may be wound complications. Improvement in the patient's condition is associated with personality change and this is paid for by a permanent brain lesion. (p. 303)

Most of these studies were concerned with standard leukotomies, a technique now largely abandoned. More recent studies reported better results and less negative side effects. An important study, which was not included in the review by Sternberg (1974) was reported by Tan, Marks, and Marset (1971). In this retrospective study, the progress of patients who had had bimedial leukotomy was compared with that of a control group of obsessional patients matched on the variables of symptom-type, onset-age, and age at treatment. Ratings were made on extracts from notes, which were available for every patient's progress in the hospital and during follow-up. All patients were followed-up for at least 5 years. At 5 year follow-up, 50% of leukotomy patients versus 23% of control patients were rated as much improved. However, the differences were not significant for obsessions, general anxiety, or depression. Further, most leukotomy patients were not cured: Only 2 patients out of 24 patients claimed complete relief from their obsessions. Twelve were readmitted at some stage during follow-up, twice in three cases and three times in one case. In addition, six patients had a second leukotomy (a full prefrontal leukotomy with five patients). Taken into account the retrospective nature of the study, the inadequate assessments, the inadequate matching on treatment related variables, and the serious side effects reported there seems little support for the conclusion of Tan *et al.* that "modified leucotomy is a useful treatment in highly selected patients with long-standing severe obsessions and anxiety" (p. 163).

Another study which was omitted in the review of Sternberg (1974) was reported by Kelly, Walter, Mitchell-Heggs, and Sargant (1972), who studied the effects of modified leukotomy on 78 patients, including 17 obsessionals. No control group was used. Eight obsessional patients showed at least some improvement on clinical ratings 6 weeks after treatment. No independent assessor was used. The results of Tan *et al.* (1971) and Kelly *et al.* (1972) corroborate the results of earlier studies on leukotomy and modified leukotomy and suggest that this type of operation may lead to serious side-effects and a questionable outcome.

2.2. Stereotactic Psychosurgery

Several studies have been reported on the progress of patients who had undergone stereotactic psychosurgical operations. Bridges *et al.* (1973) compared 24 patients with primary obsessional complaints to 24 control patients with primary complaints of depression. All patients were treated by bilateral stereotactic tractotomy. The mean duration of illness was about 10 years. Overall improvement was assessed on a five-point scale. No independent assessor was used. Psychological tests were given only at the time of follow-up, approximately 3 years after the operation. Improvement occurred in 67% of the obsessionals and 71% of the depressed patients. It was found that early onset tended to have an especially bad prognosis. It should be emphasized that no control group of obsessional patients who had not undergone psychosurgery was included. Further, the improvements achieved are poor when compared with behavior therapy. At follow-up, the mean scores on the Leyton Obsessional Inventory were 20.5 for Symptom and 9.3 for Trait. In contrast, mean scores after behavior therpay at 4.5 years follow-up were 13 for Symptom and 7 for Trait (Emmelkamp & Rabbie, 1981). Unfortunately, Bridges *et al.* did not provide pretest data on the psychological tests that makes a more adequate cross-study comparison impossible. Nevertheless, the data presented suggest that the improvements achieved were moderate at best. Finally, the finding that the bilateral stereotactic tractotomy was equally "effective" in depressed patients casts doubt on the specific "antiobsessional" effects (Foa & Steketee, 1979). In contrast, Mitchell-Heggs et al. (1976) found some differential effects across patient groups. In their study, where lower medial quadrant lesions were combined with cingulate lesions, more than 80% of obsessional patients were rated as improved, whereas the improvement rate for chronic anxiety was much lower. According to Mitchell-Heggs et al., their findings support the view that the beneficial effects are due to the interruption of certain limbic circuits.

Finally, Burzaco (1981) reported the results of stereotactic surgery in 86 obsessional patients. No control group was included. Only ratings for global improvement were reported. Although the results were reported to be favorable for about two thirds of the patients, the methodological inadequacies of this study are so grave that any conclusion is unwarranted.

Summarizing the results of the stereotactic psychosurgical operations reviewed so far, there is some evidence that these types of operation may have beneficial effects in obsessive-compulsive patients. However, since controlled studies are lacking, it is quite possible that the improvements achieved are due to other factors including additional treatment received and placebo effects. It should be noted that post-operative rehabilitation is an important part of the total treatment program and often includes behavior therapy and medication. It is reasonable to assume that psychosurgical operations may be quite susceptible to placebo effects. The history of ECT is a case in point. Johnstone, Crowe, Deakin, Frith, Lawler, McPherson, and Stevens (1981) compared a course of real ECT with a course of simulated ECT with 70 severely depressed inpatients. At one and six months follow-up there was no difference between the two groups, thus indicating that the long-term effects of ECT may be due to placebo effects. Similar conclusions were reached by Lambourn and Gill (1978), who also found hardly any difference between real ECT and simulated ECT. Presumably, placebo effects may be even more powerful with psychosurgical operations. To the best of my knowledge no one has made a serious attempt to control for placebo factors in psychosurgery.

But even if we assume that the improvements achieved are due to the surgical operation rather than to nonspecific factors, then there is still little reason to recommend this operation for obsessional patients. The improvement achieved is moderate at best and far less than that achieved with exposure in vivo and response prevention. There is no evidence that the patients who were treated by Bridges et al. (1973) and Mitchell-Heggs et al. (1976) were more severe cases than those treated in the trials examining the effects of behavior therapy reviewed in Chapter 8.

2.3. Behavior Therapy and Psychosurgery

A study on a small series of patients treated by psychosurgery in the Netherlands is of some importance. Haaijman, van Veelen, and Storm van Leeuwen (1980) treated nine patients with behavior therapy combined with intracerebral lesions made by means of semipermanent implanted intracerebral electrodes. Only in cases where behavior therapy failed was psychosurgery conducted. It has to be said that it is doubtful whether the most appropriate behavioral procedures were used. For example, one case was treated with systematic desensitization and flooding in imagination by means of a tape-recorder, treatments which are not of particular value for obsessive-compulsives. Prolonged exposure *in vivo* plus response prevention was not used "since the patient declined this" (p. 323). Two out of three patients with obsessions lost their obsessions after the implantation of electrodes but *before* the lesions were made. This suggests that the improvement may be attributed to placebo factors, although the authors discount this idea. Orbitofrontal lesions led to a reduction of anxiety and the successful application of (broad spectrum) behavior therapy subsequently. Thus, the compulsions did not disappear as a result of psychosurgery. Rather, the reduced anxiety level enhanced the efficacy of the behavioral program. Unfortunately, the study was uncontrolled, which precludes the drawing of firm conclusions with respect to the additive or synergistic effects of behavior therapy and psychosurgery.

2.4. Concluding Comment

After more than 40 years, psychosurgery still remains a controversial treatment. Although the advent of new surgical techniques has reduced the amount and seriousness of side-effects, the present appraisal of the results of psychosurgery on obsessionals must be negative. As argued by Rachman and Hodgson (1980), there is no theoretical rationale for using psychosurgery for treating obsessional disorders: "the use of surgical interventions is based on and helps perpetuate the notion that obsessional disorders are illnesses" (p. 103). Some proponents of psychosurgery rely on the work of Beech to justify the psychosurgical treatment (e.g., Haaijman *et al.*, 1980). However, it has to be emphasized that at present there is no evidence that obsessionals are different from other patients in showing elevated arousal levels. Until contrary evidence is provided, obsessional problems can better be construed as psychological problems rather than as illnesses.

III

CLINICAL APPLICATIONS

10

Clinical Assessment and Treatment Planning

1. FUNCTIONAL BEHAVIOR ANALYSIS

What occurs in clinical behavior therapy is not quite the same as what is frequently depicted in research papers. Thus far we have depicted behavior therapy of phobic and obsessive-compulsive behavior as the application of techniques. The research reviewed in the previous chapters suggests that certain general technological strategies will be applicable to a number of phobic and obsessive-compulsive patients. Some have defined behavior therapy as the application of specified techniques such as systematic desensitization and flooding apparently derived from "learning theory." However, others hold that behavior therapy can be thought of as applied general psychology. Here, the definition of behavior therapy has been modified to incorporate principles derived from other areas of (experimental) psychology. In the tradition of Shapiro (1951), who was one of the first to stress the importance of formulating and testing hypotheses, Yates (1970) relied heavily on the controlled studies of the single case as characteristic for the behavioral approach. According to the latter approach, the therapist advances hypotheses that will explain the problem behavior and devises treatments in order to test these hypotheses. Thus, according to this approach, a functional behavior analysis is a condition *sine qua non* of any treatment to be called behavior therapy.

Behavior therapy research of phobic and obsessive-compulsive behavior has been technically oriented. Actually, this approach represents more the medical than the behavioral model. Patients with the same "diagnosis" are treated with a standard package. Individual differences between patients have been neglected in the behavioral research of pho-

253

bic and obsessive-compulsive problems. Thus, a functional behavior analysis is not made, but patients are randomly assigned to treatment conditions. For this very reason some (e.g., Wolpe, 1977; Meyer & Turkat, 1979) have argued that such technology-oriented behavior therapy presents tremendous limitations for efficacious clinical practice. For example, Meyer and Turkat (1979) state that treatment "is bound to fail if the therapist does not fully analyze the client's difficulties and merely provides standardized treatment techniques" (p. 266). Similarly, Wolpe (1977) holds that outcome research as usually carried out in behavior therapy is of little or no value for the clinical behavior therapists: "practically all outcome research comparisons have involved subject groupings of uncertain and nonuniform constitution, from which few valid deductions can be made" (p. 1). According to these authors "sheep and goats" have been mixed in the outcome studies, rendering their results difficult to interpret.

While I fully agree with the necessity of conducting a functional behavior analysis of clinical cases, I disagree with the statement that most outcome research has been useless. The overriding fact is that such research has demonstrated that some treatment procedures (e.g., exposure *in vivo*) are superior to others (e.g. systematic desensitization; cognitive restructuring). It would be unfortunate if we would throw away the baby with the bath water and would still continue to treat phobic and obsessive-compulsive cases by systematic desensitization. In my view, outcome research could be improved by identifying the crucial commonalities among patients with similar problems and by specifying patients according to these commonalities.

1.1. Schemes for Behavior Analysis

The purpose of this chapter is to provide an account of the process of a functional behavior analysis. Several books on behavioral assessment have been published (e.g., Ciminero, Calhoun, & Adams, 1977; Hersen & Bellack, 1976; Mash & Terdal, 1976), but these provide a review of the various assessment instruments which are available, rather than a clinical guide on how to conduct a functional analysis. The current developments in behavioral assessment are likely to be more helpful for research purposes than for clinical use (Emmelkamp, 1981). As Meyer and Turkat (1979) point out, the emphasis in the behavioral assessment literature is on change, and not on understanding the client.

Several authors provided detailed schemes to use for behavior analysis. Kanfer and Saslow (1969) wrote a seminal paper on behavioral assessment that still provides an important source for beginning behavior therapists. Kanfer and Saslow listed several components that should be included in a behavioral analysis. In the (1) *analysis of the problem situation*, the patient's major complaints are categorized into classes of behavioral excesses and deficits and the frequency, intensity, duration, appropriateness of form, and stimulus conditions are described. Further, a (2) *clarification of the problem situation* is made. Here questions are asked about factors that maintain the problem behaviors. In the (3) *motivational analysis* a hierarchy of particular persons, events, and objects that serve as reinforcers is established. In addition, Kanfer and Saslow suggested examination of each of the following areas: (4) *developmental analysis*, (5) *analysis of self-control*, (6) *analysis of social relationships*, and (7) *analysis of the social-cultural-physical environment*. In the latter section, the norms in the patient's natural environment are taken into consideration.

Another scheme for a functional analysis that is widely used has been proposed by Lazarus (1973). In his paper, "Multimodal behavior therapy: treating the BASIC ID," Lazarus states that "patients are troubled by a multitude of *specific* problems which should be dealt with by a similar multitude of *specific* treatments" (p. 404). In his view, assessment of the following seven modalities provides a systematic framework for conceptualizing presenting problems within a meaningful context: (1) Behavior, (2) Affect, (3) Sensation, (4) Imagery, (5) Cognition, (6) Interpersonal Relationship, and (7) Drugs. The first letters of each modality form the acronym BASIC ID.

Meyer and Turkat (1979) propose a behavior analysis matrix as a framework for eliciting a description of the individual's difficulties: (1) the stimuli that produce the response, (2) the response components, and (3) the consequences of the response are specified and the cognitive, autonomic, motoric, and environmental variables that serve as stimulus, response, or consequence are examined.

While the elaborate schemes of Kanfer and Saslow (1969), Lazarus (1973), and Meyer and Turkat (1979) suggest the multitude of factors that might be considered in behavioral interviewing, they provide few guidelines on how this information should be used for treatment planning. Further, information on some of the components of their schemes are unnecessary for treatment planning with the majority of phobic and obsessive-compulsive patients. For example, psychophysiological data of autonomic reactions of phobic patients will be difficult to investigate for clinicians in consulting room practice. Usually, psychophysiological assessment will not be feasible, and if time and equipment are available, the information provided will be of little use for treatment planning. Lazarus (1973) argues that durable results are in direct proportion to the number of specific modalities dealt with. Since his own treatment strategy resembles more a shotgun approach than a scientific analysis of the patient's problems, it is difficult to see how this may form evidence to support his supposition. Actually, Lazarus applies a number of different therapeutic strategies in a cookbook manner, without practicing a functional behavior analysis.

1.2. Diagnosis versus Functional Behavior Analysis

Generally, a diagnosis is of little use for making a functional analysis. Apparently homogeneous problems may be caused by different factors and may be maintained by different factors. The procedures for analyzing behavior in functional-analytic terms are described in detail further on. However, for purposes of the present discussion, we will consider a few cases with the same diagnosis (i.e., agoraphobia) that illustrate the complexity of a functional analysis and justify the need for careful analyses of such cases.

The following patients were all troubled by agoraphobia. They were afraid of walking, leaving home, mixing in crowds, and avoided buses and trains. Thus, as far as their responses in these situations are considered, these patients were quite similar. The (implicit) behavioral analysis on which most behavioral treatments (e.g., flooding, systematic desensitization, exposure *in vivo*) are based is depicted in Figure 48.

A number of different stimuli provokes anxiety that motivates escape and avoidance behavior. This chain of events is hypothesized to be reinforced by anxiety reduction (negative reinforcement). According to this model prolonged exposure *in vivo* should lead to extinction of anxiety. Eventually, the patient will experience that nonavoidance also will lead to anxiety reduction.

The first patient, for whom this model did not hold, is a 38-year-old agoraphobic woman. Prolonged exposure to the various stimuli did not work in her case. She remained as anxious as before both during the treatment sessions and afterwards. Further analysis revealed that she cognitively avoided actual exposure. Thus, for this patient at least, the functional analysis (Figure 48) failed in that it did not incorporate the

Figure 48. Behavioral analysis of agoraphobia.

all important role of covert events. Had this been clear at the start of treatment, the focus of treatment probably would have been on this cognitive avoidance as well.

A second example that illustrates the simplistic nature of the functional analysis (Figure 48) involves an agoraphobic woman. In her case it was hypothesized that attention from her husband rather than anxiety reduction was the reinforcement strengthening her phobic behavior. This unhappily married woman felt emotionally neglected by her husband. The only way she felt she could force him to spend some time with her was by being phobic and being unable to do anything alone. Treatment directed at changing the avoidance behavior of this patient is probably doomed to fail since the important reinforcing agent (attention from husband) is neglected. In this case it would be probably wise to focus on the unhappy marriage.

The third example illustrates other ways in which environmental factors may influence phobic behavior. A male agoraphobic patient was very dependent, a trait reinforced by his parents. Although this patient had been married for seven years, he regularly went to his parents' house at night when he got a panic attack. Since he was unable to drive alone, his wife and two children had to accompany him on these nightly trips. Further analysis revealed that he still had been allowed to sleep in his parents' bed when he was already engaged to his wife. Obviously, in this case, treatment plans had to take into account the reinforcing role of his parents.

In another male agoraphobic patient the primary reinforcing agent of his agoraphobia was found to be abstinence from intercourse. The agoraphobic complaints started after an unsuccessful coitus attempt with his wife which led the patient to think of himself as being impotent. After that night, he got palpitations, became anxious, and as a result of this finally became housebound. The effect of all these complaints was that his wife seriously thought he had a cardiac disease, which led her to abandon sexual intercourse. The "physical" complaints provided the patient an excuse to prevent further sexual failure.

The last example involves a female aged 40. Analysis of her case revealed that social anxiety and the avoidance of situations in which she felt ridiculed led to the development and maintenance of her agoraphobia. She was convinced that she was talked about and laughed at behind her back. She found it terrible when she had to assist her husband in the shop, but she did not dare to tell him. When her children were grown and her husband increasingly insisted upon her assistance, she got a panic attack in the shop that led to her agoraphobia. By being agoraphobic she was excused from having to assist her husband in the shop.

The examples listed above are not meant to be exhaustive with respect to factors involved in a functional analysis, but were provided to demonstrate that a diagnosis (i.e., agoraphobia) is not the same as a functional analysis. The functional analyses of these cases revealed that different factors were involved in the various cases, which resulted in different treatment for the man who avoids sexual failure by being agoraphobic and for the agoraphobic man with overprotective parents. For the sake of simplicity, I only mentioned the most obvious factors that were related to the development and maintenance of agoraphobia. Actually, in most instances more than one factor played a role as is often the case with clinical patients.

1.3. Macroanalysis

The aim of the functional analysis is to map out the various problem areas, to establish the relationships between them, and to arrive at a treatment strategy. Often the patients come with more than one problem. They are not only agoraphobic, but at the same time are unable to handle the children, they are depressed, and suffer from migraine. A patient may have obsessions of causing accidents, and additionally may be seriously bothered by feelings of inferiority. Another patient applied for treatment for his obsessional doubting and unassertiveness. Even when the patient presents a neatly defined problem (phobia or obsession) other problems may also appear to play an important part. It is not always easy to convince the patient of the necessity to discuss other problems as well as the original complaint. For example, a young female agoraphobic appeared to be regularly beaten up by her husband. The agoraphobia fluctuated according to the marital rows. Nevertheless, this patient wished to be treated for her agoraphobia only and the rest was "none of the therapist's business."

It is useful to distinguish two phases in the functional analysis: macroanalysis and microanalysis. Macroanalysis deals with relationship *between* the various problem areas. The therapist tries to map out the different problems and to determine the functional relationships between them. Microanalysis, on the other hand, deals with the functional analysis *within* one problem area only. These phases, however, often overlap during the process of functional analysis.

The aim of macroanalysis is to place the various problem areas in a wider frame and finally to formulate a hypothesis of why the patient "is as he is." The therapist tries to understand how the patient's problems are related.

Although behavior therapists usually pay attention to the microanalysis of phobic and obsessive-compulsive behavior, the macroanalysis is often passed by. Frequently, this approach results in emphasis on the end result of a complex behavioral chain, which can obscure the underlying problem.

It is often far from easy to determine which is cause and which is effect. As yet, the behavior therapist has little in the way of scientifically based procedures for deciding which of the problems will be the most effective focus in treatment. The process of the macroanalysis can be illustrated with the following example.

A woman presents the following problems in her interview: she is socially anxious, which expresses itself in fear of criticism. She is afraid to visit or receive people. In addition, she has sexual and marital difficulties, she suffers from insomnia, and is depressed. Which of the problem areas should be tackled first? In order to decide which problem to treat first the therapist has to apply macroanalysis. For this purpose the therapist generates a number of hypotheses which he subsequently tests in the following interviews. One hypothesis may be that the constant criticism of her partner has made her afraid of criticism in general and that as a consequence she sleeps badly and has become increasingly depressed. Her sexual problems could also be caused by the unsatisfactory marital situation, which is depicted schematically in Figure 49. If this model holds, then the following hypotheses should hold too:

1. The social anxiety started after the patient had been seeing her husband regularly. Should it appear that the patient was socially anxious long before having met her husband, the model would become unsettled.
2. The patient worries about either the relationship with her husband, or about (the lack of) social contact, or about both which causes the insomnia.
3. The patient became depressed only after some time. If the patient had been depressed before she had met her husband, the model does not hold either.

In succeeding interviews, the therapist will try to test these hypotheses. He will try to gather more information about the developmental history of the various problems. Soon it appears that the model does not hold. The patient has been socially anxious for as long as she can remember. She grew up isolated on a farm and had never had any friends. At school, she was often teased. Further questioning about the sexual relationship yields the following information. She feels she is

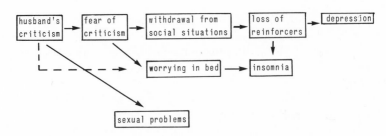

Figure 49. Hypothesized functional analysis.

being looked at and has been afraid of undressing before her husband from the day they were married. In the course of her marriage, the depressed mood developed. On the one hand, the insomnia seems to be related to worrying about problems in social situations, on the other hand to quarrels with her husband about her not wanting to have sex.

On the strength of the gathered information, a schematic model (see Figure 50) can be constructed.

On the one hand, the patient's fear of criticism and of being looked at leads to the avoidance of social contact, and, on the other hand, to the sexual and marital problems. Both the marital problems and her social withdrawal lead to the loss of essential reinforcers. Her husband goes out more and more and the few friends the patient had visited her less and less. This loss of potential reinforcers is assumed to cause the depression and insomnia.

On the basis of this model it is the social anxiety that should be treated. It is hypothesized that when the fear of being looked at is reduced, the other problems will either decrease by themselves or become easier to treat. It might be necessary to involve the husband in the treatment, because his criticizing constantly reinforces her feelings of inferiority.

It should be noted that this is also a hypothesis. The treatment can be considered to be an empirical validation of the theoretical model. The

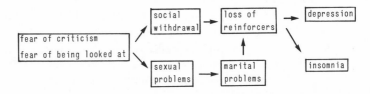

Figure 50. Revised functional analysis.

functional analysis is not necessarily restricted to the first few interviews. Information obtained during treatment may provide important data to devise new hypotheses. The following example may illustrate this.

The patient is a young woman who is afraid of aggression. Further analysis reveals that this fear is limited to aggression in bars. The patient has been avoiding bars for a long time. The patient relates two traumatic experiences in bars in which she happened to witness fights, which gave rise to her anxiety. The patient was reluctant to discuss other matters (e.g., her relationship). Because a relatively simple phobia seemed to be the case, an exposure *in vivo* program was decided upon. The patient visited several "creepy" establishments, first accompanied by the therapist and then on her own. At first she was anxious, but this dissipated with time. For homework, the patient was assigned to visit bars with her partner. In the next session, she said her homework assignment had been unsuccessful. She realized that her anxiety had little to do with aggression in bars, as she had thought up to that moment. Now, she attributed the anxiety to the fact that her partner might "misbehave" in bars. In the following interviews it was possible to discuss the "underlying problem" (uncertainty concerning her relationship; fear that her partner might leave her). The fear of aggression and her avoiding bars resulted in her partner staying at home at night which reduced the uncertainty about their relationship.

In those cases in which the therapist suspects additional problems that the patient denies, it is of little or no avail to force the therapist's opinion on the patient. If in the course of the treatment the problem appears not to be as simple as the patient thinks, he or she may be sooner inclined to go into other problems. In practice, this means that the therapist sometimes has to work with an incomplete analysis.

1.3.1. When to Carry Out Macroanalysis?

In the case of specific phobias, it is tempting to start treatment immediately. On closer inspection, however, specific phobias often appear not to be so simple. A well-known case is the man who had a bridge phobia (Lazarus, 1971). Further analysis in this case revealed that the underlying problem was criticisms by the patient's mother. In my clinical experience, specific phobias are often more complex than they originally seem. For example, a "simple" thunderstorm phobia appeared to be related to marital difficulties. An analysis of a urination phobia revealed that the anxiety was related to unassertiveness; fear of being lesbian was related to marital conflict. Thus, a functional analysis is also recommended in cases with "simple phobias."

To sum up, a functional analysis should be an essential part in the treatment of phobic and obsessive-compulsive patients. The formulation of the patient's problem arrived at by the therapist is linked as closely as possible to information obtained in the interview. Starting with the first interview a continuous process of hypothesis validation by the therapist takes place. The final clinical validation consists of the (successful) application of the therapeutic strategy, which logically stems from the theoretical model.

2. FUNCTIONAL ANALYSIS OF RELATIONSHIP PROBLEMS

Although a number of phobic and obsessional patients have marital problems, this does not indicate that the problems in the relationship caused the phobic/obsessive-compulsive problems. In such cases there are several possibilities that deserve close scrutiny by the therapist before treatment planning.

2.1. Relationship between Phobic/Obsessive-Compulsive Behavior and Marital Problems

2.1.1. Phobic/Obsessive-Compulsive Problems and Relationship Problems Are Unrelated

In these cases both types of problems follow an independent course. Often patients were already phobic/obsessive-compulsive before they met their spouses. Usually, the relationship problems involve other areas than the phobic/obsessive-compulsive problems. There is no reason to treat the relationship problems first, unless the patient so requests.

2.1.2. Phobic/Obsessive-Compulsive Problems Lead to Relationship Problems

Here, the marital distress is the result of the phobic/obsessive-compulsive problems. Partners get along quite well until the patient becomes phobic/obsessive-compulsive. The development of the phobic/obsessive-compulsive problems appears to be unrelated to marital distress. The phobic/obsessive-compulsive problems place a heavy stress on the relationship leading to increasing marital distress. For example, partners of agoraphobics have to accompany the patient everywhere. If these partners are not allowed to do things on their own, arguments and dissatisfaction with the marriage might ensue. Or, in the case of obsessional patients, the lives some spouses of patients are forced to live may be unacceptable to them. For example, some partners of obsessional patients may have to assist the patient in cleaning the house until past midnight, or to reassure the patient every few minutes. It is difficult to see how such conditions can lead to a mutually satisfying relationship. Here, treatment might be directed to the phobic/obsessive-compulsive disorders which eventually may lead to increased marital satisfaction.

2.1.3. Causative and Maintaining Role of Relationship Problems

In some cases the marital conflict is quite overt and clearly related to the phobic/obsessive-compulsive disorders. In others, however, the marital conflict might be less clear and may even be denied by the patient. According to system-theorists, phobic/obsessive-compulsive problems should be regarded as a result of inadequate interactions. A basic assumption is that psychiatric symptoms have interpersonal meaning in relationship. Thus, it is assumed that phobic/obsessive-compulsive symptoms reflect relationship conflict. Several behavior therapists also stress the importance of interpersonal conflicts in the development and maintenance of phobic and obsessive-compulsive problems. For example, Goldstein and Chambless (1980) found some evidence that agoraphobia onset was related to high interpersonal conflict. They proposed that the phobic symptoms are the result of psychological avoidance behavior in conflict situations:

> Usually because of his/her unasssertiveness the agoraphobic has found himself/herself in an unhappy seemingly irresolvable relationship under the domination of a spouse or parent. The urges to leave and the fears of being on her/his own balance out, and the agoraphobic is trapped in this conflict, unable to move and lacking the skills to change the situation. (Chambless & Goldstein, 1980, p. 324)

Similarly, the symptoms of some obsessive-compulsive patients are also the result of inability to deal with interpersonal stress or reflections of marital dissatisfaction. Further, with some patients the phobic/obsessive-compulsive symptoms may provide a mighty weapon to control the relationship. Ideally, in these instances, treatment should be aimed at the marital problems, although this might lead to many difficulties.

2.1.4. Phobic/Obsessive-Compulsive Problems Are Functionally Autonomous

Although relationship difficulties may have played a part in the development of the phobic/obsessive-compulsive problems, this does not necessarily mean that relationship difficulties still actually affect these symptoms. In some patients, temporary marital distress led to the development of phobic/obsessive-compulsive complaints. However, these problems have been resolved in the mean time and the phobic/obsessive-compulsive problems are maintained by other factors. Obviously, marital treatment will be of little use in these instances.

2.1.5. Phobic/Obsessive-Compulsive Problems Are Maintained by Relationship Factors

In other patients the development of phobic/obsessive-compulsive symptoms is unrelated to relationship difficulties, but relationship factors play a part in maintaining these behaviors. Spouses, who gain from the partner's phobic/obsessive-compulsive problems in one way or another, may resist improvement in the patient. Some spouses fear changes in the relationship pattern, which can result in overt resistance or more subtle obstruction. Often a relationship pattern developed while the patient was dependent on the spouse and the prospective change of this pattern may make the spouse of the patient considerably anxious. Further, some spouses may have become phobic themselves as a result of the avoidance behavior of the patient but were quite able to conceal this from their partner. Finally, in other cases, spouses may desire improvement of the phobic/obsessive-compulsive complaints but are very responsive to the phobic/obsessive-compulsive behavior, thus reinforcing it. Since in all these instances the spouse's behavior can render treatment of the phobic/obsessive-compulsive behavior useless, it might be necessary to focus on both the relationship and the phobic/obsessive-compulsive problems.

2.1.6. Reciprocal Relationship

This last category of patients is most difficult to treat. Here phobic/obsessive-compulsive problems and relationship problems reciprocally influence each other, the result of which is a vicious circle. Relationship problems lead to phobic problems which in turn affect negatively the relationship and so on. Thus both patient and partner are caught in a spiral. Generally, unless relationship problems and phobic/obsessive-compulsive problems are treated simultaneously, treatment of either problem by itself is doomed to fail.

2.1.7. Concluding Comment

Thus the relationship between marital conflict and phobic/obsessive-compulsive behavior is often complex. It is necessary to determine the functional relationship (if any) between these problem areas before focusing on either of them as treatment target.

It is important to note that lack of (reported) arguments or marital distress does not necessarily mean that relationship factors are not involved. In evaluating the part played by relationship factors in causing and/or maintaining the phobic/obsessive-compulsive behavior, the therapist must evaluate multiple aspects of marital functioning. To conduct this assessment, we recommend the therapist use the models formulated above as hypotheses.

2.2. Assessment Of Marital Dysfunction

To assess a marital relationship, the therapist may use questionnaires or standard behavioral observation. While these instruments may be quite useful for couples who are treated for marital discord, they are of little use in terms of information provided with respect to a functional analysis of phobic/obsessive-compulsive behavior. The objective of marital assessment with phobic and obsessive-compulsive patients is to explore the connection between specific relationship behaviors and the target complaint. The behavioral marriage literature does little to help the therapist with this specific task. The marital adjustment or marital satisfaction questionnaires are generally of little use for this purpose.

2.2.1. Questionnaires

The widely used Locke-Wallace Marital Adjustment Scale (MAS) (Locke & Wallace, 1959) is a self-report inventory which has been found to discriminate reliably between distressed and nondistressed couples. However, there is some evidence that this instrument is highly influenced by social desirability factors. Thus, if patients are reluctant to admit marital problems in the interview, it is unlikely that their scores on this questionnaire will provide the therapist with more accurate information. There is no reason not to assume that other marital questionnaires are affected as much by demand characteristics and social desirability factors. Further, another limitation of these questionnaires—even more important for the present discussion—is that no information is obtained as to how such relationship problems are related to the phobic/obsessive-compulsive behavior.

2.2.2. Behavioral Observation

The same precautions that we discussed in regard to marital questionnaires also apply to behavioral observation of a couple's interaction.

Behavioral observation in the area of marital interaction usually involves assessment of problem-solving discussions in the laboratory. It is generally assumed that these laboratory tasks are related to problem-solving in the natural environment of the couple, although data to support this supposition are few. The two most widely used instruments for evaluating couples interactions are the Marital Interaction Coding System (MICS), developed by Hops, Wills, Patterson, and Weiss (1972) and the Couples Interaction Scoring System (CISS) developed by Gottman (1979). In my opinion, the assessment of a couple's interaction along these lines is a misguided endeavor from the point of view of a functional behavior analysis. Similarly, to the questionnaires discussed above, these interaction tasks may be influenced by social desirability factors and do not offer information with respect to the functional connection between the various problem areas. At best, behavioral observation of a couple's interaction may provide some information that may be useful in developing a profile of problem-solving behavior. However, the validity is unknown and the latter objective by itself does not justify the efforts and costs involved.

2.2.3. Interview

The interviews that the therapist holds with the patient are presumably most informative with respect to a functional analysis. Of course, one should not lose sight of the fact that the patient—intentionally or not—may distort the information. However, when the therapist wishes to pursue information with respect to the functional relationship between relationship factors and phobic/obsessive-compulsive complaints, there are no other assessment alternatives available. Usually, such general questions as, "Are you satisfied with your marriage" are of little use since most patients, even the most marital-distressed ones, will answer in the affirmative. The information that is needed must be more specific. It is often useful to have the patient relate the development of the problem, especially the first instance that he became anxious. If the first occurrence of the problem is reported by the patient, the therapist has to determine if the patient's spouse was involved, either as an antecedent or as a consequence. Further, detailed information about the current role of the patient's partner is needed. Here again, the question to ask is whether or not the partner provides antecedents or consequences that affect the occurrence of the phobic/obsessive-compulsive behavior.

It is very important for the patient to be as specific as possible. Eliciting this type of detailed information from the patient can be a laborious process, which requires a lot of tact and interviewing skills on the part of the therapist. If the patient is very reluctant to provide the therapist with this information, the therapist should not force him to do so. Especially in the first sessions, it is important to build a therapeutic relationship. However, this may be disturbed by too much pressure on the part of the therapist. If the therapist has the idea that relationship factors are involved, but the patient is uncooperative in providing the necessary information, he may choose between two alternatives: either leaving the subject for the time being with the option of returning to it after some time, or inviting the patient's partner for further assessment. Although the latter strategy has several advantages to recommend it, this approach might be too threatening for some patients (and their partners). One of the advantages of seeing the patient's partner (either alone or together with the patient) is to have another opportunity to gather information with respect to the connection between relationship factors and the phobic/obsessive-compulsive complaints. Perhaps even more important, the conjoint interview provides observational data that may add to the information provided by the spouse.

2.3. Treatment Planning

When the functional analysis reveals that the phobic/obsessive-compulsive behavior is controlled by relationship factors, the question remains whether marital therapy is the best option. Consider the following obsessive-compulsive woman seen for therapy. The macroanalysis revealed that relationship problems elicited and were partly maintaining the obsessive-compulsive behavior. However, since this patient appeared also to be highly unassertive, it was decided to deal with the unassertiveness. We felt that this patient needed training in assertiveness skills to make her better able to express requests and opinions toward her spouse. It is our opinion that in a number of instances marital problems are better treated individually rather than conjointly.

It should be remembered that the association between marital distress and phobic/obsessive-compulsive problems offers the therapist no particular guidelines in terms of treatment planning. Even if the functional analysis reveals that these problems are causally related, there is no reason to expect that treatment of relationship problems will lead to improvement of the phobic/obsessive-compulsive behavior. Since there are no tested guidelines on when to begin with either marital therapy or treatment of the phobic/obsessive-compulsive behavior, the therapist must make the decision on the basis of the presented information and must rely on his clinical intuition. Usually, it is not a question of offering one therapy to the exclusion of the other, but rather what to focus on first. Generally, the therapeutic intervention—or the sequencing of therapeutic interventions—should be chosen on the basis of what will provide the speediest improvement.

2.3.1. Marital Treatment

When a decision is made to work dyadically with the patient, further information is requested in order to decide which type of marital treatment is most suited to this particular couple. Generally, it makes little sense to treat phobic/obsessive-compulsive patients with canned procedures (e.g., communication and problem-solving training or contingency contracting), unless the analysis indicates that these approaches are necessary.

In some cases the partner may be invited to act as cotherapist. In general, such an approach must be discouraged when there is so much animosity between the partners that homework exercises are likely to lead to further arguments and increased tension. In these instances it is quite likely that treatment may exacerbate rather than alleviate the problems. To summarize, a thorough assessment is essential to identify the relationship variables that control the phobic/obsessive-compulsive behavior and to select the appropriate therapeutic intervention.

If treatment is to focus on the relationship, this must be made clear to the couple. The therapist must describe what is involved in marital treatment and explain how it differs from what the patient initially requested. When the patient and/or the spouse are reluctant to accept the offer of marital therapy, it seems therapeutically wise to (re)focus treatment on the phobic/obsessive-compulsive problems. In my opinion it does not make sense to "sell" the treatment to the couple. One might reasonably question the feasibility of marital therapy for an unmotivated couple. It may be argued that there is little danger in starting marital therapy, regardless of the commitment of the couple to this therapeutic approach, since, if marital treatment does not work, one could still treat the phobic/obsessive-compulsive problems directly. Unfortunately, failure of marital therapy can have negative consequences for both partners, eventually resulting in their dropping out of treatment.

3. PATHOLOGICAL GRIEF REACTIONS

In a number of cases there is a relationship between pathological grief and phobias and compulsions, even if the patient will not usually perceive this relationship. Questions, then, that are important for the functional analysis are: Does the unresolved grief lead to phobic behavior or are they relatively independent problem areas? It also occurs that the original grief reactions may have led to the development of the phobia, while the phobia has become functionally autonomous in the course of time. It is necessary to determine how far the phobia has become separated from its original source, particularly in the case of chronic phobias.

3.1. Treatment Planning

Of course, a functional analysis may have important implications for treatment planning. When the phobia still feeds on the unresolved grief it is natural to consider grief therapy (see Ramsay, 1979). In a number of cases the phobic complaints appear to improve by themselves after the successful treatment of pathological grief. When the problems are independent, they will probably have to be dealt with separately. In those cases where unresolved grief was the cause but now has become independent from the phobia, it makes sense to disregard the grief reactions and to focus on the direct treatment of the phobia first.

To say that a functional analysis in such cases is important does not necessarily imply that it makes sense (or is practically feasible) to gather in detail all information related to the unresolved grief. Rather, the task of the therapist is to judge how far there is still a question of pathological grief. To pursue such information in too much detail could even develop into a grief therapy. By means of such detailed questions the therapist confronts the patient with painful stimuli, which the latter would rather avoid. When the patient becomes emotional, the therapist can do little but "finish his work," leaving the functional analysis as it is.

It is not always possible to make a functional analysis in advance: the feelings may be so painful to the patient that he does not dare mention them to the therapist. In such a situation the therapist can do little but start treatment of the phobia or compulsion. The therapist will still be left with the feeling that there is more to it, but it is of little use to force the patient at this stage. If in the course of the treatment it becomes clear to the patient that there are other problems involved, these can still be discussed. Further, the fact that, during the first few sessions, the therapeutic relationship has not yet developed into what it should be, may make it difficult for the patient to relate such painful emotional experiences to an almost complete stranger. By taking the patient's complaint (phobia or compulsion) seriously and focusing treatment on this complaint, the therapist can create a climate which may enable the patient to relate these experiences. It is wise for the therapist to communicate some of his reservations about the efficacy of the "symptomatic" treatment: "I think we should start a program to deal with your anxiety. But we might come upon other factors which may affect your complaints . . . then I think it would be useful to stop and reconsider the treatment planning."

3.2. Clinical Examples

The following example clearly shows how in the course of treatment the patient herself realizes that other factors are involved. Mrs. G., a depressed widow, was referred to us for treatment of her obsessive-compulsive behavior. She suffered from checking compulsions. In addition to the usual rituals like checking the gas, electricity, etc., she also continually checked to see whether her only child was still breathing. Further, she was seriously affected by compulsive doubting and obsessional slowness and to a lesser degree by cleaning compulsions. The patient felt that nonperformance of rituals would cause something terrible to happen to her child, her parents, or herself. For years, the patient had suffered from these rituals, which had become worse the last 4 years after the death of her husband.

Treatment consisted of an intensive exposure program in the patient's home with the therapist confronting her with all kinds of situations that triggered her rituals. After two weeks, the patient was almost symptom free as far as her rituals were concerned. However, the patient reported an increase in depressed mood and loneliness. In subsequent sessions, it became clear that these feelings stemmed from unresolved grief. Years before she had had an affair with a married man and stopped seeing him because he did not want to divorce his wife. He did not leave her alone, however, but kept checking whether she met other men and prophesied that she would never become happy with somebody else. She had never had the same feelings for anybody else, not even for her husband. She had never been able to really express her feelings for this man to her husband. It was hypothesized that the rituals had functioned to avoid painful feelings related to the affair. Consequently, grief therapy was decided upon.

Treatment does not always progress as smoothly as in the case just described, which can be illustrated in the following example.

The patient had been agoraphobic for 5 years. Her complaints started after the sudden death of her baby. She was afraid to do things on her own and was afraid to go out by herself. In addition, she had obsessions concerning the death of her husband, her children, and herself. Her husband had to telephone her often during the day to let her know that he was all right. Every siren she heard made her think that something had happened to one of her children. The loss of her child persisted, and she continually ruminated about her. When it was cold, she wondered whether the child felt cold in the cemetery, and when it was raining whether the child was lying in a pool of water. She claimed that she did not have feelings of guilt about her child's death but about "having her taken away and having a heavy stone put on top of her." Treatment of her agoraphobia by exposure *in vivo* had little therapeutic effect. Even after a number of interviews the patient failed to see the need for grief therapy, and treatment had to be discontinued.

3.3. Concluding Remarks

In cases in which the therapist suspects that there is a clear relationship between grief and phobia or compulsion and the patient agrees, the therapist does well not to promise the patient that his phobic/compulsive complaints will vanish as a result of grief therapy: "Your phobic complaints may be reduced through grief therapy but this is not certain. We may have to apply a separate treatment to overcome your anxieties after we have finished your grief therapy . . . but this is of course difficult to tell in advance." In this way the therapist can prevent disillusion on the part of the patient when the grief therapy has no immediate effect on the phobic or compulsive complaints. Otherwise a patient may drop out of treatment prematurely, which might have been prevented if the therapist had been more reticent about the expected results of the treatment.

It is not always easy to judge how far it is necessary to go into pathological grief. Even in those cases where there is a clear relationship between unresolved grief and the development of phobic or obsessive-compulsive problems and this grief still seems to play an important part, the pros and cons of such treatment should be considered. Grief therapy is an emotionally painful treatment, the effects of which have still not been sufficiently investigated. There are not sufficient data available on the effects of grief therapy in more complex cases than discussed here. In any case, it is my experience that the phobic/compulsive complaints do not always disappear as a matter of course after successful grief therapy. On the other hand, we have sometimes seen improvement of phobic-compulsive complaints presumably caused by unresolved grief without having dealt with the grief (See Mrs. G., p. 270). To summarize, even when the functional analysis reveals the influence of pathological grief on the development of the phobic-compulsive problems, this does not necessarily mean that grief therapy should be the treatment of choice.

3.4. Inadequate Emotional Processing

Sometimes phobias and compulsions are linked to other painful emotional experiences that have not been sufficiently overcome. This is often the case with patients who in their youth felt emotionally neglected and who try to avoid the memory of these painful emotional experiences (cognitive avoidance). We have successfully treated a (limited) number of cases with a procedure which aimed at breaking down the cognitive avoidance in order to achieve habituation to the negative emotions (prolonged exposure to past experiences).

The same issues that have been discussed when we dealt with pathological grief also apply to this category of patients. In my opinion pathological grief is only one variant of inadequate emotional processing (Rachman, 1980). Thus, even if a clear relationship exists between inadequate emotional processing of past experiences and phobic or obsessive-compulsive complaints, this does not imply that treatment by "imaginal confrontation" is indicated.

4. TREATMENT PLANNING

Even when the functional analysis reveals that there are underlying problems that elicit the phobic/obsessive-compulsive behavior, this does not mean that the focus should always be on the underlying circumstances. There are several reasons why it might be therapeutically wise to delay treatment of these problems for some time and to initially focus treatment on the phobic/obsessive-compulsive behavior.

First, in some instances the therapist has a clear idea why the patient functions as he does, but the patient is not yet ready to accept this formulation of his problems. In some cases the patient does not agree with the therapist's formulation of the problem. It is important to note that the therapist should formulate his functional analysis as a hypothetical model. If the patient does not agree with the therapist's formulation of the problem, the therapist may best proceed by following the patient's line and treating the phobic/obsessive-compulsive problems directly. Assuming that the functional analysis is accurate, it is reasonable to argue that treatment is doomed to fail. However, it is my belief that it is better to change the focus of treatment when the patient himself feels that the treatment is a failure than to have the therapist persuade him.

The therapist should never utter such disdainful comments as, "Well, you will see that I will be put in the right." Rather, the therapist may say something like: "Well, it may be worthwhile to have a look and see whether we can treat your phobic/obsessive complaints directly. Should treatment fail we can as yet consider other possibilities."

A second possibility is that the patient accepts the therapist's formulation of the problem but still prefers treatment for his phobic/obsessive complaints only. In these cases, too, the therapist had better proceed as outlined above. Thus, the patient's request for direct treatment of his phobic/obsessive-compulsive complaints is granted.

In other cases, it may even be better to conceal the functional analysis, when there are reasons to assume that the behavioral formulation may be too threatening for the patient. For example, after just a few minutes in the first interview, an unmarried socially isolated obsessive-compulsive female patient started to bombard the therapist with these statements: "You should not think that I am sexually frustrated" and "I can get as many friends as I would like, but I hate people." It is probably foolish to try to convince this patient that these may be problem areas that are related to her obsessive-compulsive behavior and that deserve treatment separately. With such cases, it may be better to wait until a therapeutic relationship has developed and the patient trusts the therapist.

Further, in some cases the phobic and obsessive-compulsive problems by themselves may limit fruitful intervention in other areas and therefore have to be dealt with first. For example, it might be hypothesized that the obsessional complaints of a patient who is totally housebound as a result of his harming obsessions are related to his social anxiety and unassertiveness. However, the latter problems may prove to be difficult to treat unless the patient is less troubled by his obsessions and is able to leave his home and meet people. So, in this case at least, it would be ill advised to start treating social anxiety in a vacuum of social relationships.

Finally, in a number of instances there is no reason to suppose that treatment of the phobic/obsessive-compulsive behavior will be impeded by the other problems. Often other problems were in some way related to the development of the phobic/obsessive-compulsive problems, but at the moment these problems control the phobic/obsessive-compulsive behavior neither as an antecedent nor as a consequence. Although the other problems may still need separate treatment, in order to prevent relapse in the future, there is no need to handle these problems before the phobic/obsessive-compulsive complaints have been dealth with. For example, an agoraphobic patient became anxious for the first time after critical comments of her boss. Although it is reasonable to assume that the unassertiveness of the patient led to the agoraphobia, there was no evidence that the unassertiveness was maintaining the phobia. In the meantime the patient got married and had children, which made her give up her job. Although this patient was still very unassertive, there was no reason to postpone treatment for her phobia, since the agoraphobic complaints appeared to have become functionally autonomous from the original eliciting condition. At a later stage, her unassertiveness can still be dealt with and probably more fruitfully. When the patient is no longer troubled by her agoraphobia, she may be in a better opportunity to rehearse newly learned assertive behavior *in vivo* and discuss her failures with her therapist.

The therapist should never forget that the functional analysis is a hypothetical formulation of the patient's problem. Recently, we were reminded of this when treating an obsessive-compulsive young man whose problems started just after a prolonged period of hospitalization during which time he felt abandoned by his friends. His friends did not visit him in the hospital, which caused him to withdraw from all social contacts afterwards. It was hypothesized that his obsessive-compulsive complaints were functional in avoiding criticism and social failure. For reasons that have already been discussed above, we decided to start treating his obsessive-compulsive complaints by exposure *in vivo* and response prevention, and to focus on his social withdrawal later on. Totally unexpected, however, the successful treatment of his obsessional complaints resulted in improved social relationships without any intervention on the part of the therapist in this area. Although this may indicate a failure in our functional analysis, it is equally plausible that improvements of his obsessive-compulsive problems led to enhanced feelings of self-efficacy, which generalized to a better handling of social situations.

One final word of caution should be made. If treatment is directed to the "underlying problem" the therapist should carefully monitor changes in the phobic/obsessive-compulsive behavior. It is quite possible that treatment results in improvement of related problems without affecting the phobic/obsessive-compulsive behavior. If the latter is the case the treatment goals should be rediscussed. It may be that treatment of the original complaint may be postponed, since improvement in the other areas of functioning is found at least as important as improvement of the phobic/obsessive-compulsive behavior. Alternatively, the end result of this reanalysis might also be that the phobic/obsessive-compulsive problems are as yet to be dealt with.

In writing this chapter, I had to speculate well beyond available data. Unfortunately, research in the area of functional behavior analysis and treatment planning is lacking. The clinician has to base his decisions on little more than hunches based on observed coincidences of target responses and consequences and on his experience with similar cases. To be honest, there is no evidence that treatment based on a thorough functional analysis is superior to treatment for the "symptomatic" behavior only. In planning therapeutic interventions, it is important to take into account the probability of effect of a particular treatment approach. It should be remembered that exposure procedures proved to be effective in *unselected* phobic and obsessive-compulsive patients. Unfortunately, the effect of most other procedures are unknown with phobic and obsessive-compulsive patients, which should be acknowledged in the process of treatment planning.

5. DATA GATHERING

5.1. Behavioral Interview

The behavioral interview forms the most important source of information. In the initial interview the therapist will attempt to form a picture of the patient's problem(s). Other sources of data gathering (e.g., behavioral diary, self-report questionnaires, behavioral observation) depend on information gathered and hypotheses formulated during the interview. Furthermore, information from questionnaires and from behavioral observation will usually be followed by further queries during subsequent interviews. The interview offers the opportunity to pursue information in greater detail than is possible in questionnaires. In the interview, the therapist will devote some time to both specific circumstances that elicited the phobic or obsessive-compulsive reactions and environmental consequences, information that is usually not provided by questionnaires. Since it is necessary to go into detail into the eliciting conditions, the behavioral and cognitive responses, and the consequences on a number of different occasions, neither questionnaires nor behavioral observation by themselves will provide the information necessary for a functional behavior analysis.

During the interview the therapist continuously tries to understand the patient's problems. Therefore, standard questions are usually of little avail. Novices are often so anxious not to miss essential information that they formulate a number of questions in advance. A disadvantage of this strategy is that they are often so preoccupied with their questions that they lack the flexibility that is needed. As a result of this rigid interview approach they miss important nuances, and essential information is often lost. It is important for the therapist to listen with a "second ear" and to continuously try to understand the patient's problems. Of course, it may be useful to check a number of standard problem areas that are often related to the target problem in order to be sure not to overlook important events. Mostly, however, this information comes up spontaneously in the course of the interview.

To gather the necessary information, an empathic attitude on the part of the therapist is required. Especially in the first interview, an empathic attitude may be more productive than mere questioning. Therapists who are excessively preoccupied with pursuing information are likely to be regarded as insensitive. Having to answer a number of standard questions may often be an experience that is unpleasant; and, if the experience is sufficiently negative for the patient, he may not return. I am not advocating a total avoidance of direct questioning during the initial interview but recommend that the therapeutic relationship be the primary focus of an initial interview. It is a common misconception that empathy is similar to nondirective reflection of feelings. Selective direct questioning and comments in areas important to the patient often convey the impression that the therapist understands the patient's problems. For example, when a patient relates that he is anxious when walking outside, the therapist may ask whether the same feelings occur during shopping and traveling on a bus. Two ends are served by such direct questions: first, the therapist may demonstrate that he has experience with similar patients and understands the patient; second, if the patient does not have problems in these situations, he has the opportunity to correct the therapist.

To understand the problem fully, it is necessary to have an overview of the developmental history of the problem. Such information presents the therapist with a more detailed picture of the early eliciting and reinforcing stimuli controlling the behavior. If the information is not spontaneously forthcoming, questions should be focused on elucidating the etiology of the problem. The events marking the inception of the phobic/obsessive-compulsive problems often provide valuable clues regarding variables that are controlling these problems.

Since it is necessary to determine which specific conditions actually affect the problem behavior, the therapist should also pursue information about what is currently controlling this behavior. Since so many factors may be involved, it is not possible to list them all, although some of them are discussed throughout this chapter. An important source of information may be provided by the behavioral diary. This diary can supply the therapist useful information regarding eliciting and reinforcing stimuli currently controlling the phobic/obsessive-compulsive behavior. Patients are instructed to fill out their diary regularly, if possible, each hour. Ideally, the diary should provide the therapist with information regarding situations that are related to the phobic/obsessive-compulsive behavior either as an antecedent or as a consequence. Since most patients have difficulty in writing accounts of their experiences, it is important that the therapist is as explicit as possible in specifying the type of data that are needed. It is recommended to design recording forms that are tailor-made to the individual needs of the patients and that contain specific questions that are particularly relevant for this patient. For example, with some patients it may be necessary to obtain very specific information regarding behavior in social situations whereas for others assessment of cognitive events is of primary importance. Thus, it is recommended that the therapist be flexible in using the behavioral diary as an assessment instrument. It is important that the patient fills out his diary regularly throughout the day so that they do not need to recall events. Inspection of the diary may reveal significant associations between problem behavior and particular events. This may provide the therapist with clues about factors that are related to the phobic/obsessive-compulsive behavior. In our experience, identification of these factors along these lines is extremely useful in planning therapeutic interventions.

5.2. Questionnaires

Questionnaires can be used to supplement and follow-up on data gathered during the interview. Rather than having patients complete a number of standard questionnaires, the choice of questionnaire(s) to be used should be determined by the problems of the patient. Questionnaires are useful as: (1) information gathering, (2) a tool to help in testing hypotheses, and (3) a measurement of therapy outcome.

5.2.1. Information Gathering

Questionnaires can be used to supplement information gathered during the interview. For example, the therapist may need specific information regarding situations that patients fear (Fear Survey Schedules), situations in which patients are unassertive (Assertiveness Scales), or situations in which patients are troubled by obsessive-compulsive behavior (Obsessional Questionnaires). Of course, the therapist could ask each question of the questionnaire during the interview, but this information is obtained more easily through questionnaires. Thus, in these instances questionnaires present a low-effort and low-cost method of gathering information. Usually the information provided by the questionnaires will lead to further queries in subsequent interviews. Questionnaire data may direct the therapist to related situations that require further exploration in the interview.

5.2.2. Hypotheses Testing

In addition to information gathering, questionnaires can be used to test hypotheses that were formulated during the interview. For example, during the interview the therapist might hypothesize that the patient is highly unassertive. To test this hypothesis an assertiveness questionnaire may be used. Or, to take another example, the therapist may hypothesize that the patient needs to try to make a good impression. In this case he might test this hypothesis by requesting that the patient fill out a social desirability questionnaire.

5.2.3. Measurement of Therapy Outcome

It is important for the therapist to know whether a particular therapeutic intervention leads to improvement of the target behavior. For this purpose, questionnaires can be used, but it should be emphasized that improvements on a questionnaire do not necessarily imply real clinical improvement. Recently, I contacted a former behavior therapist about one of my patients who was still considerably phobic. This therapist attempted to convince me about her improvement by enumerating "change scores" on questionnaires that she had filled out. That the patient herself was still considerably handicapped by her phobia did not matter very much, since the assessment had revealed that she was cured!

When the therapist decides to use questionnaires as an assessment instrument for one of the purposes listed above, it is important to elicit cooperation regarding the assessment from the patient. It is important that the therapist emphasizes the utility and relevance of filling out questionnaires for treatment planning and evaluation of outcome. Since its function is obvious to the therapist, the patient cannot be expected to understand the necessity for assessment. In designing assessment procedures, the therapist must consider whether the information being requested of the patient is, indeed, essential to the treatment process. If the patient views the filling out of questionnaires as an integral part of his treatment, this will increase the patient's commitment to produce accurate data.

To summarize, in contrast to research studies, routine use of questionnaires is not recommended for use in clinical practice. In presenting questionnaires, it should be made clear to the patients that the assessment is a functional necessity for their treatment. Even with a full explanation, assessment may be viewed to be less necessary from the patient's perspective. Assuming that the information provided by questionnaires is indeed essential to the treatment process, the therapist must be firm in requiring the participation of the patient. Although the therapist must be empathetic about the amount of effort involved in filling out the questionnaires, he should make clear that treatment can only commence after the necessary information is required.

5.3. Behavioral Observation

In general, standard laboratory tests yield little useful information sufficient for making a functional analysis. On the other hand, behavioral observation in the patient's natural environment may often be valuable. Visiting the home of obsessive-compulsive patients often yields more information than a number of interviews in the office. The compulsive behavior may have become so "normal" that the patient forgets to mention it. For example, a patient applied for treatment for fear of contamination, cleaning, and checking rituals and provided a number of examples. When visiting the patient's home a lot of items could be added to the list. The floors were littered with "contaminated" objects, most of which had been there for weeks, which the patient was afraid to touch. In addition, there was a room especially for contaminated objects. Years before the patient had put away all these contaminated objects and she never entered this room any more. Moreover, the patient appeared to suffer seriously from a hoarding compulsion and from a compulsion to buy things: cupboards contained newspapers years old that the patient could not throw away. In addition, she had hoarded loads of provisions and appeared to feel forced to buy everything on sale (for example, books which she never read because she was afraid to touch them). In other cases patients appeared to have developed special postures and to touch objects in a special way, which had become so ordinary that they were not mentioned in the office.

5.4. Concluding Comment

The functional analysis has to be of practical value for the therapy. This means that the therapist has to restrict the issues that are raised. Although it is difficult to give general guidelines (one patient simply happens to be more complex than another), usually three or four interviews will do. Some therapists are inclined to prolong this phase unnecessarily; they are uncertain whether they may have overlooked an essential point and overburden their patients with questionnaires without any new essential material being revealed.

Although the therapist feels that much—and probably essential—material has not come up, it still often makes sense to start treatment. In the course of the treatment important information may be as yet revealed. It is questionable whether this information would have presented itself had the therapist prolonged the number of interviews. The patient may become demotivated when treatment is postponed—for his complaints do not change—which may lead to a discontinuance of treatment.

Treatment of Phobic Disorders

In this chapter we are concerned primarily with the clinical application of exposure *in vivo* procedures. Treatment procedures as applied in experimental studies are not always directly comparable to the clinical application. As we have already discussed in the previous chapter, a functional behavior analysis is not made, but patients are randomly assigned to treatment conditions. In research studies all patients have to be treated in the same manner. The research requirements usually leave little room for individual variation within the procedures applied. Number of sessions, duration of sessions, spacing of sessions, and degree of therapist involvement all have to be specified before the start of the study. The goal of the present chapter is to provide some clinical guidelines on how to conduct exposure *in vivo* procedures.

1. SPECIFIC PHOBIAS

With specific phobias, exposure *in vivo* is easy to apply. The stimulus situations that elicit anxiety reactions are usually quite clear (e.g., balconies of buildings in the case of acrophobia, large dogs in the case of dogphobia, etc.). Treatment consists of rapid exposure to the feared object or situation. The therapist accompanies the patient to the feared situation and encourages him to stay there until he feels better. In most cases therapeutic effects are achieved within a few sessions of prolonged exposure *in vivo*.

With dental phobics a more gradual approach is to be preferred. The successful application of self-controlled exposure *in vivo* was described already in 1962 by a dentist (Borland): "the dentist encourages the patient to try a little more each time while still allowing him to set his own pace. Above all, each additional venture on the part of the patient must stop short of arousing any real panic, since each experience must illustrate to him that there is really not so much to be afraid of."

Generalization of improvement outside the treatment setting is an essential requirement of successful therapy. Therefore, therapists have to leave their office and to apply exposure *in vivo* in real life situations. With rapid exposure *in vivo,* instructing patients to confront feared situations by themselves usually will not do. In most cases it is therapeutically wise to accompany the patient during actual practice to make sure that anxiety really decreases when the patient enters the phobic situation or handles feared objects.

2. AGORAPHOBIA

With agoraphobics two major variants of exposure *in vivo* can be distinguished: (1) self-controlled exposure *in vivo,* and (2) prolonged exposure *in vivo.* With *self-controlled exposure in vivo* patients have to confront the feared situation (e.g., walking on the street) until they feel tense. Then, they are allowed to return. Although patients are allowed to avoid the phobic situation, they have to practice again and again until the 90-minute session is over. The instructions patients receive are depicted in Table 14.

With *prolonged exposure in vivo* patients have to walk outside until anxiety declines; thus they are not allowed to return when feeling anxious but they have to stay there until they feel better. Other situations that are included in the treatment sessions are shopping in department stores and supermarkets and riding in buses. The therapist is less and less frequently present during the exposure *in vivo* periods. The reason for less involvement of the therapist during actual practice is to make the *in vivo* practice more difficult for the patients. Knowing that a therapist is nearby prevents actual exposure to distressing situations (i.e., being alone) for a substantial number of agoraphobics. Generally, therapists are very "pushy" in leading patients to confront their feared situations.

2.1. Self-Controlled Exposure versus Prolonged Exposure

There are no clear guidelines whether self-controlled or prolonged exposure should be applied. While self-controlled exposure *in vivo* may offer several advantages (e.g., easy to apply by the patients themselves,

Table 14. Instructions for the Self-observation Procedure[a]

When you are troubled by fear, the best treatment is to practice in those situations in which the fear occurs. When you practice *systematically* and *persistently*, you will experience a decrease of your fear. For those people who are fearful of going into the street alone the treatment procedure is as follows:

1. Each treatment session takes 90 min of your time. It is very important that you stick to these times. It is necessary to choose these times when you have nothing else to do and when you are at home alone. During treatment hours, you are therefore not allowed to receive any guests.

2. Since you will have to practice 90 min *in one session*, you *cannot* practice 30 min in the morning and then do the remainder in the afternoon. In that case, it is very likely your fear will increase rather than decrease. When you are tired of walking, you may, of course, rest for a few minutes.

3. Go into the street alone and start walking until you feel uncomfortable or tense. Then return to your home immediately. (Taking the dog and a bicycle with you is not permitted.)

4. Note the time that you are out on the street. Take a notebook in which you write down this period of time.

5. After this go outside again. Again, walk until you become tense or anxious. Then return to your home immediately, and, as before, write down the time that you have spent out on the street.

6. Continue practicing until 90 min have passed by.

7. Copy down the times you have scored during the last three practice sessions on the special form. Put this form in an envelope and send it to us that same day. We can then check how you are coming along. Postage is free.

8. It is very important to write down the times you have scored. In this way, you can see for yourself how much progress you have made. Research has shown that people who write down their times improve more than people who do not.

9. You are supposed to try to enlarge the distance you walk away from your home. Therefore, you are not allowed to walk in circles. You are not allowed to do any shopping or any talking to friends and acquaintances. Your therapist will make an agreement with you on which route you should take.

10. *Progress will not always continue at the same pace.* You should not let yourself be discouraged by this fact. Some people might notice rapid initial progress and later on a decrease. Usually this is only a temporary problem. You might feel better on one day than on the other. You must nevertheless continue to practice.

[a] From "Exposure *In Vivo* Treatments by P. M. G. Emmelkamp in A. Goldstein and D. Chambless (Eds.) *Agoraphobia: Multiple Perspectives on Theory and Treatment.* Copyright 1982 by Wiley. Reprinted by permission.

less therapist involvement, prevention of generalization problems from consulting room to the natural environment) there are also some contraindications. First, when patients have to practice from their own homes, some agoraphobics have considerable difficulty in walking again and again along the houses of their neighbors, especially when living in a small community. This problem may sometimes be dealt with by having the patients first practice from another base (for instance, the clinic).

Second, although feedback of the time stayed in the phobic situation may be reinforcing when progress is made, it may work against the therapy if little or no progress is made: several patients became depressed by seeing little progress. Finally, another difficulty with self-controlled exposure is that patients may avoid going into the street by spending their time drinking coffee or going to the toilet. We found it extremely useful to have our patients send in their notes immediately after their home practice. If the therapist did not receive the notes in time, patients were pressed to do so. As a general rule, if after a few sessions of self-controlled exposure *in vivo* no progress is made, other procedures should be considered.

With the self-observation procedure, frequency and spacing of therapist contacts differ from patient to patient. For some agoraphobics only a few sessions with the therapist present are necessary before they are able to apply the procedure on their own. On the other hand, other patients need much more support and it may take considerable time before the therapist can fade out. Even if patients are able to apply the procedure on their own it is advisable to have regular telephone contact in order to stimulate patients to carry on.

The mechanisms by which the self-observation procedure achieves its results are still not clear. One important aspect seems to be the mastery experience that patients get when they apply the procedure. In contrast with their earlier avoidance they now learn coping behavior to deal with their anxiety. Anxiety no longer "overcomes" them; they now have a method to control their anxiety.

Although for some patients, who do not benefit from the self-observation procedure, prolonged exposure *in vivo* may offer a solution, prolonged exposure *in vivo* has also several disadvantages. First, not all patients can be persuaded to undergo this form of treatment. For instance, one of our patients hid in the cellar out of fear of being sent into the street for a prolonged period with no possibility for escape. In addition, a few agoraphobics urinate or defecate when becoming anxious during an exposure session. Since repeated experiences of this kind may enhance the anxiety, self-controlled exposure *in vivo* may be more useful in such cases.

2.2. Prolonged Exposure in Vivo

In this section some clinical guidelines for conducting prolonged exposure *in vivo* are provided. Before actual exposure *in vivo* can commence, patients have to understand the rationale of this particular approach. Here follows an example of the rationale for prolonged exposure *in vivo* that we use in our group therapy for agoraphobia.

2.2.1. Rationale

You have all come here with similar problems. You all become anxious when walking, shopping, etc. You are afraid of panic attacks or of fainting spells. Most of you start to tremble or get palpitations when you find yourself in such situations and some of you even may fear going crazy.

Anxiety is in principle a useful mechanism. Anxiety leads to physical sensations like palpitations, shortness of breath, tightness of the chest, dizziness, trembling, etc. These sensations are quite terrible and make you want to get out of such dangerous situations. Anxiety as a reaction to real danger (e.g., a loose tiger) can be extremely useful and a very functional warning signal. This can be compared with toothache. The pain can be terrible, but useful because it is an indication that you have a cavity. Unfortunately, you become anxious in situations in which this warning signal is of no use.

In fact, your anxiety arises from experiences in the past. Most of you reported on the first anxiety attack. After that traumatic experience you started to avoid the situations in which it had occurred and subsequently you avoided other situations as well in which it possibly could happen also. Because of this sort of experience you now become anxious in situations like walking alone, shopping in busy stores, waiting, travelling by bus, etc., which in fact are not dangerous at all. It is this anxiety that causes your physical sensations like dizziness, palpitations, and shortness of breath. These sensations themselves are likely to make you even more anxious: "Oh, I am going to faint, . . . have a heart-attack, . . . I am going to die." So, even though you are all healthy, you think you have to be careful because something might happen to you.

In this group we will not go into the development of your anxiety. Rather we will deal with the situation which currently maintains your anxiety. In certain situations you become anxious because you are convinced that something terrible is going to happen. You continuously avoid or try to escape from such situations. In this way you will never notice that nothing terrible happens when you remain in these situations long enough. You will continue to be convinced that terrible things are going to happen if you go on avoiding these situations. The more you avoid these situations, the more convinced you become. The very reason your anxiety does not diminish is because you have never tried to see whether the terrible things which you expect *really* occur.

This treatment is focused on helping you to get through these anxiety arousing situations so that you may see that your anxiety is unfounded. You might have some pretty bad times and it will cost you a lot of effort to stay in the phobic situations. A lot of patients before you have gone through this as well with quite good results.

What we are going to do is put ourselves in these difficult situations and *stay* there till the anxiety has subsided. Thus, you are no longer allowed to escape from these situations, since this will maintain or perhaps even increase your anxiety. Take, for example, this housewife who decides to enter a supermarket after some hesitation and becomes anxious. If she immediately runs out, it will cost her more effort to enter the supermarket a next time. She may even send her son or daughter to avoid going to the supermarket. The next time when she is forced to go shopping it will be very difficult if not well-nigh impossible for her to do so. Thus, when you become anxious in certain situations it is very important for you to stay there and not try to escape. Of course, as a result of your anxiety you may experience palpitations, start to perspire, become dizzy, etc. However, the anxiety and the accompanying sensations will gradually diminish when you stay in the anxiety-arousing situations long enough.

Although it is important for the patient to understand the rationale, the therapist must not expect the patients to fullheartedly agree with the notion that the anxiety will decrease when staying in the phobic situations long enough. It is of no use to prolong the discussion at length or to try to convince the patient rationally of the rightness of this notion. The best way to convince the patients is to confront them with the anxiety-arousing situations: Experience is the best teacher.

2.2.2. Microanalysis

It is important to find out what exactly the patient is afraid of. Although most agoraphobics are afraid of crowds, other situations that are feared differ from patient to patient. One patient is afraid of quiet alleys outside the town center, another of walking past water, and a third is afraid of unfamiliar places. Still other patients are afraid to be in places where they cannot take a bus or taxi to flee home in case of "emergency."

It is useful to observe patients during their first practice session. It is especially important to watch how fast or slow a patient is walking. Some patients walk very fast in order to finish the assignments as quickly as possible. Other patients, however, walk slowly for fear of falling.

Furthermore, it is good to pay attention to subtle avoidance behavior during practice. Some people keep looking down for fear of stumbling or in order to avoid eye contact. For instance, in one of our social-anxious agoraphobics treatment by prolonged exposure to busy high street did not lead to any anxiety reduction. Discussion after the exposure session revealed that the patient had continuously avoided looking at other people, thus preventing real exposure to the distressing stimuli. The next session the patient had to walk along the same route, but now she was instructed to make eye contact. Although exposure carried out like this initially led to considerably more anxiety than on the previous occasion, the anxiety finally dissipated. Other subtle forms of avoidance behavior may include taking pills, wearing sunglasses, talking to someone, or running. Other tricks to avoid or reduce anxiety are walking close to shops, because it gives "support," looking at shop windows to seek diversion, chewing gum, and leaning against something, and things like that. In addition, real exposure may still be avoided through cognitive avoidance, for example by such thoughts as: "There is a hospital." . . . "My sister lives there." . . . "A general practitioner lives there." . . . "If something goes wrong there will be help." If exposure is to be meaningful the more subtle forms of avoidance behavior will also have to be dealt with.

2.2.3. Exposure Sessions

Although treatment by prolonged exposure *in vivo* looks simple, it is not so easy to apply. First of all, it is extremely important to confront the patient with distressing stimuli continuously, without escape or avoidance. Novices often have their patients walk for a few minutes in the street, visit a supermarket for a few minutes, ride in a bus for a few minutes and so on until the session is over. Although the exposure session is prolonged, actual exposure to each separate situation is short. Thus, it is not surprising that exposure along these lines often leads to failure. The effects of such an exposure may be that patients repeatedly escape when they are still anxious in a particular situation. It is essential that patients remain in one situation (for example in a bus) until anxiety is declined before entering a new situation (for example shopping). These guidelines imply that *in vivo* treatment—even when conducted in groups—should be tailor-made to the needs of each individual patient. If a patient has to practice travelling by bus, it is important to choose a route that is long enough so that anxiety-reduction can take place. Often, the distance from or to a safe point (hospital, home) is also important. Generally, patients find it more difficult to travel on out-of-town buses than on city buses. In supermarkets, it is important for the patient to practice during rush hours and to stand in the longest line at the check-out counters. For most agoraphobic patients, waiting is awful and it is advisable to pay necessary attention to it. Other situations where waiting can be practiced are bus stops, waiting-rooms, postoffices, etc.

Deliberate anxiety provocation is not necessary. In contrast with our earlier view when we adopted a flooding strategy, prolonged exposure might be accomplished along a hierarchy from less to more distressing situations. However, it is essential that the situations a patient is exposed to during a particular session are of the same subjective anxiety level. Otherwise, habituation to the distressing situations may be prevented since patients may repeatedly feel relief because of their exposure to situations that do not evoke anxiety.

It is important to formulate the assignments as specifically as possible. For example, a vague formulated assignment like "Go shopping in a department store" offers the patient opportunity enough to "avoid." It is better to indicate exactly what is expected of him. For example: "Go to department store X and walk about on the ground floor until you feel at ease. After that go to the first floor and walk about, keeping as far away from the escalators as possible, until you feel at ease. Then go to the next floors and do the same. If there are special situations which you find very difficult, stay there and wait until the pressure has dropped."

It is advisable for the patient to help formulate the assignments as much as possible. On the one hand, this increases the patient's concern for his assignment. Moreover, it becomes more difficult for the patient not to carry out his assignment because he has helped formulate it.

While discussing the assignments, the therapist must not allow himself to be led too easily by the patient's avoidance behavior (such as discussing, becoming afraid, weeping). Often patients are glad to have carried out assignments which at first they were afraid of. On the other hand, the therapist must not demand too much. Especially if a patient is "doing fine" it is tempting to make high demands which, if the patient fails to carry out an assignment, may lead to disappointment and relapse.

The speed at which exposure *in vivo* can be carried out varies from patient to patient. It is important for every patient to practice at his own pace and not to hurry so that anxiety-reduction can be clearly felt. In the case of group treatment, too, it is important not to go beyond what the patients can handle. Some patients are jealous of the progress of other patients. Therefore, it is important for the therapist to keep explaining that the patients' problems cannot be compared.

It is important for the patient to practice outside of therapy sessions as well, but the rate at which this occurs depends on the frequency of the therapy sessions and on the patient's personal circumstances. If the patient practices in his natural environment there must be enough time for anxiety reduction. When formulating the homework assignments, care must be taken not to choose assignments that are too difficult. As a general rule it makes sense not to go beyond what has been practiced during the therapy session. Assignments that are too difficult are a reason for some patients not to carry out their homework at all.

When agoraphobia is associated with cardiac neurosis, exposure *in vivo* to situations that patients avoid is usually of little benefit. Often exposure *in vivo* may lead to some improvements, but one experience of palpitations may negate the improvements achieved. In these cases, exposure to internal stimuli and palpitations that are deliberately provoked by the therapist might be more useful than exposure to the situations which they avoid. This can be achieved by having the patient do physical exercises that trigger palpitations or by provoking hyperventilation deliberately, first in the therapist's office and then by the patient at home.

Clinically, various treatments often have to be combined. Although it sometimes is useful to start with the second treatment only after the first treatment is finished, in other cases it may be better to use various procedures concurrently. For instance, a social-anxious agoraphobic patient may receive assertiveness training in the clinic while she conducts an exposure *in vivo* homework program concurrently on her own. Social situations of increasing difficulty may be included in the exposure *in vivo* program after the successful performance of the appropriate social skills during the assertiveness training sessions.

3. SOCIAL ANXIETY

It is important when treating social anxiety to pay attention to avoidance behavior. Characteristically, most patients avoid attracting attention, and this is expressed in various ways. Patients who are afraid of blushing often wear scarfs and turtleneck sweaters, use a lot of makeup, and are inclined to sit in dark places. Some men wear their hair long and grow a beard so that their faces can hardly be seen. Usually, socially anxious patients wear inconspicuous clothes.

When patients go out they often wear sunglasses and feel they must have something in their hand (e.g., a bag). Some patients often look back to see if they are being observed. Groups of children or construction workers are avoided because they may laugh at the patient. Most patients do not go to parties. A number of socially anxious patients do not dare leave their house at all for fear of what people might think of them. Most patients avoid eye contact.

Whether or not they know people well is often influential on the anxiety: Some patients are more afraid of people they know well, while others are afraid of people they do not know.

During exposure *in vivo*, it is important to take specific fear-provoking stimuli and specific avoidance behavior of a patient into account, although in practice this may present problems. Socially anxious patients are often unsystematically exposed to those daily life situations they fear without them showing definitive improvement. A systematic and prolonged exposure in real life situations is difficult to arrange.

Group treatment offers an excellent opportunity to socially anxious patients to confront their feared situations in the group. For example, patients who are afraid of blushing have to sit in front of others while wearing an open blouse until anxiety dissipates. Others who fear that their hands may tremble have to write on the blackboard and to serve tea to the group. Or to give another example, patients who fear that they might stutter (but in fact rarely do) have to give a speech in front of the group.

In our exposure groups for social phobics an important part of treatment consists of actual exposure *in vivo* in "town." Patients and therapist go to the town center where the patients have to perform a number of difficult tasks. They have to practice these assignments again and again (in different shops, bars etc.) until they feel better. Examples of assignments that can be used are the following:

1. Go to a hi-fi store (not in a department store) and let a clerk inform you extensively about color TV sets. Inquire about the advantages and disadvantages of the different makes, the longevity, the price, and guarantee, etc.
2. Go to a supermarket and buy *one* article, hold the right amount of money in your hand and ask another customer if you could go first at the check-out counter. If the answer is "no" try again at another counter.
3. Go to a travel agency and inquire about trips to Portugal for a certain period of time previously decided upon. You want to go as cheap as possible. Ask, for example, whether it is possible to travel by charter-flight without having to take an all-inclusive trip.
4. Go to an established record shop and ask one of the assistants for medieval music. Select one record from this category and ask to listen to it. Listen to a part of it. Do not buy anything.
5. Visit a busy department store with an alarm clock section. Set off at least one of the alarms. Do not buy it.
6. Buy a piece of cheese in a busy shop and ask if you may taste it first.
7. Ask a number of people in the street where they bought their coat, bag, tie, etc.
8. Go into a bar and start a conversation with a stranger.
9. Go to a telephone booth. Call up a civil servant and ask for detailed information about passports, bus tickets, their policy on equal rights for women, the town's new traffic plan, etc.
10. Go to a bar and ask to use the phone. Only use the phone; do not order anything.
11. Enter a shoe store. Ask someone to help you. Try on at least five pairs of shoes, but do not buy any.

12. Stand in line at the supermarket and give the person in front of you a compliment.
13. Go into a store and change $25 for two tens and five ones. Do not buy anything.
14. Walk in a straight line through a busy street. Do not step aside for anyone and look passers-by straight in the eyes.
15. Walk through a busy street and give someone of the opposite sex about your own age a smile.
16. Go to the butchers and buy some meat (not minced meat). Pay attention to the scales. If the butcher asks, "Alright if it's a bit more?" Tell him you would rather have the exact amount. If he does not say anything and you check the scales and see that it is too much, inform the butcher about this and tell him you want the exact amount you have asked for. If you did not have the chance to check the scales ask the butcher the weight and then insist on the right amount.
17. Stop a person in the street and ask him the way to the Tourist Information Bureau. Pick someone who looks like a difficult type. To make sure you understood the directions, repeat the information to the person.
18. Take a ride on a city bus. Say to the driver: "I have to go to the _____ street. Can you tell me where to get out?" If possible take a seat with your back to the driver. After a while ask the person opposite you if he/she would mind changing places.
19. Buy something. Pay with a check and say that you have forgotten your identification card.

It should be stressed that treatment has to be adapted to the individual needs of the patient. The therapist should choose those assignments that are beneficial to a particular individual. Often a hierarchy has to be made because some of the tasks are too difficult to start with.

Usually, anxiety does not dissipate during one task because of its short duration. Therefore, patients have to practice various tasks of the same sort and of the same subjective anxiety level *without any break* until they feel better, which means that exposure *in vivo* sessions may last up to 3 hours.

Massed exposure sessions are to be preferred to spaced sessions. A useful format is to have 3-hour sessions three times a week.

When patients succeed in overcoming their anxiety during the exposure session they frequently invent even more difficult tasks for themselves and their group members than those suggested by the therapist. For example, one of our patients who was afraid of trembling was instructed to talk with a stranger in a bar. When she successfully accomplished the assignment she offered him a drink which she managed to serve without trembling. Her "courage" stimulated others to think out more difficult tasks for themselves. A friendly competitiveness is common in exposure groups.

In most cases specific programs must be instituted as homework to foster generalization from the treatment setting to the natural environment. In the course of the treatment program, patients receive homework assignments appropriate to their individual needs. The exposure principle can be applied to many social situations (e.g., friends, family, work setting). The therapist and patient select a task which is not too difficult for the patient to perform in real life so that he is likely to succeed in handling it. Each successful performance will increase the patient's self-confidence, which sets the stage for further performance attempts.

It is important to note that the effects of exposure *in vivo* programs with socially anxious patients have not yet been evaluated. While a number of patients derive some benefit from exposure *in vivo*, often other treatments such as cognitive restructuring and social skills training have to be added. Further, for some patients group treatment is too threatening and these patients need an individual program first before they can participate in a group program.

12

Treatment of Obsessive-Compulsive Disorders

In this chapter information necessary for the microanalysis of obsessive-compulsive behavior and the subsequent treatment will be discussed. Although often a comprehensive treatment should be applied, we will limit our focus here to the treatment of the obsessive-compulsive behavior *per se* through exposure and response prevention.

1. PREPARATION FOR TREATMENT

1.1. Microanalysis

As a first step in the microanalysis we need to determine what external stimuli or internal stimuli (thoughts) give rise to the obsessive-compulsive behavior. Questions to be asked are: "Can you give me a full account when you have to wash your hands?" and "When you start to wash your hands what do you think about?" It is often extremely helpful to have the patient give a detailed account of the previous day starting with his wakening and ending with his falling asleep.

With washing rituals, the therapist should gather information with respect to the reason why a patient feels contaminated: "You say you feel dirty when you touch an apple, can you tell me why?" Or in the case of checking rituals the therapist may ask what would happen if the patient failed to perform his rituals. Such questions might provide the therapist with information concerning the obsessional thoughts underlying the problem.

The therapist should be alert to the possibility that the patient may find it difficult to relate certain aspects of the problem, especially related to toilet rituals and sexual issues. The therapist should discuss these topics in a matter-of-fact way thus demonstrating that the patient does not have to feel ashamed about it. Similarly, with harming obsessions the therapist may prompt information by direct questioning. For example, with a patient who is afraid of knives and has serious difficulties in discussing this topic the therapist may ask: "A lot of people who are afraid of knives have obsessions to kill people; I wonder whether you are an exception?" Often such a frank statement on the part of the therapist will enhance further communication.

Special attention should be devoted to situations that patients avoid because of their difficulties. The therapist should keep in mind that apart from active avoidance (rituals), often a lot of passive avoidance is involved. Patients with washing rituals will go to great length to prevent contamination. Similarly, checkers will avoid situations that may trigger their rituals; that is, they avoid being alone, driving, using matches, and being the last one to go to bed. Further, it is important to determine whether family members have taken over former responsibilities of the patient or give constant reassurance, which maintain the problem.

The content of the ritual is another important aspect that needs to be attended to in the initial interviews. How long does the ritual take? Does the patient have to do things in a special sequence? What happens when he is interrupted during the performance of a ritual? The therapist should not expect that the performance of the ritual can be explained according to common logic. One of our patients had to wash her hands 25 times each time she felt contaminated. When asked why she was able to stop after 25 times she frankly replied: "You don't expect me to go on forever?"

To illustrate the detailed information that is required for treatment planning, the following case is presented. The information was gathered in two interviews, one in the office and the second in the home of the patient. Additionally, the hierarchy of exposure tasks that was based on the information gathered during the initial interview is presented. For illustrative purposes a relatively simple case was chosen.

1.2. Case Example

The patient is a 27-year-old unmarried nurse, who had suffered increasingly from fear of contamination and compulsive washing since she was 14 years old. Before being referred to us she had been treated with systematic desensitization without any success for two years.

1.2.1. Information Gathering

The functional analysis revealed that the complaints stemmed from problems with her parents. At first she had an aversion to kissing or touching her parents and did not like to go out with them. In the same period she no longer wanted to make use of the toilet, because her parents used it as well.

Eight years ago, when she moved to city X where she got a job in a hospital, the problem became more serious. The heart of the problem is contamination by objects from the parental home in city A. Letters from city A are thrown away in a special garbage can in the corridor. Everything she has touched before washing her hands is cleaned thoroughly or disposed of.

She washes her hands with disinfecting soap in a ritualistic, stereotype manner which lasts for about eight minutes. If she has touched "contaminated" material she must perform this ritual three times or take a shower in a ritualistic way.

When going to visit her parents, she gets dressed in the attic where special clothes for this occasion are kept. Her housemate opens all the doors and the patient goes up to the attic wearing nothing but wooden shoes. Except for this occasion she never visits the attic. The attic and the garbage can in the corridor have become secondary anxiety-provoking stimuli. She is afraid of using the sink under the attic stairs; instead she washes in the kitchen. She also feels that the ceiling of her room, which is under the attic, is contaminated.

Foodstuffs are stored in the living room because the kitchen leads to the corridor. The attic door and the garbage can are avoided; she walks via a "special route" through the corridor, with her hands high above her head. She is afraid to speak in the corridor. If this ever happens she brushes her teeth thoroughly.

She never walks barefoot, because she has walked there when wearing contaminated shoes. She wears her sleeves rolled up to prevent contamination. Her clothes are washed in the hospital laundry (often several times).

She avoids contact with her housemate because the latter makes use of the garbage can in the corridor and sometimes goes upstairs to the attic. They used to have dinner together but never do anymore. She has not received any friends for a year for fear they might be contaminated.

Avoidance is not limited to her home. Streets in which there are litterbins are avoided, because she used to throw away mail from city A in these bins. Normally, she avoids stations and trains, except when she occasionally (specially dressed) travels to her parents' home. Further, she avoids people who she knows have recently travelled by train. If she sees a person with a train ticket near the coffee-machine, she refuses to drink coffee. She is afraid to touch money, which she suspects of having come from the station. For the same reason she is afraid to touch newspapers she sees lying about. In the hospital, she checks registrations to see whether patients are connected to the railway company. If such is the case, she avoids them as much as possible.

Situations connected to city A in any way at all are avoided. For example a bank affiliation, which has its head office in city A is avoided, because it receives mail daily from city A.

1.2.2. Hierarchy Construction

On the basis of a microanalysis such as this, a hierarchy was constructed: the patient rates the anxiety level of a number of items from 0 to 100 (0 = no anxiety; 100 = maximal anxiety). Both the extent of exposure and the extent of response prevention are structured into one hierarchy. In this case study, the patient is not allowed to perform her rituals after exposure to each item, and is informed of this in advance. The final hierarchy presented to the patient was as follows:

	Anxiety level
1. From now on, no more checking to see if patients are connected to the railway company.	10
2. Visit a contaminated bank and ask for information extensively.	20
3. Wash hands "normally" with everyday soap within 30 seconds.	20
4. Walk barefoot through the room.	25
5. Touch and read newspapers lying about in the waiting-rooms.	30
6. Talk in the corridor and do not brush your teeth afterward.	35
7. Do not walk about with rolled up sleeves.	35
8. Do not walk with your hands in the air in the corridor.	35
9. Wash your clothes at home instead of at the hospital.	35
10. Store foodstuffs in the kitchen.	40
11. Invite people to your room.	40
12. Have dinner with your housemate.	40
13. Touch your ceiling for a period of time.	40
14. Walk directly to the sink under the attic stairs without following the special route and wash there from now on.	45
15. Walk barefoot through the corridor.	45
16. Touch and hold the garbage can in the corridor.	65
17. Visit friends who have just traveled by train.	70

18. Touch "station money" extensively and put it in with the other money in your purse.   75
19. Touch and hold the litter bins in the streets.   75
20. Feel the attic door.   80
21. Hold letters from city A.   80
22. Leave letters from city A lying about in your room.   85
23. Push your hands into the garbage can and stir about.   90
24. Show friends your attic.   90
25. Walk about the station for a long time and touch as many people as possible.   95
26. Travel by train wearing normal clothes.   95
27. Rub your naked body all over with letters from city A.   95
28. Put on the special clothes from the attic and wear these at home for a few days, contaminating everything.   95
29. Wear these special clothes outside the house, to the hospital, when visiting friends, and touch everything as often as possible.   95
30. Travel to city A by train wearing *normal* clothes and visit your parents. Touch and hold *everything* and keep wearing these clothes when back at home. Do not wash or shower for at least two days.   100

Treatment in this case involved three exposure sessions in the company of the therapist, but most tasks were accomplished as homework assignments. Treatment was highly successful. Within a few weeks the patient could manage the most difficult tasks and resume a normal life.

Often different dimensions of obsessive-compulsive behavior can be distinguished for which different hierarchies could be constructed. For instance, separate hierarchies can be constructed for washing, checking, or hoarding, respectively. However, we have found it more useful to combine the items into one hierarchy, because the only relevant criterion for progress with the *in vivo* exercises seems to be the anxiety experienced. Sometimes, during treatment, changes in the hierarchy have to be made. For instance, the anxiety experienced when carrying out difficult items cannot often be estimated adquately at the start of the treatment, while after some practice a finer discrimination of the top-items of the hierarchy may as yet be achieved.

1.3. Explanation of Treatment Rationale

Before starting actual treatment, it is important for the patient to understand the rationale of treatment. Although it can be useful to explain that the anxiety and compulsions are the result of past learning experiences, an extensive theoretical explanation in terms of conditioning is of little value. The treatment is explained using one or more examples given by the patient. It is necessary that the patient understands that his problem is maintained through passive and active avoidance. To illustrate this, an example of the explanation of treatment given to a patient suffering from fears of contamination and washing rituals is provided:

> Washing your hands immediately after you feel contaminated may indeed reduce your anxiety. In the long run, however, you gain nothing by this. As you have seen, more and more situations have became anxiety-provoking that now lead you to avoid them. On an increasing number of occasions you felt the urge to wash your hands to achieve anxiety-relief. By continually avoiding anxiety-provoking situations, you will not notice that anxiety also reduces when you touch contaminated material without washing your hands afterward. If you do not give in to the urge to wash, it will take longer, maybe even some hours, for your anxiety to reduce. Eventually, however, anxiety will be reduced. When you expose yourself to contaminated situations a number of times, without performing your washing ritual, you will notice that, in the long run, you will get used to these situations and they will no longer be anxiety-provoking.

Explain to the patient that exposure will be gradual, starting with relatively easy situations. To see just how much the patient has understood the rationale, it may be useful to have him write it down in his own words when he is at home. If, at the following session, it appears that the rationale is still not understood, it can be explained one more time.

2. EXPOSURE *IN VIVO*

The principle of exposure is often easier to state than to carry out in practice. To what exactly do patients have to be exposed during treatment? In the case of fear of contamination, it is often easy to determine to what stimuli patients have to be exposed, but in the case of checkers it is much more complicated to carry out an exposure program.

2.1. Checking Compulsions

It is characteristic of most checkers to be afraid of harming themselves or other people. It is essential that they themselves feel responsible. Exposure, then, must be aimed at bringing them into situations in which they are responsible. For this reason, exposure in the presence of the therapist is often not a genuine exposure, for the patient can easily transfer the responsibility for the action to the therapist.

In addition, it is important to notice that the nature of the exercises often excludes the repetition of the same exercise during one session. For example, the checking of gas can be done only once during an exposure session. If the patient is assigned to do this more often, it is no longer genuine exposure, for when the patient carries out the assignment a second time, he is in fact checking whether he has done it right the first time and is thus reassured. Instead of carrying out such an exercise several times during one session, it is better to do this only once, after which the patient has to leave the house and is not allowed to return for at least a few hours. In the case of practicing checking items at his work, it is important that the patient is the last one to go home so that he is responsible.

Now I will give a number of examples of exposure assignments for patients with frequently occurring checking compulsions.

If patients are afraid to cause traffic accidents they are assigned to drive along difficult routes by themselves without going back to check whether they have not caused an accident. They are not allowed to read newspapers or call the police to check if an accident has occurred.

When patients are afraid that their actions harm other people (by means of glass splinters, pins, etc.), the exposure consists of having them break glass, drop pins, or leave knives laying about.

In the case of patients who are afraid to say insulting things about people and who have to check whether they have not lost notes that may be insulting, the patient has to walk around in town, having notes with insulting remarks about certain people with him. He is not allowed to check whether he has lost any notes. A more difficult assignment is to have the patient drop these notes without picking them up afterward.

2.2. Cleaning Compulsions

In the case of an exposure program for cleaning compulsions, treatment usually consists of two elements: first, the patient is exposed to "dirt" without being allowed to clean it. Second, the treatment aims at teaching the patient to clean in a nonritualistic way. It is important that both elements are practiced separately. If a patient is first exposed to dirt and immediately afterwards allowed to clean it, the exposure element is of little or no use, because the cleaning reduces the fear. A few examples of assignments for this kind of patients may clarify this:

1. Do not mop the floor of your bathroom for a week. After this, clean it within three minutes, using an ordinary mop. Use this mop for other chores as well without cleaning it.

2. Clean the window sill with a few broad sweeps within 20 seconds. The sill is cleaned in this way only once every other week.
3. Buy a fluffy mohair sweater and wear it for a week. When taking it off at night do not remove the bits of fluff. Do not clean your house for a week.
4. Dust the doormat in your livingroom. Do not clean the house for a week.
5. You, your husband, and children all have to keep shoes on. Do not clean the house for a week.
6. Do not have your children go upstairs naked, but let them undress in their bedroom. Do not clean the bedrooms for a week.
7. (The week after) Clean the playroom within ten minutes (only with the vacuum cleaner, no dusting).
8. Vacuum the house within 50 minutes (livingroom, kitchen, hall, and bedrooms) without doing things twice.
9. Drop a cookie on the contaminated floor, pick the cookie up and eat it.
10. Drop your knives and forks on the floor and use them for dinner.
11. Leave the sheets and blankets on the floor and then put them on the beds. Do not change these for a week.

If patients are afraid to be contaminated by specific stimuli (e.g., cancer, venereal disease), their houses have to be contaminated with such stimuli. For example, with objects from a "contaminated" ward, such as a nurse's apron, all kinds of utensils, foods, beds, and clothes can be contaminated.

2.3. Precision

With patients who are compulsively precise, exposure consists of putting all kinds of objects into disarray and changing precise habits. Some assignments could be:

1. Leave newspapers and clothes lying around in the living room for a week.
2. Change the positions of the objects on the dressing table in an arbitrary way.
3. Put plates, cups, and pans in another place (slovenly).
4. Invite people for the weekend and have the whole house in disarray.

5. Pull a pillowcase from the middle of a pile of pillowcases and leave the pile as it is.
6. Do not iron your clothes for a week and wear unironed shirts and blouses.
7. Put your books and records in the wrong places.
8. Change the locations of the couch and the dining table within 20 minutes and leave them like that.
9. Hang your paintings aslant.
10. Put all kinds of things in different places and in different positions (picture frames, plants, tablecover, paintings).
11. Be ten minutes late for an appointment without giving an explanation or making excuses.
12. Throw the pillows on the beds and leave them as they fall.
13. Put on a checked shirt and roll up the sleeves in such a way that there are more checks visible on the one than on the other sleeve.
14. Put the chairs visibly askew.
15. Shower at night instead of in the morning.
16. Go to work at varying times.

2.4. Compulsions Related to Death

With some patients rituals are triggered by thoughts about death and deceased people. Hence all kinds of situations that may evoke thoughts about death are avoided, such as reading newspapers (the obituaries), watching television, or going to a cemetery. The rituals are often very subtle and may consist of "touching wood," mentioning particular numbers or proverbs, expressing neutralizing thoughts to oneself, turning one's head away (from a cemetery), repeating whatever one was occupied with, etc. Of course, it is pointed out to the patient that he must get rid of these rituals. Some of the exposure assignments could be:

1. Read the obituaries in the newspapers.
2. Cut out an arbitrary obituary and keep it with you all week.
3. Go to a cemetery and read the epitaphs with care.
4. Sit down on a tombstone.
5. Keep a card with the name and a picture of your deceased father with you.
6. Sit down in the chair of your deceased father.
7. Put on a suit of your deceased father and wear it all week.
8. Follow a funeral procession.
9. Go to a cremation.

With other patients thoughts about death evoke feelings of guilt rather than fear. For example, a 40-year-old patient had compulsive thoughts about offending the dead. He continually wondered whether a particular thought, action, or remark did offend the dead (especially his father-in-law), which caused him to feel guilty. He attempted to get rid of his guilt feelings through rituals (repetition), asking for reassurance, etc. Treatment in this case consisted in part of offending the dead, both at home and at the cemetery. In such cases it is essential that exposure evokes the feelings of guilt.

2.5. Doubting

Even though doubting is a common characteristic of many obsessive-compulsives, for some patients it is the essential feature of their disorders. Generally, treatment in these cases involves exposure to situations in which the patients have to take decisions by themselves and are not allowed to reconsider these decisions. Some examples of exposure assignments could be:

1. You alone have to decide what clothes to wear (within two minutes).
2. You yourself have to decide what coat to put on (within one minute). Go out in this coat and do not return to change it.
3. Become a member of one of the five following societies (give list to patient).
4. Buy a new pair of trousers in shop X within 15 minutes without looking in other shops first. Do not try on more than two pairs. Do not ask for advice. Do not exchange the trousers.
5. Buy a book in shop X within ten minutes. Do not exchange it.
6. Buy shoes in shop X. Do not try on more than five pairs. Do not exchange them.
7. Apply for job X. If the company wants to hire you, decide within 24 hours and call them immediately.
8. Decide before next week where to go on holiday.
9. Go to ten insurance companies and ask for advice about furniture insurance. Read everything twice, thoroughly, and then decide. Sent the letter at once.
10. Have youself informed about record players in two different shops (no longer than 15 minutes in each). After this decide within 30 minutes and buy the one you want at once.
11. You and your wife go to a film tonight. Look in the newspapers to see what films are shown (five minutes) and book reservations by telephone. Do not debate with your wife.

Exposure in these cases presents special problems because the patient has to take important decisions all by himself without appealing for reassurance from his partner. In these cases it is always useful to inform the patient's partner about the rationale of the treatment. If such a program is to be carried out, the cooperation of the partner is required.

2.6. Compulsive Buying and Hoarding

Compulsive buying may be treated by exposure to situations in which patients have ample opportunity to buy but are not allowed to do so. Typically, patients having a lot of money with them are brought into situations in which they are tempted to buy (e.g., in a shopping mall) but have to stay there without buying anything until the discomfort has dropped. Treatment of compulsive hoarding involves throwing out all kinds of superfluous objects. Patients who suffer from this compulsion may have cupboards full of ten-year-old cash slips, old notes, hundreds of pairs of shoes, underwear, and clothes which in extreme cases may fill whole rooms. None of these things will ever be used but the patient is afraid to throw them away in case they might come in handy. Here therapist-assisted exposure in often required to help the patient throw away these objects.

2.7. Asking for Reassurance

Asking for reassurance is a frequently occurring phenomenon with obsessionals and has the same function as the rituals. If a patient feels uncertain or afraid he may calm down (temporarily) through reassurance. In the microanalysis of the compulsive behavior the therapist must determine how far the patient asks for reassurance. If it occurs, due attention must be paid to it during treatment. Looking for reassurance can consist of asking relatives, people involved, or experts, but also looking up items in newspapers, encyclopedias. It is explained to the patient on the basis of the anxiety-reduction model how by asking for reassurance the anxiety is maintained. The patient is instructed to stop this. It is often necessary to inform relatives about the necessity to stop giving reassurance, and in some cases it can be useful to teach them by means of role-playing how to deal with such questions: "I know you feel terrible, but Dr. E. instructed us not to give in to your questions."

2.8. Compulsive Breaking

Although it often occurs that patients are afraid of breaking things, the reverse (being compelled to break things) is rare. One of our patients could not go past windows, mirrors, and other glassware without feeling the urge to break these, which, indeed, he frequently did. In this case, treatment involved exposure to situations in which the urge to break things was provoked but not allowed to be satisfied (response prevention). The therapist accompanied the patient to his home, where the patient had to touch windows and mirrors, to hold glasses and to touch the TV screen, etc. Although the exposure provoked the urge to break things, this urge and the accompanying discomfort diminished after some time. Treatment along these lines proved to be highly success-ful. After 10 sessions the patient was symptom free and was able to resume a normal life, eat from regular plates and drink from normal glasses, watch television, go past shopwindows, etc.

2.9. Self-Controlled Exposure

It is important, with self-controlled exposure, to establish fixed times at which the patient has to do his assignments. As a rule, we prescribe two-hour sessions without a break. The patient must be at home alone so that he can practice without being disturbed. During these two hours, the patient has to carry out the assignments. He may pass on to the next assignment only when the anxiety/tension arising from the preceding assignment has diminished to a reasonable extent. In the discussion with the therapist, the practice session is talked about in detail and a close look is taken at the new assignments. If the patient has not done his homework (which rarely happens), the therapist asks for the reason and sends the patient home to do it (except in exceptional cases, when there is a real cause for talking somewhat longer; for example, with the death of the patient's mother).

The assignments are written down on separate notecards. It is very important that they be clearly formulated. A formulation such as "Leave your house at 10 A.M. without checking the gas, electricity, water, and doorlocks, go to A and do not return before midnight," is clearer than "Do not check when you leave the house."

There are no general guidelines with respect to the number of situations a hierarchy should consist of and the number of situations per homework session. It depends on the patient and on how difficult the assignments are. Some patients are quick to perceive the basic principle and apply this in other situations as well. Other patients, however, do not generalize at all and have to practice every situation separately, which may have absurd consequences. One patient was able to sit on the floor and pick up things from the floor without experiencing any anxiety during her homework sessions, but could not do it out of these sessions.

Here, the instruction cards of the therapist had become safety signals. At the end of her treatment this patient asked for copies of the instruction cards so as to give these to her neighbors, in case her own cards would be lost in a fire. Clearly, treatment had been less successful than we would have wished it to be. In similar cases we have found a fading procedure to be useful. First the therapist writes down the assignments on cards, later on he only gives oral instructions. After this, the patient himself devises assignments, which he discusses with the therapist. In the last phase, treatment is left entirely in the hands of the patient. The patient has to devise assignments himself and carry them out without consulting his therapist.

Not every assignment can be practiced within the two-hour sessions. For example, a visit from or to certain people cannot easily be arranged in the sessions. In such cases the patient has to carry out the assignment outside the session hours, but always keeping the hierarchy in mind.

If assignments have been practiced well enough, the patient has to maintain them in his daily life. If, for example, a patient has learned to leave his house without checking, he should keep on doing this; or when a patient has learned to wash in a nonritualistic way, he should henceforth wash in a normal way.

2.10. Practical Guidelines

The following items provide some practical tips for carrying out the exposure treatment.

1. The hierarchy that has been established at the beginning of the treatment has to be flexible. There are often circumstances that make it necessary to adjust the assignments or add new ones.

2. The therapist must be empathetic yet firm. During the exposure part of treatment, negotiations about the necessity of (carrying out) one or more assignments have to be avoided as much as possible. If the patient disregards certain items or has "rational" objections, the therapist must not give in too easily. The patient's objections against certain assignments can often be regarded as avoidance behavior.

3. If the assignments do not yield the desired results as quickly as the patient would like, the following encouragement may help: "You cannot expect to be rid of a habit that you have had for years within just a few days. Instead of thinking that all this makes no sense, it is more rational to conclude that you need more practice before having mastered it completely."

4. The patient must not be satisfied if an assignment goes well once or for a short period of time: the patient has to go on practicing in

order to diminish the chance of relapse until it poses no more problems in daily life.

5. If the anxiety reduces during practice, but the obsessive thoughts do not disappear soon, which disconcerts the patient, the following remark may be helpful: "With a number of patients such obsessions diminish in the course of time. For the time being I am satisfied with the fact that the anxiety reduces during practice. Should it appear after some time and you are still troubled by these obsessions, we will have to deal with them separately."

6. Often the patients think the proposed assignments are "overdone" and say that nobody they know is as slovenly, dirty, or careless as the therapist instructs them to be. It should be explained, then, that the assignments may aid them to overcome their anxiety but are not meant as a standard for their future life. At the end of treatment the patients are free to choose how to lead their own lives without this choice being governed by their fear, as now often is the case.

7. At the end of treatment it is sensible to point out to the patients that they may sooner or later experience a (slight) relapse. However, they know how to deal with such a relapse: They should not avoid anxiety-provoking situations but expose themselves to these without rituals until the anxiety is reduced.

3. COURSE OF THERAPEUTIC INTERVENTION

In the case description that follows, we will trace a course of therapy that illustrates the use of self-controlled exposure *in vivo*.

3.1. Information Gathering (Sessions One and Two)

Julia is a 28-year-old unmarried female who works and lives in a home for aged persons. Her obsessive-compulsive behavior involves both washing and checking.

Julia is afraid of cleaning products like cleansers, detergents, liquid ammonia, and turpentine; products she has to use daily in her work. She is afraid that by touching these products she may contaminate other people (colleagues, patients). In addition, she is afraid of having cracked or chipped plates, cups and saucers, glasses, and such that might harm other people. Furthermore, she is afraid of having unknowingly turned on the gas or of having cut the gas or electricity cable. She avoids sharp objects like tacks, knitting needles, pins, knives, and such for fear of leaving them lying about and thus possibly causing an accident to some other person. Lastly, Julia is afraid of having set a fire, especially in places she can no longer check like summer houses, trains, and rooms of patients or personnel. She never carries matches with her and when other people use either a match or a lighter she asks them to put these away safely.

Julia avoids cleaning products and situations that might contaminate her. To make sure that she is not contaminated, she washes her hands about 30 times a day, changes into clean clothes if she happens to have come in contact with cleaning products or other contaminated material, and checks cups and plates carefully before putting them away after having done the washing. She is afraid to set a glass on the edge of a table and requests people who do this to move their glasses. To avoid coming in contact with cleaning products, gas, and electricity, she avoids the kitchen as much as possible. The patient was referred to us when she was no longer able to do her work. She could not walk or travel unaccompanied and was unable to go shopping by herself for fear of accidentally injuring other people. She came to the therapy sessions accompanied by her boyfriend.

3.2. Third Session

In the third session, the assignments formulated by the therapist were scored according to the degree of anxiety they evoked, and a hierarchy was set up. Julia accepted the rationale of the treatment. It was agreed that she would practice for at least two hours uninterrupted twice a week. At the end of the sessions, the following assignments (for which an anxiety level was rated between 0–10) were given to her to practice in the first two homework sessions.

1. Drink from a cup without first checking to see or asking people whether it is chipped.
2. Tap the liquid detergent against the liquid ammonia without washing your hands. Do not ask anybody whether this might be dangerous — no reassurance.
3. Lift the ammonia bottle by the cap without washing your hands afterward — no reassurance.
4. Hold the cloth drenched in ammonia tightly without washing your hands afterward — no reassurance.
5. Pour detergent into the washing machine without washing your hands afterward. Do not wipe your hands on your clothes and do not change into clean clothes — no reassurance.
6. Throw a used coffee filter into the trash and do not wash your hands afterward.

7. Hold the clean wash before hanging against your clothes and let it dry. Do not wash—no reassurance.
8. Light a match in your room and blow it out. Put it into the ashtray and leave your room. Do not check to see if it is out—no reassurance.
9. Walk along the engine room of a train and calmly take a look inside—no reassurance.
10. Take a box of pins along with you into the train. Do not check to see if you still have it.
11. Put dirty washing into the laundry basket without washing your hands afterward—no reassurance.
12. Put dirty laundry into the washing machine without washing your hands—no reassurance.
13. Hang up clean clothes. Do not wash your hands in advance — no reassurance.

3.3. Session Four

Everything went quite well the week before. Although Julia had anxious thoughts, she no longer panicked at the merest trifles and soon began to lose her anxiety. She was so satisfied that she even went so far as to come to the hospital by train all by herself.

She had fulfilled all the assignments without any difficulties. She was glad that she no longer needed reassurance from others for the least little thing. She had even done two assignments which were programmed for the following week. Together with Julia the following assignments were selected for practice in the next two sessions (anxiety level ranged from 10–30). All items included "no reassurance," but this has been omitted for sake of space.

14. Rub a handful of detergent between your hands and rub it into your clothes. Do not wash your hands or change into clean clothes.
15. Go to the toilet without washing your hands afterward.
16. Hang your pants, which have just been washed, over the potato-container without checking to see if it is dirty. Do not rewash your pants.
17. Hold the bottle of bleach in your hands and then go and make coffee without first washing your hands.
18. Rub dirty laundry against your clothes. Do not wash your hands or change your clothes.
19. Rub the dish cloth in your hands and then eat something without washing your hands.

20. Mix your towel with the dirty laundry and then use it again normally. Do not wash your hands.
21. Rub the dust cloth between your hands and then have something to eat without first washing your hands.
22. Do not ask people to put away tacks, pins, needles, knives, medicine, and such any more.
23. Turn the gas on and off. Do not check to see if they are really turned off.
24. Leave a bottle of aspirin behind in the train.
25. Do not wash your hands "just in case" any more.
26. Hold onto the dishwasher knobs without checking to see if they are still in the right position.
27. Do not wash your hands when you wake up in the morning.
28. When visting someone, pull a plug out of its socket and then plug it in again at once. Do not check.

3.4. Session Five

All the assignments were done without difficulty, except for assignment Number 14, which she had not had the opportunity to do. It was agreed that she would start with this assignment at the first following practice session. She often no longer stops to think about things. For example, she had dusted and had "forgotten" to wash her hands afterwards. She no longer washes her hands between actions. She is no longer bothered by gas and electricity knobs. This last week she also went shopping alone again. The following assignments were agreed upon for the next two practice sessions (anxiety level range: 30–40).

29. Rub your hands against the fire hose. Do not check to see if it is broken.
30. Rub your hands firmly against the hoses of the gas stove. Do not return to check if everything is still in order.
31. Set the table, drop the silverware on the floor, pick it up, and lay it on the table without washing it.
32. Put the dishes into the cupboard without checking to see if there are pieces missing.
33. Pick up the dishes quickly, without checking to see whether they are chipped.
34. Go into the train and sit beside someone who looks "dirty." Accidently nudge him with your elbow and do not clean your clothes afterwards.
35. Borrow a book and put a pin in it. Remove the pin after 30 minutes. Return the book without checking to see if you have removed the pin.

36. Remove a tack from the bulletin board and put it on the table.
37. Sprinkle detergent on the toilet seat, blow it off, do not clean the toilet or wash your hands. Do not change into clean clothes.
38. Go to a supermarket alone and buy two bottles of soda. Do not check to see if you have chipped anything.
39. Buy a bottle of bleach, liquid ammonia, and cookies. Put them all into one bag. Do not wash your hands. Eat the cookies.
40. Clean the sink with cleanser, rinse it off once quickly, and do not check it again.
41. Get into the train near the engine. Do not ask anybody whether you have touched anything.
42. Touch the knobs on the fire extinguisher without checking to see whether the knobs are still in the right position.
43. Lay a knife near the rubber gas hose. Do not go back to check.

3.5. Session Six

Julia had not done her assignments because the atmosphere had become tense in her department. One of her colleagues told her that they could no longer stand having to reassure her all the time, even though they had noticed this happened less often than it used to.

Julia then decided not even to ask for reassurance any more, which was applauded by the therapist. After ten minutes the patient was sent back home to do her assignments.

3.6. Session Seven

The assignments had gone well. Julia feels excellent and if she sometimes still has a nagging thought she tells herself that she has done nothing wrong and she is sure of herself. The thoughts do not cause tension any more.

Julia does not feel like continuing because she can do it alone now and she thinks the assignments are "stupid." The therapist shows that the assignments she now finds "stupid" she first found difficult, and that the most difficult are still to come. After this Julia reluctantly agrees to continue.

The following assignments were given to her for the next two practice sessions (anxiety level range: 40–50).

44. Visit somebody's room and leave a pin there.
45. Lean against a dirty car without washing your clothes afterward.
46. Lean against a dirty wall without washing your clothes afterward.

47. Pass a knife over the gas pipe. Do not return to check if the pipe was cut.
48. Pass the blunt edge of a knife over the gas hoses in the kitchen. Do not check to see if they are uncut.
49. Go to a supermarket alone and buy some matches. Put them in your pocket and do not check to see whether you have lit one.
50. Touch the cables of an advertisement sign and do not return to check if something is wrong.
51. Touch the contact plate near the towing bracket of a car.
52. Take some knitting needles with you in your canvas bag and walk through busy stores without checking to see whether the needles are sticking out.
53. In the train, take a pin out of a full pinbox and drop it under the seat. Go and sit in another compartment without checking.
54. Touch the pins in the harmonica part of a train. Do not look to see if you have damaged them.
55. Light a match in the train and put it in the ashtray while it is still burning. Go and sit in another compartment immediately without looking to see if the match is out.
56. Leave the box of matches on the train.
57. Lay your sweater down on the floor in the movies and put it on again without first dusting it off.
58. Enter a supermarket alone and brush past the bottles with your shopping cart. Do not check for chips.
59. Set a glass on the table in such a way that one-third of its sticks out over the edge. Leave it like that.
60. Break a glass in your room. Throw the pieces into the trash can and vacuum the splinters in 15 seconds.

3.7. Session Eight

Julia was very happy. All the assignments had gone well once more and without any difficulties. As a surprise she had brought along a bottle of bleach for the therapist which she triumphantly held in her hand. Julia says she no longer asks people for reassurance ("I just simply won't"), and lately she is told not to throw down the plates so roughly on the table, because "they might break."

Julia is back at work again, a fact which she is very pleased about. While selecting the last assignments she says that she cannot imagine that the items which she scored a "100" are so difficult. The remaining assignments are given for the next two practice sessions (anxiety level range: 60–100).

61. Look after the patients without washing your hands or changing your clothes.
62. Put a tack near the rubber hose of the gas stove. Do not check.
63. Go into a large department store and turn all the knobs on the washing machines and gas stoves. Do not check to see if they are still in the right position.
64. At your work, touch all the buttons on the switchboard at length and do not check to see if everything is still all right.
65. Hold the cleanser cap in your hands, then eat a cookie without washing your hands.
66. Refill your car with gas yourself without washing your hands.
67. Take an electric cord plug apart and put it back together again.
68. Break a bottle at the station. Throw the pieces away in a trash can and do not wash your hands.
69. Rub a cloth soaked with turpentine over your pants. Do not wash your hands or put on clean clothes.
70. Clean out the cupboard containing all the "dangerous" cleaning products and then have a cookie without washing your hands.
71. Wipe off all the doorknobs in your home with a cloth drenched in ammonia. Do not wash your hands.

3.8. Session Nine: Evaluation

Again all the assignments had gone well. Nothing appears to be difficult any more. The questionnaires and rating scales showed the same results. Improvement was maintained up to 6-months follow-up.

References

Abe, K., & Masui, T. Age-sex trends of phobic and anxiety symptoms in adolescents. *British Journal of Psychiatry*, 1981, *138*, 297–302.

Agras, S., Sylvester, D., & Oliveau, D. The epidemiology of common fears and phobias. *Comprehensive Psychiatry*, 1969, *10*, 151–156.

Agras, W. S. Transfer during systematic desensitization therapy. *Behaviour Research and Therapy*, 1967, *5*, 193–199.

Agras, W. S., Leitenberg, H., & Barlow, D. H. Social reinforcement in the modification of agoraphobia. *Archives of General Psychiatry*, 1968, *19*, 423–427.

Agras, W. S., Leitenberg, H., Barlow, D. H., & Thomson, L. E. Instructions and reinforcement in the modification of neurotic behavior. *American Journal of Psychiatry*, 1969, *125*, 1435–1439.

Agras, W. S., Leitenberg, H., Wincze, J. P., Butz, R. A., & Callahan, E. J. Comparison of the effects of instructions and reinforcement in the treatment of a neurotic avoidance response: A single case experiment. *Journal of Behavior Therapy and Experimental Psychiatry*, 1970, *1*, 53–58.

Agras, W. S., Leitenberg, H., Barlow, D. H., Curtis, N. A., Edwards, J., & Wright, D. Relaxation in systematic desensitization. *Archives of General Psychiatry*, 1971, *25*, 511–514.

Agras, W. S., Chapin, H. N., & Oliveau, D. C. The natural history of phobia: Course and prognosis. *Archives of General Psychiatry*, 1972, *26*, 315–317.

Agulnik, P. The spouse of the phobic patient. *British Journal of Psychiatry*, 1970, *117*, 59–67.

Aitken, R. C. B., Lister, J. A., & Main, C. J. Identification of features associated with flying phobia in aircrew. *British Journal of Psychiatry*, 1981, *139*, 38–42.

Akhtar, S., Wig., N. H., Verma, V. K., Pershod, D., & Verma, S. K. A phenomenological analysis of symptoms in obsessive-compulsive neuroses. *British Journal of Psychiatry*, 1975, *127*, 342–348.

Alden, L., & Cappe, R. Nonassertiveness: Skill deficit or selective self-evaluation. *Behavior Therapy*, 1981, *12*, 107–114.

Alden, L., & Safran, J. D. Irrational beliefs and nonassertive behavior. *Cognitive Therapy and Research*, 1978, *4*, 357–364.

Alden, L., Safran, J., & Weideman, R. A comparison of cognitive and skills training strategies in the treatment of unassertive clients. *Behavior Therapy*, 1978, *8*, 843–846.

Allen, G. J. The behavioral treatment of test anxiety: Therapeutic innovations and emerging conceptual changes. In M. Hersen, R. M. Eisler, & P. M. Miller (Eds.), *Progress in Behavior Modification* (Vol 9). New York: Academic Press, 1980.

Alsen, V. Entstehungsbedingungen des phobisch-anankastischen Syndroms. *Archiv für Psychatrie und Nervenkrankheiten*, 1970, *213*, 246–263.

Ananth, J., & van den Steen, N. Systematic studies in the treatment of obsessive compulsive neurosis with tricyclic antidepressants. *Current Therapeutic Research*, 1977, *21*, 495–501.

Ananth, J., Solyom, L., Solyom, C., & Sookman, D. Doxepin in the treatment of obsessive compulsive neurosis. *Psychosomatics*, 1975, *16*, 185–187.

Andersen, B. L. A comparison of systematic desensitization and directed masturbation in the treatment of primary orgasmic dysfunction in females. *Journal of Consulting and Clinical Psychology*, 1981, *49*, 568–570.

Anderson, M. P., & Borkovec, T. D. Imagery processing and fear reduction during repeated exposure to two types of phobic imagery. *Behaviour Research and Therapy*, 1980, *18*, 537–540.

Andrews, J. D. W. Psychotherapy of phobias. *Psychological Bulletin*, 1966, *66*, 455–480.

Annesley, P. T. Nardil response in a chronic obsessive-compulsive. *British Journal of Psychiatry*, 1969, *115*, 748.

Appleby, I. L., Klein, D. F., Sachar, E. J., & Levitt, M. Biochemical indices of lactate-induced panic: A preliminary report. In D. F. Klein & J. G. Rabkin (Eds.), *Anxiety: New research and concepts*. New York: Raven Press, 1981.

Argyle, M., Bryant, B. M., & Trower, P. Social skills training and psychotherapy: A comparative study. *Psychological Medicine*, 1974, *4*, 435–443.

Arkowitz, H. Measurement and modification of minimal dating behavior. In M. Hersen, R. M. Eisler, & P. M. Miller (Eds.), *Progress in behavior modification* (Vol. 5). New York: Academic Press, 1977.

Arkowitz, H., Lichtenstein, E., McGovern, K., & Hines, P. The behavioral assessment of social competence in males. *Behavior Therapy*, 1975, *6*, 3–13.

Arrindell, W. A. Dimensional structure and psychopathology correlates of the fear survey schedule (FSS-111) in a phobic population: A factorial definition of agoraphobia. *Behaviour Research and Therapy*, 1980, *18*, 229–242.

Ascher, L. M. *Employing paradoxical intention in the treatment of agoraphobia*. Paper presented at the American Association of Behaviour Therapy meeting, New York, November 1980.

Ascher, L. M., & Clifford, R. E. Behavioral considerations in the treatment of sexual dysfunction. In M. Hersen, R. M. Eisler, & P. M. Miller (Eds.), *Progress in Behavior Modification* (Vol. 3). New York: Academic Press, 1976.

Asso, D., & Beech, H. R. Susceptibility to the acquisition of a conditioned response in relation to the menstrual cycle. *Journal of Psychosomatic Research*, 1975, *19*, 337–344.

Bajtelsmit, J. W., & Gershman, L. Covert positive reinforcement: Efficacy and conceptualization. *Journal of Behavior Therapy and Experimental Psychiatry*, 1976, *7*, 207–212.

Bandura, A. *Principles of behavior modification*. New York: Holt, Rinehart & Winston, 1969.

Bandura, A. Self-efficacy: Toward a unifying theory of behavioral change. *Psychological Review*, 1977, *84*, 191–215.

Bandura, A. On paradigms and recycled ideologies. *Cognitive Therapy and Research*, 1978, *2*, 79–103.

Bandura, A., & Adams, N. E. Analysis of self-efficacy theory of behavioral change. *Cognitive Therapy and Research*, 1977, *1*, 287–310.

Bandura, A., & Barab, P. G. Processes governing disinhibitory effects through symbolic modeling. *Journal of Abnormal Psychology* 1973, *82*, 1–9.

Bandura, A., & Menlove, F. L. Factors determining vicarious extinction of avoidance behavior through symbolic modeling. *Journal of Personality and Social Psychology*, 1968, *8*, 99–108.

Bandura, A., Adams, N. E., & Beyer, J. Cognitive processes mediating behavioral change. *Journal of Personality and Social Psychology*, 1977, *35*, 125–139.

Bandura, A., Adams, N. E., Hardy, A. B., & Howells, G. N. Test of the generality of self-efficacy theory. *Cognitive Therapy and Research*, 1980, *4*, 39–66.

Bandura, A., Jeffery, R. W., & Gajdos, E. Generalizing change through participant modeling with self-directed mastery. *Behaviour Research and Therapy*. 1975, *13*, 141–152.

Barlow, D. H., Leitenberg, H., Agras, W. S., & Wincze, J. P. The transfer gap in systematic desensitization: An analogue study. *Behaviour Reserch and Therapy*, 1969, *7*, 191–196.

Barlow, D. H., Agras, W. S., Leitenberg, H., & Wincze, J. P. An experimental analysis of the effectiveness of "shaping" in reducing maladaptive avoidance behavior: an analogue study. *Behaviour Research and Therapy*, 1970, *8*, 165–173.

Barrett, C. L. Systematic desensitization versus implosive therapy. *Journal of Abnormal Psychology*, 1969, *74*, 587–592.

Barrios, B. A. Note on demand characteristics in analogue research on small animal phobias. *Psychological Reports*, 1978, *42*, 1264–1266.

Barrios, B. A. *Modeling and desensitization approaches to heterosocial skills training: An analysis of the relevance of self-efficacy theory.* Paper presented to the American Association of Behavior Therapy, New York, November 1980.

Barrios, B. A., Ginter, E. J., Scalize, J. J., & Miller, F. G. Treatment of test anxiety by applied relaxation and cue-controlled relaxation. *Psychological Reports*, 1980, *46*, 1287–1296.

Bass, B. A. An unusual behavioral technique for treating obsessive ruminations. *Psychotherapy: Theory, Research and Practice*, 1973, *10*, 191–193.

Bauer, R. M., & Craighead, W. E. Psychophysiological responses to the imagination of fearful and neutral situations: The effects of imagery instructions. *Behavior Therapy*, 1979, *10*, 389–403.

Becker, H. G., & Costello, C. G. Effects of graduated exposure with feedback of exposure times on snake phobias. *Journal of Consulting and Clinical Psychology*, 1975, *43*, 478–484.

Bedell, J. R., Archer, R. P., & Rosman, M. Relaxation therapy, desensitization, and the treatment of anxiety-based disorders. *Journal of Clinical Psychology*, 1979, *35*, 840–843.

Beech, H. R. Ritualistic activity in obsessional patients. *Journal of Psychosomatic Research*, 1971, *15*, 417–422.

Beech, H. R., & Liddell, A. Decision-making, mood states and ritualistic behaviour among obsessional patients. In H. R. Beech (Ed.), *Obsessional states*. London: Methuen, 1974.

Beech, H. R., & Perigault, J. Toward a theory of obsessional disorder. In H. R. Beech (Ed.), *Obsessional states*. London: Methuen, 1974.

Beech, H. R., & Vaughan, M. *Behavioral treatment of obsessional states*. New York: Wiley, 1978.

Beiman, I. The effects of instructional set on physiological response to stressful imagery. *Behaviour Research and Therapy*, 1976, *14*, 175–180.

Beiman, I., Israel, E., & Johnson, S. During training and post-training effects of live and taped extended progressive relaxation, self-relaxation, and electromyogram feedback. *Journal of Consulting and Clinical Psychology*, 1978, *46*, 314–321.

Beiman, I., O'Neil, P., Wachtel, D., Frugé, E., Johnson, S., & Feuerstein, M. Validation of a self-report/behavioral subject selection procedure for analog fear research. *Behavior Therapy*, 1978, *9*, 169–171.

Bellack, A. S., & Hersen, M. Self-report inventories in behavioral assessment. In J. D. Cone & R. P. Hawkins (Eds.), *Behavioral Assessment: New directions in clinical psychology*. New York: Brunner/Mazel, 1977.

Bellack, A. S., Hersen, M., & Lamparski, D. Role play test for assessing social skills: Are they valid? Are they useful? *Journal of Consulting and Clinical Psychology*, 1979, *47*, 335–342.

Beloff, H. The structure and origin of the anal character. *Genetic Psychological Monograph,* 1957, *55,* 141–172.

Benjamin, S., Marks, I. M., & Huson, J. Active muscular relaxation in desensitization of phobic patients. *Psychological Medicine,* 1972, *2,* 381–390.

Bernardt, B. W., Silverstone, T., & Singleton, W. Behavioural and subjective effects of beta-adrenergic blockade in phobic subjects. *British Journal of Psychiatry,* 1980, *137,* 452–457.

Berney, T., Kolvin, I., Bhate, S. R., Garside, R. F., Jeans, J., Kay, B., & Scarth, L. School phobia: A therapeutic trial with clomipramine and short-term outcome. *British Journal* of Psychiatry, 1981, *138,* 110–118.

Bernstein, D. A. Manipulation of avoidance behavior as a function of increased or decreased demand on repeated behavioral tests. *Journal of Consulting and Clinical Psychology,* 1974, *42,* 896–900.

Bernstein, D. A., & Nietzel, M. T. Procedural variations in behavioral avoidance tests. *Journal of Consulting and Clinical Psychology,* 1973, *41,* 165–174.

Bernstein, D. A., & Nietzel, M. T. Behavioral avoidance tests: The effects of demand characteristics and repeated measures on two types of subjects. *Behavior Therapy,* 1974, *5,* 183–192.

Bianchi, G. N. Origins of disease phobia. *Australian and New Zealand Journal of Psychiatry,* 1971, *5,* 241–257.

Bindra, D. *Motivation: A Systematic Reinterpretation.* New York: Ronald Press, 1959.

Black, A. The natural history of obsessional neurosis. In H. R. Beech (Ed.), *Obsessional states.* London: Methuen, 1974.

Blackwell, B. Hypertensive crisis due to mono-amine oxidase inhibitors. *Lancet,* 1963, *2,* 849–851.

Blanchard, E. B. The relative contributions of modeling, informational influences, and physical contact in the extinction of phobic behavior. *Journal of Abnormal Psychology,* 1970, *76,* 55–61.

Blanchard, E. B., & Abel, G. G. An experimental case study of the biofeedback treatment of a rape-induced psychophysiological cardiovascular disorder. *Behavior Therapy,* 1976, *7,* 113–119.

Bland, K., & Hallam, R. S. Relationship between response to graded exposure and marital satisfaction in agoraphobics. *Behaviour Research and Therapy,* 1981, *19,* 335–338.

Blankstein, K. R. Heart rate control, general anxiety, and subjective tenseness. *Behavior Therapy,* 1975, *6,* 699–700.

Bleijenberg, G. Rational-emotive therapy and behavior therapy with compulsive checkers. An outpatient study. In I. Hand (Ed.), *Obsessions and compulsions: Recent advances in behavioral analysis and therapy.* New York: Springer, in press.

Blom, B. E., & Craighead, W. E. The effects of situational and instructional demands on indices of speech anxiety. *Journal of Abnormal Psychology,* 1974, *83,* 667–674.

Boelens, W., Emmelkamp, P., MacGillavry, D., & Markvoort, M. A clinical evaluation of marital treatment: Reciprocity counseling vs. system-theoretic counseling. *Behavioral Analysis and Modification,* 1980, *4,* 85–96.

Boersma, K., den Hengst, S., Dekker, J., & Emmelkamp, P. M. G. Exposure and response prevention in the natural environment: A comparison with obsessive-compulsive patients. *Behaviour Research and Therapy,* 1976, *14,* 19–24.

Bolles, R. C. Species—specific defence reactions and avoidance learning. *Psychological Review,* 1970, *77,* 32–48.

Bootzin, R. R., & Lick, J. R. Expectancies in therapy research: Interpretive artifact or mediating mechanism. *Journal of Consulting and Clinical Psychology,* 1979, *47,* 852–855.

Borkovec, T. D. Effects of expectancy on the outcome of systematic desensitization and implosive treatments for analogue anxiety. *Behavior Therapy*, 1972, *3*, 29–40.

Borkovec, T. D. The role of expectancy and physiological feedback in fear research: A review with special reference to subject characteristics. *Behavior Therapy*, 1973, *4*, 491–505.

Borkovec, T. D. Physiological and cognitive processes in the regulation of anxiety. In G. E. Schwartz & D. Shapiro (Eds.), *Consciousness and self-regulation: Advances in research* (Vol 1). New York: Plenum, 1976.

Borkovec, T. D., & Nau, S. D. Credibility of analogue therapy rationales. *Journal of Behavior Therapy and Experimental Psychiatry*, 1972, *3*, 257–260.

Borkovec, T. D., & Rachman, S. The utility of analogue research. *Behaviour Research and Therapy*, 1979, *17*, 253–261.

Borkovec, T. D., & Sides, J. K. Critical procedural variables related to the physiological effects of progressive relaxation: A review. *Behaviour Research and Therapy*, 1979, *17*, 119–125.

Borkovec, T. D., Weerts, T. C., & Bernstein, D. A. Behavioral assessment of anxiety. In A. Ciminero, K. Calhoun, & H. E. Adams (Eds.), *Handbook of behavioral assessment*. New York: Wiley, 1977.

Borkovec, T. D., Stone, N. M., O'Brien, G. T., & Kaloupek, D. G. Evaluation of a clinically relevant target behavior for analogue outcome research. *Behavior Therapy*, 1974, *5*, 504–514.

Borland, L. R. Odontophobia—inordinate fear of dental treatment. *Dental Clinics of North America*, 1962, *6*, 683–695.

Boudewyns, P. A., & Wilson, A. E. Implosive therapy and desensitization therapy using free association in treatment of inpatients. *Journal of Abnormal Psychology*, 1972, *79*, 252–268.

Boulougouris, J. C., & Bassiakos, L. Prolonged flooding in cases with obsessive-compulsive neurosis. *Behaviour Research and Therapy*, 1973, *11*, 227–231.

Boulougouris, J. C., Marks. I. M., & Marset, P. Superiority of flooding (implosion) to desensitization for reducing pathological fear. *Behaviour Research and Therapy*, 1971, *9*, 7–16.

Boulougouris, J. C., Rabavilas, A. D., & Stefanis, C. Psychophysiological responses in obsessive-compulsive patients. *Behaviour Research and Therapy*, 1977, *15*, 221–230.

Bourque, P., & Ladouceur, R. An investigation of various performance-based treatments with acrophobics. *Behaviour Research and Therapy*, 1980, *18*, 161–170.

Bowen, R. C., & Kohout, J. The relationship between agoraphobia and primary affective disorders. *Canadian Journal of Psychiatry*, 1979, *24*, 317–322.

Brandrup, E., & Vanggaard, T. LSD treatment in a severe case of compulsive neurosis. *Acta Psychiatria Scandinavia*, 1977, *55*, 127–141.

Branham, L., & Katahn, M. Effectiveness of automated desensitization with normal volunteers and phobic patients. *Canadian Journal of Behavioral Sciences*, 1974, *6*, 234–245.

Bregman, E. An attempt to modify the emotional attitudes of infants by the conditioned response technique. *Journal of Genetic Psychology*, 1934, *45*, 169–196.

Brickner, R., Rosner, A., & Munro, R. Physiological aspects of the obsessive state. *Psychosomatic Medicine*, 1940, *2*, 369–383.

Bridges, P. K., Goktepe, E. O., & Maratos, J. A comparative review of patients with obsessional neurosis and with depression treated by psychosurgery. *British Journal of Psychiatry*, 1973, *123*, 663–674.

Broadhurst, A. It is never too late to learn: An application of conditioned inhibition to obsessional ruminations in an elderly patient. In H. J. Eysenck (Ed.), *Case studies in behaviour therapy*. London: Routledge & Kegan Paul, 1976.

Brody, B. Freud's case load. *Psychotherapy: Theory, Research and Practice,* 1970, *7,* 8–12.

Bryant, B., & Trower, P. E. Social difficulty in a student sample. *British Journal of Educational Psychology,* 1974, *44,* 13–21.

Buglass, D., Clarke, J., Henderson, A. S., Kreitman, N., & Presley, A. S. A study of agoraphobic housewives. *Psychological Medicine,* 1977, *7,* 73–86.

Burish, T. G., & Horn, P. W. An evaluation of frontal E M G as an index of general arousal. *Behavior Therapy,* 1979, *10,* 137–147.

Burrell, R. H., Culpan, R. H., Newton, K. J., Ogg, G. J., & Short, J. H. W. Use of bromazepam in obsessional, phobic and related states. *Current Medical Research and Opinion,* 1974, *2,* 430–436.

Burzaco, J. *Stereotactic surgery in the treatment of obsessive-compulsive neurosis.* Paper presented to the Third World Congress of Biological Psychiatry, Stockholm, July 1981.

Butollo, W., Burkhardt, P., Himmler, C., & Müller, M. *Mehrdimensionale Verhaltenstherapie und Beta-Blocker bei funktionellen Dysrytmien und chronischen körperbezogenen Angstreaktionen.* Paper read at die Tagung der deutschen Konferenz für psychosomatische Medizin, Cologne, 1978.

Calef, R. A., & MacLean, G. D. A comparison of reciprocal inhibition and reactive inhibition therapies in the treatment of speech anxiety. *Behavior Therapy,* 1970, *1,* 51–58.

Canter, A., Kondo, C. Y., & Knott, J. R. A comparison of EMG feedback and progressive muscle relaxation training in anxiety neurosis. *British Journal of Psychiatry,* 1975, *127,* 470–477.

Capstick, N. Clomipramine in the treatment of the true obsessional state: A report on four patients. *Psychosomatics,* 1975, *16,* 21–25.

Capstick, N., & Seldrup, J. Obsessional states: A study in the relationship between abnormalities occurring at the time of birth and the subsequent development of obsessional symptoms. *Acta Psychiatrica Scandinavia,* 1977, *56,* 427–434.

Carey, M. S., Hawkinson, R., Kornhaber, A., & Wellish, C. S. The use of clomipramine in phobic patients: Preliminary research report. *Current Therapeutic Research,* 1975, *17,* 107–110.

Carmody, T. P. Rational-emotive, self-instructional, and behavioral assertion: Facilitating maintenance. *Cognitive Therapy and Research,* 1978, *2,* 241–253.

Carr, A. T. Compulsive neurosis: A review of the literature. *Psychological Bulletin,* 1974, *81,* 311–318.

Carr, A. T. The psychopathology of fear. In W. Sluckin (Ed.), *Fear in animals and man.* New York: Van Nostrand Reinhold, 1979.

Carroll, D., Marzillier, J. S., & Watson, F. Heart rate and self-report changes accompanying different types of relaxing imagery. *Behaviour Research and Therapy,* 1980, *18,* 273–279.

Carver, C. S., & Blaney, P. H. Avoidance behavior and perceived arousal. *Motivation and Emotion,* 1977, *1,* 61–73. (a)

Carver, C. S., & Blaney, P. H. Perceived arousal, focus of attention, and avoidance behavior. *Journal of Abnormal Psychology,* 1977, *86,* 154–162. (b)

Catts, S., & McConaghy, N. Ritual prevention in the treatment of obsessive-compulsive neurosis. *Australia and New Zealand Journal of Psychiatry,* 1975, *9,* 37–41.

Cautela, J. R. Covert reinforcement. *Behavior Therapy,* 1970, *2,* 192–200.

Cautela, J. R. Covert processes and behavior modification. *Journal of Nervous and Mental Diseases,* 1973, *157,* 27–36.

Cautela, J. R., & Wall, C. C. Covert conditioning in clinical practice. In A. Goldstein & E. B. Foa (Eds.), *Handbook of behavioral interventions.* New York: Wiley, 1980.

Chambless, D. L., & Goldstein, A. The treatment of agoraphobia. In A. Goldstein and E. B. Foa (Eds.), *Handbook of behavioral interventions.* New York, Wiley, 1980.

Change-Liang, R., & Denney, D. R. Applied relaxation as training in self-control. *Journal of Counseling Psychology*, 1976, *23*, 183–189.

Chaplin, E. W., & Levine, B. A. *The effects of total exposure duration and interrupted versus continuous exposure in flooding.* Paper presented at the 14th annual convention of the American Association of Behavior Therapy, New York, November 1980.

Ciminero, A. R., Calhoun, K. S., & Adams, H. E. (Eds.), *Handbook of behavioral assessment.* New York: Wiley, 1977.

Ciminero, A. R., Doleys, D. M., & Williams, C. L. Journal literature on behavior therapy 1970–1976: An analysis of the subject characteristics, target behaviors, and treatment techniques. *Journal of Behavior Therapy and Experimental Psychiatry*, 1978, *9*, 301–308.

Clark, J. V., & Arkowitz, H. Social anxiety and self-evaluation of interpersonal performance. *Psychological Reports*, 1975, *36*, 211–221.

Cloninger, C. R., Martin, R. L., Clayton, P., & Guze, S. B. A blind follow-up and family study of anxiety neurosis: Preliminary analysis of the St. Louis 500. In D. F. Klein & J. Rabkin (Eds.), *Anxiety: New research and changing concepts.* New York: Raven Press, 1981.

Cobb, J., McDonald, R., Marks, I., & Stern, R. Marital versus exposure therapy: Psychological treatments of co-existing marital and phobic-obsessive problems. *Behavioural Analysis and Modification*, 1980, *4*, 3–16.

Cobb, J. P., & Marks, I. M. Morbid jealousy featuring as obsessive-compulsive neurosis: Treatment by behavioural psychotherapy. *British Journal of Psychiatry*, 1979, *134*, 301–305.

Colgan, A. A pilot study of anafranil in the treatment of phobic states. *Scottish Medical Journal*, 1975, *20*, 55–60.

Condon, T. J., & Allen, G. J. Role of psychoanalytic merging fantasies in systematic desensitization: a rigorous methodological examination. *Journal of Abnormal Psychology*, 1980, *89*, 437–443.

Cone, J. D. Confounded comparisons in triple response mode assessment research. *Behavioral Assessment*, 1979, *1*, 85–95.

Connolly, J. F. Tonic physiological responses to repeated presentations of phobic stimuli. *Behaviour Research and Therapy*, 1979, *17*, 189–196.

Connolly, J., Hallam, R. S., & Marks, I. M. Selective association of fainting with blood-injury phobias. *Behavior Therapy*, 1976, *7*, 8–13.

Cooper, A. J. Disorders of sexual potency in the male: A clinical and statistical study of some factors related to short-term prognosis. *British Journal of Psychiatry*, 1969, *115*, 709–719.

Cooper, J. The Leyton obsessional inventory. *Psychological Medicine*, 1970, *1*, 48–64.

Cooper, A., Furst, J. B., & Bridger, W. H. A brief commentary on the usefulness of studying fear of snakes. *Journal of Abnormal Psychology*, 1969, *74*, 413–414.

Cooper, J. E., Gelder, M. G., & Marks, I. M. Results of behaviour therapy in 77 psychiatric patients. *British Medical Journal*, 1965, *1*, 1222–1225.

Cooper, J. E., & Kelleher, M. Y. The Leyton Obsessional Inventory: A principal component analysis on normal subjects. *Psychological Medicine*, 1973, *3*, 204–208.

Cornish, R. D., & Dilley, J. S. Comparison of three methods of reducing test anxiety: Systematic desensitization, implosive therapy, and study counseling. *Journal of Counseling Psychology*, 1973, *20*, 499–503.

Counts, D. K., Hollandsworth, J. G., & Alcorn, J. D. Use of electromyographic biofeedback and cue-controlled relaxation in the treatment of test anxiety. *Journal of Consulting and Clinical Psychology*, 1978, *46*, 990–996.

Coursey, R. D. Electromyographic feedback as a relaxation technique. *Journal of Consulting and Clinical Psychology*, 1975, *43*, 825–834.

Craighead, L. W. Self-instructional training for assertive-refusal behavior. *Behavior Therapy*, 1979, *10*, 529–542.

Craighead, W. E., & Craighead, L. W. Instructional demand and anxiety level: Effects on speech anxiety. *Behavior Modification*, 1981, *5*, 103–117.

Crisp, A. H. "Transference," "symptom emergence" and "social repercussion" in behaviour therapy. *British Journal of Medical Psychology*, 1966, *39*, 179–196.

Crowe, R. C., Pauls, D. L., Venkatesh, A., Van Valkenburg, C., Noyes, R., Martins, J. B., & Kerber, R. E. Exercise and anxiety neurosis. *Archives of General Psychiatry*, 1979, *36*, 652–653.

Crowe, M. J., Marks, I. M., Agras, W. S., & Leitenberg, H. Time-limited desensitization implosion and shaping for phobic patients: A cross-over study. *Behaviour Research and Therapy*, 1972, *10*, 319–328.

Curran, J. P. Skills training as an approach to the treatment of heterosexual-social anxiety: A review. *Psychological Bulletin*, 1977, *84*, 140–157.

Curtis, G. C., Buxton, M., Lippman, D., Nesse, R., & Wright, J. "Flooding in vivo" during the circardian phase of minimal cortisol secretion: Anxiety and therapeutic success without adrenal corticol activation. *Biological Psychiatry*, 1976, *11*, 101–107.

Curtis, G. C., Nesse, R., Buxton, M., & Lippman, D. Plasma growth hormone: effect of anxiety during flooding in vivo. *American Journal of Psychiatry*, 1979, *136*, 410–414.

Damas-Mora, J., Davies, L., Taylor, W., & Jenner, F. A. Menstrual respiratory changes and symptoms. *British Journal of Psychiatry*, 1980, *136*, 492–497.

Davison, G. C. Systematic desensitization as a counterconditioning process. *Journal of Abnormal Psychology*, 1968, *73*, 91–99.

Davison, G. C., & Wilson, G. T. Processes of fear-reduction in systematic desensitization: Cognitive and social reinforcement factors in humans. *Behavior Therapy*, 1973, *4*, 1–21.

De Csipkes, R. A., & Rowe, W. Taped vs. "live" desensitization and level of autonomic arousal. *Journal of Clinical Psychology*, 1978, *34*, 740–743.

Dee, C. Instructions and the extinction of a learned fear in the context of taped implosive therapy. *Journal of Consulting and Clinical Psychology*, 1972, *39*, 123–132.

Deffenbacher, J. L. Relaxation in vivo in the treatment of test anxiety. *Journal of Behavior Therapy and Experimental Psychiatry*, 1976, *7*, 289–292.

Deffenbacher, J. L., & Hahnloser, R. M. Cognitive and relaxation coping skills in stress inoculation. *Cognitive Therapy and Research*, 1981, *5*, 211–215.

Deffenbacher, J. L., & Parks, D. H. A comparison of traditional and self-control desensitization. *Journal of Counseling Psychology*, 1979, *26*, 93–97.

Deffenbacher, J. L., & Payne, D. M. J. Two procedures for relaxation as self-control in the treatment of communication apprehension. *Journal of Counseling Psychology*, 1977, *24*, 255–258.

Deffenbacher, J. L., & Shelton, J. L. Comparison of anxiety management training and desensitization in reducing test and other anxieties. *Journal of Counseling Psychology*, 1978, *25*, 277–282.

Deffenbacher, J. L., Mathis, H., & Michaels, A. C. Two self-control procedures in the reduction of targeted and nontargeted anxieties. *Journal of Counseling Psychology*, 1979, *26*, 120–127.

Deffenbacher, J. L., Michaels, A. C., Michaels, T., & Daley, P. C. Comparison of anxiety-management training and self-control desensitization. *Journal of Counseling Psychology*, 1980, *27*, 232–239.

Delius, S. J. Irrelevant behaviour, information processing and arousal homeostasis. *Psychologische Forschung*, 1970, *33*, 165–188.

De Moor, W. Systematic desensitization vs. prolonged high intensity stimulation (flooding). *Journal of Behavior Therapy and Experimental Psychiatry*, 1970, *1*, 45–52.

Dennerstein, L., & Burrows, G. D. Affect and the menstrual cycle. *Journal of Affective Disorders*, 1979, *1*, 77–92.

Denney, D. R., & Rupert, P. A. Desensitization and self-control in the treatment of test anxiety. *Journal of Counseling Psychology*, 1977, *24*, 272–280.

Denney, D. R., & Sullivan, B. J. Desensitization and modeling treatments of spider fear using two types of scenes. *Journal of Consulting and Clinical Psychology*, 1976, *44*, 573–579.

Derogatis, L. R. SCL.90: *Administration, scoring and procedures manual—I for the R[evised] version*. Johns Hopkins University School of Medicine, Clinical Psychometrics Research Unit, Baltimore, 1977.

Derry, P. A., & Stone, G. L. Effects of cognitive-adjunct treatments on assertiveness. *Cognitive Therapy and Research*, 1979, *3*, 213–223.

De Silva, P., Rachman, S., & Seligman, M. E. P. Prepared phobias and obsessions: Therapeutic outcome. *Behaviour Research and Therapy*, 1977, *15*, 65–78.

De Silva, F. R. P., & de Wijewickrama, H. S. Clomipramine in phobic and obsessional states. *New Zealand Medical Journal*, 1976, *4*, 4–6.

De Voge, J. T., & Beck, S. The therapist-client relationship in behavior therapy. In M. Hersen, R. M. Eisler, & P. M. Miller (Eds.), *Progress in behavior modification* (Vol. 6). New York: Academic Press, 1978.

Dijkema, S. *Een psychometrische evaluatie van de D-schaal van Zung, de Leyton Obsessional Inventory en de Fear Survey Schedule*. Unpublished manuscript, University of Groningen, 1978.

Di Loreto, A. O. *Comparative psychotherapy: An experimental analysis*. Chicago: Aldine, 1971.

Donovan, T. R., & Gershman, L. Experimental anxiety reduction: Systematic desensitization versus a false-feedback expectancy manipulation. *Journal of Behavior Therapy and Experimental Psychiatry*, 1979, *10*, 173–179.

Dormaar, M., & Dijkstra, W. *Systematic desensitization in social anxiety*. Paper read at the Conference of the European Association of Behaviour Therapy, 1975.

Dowson, J. H. The phenomenology of severe obsessive-compulsive neurosis. *British Journal of Psychiatry*, 1977, *131*, 75–78.

Dyckman, J. M., & Cowan, P. A. Imagining vividness and the outcome of in vivo and imagined scene desensitization. *Journal of Consulting and Clinical Psychology*, 1978, *48*, 1155–1156.

D'Zurilla, T. J., Wilson, G. T., & Nelson, R. A preliminary study of the effectiveness of graduated prolonged exposure in the treatment of irrational fear. *Behavior Therapy*, 1973, *4*, 672–685.

Elder, J. P., Edelstein, B. A., & Fremouw, W. Client by treatment interactions in response acquisition and cognitive restructuring approaches. *Cognitive Therapy and Research*, 1981, *5*, 203–210.

Ellis, A. *Reason and emotion in psychotherapy*. New York: Lyle-Stuart, 1962.

Ellis, A. A note on the treatment of agoraphobics with cognitive modification with prolonged exposure *in vivo*. *Behaviour Research and Therapy*, 1979, *17*, 162–164.

Emmelkamp, P. M. G. Self-observation versus flooding in the treatment of agoraphobia. *Behaviour Research and Therapy*, 1974, *12*, 229–237.

Emmelkamp, P. M. G. Effects of expectancy on systematic desensitization and flooding. *Behavioral Analysis and Modification*, 1975, *1*, 1–11. (a)

Emmelkamp, P. M. G. Face-validity and behaviour therapy. *Behavioral Analysis and Modification*, 1975, *1*, 15–19. (b)

Emmelkamp, P. M. G. Phobias: Theoretical and behavioural treatment considerations. In J. C. Boulougouris & A. D. Rabavilas (Eds.), *The treatment of phobic and obsessive compulsive disorders*. New York: Pergamon, 1977.

Emmelkamp, P. M. G. The behavioral study of clinical phobias. In M. Hersen, R. M. Eisler, & P. M. Miller (Eds.), *Progress in behavior modification* (Vol. 8). New York: Academic Press, 1979.

Emmelkamp, P. M. G. Relationship between theory and practice in behavior therapy. In W. De Moor & H. Wijngaarden (Eds.), *Psychotherapy*. Amsterdam: Elsevier, 1980. (a)

Emmelkamp, P. M. G. Agoraphobics' interpersonal problems: Their role in the effects of exposure *in vivo* therapy. *Archives of General Psychiatry*, 1980, *37*, 1303–1306. (b)

Emmelkamp, P. M. G. *The effectiveness of exposure in vivo, cognitive restructuring and assertive training in the treatment of agoraphobia.* Paper read at the conference of the American Association of Behavior Therapy, New York, November 1980. (c)

Emmelkamp, P. M. G. The current and future status of clinical research. *Behavioral Assessment*, 1981, *3*, 249–253.

Emmelkamp, P. M. G. Anxiety and fear. In A. Bellack, M. Hersen, & A. Kazdin (Eds.), *International handbook of behavior modification and therapy*. New York: Plenum Press, 1982. (a)

Emmelkamp, P. M. G. Exposure in vivo treatments. In A. Goldstein & D. Chambless (Eds.), *Agoraphobia: Multiple perspectives on theory and treatment*. New York: Wiley, 1982. (b)

Emmelkamp, P. M. G. Recent developments in the behavioral treatment of obsessive-compulsive disorders. In J. Boulougouris (Ed.), *Learning theories approaches in psychiatry*. New York: Wiley, 1982. (c)

Emmelkamp, P. M. G. Obsessive-compulsive disorders: A clinical-research approach. In I. Hand (Ed.), *Obsessions and compulsions—recent advances in behavioral analysis and modification*. New York, Springer, 1982. (d)

Emmelkamp, P. M. G., & Boeke-Slinkers, I. Demand characteristics in behavioral assessment. *Psychological Reports*, 1977, *41*, 1030. (a)

Emmelkamp, P. M. G., & Boeke-Slinkers, I. *The contribution of therapeutic instruction to systematic desensitization with low-fearful and high-fearful subjects.* Unpublished manuscript. University of Groningen, 1977. (b)

Emmelkamp, P. M. G., & Cohen-Kettenis, P. Relationship of locus of control to phobic anxiety and depression. *Psychological Reports*, 1975, *36*, 390.

Emmelkamp, P. M. G., & Emmelkamp-Benner, A. Effects of historically portrayed modeling and group treatment on self-observation: A comparison with agoraphobics. *Behaviour Research and Therapy*, 1975, *13*, 135–139.

Emmelkamp, P. M. G., & Giesselbach, P. Treatment of obsessions: Relevant vs. irrelevant exposure. *Behavioural Psychotherapy*, 1981, *9*, 322–329.

Emmelkamp, P. M. G., & Kwee, K. G. Obsessional ruminations: A comparison between thought-stopping and prolonged exposure in imagination. *Behaviour Research and Therapy*, 1977, *15*, 441–444.

Emmelkamp, P. M. G., & Kraanen, J. Therapist controlled exposure *in vivo* versus self-controlled exposure *in vivo:* A comparison with obsessive-compulsive patients. *Behaviour Research and Therapy*, 1977, *15*, 491–495.

Emmelkamp, P. M. G., & Kuipers, A. Agoraphobia: A follow-up study four years after treatment. *British Journal of Psychiatry*, 1979, *134*, 352–355.

Emmelkamp, P. M. G., & Mersch, P. P. Cognition and exposure in vivo in the treatment of agoraphobia: Short-term and delayed effects. *Cognitive Research and Therapy*, 1982, *6*, 77–90.

Emmelkamp, P. M. G., & Rabbie, D. Psychological treatment of obsessive-compulsive disorders: A follow-up 4 years after treatment. In B. Jansson, C. Perris, & G. Struwe (Eds.), *Biological Psychiatry*. Amsterdam: Elsevier, 1981.

Emmelkamp, P. M. G., & Rabbie, D. Perceived parental characteristics of checkers and washers. Manuscript in preparation, 1982.

Emmelkamp, P. M. G., & Straatman, H. A psychoanalytic reinterpretation of the effectiveness of systematic desensitization: Fact or fiction? *Behaviour Research and Therapy*, 1976, *14*, 245–249.

Emmelkamp, P. M. G., & Ultee, K. A. A comparison of successive approximation and self-observation in the treatment of agoraphobia. *Behavior Therapy*, 1974, *5*, 605–613.

Emmelkamp, P. M. G., & van der Heyden, H. The treatment of harming obsessions. *Behavioural Analysis and Modification*, 1980, *4*, 28–35.

Emmelkamp, P. M. G. & van der Hout, A. Failure in treating agoraphobia. In E. B. Foa & P. M. G. Emmelkamp (Eds.), *Failures in behavior therapy*. New York: Wiley, 1982.

Emmelkamp, P. M. G., & Walta, C. The effects of therapy-set on electrical aversion therapy and covert sensitization. *Behavior Therapy*, 1978, *9*, 185–188.

Emmelkamp, P. M. G., & Wessels, H. Flooding in imagination vs. flooding *in vivo:* A comparison with agoraphobics. *Behaviour Research and Therapy*, 1975, *13*, 7–16.

Emmelkamp, P. M. G., Kuipers, A., & Eggeraat, J. Cognitive modification versus prolonged exposure *in vivo:* A comparison with agoraphobics. *Behaviour Research and Therapy*, 1978, *16*, 33–41.

Emmelkamp, P. M. G., van de Helm, M., van Zanten, B., & Plochg, I. Contributions of self-instructional training to the effectiveness of exposure *in vivo:* A comparison with obsessive-compulsive patients. *Behaviour Research and Therapy*, 1980, *18*, 61–66.

Emmelkamp, P. M. G., van de Helm, M., MacGillavry, D., & van Zanten, B. Marital therapy with clinically distressed couples: A comparative evaluation of system-theoretic, contingency contracting and communication skills approaches. In N. Jacobson & K. Hahlweg (Eds.), *Marital therapy and interaction*. New York: Guilford Press, 1982.

Emmelkamp, P. M. G., van der Hout, A., & de Vries, K. *Assertive training for agoraphobics.* Manuscript in preparation, 1982.

Engel, B. T. Operant conditioning of cardiac function: Some implications for psychosomatic medicine. *Behavior Therapy*, 1974, *5*, 302–303.

English, H. Three cases of the "conditioned fear response." *Journal of Abnormal and Social Psychology*, 1929, *34*, 221–225.

Engum, E. S., Miller, F. D., & Meredith, R. L. An analysis of three parameters of covert positive reinforcement. *Journal of Clinical Psychology*, 1980, *36*, 301–309.

Errera, P., & Coleman, J. V. A long-term follow-up study of neurotic phobic patients in a psychiatric clinic. *Journal of Nervous and Mental Disease*, 1963, *136*, 267–271.

Ersner-Hershfield, R., & Kopel, S. Group treatment of preorgasmic women: Evaluation of partner involvement and spacing of sessions. *Journal of Consulting and Clinical Psychology*, 1979, *47*, 750–759.

Escobar, J. I., & Landbloom, R. P. Treatment of phobic neurosis with clomipramine: A controlled clinical trial. *Current Therapeutic Research*, 1976, *20*, 680–685.

Esse, J. T., & Wilkins, W. Empathy and imagery in avoidance behavior reduction. *Journal of Consulting and Clinical Psychology*, 1978, *46*, 202–203.

Evans, P. D., & Kellam, A. M. P. Semi-automated desensitization: A controlled clinical trial. *Behaviour Research and Therapy*, 1973, *11*, 641–646.

Evans, L., & Moore, G. *The treatment of phobic anxiety by zimelidine.* Paper presented to the Depression Symposium, Corfu, April 1980.

Everaerd, W. T. A. M., Rijken, H. M., & Emmelkamp, P. M. G. A comparison of "flooding" and "successive approximation" in the treatment of agoraphobia. *Behaviour Research and Therapy*, 1973, *11*, 105–117.

Everaerd, W., Stufkens-Veerman, I., Van der Bout, J., Hofman, A., Syben-Schrier, M., & Schacht, H. Unpublished manuscript, University of Utrecht, 1977.

Falloon, I. R. H., Lindley, P., McDonald, R., & Marks, I. M. Social skills training of out-patient groups: A controlled study of rehearsal and homework. *British Journal of Psychiatry*, 1977, *131*, 599–609.

Fazio, F. Implosive therapy with semiclinical phobias. *Journal of Abnormal Psychology*, 1972, *80*, 183–188.

Fenichel, O. *Psychoanalytic theory of neurosis*. New York: Norton, 1977.

Fine, S. Family therapy and a behavioral approach to childhood obsessive-compulsive neurosis. *Archives of General Psychiatry*, 1973, *28*, 695–697.

Finger, R., & Galassi, J. P. Effects of modifying cognitive versus emotiality responses in the treatment of test anxiety. *Journal of Consulting and Clinical Psychology*, 1977, *45*, 280–287.

Finney, J. C. Maternal influences on anal or compulsive character in children. *Journal of Genetic Psychology*, 1963, *103*, 351–367.

Fisher, S., & Greenberg, R. P. *The scientific credibility of Freud's theories and therapy*. New York: Basic Books, 1977.

Flannery, R. B. A laboratory analogue of two covert reinforcement procedures. *Journal of Behavior Therapy and Experimental Psychiatry*, 1972, *3*, 171–177.

Flor-Henry, P. Yeudall, L. T., Koles, Z. J., & Howarth, B. G. Neuropsychological and power spectral EEG investigations of the obsessive-compulsive syndrome. *Biological Psychiatry*, 1979, *14*, 119–130.

Foa, E. B., & Chambless, D. L. Habituation of subjective anxiety during flooding in imagery. *Behaviour Research and Therapy*, 1978, *16*, 391–399.

Foa, E. B., & Goldstein, A. Continuous exposure and complete response prevention in the treatment of obsessive-compulsive neurosis. *Behavior Therapy*, 1978, *9*, 821–829.

Foa, E. B., & Steketee, G. S. Obsessive-compulsives: Conceptual issues and treatment interventions. In M. Hersen, R. M. Eisler, & P. M. Miller (Eds.), *Progress in Behavior Modification* (Vol. 8). New York: Academic Press, 1979.

Foa, E. B., Blau, J. S., Prout, M., & Latimer, P. Is horror a necessary component of flooding (implosion)? *Behaviour Research and Therapy*, 1977, *15*, 397–402.

Foa, E. B., Steketee, G., & Groves, G. Use of behavioral therapy and imipramine: A case of obsessive-compulsive neurosis with severe depression. *Behavior Modification*, 1979, *3*, 419–430.

Foa, E. B., Jameson, J. S., Turner, R. M., & Payne, L. L. Massed vs. spaced exposure sessions in the treatment of agoraphobia. *Behaviour Research and Therapy*, 1980, *18*, 333–338.

Foa, E. B., Steketee, G., & Milby, J. B. Differential effects of exposure and response prevention in obsessive-compulsive washers. *Journal of Consulting and Clinical Psychology*, 1980, *48*, 71–79.

Foa, E. B., Steketee, G., Turner, R. M., & Fischer, S. C. Effects of imaginal exposure to feared disasters in obsessive-compulsive checkers. *Behaviour Research and Therapy*, 1980, *18*, 449–455.

Fodor, I. G. The phobic syndrome in women. In V. Franks & V. Burtle (Eds.), *Women in therapy*. New York: Brunner/Mazel, 1974.

Fontana, D. Some standardization data for the Sandler-Hazari Obsessionality Inventory. *British Journal of Medical Psychology*, 1980, *53*, 267–275.

Foulds, G. A. *Personality and Personal Illness*. London: Tavistock Publications, 1965.

Fransella, F. Thinking and the obsessional. In H. R. Beech (Ed.), *Obsessional states*. London: Methuen, 1974.

Fredrikson, M., Hugdahl, K., & Öhman, A. Electrodermal conditioning to potentially phobic stimuli in male and female subjects. *Biological Psychology*, 1976, *4*, 305–314.

Freedman, A. M. Psychopharmacology and psychotherapy in the treatment of anxiety. *Pharmakopsychiatrie*, 1980, *13*, 277–289.

Freeman, W., & Watts, J. W. *Psychosurgery*. New York: Oxford University Press, 1950.

Fremouw, W. J., & Zitter, R. E. A comparison of skills training and cognitive restructuring—relaxation for the treatment of speech anxiety. *Behavior Therapy*, 1978, *9*, 248–259.

Freud, S. Further remarks on the neuro-psychoses of defence. *Standard edition* (Vol. III). London: Hogarth Press, 1966. (Originally published, 1896.)

Freud, S. Character and anal erotism. *Standard edition* (Vol IX). London: Hogarth Press, 1966. (Originally published, 1908.)

Freud, S. Analysis of a phobia in a five-year old boy. *Standard Edition* (Vol X). London: Hogarth Press, 1966. (Originally published, 1909.) (a)

Freud, S. Notes upon a case of obsessional neurosis. *Standard edition* (Vol X). London: Hogarth Press, 1966. (Originally published, 1909.) (b)

Freud, S. The disposition to obsessional neurosis. *Standard edition* (Vol. XII). London: Hogarth Press, 1966. (Originally published, 1913.)

Freud, S. Inhibitions, symptoms and anxiety. *Standard edition*. (Vol XX). London: Hogarth Press, 1966. (Originally published, 1926.)

Freud, S. Turnings in the world of psycho-analytic therapy. In *Collected papers* (Vol. 2). London: Hogarth Press, 1966. New York: Basic Books, 1959.

Friedman, J. H. Short-term psychotherapy of "phobia of travel." *American Journal of Psychotherapy*, 1950, *4*, 259–278.

Fry, W. F. The marital context of an anxiety syndrome. *Family Process*, 1962, *1*, 245–252.

Galassi, J. P., Frierson, H. T., & Sharer, R. Behavior of high, moderate, and low test anxious students during an actual test situation. *Journal of Consulting and Clinical Psychology*, 1981, *49*, 51–62.

Gardner, F. L., McGowan, L. P., DiGiuseppe, R., & Sutton-Simon, K. *A comparison of cognitive and behavioral therapies in the reduction of social anxiety.* Paper presented to the American Association of Behavior Therapy, New York, November 1980.

Gardos, G. Is agoraphobia a psychosomatic form of depression? In D. F. Klein & J. Rabkin (Eds.), *Anxiety: New research and changing concepts*. New York: Raven Press, 1981.

Garssen, B. Role of stress in the development of the hyperventilation syndrome. *Psychotherapy and Psychosomatics*, 1980, *33*, 214–225.

Gatchel, R. J. Therapeutic effectiveness of voluntary heart rate control in reducing anxiety. *Journal of Consulting and Clinical Psychology*, 1977, *45*, 689–691.

Gatchel, R. J., Hatch, J. P., Maynard, A., Turns, R., & Taunton-Blackwood, A. Comparison of heart rate biofeedback and systematic desensitization in reducing speech anxiety: Short- and long-term effectiveness. *Journal of Consulting and Clinical Psychology*, 1979, *47*, 620–622.

Gatchel, R. J., Hatch, J. P., Watson, P. J., Smith, D., & Gaas, E. Comparative effectiveness of voluntary heart rate control and muscular relaxation as active coping skills for reducing speech anxiety. *Journal of Consulting and Clinical Psychology*, 1977, *45*, 1093–1100.

Gatchel, R. J., & Proctor, J. D. Effectiveness of voluntary heart rate control in reducing speech anxiety. *Journal of Consulting and Clinical Psychology*, 1976, *44*, 381–389.

Gauthier, J., & Marshall, W. L. The determination of optimal exposure to phobic stimuli in flooding therapy. *Behaviour Research and Therapy*, 1977, *15*, 403–410.

Gay, M. L., Hollandsworth, J. G., & Galassi, J. P. An assertiveness inventory. *Journal of Counseling Psychology*, 1975, *22*, 340–344.

Gelder, M. G. Behavioral treatment of agoraphobia: Some factors which restrict change after treatment. In J. C. Boulougouris & A. D. Rabavilas (Eds.), *The treatment of phobic and obsessive compulsive disorders.* New York: Pergamon Press, 1977.

Gelder, M. G., Bancroft, J. H., Gath, D. H., Johnston, D. W., Mathews, A. M., & Shaw, P. M. Specific and non-specific factors in behaviour therapy. *British Journal of Psychiatry*, 1973, *123*, 445–462.

Gelder, M. G., & Marks, I. M. Severe agoraphobia: A controlled prospective trial of behaviour therapy. *British Journal of Psychiatry*, 1966, *112*, 309–319.

Gelder, M. G., & Marks, I. M. Desensitization and phobias: A crossover study. *British Journal of Psychiatry*, 1968, *114*, 323–328.

Gelder, M. G., Marks, I. M., & Wolff, H. H. Desensitization and psychotherapy in the treatment of phobic states: A controlled enquiry. *British Journal of Psychiatry*, 1967, *113*, 53–73.

Gentry, W. D. In vivo desensitization of an obsessive cancer fear. *Journal of Behavior Therapy and Experimental Psychiatry*, 1970, *1*, 315–318.

Gillan, P., & Rachman, S. An experimental investigation of desensitization in phobic patients. *British Journal of Psychiatry*, 1974, *124*, 392–401.

Girodo, M., & Henry, D. R. Cognitive, psychological and behavioral components of anxiety in flooding. *Canadian Journal of Behavioral Sciences*, 1976, *8*, 224–231.

Girodo, M., & Roehl, J. Cognitive preparation and coping self-talk: Anxiety management during the stress of flying. *Journal of Consulting and Clinical Psychology*, 1978, *46*, 978–989.

Gittelman-Klein, R., & Klein, D. F. Controlled imipramine treatment of school phobia. *Archives of General Psychiatry*, 1971, *25*, 204–207.

Glasgow, R. E., & Arkowitz, H. The behavioral assessment of male and female social competence in dyadic heterosexual interactions. *Behavior Therapy*, 1975, *6* 488–498.

Glass, C. R., Gottman, J. M., & Shmurak, S. H. Response acquisition and cognitive self-statement modification approaches to dating-skills training. *Journal of Counseling Psychology*, 1976, *23*, 520–526.

Glenn, S. S., & Hughes, H. H. Imaginal response events in systematic desensitization: A pilot study. *Biological Psychology*, 1978, *7*, 303–309.

Glogower, F. D., Fremouw, W. J., & McCroskey, J. C. A component analysis of cognitive restructuring. *Cognitive Therapy and Research*, 1978, *2*, 209–223.

Gochman, I. R., & Keating, J. P. Misattribution to crowding: Blaming crowding for non-density-caused events. *Journal of Nonverbal Behavior*, 1980, *4*, 157–175.

Golden, M. A measure of cognition within the context of assertion. *Journal of Clinical Psychology*, 1981, *37*, 253–262.

Goldfried, M. R. Systematic desensitization as training in self-control. *Journal of Consulting and Clinical Psychology*, 1971, *37*, 228–234.

Goldfried, M. R., Decenteceo, E. T., & Weinberg, L. Systematic rational restructuring as a self-control technique. *Behavior Therapy*, 1974, *5*, 247–254.

Goldfried, M. R., & Goldfried, A. P. Importance of hierarchy content in the self-control of anxiety. *Journal of Consulting and Clinical Psychology*, 1977, *45*, 124–134.

Goldfried, M. R., & Sobocinski, D. The effect of irrational beliefs on emotional arousal. *Journal of Consulting and Clinical Psychology*, 1975, *43*, 504–510.

Goldfried, M. R., & Trier, C. S. Effectiveness of relaxation as an active coping skill. *Journal of Abnormal Psychology*, 1974, *83*, 348–355.

Goldfried, M. R., Linehan, M. M., & Smith, J. L. The reduction of test anxiety through rational restructuring. *Journal of Consulting and Clinical Psychology*, 1978, *37*, 228–234.

Goldstein, A. J. Learning theory insufficiency in understanding agoraphobia. A plea for empiricism. *Proceedings of the European Association for Behaviour Therapy*, Munich: Urban & Schwarzenberg, 1973.

Goldstein, A. J., & Chambless, D. L. A reanalysis of agoraphobia. *Behavior Therapy*, 1978, *9*, 47–59.

Goodstein, R. K., & Swift, K. Psychotherapy with phobic patients: The marriage relationship as the source of symptoms and focus of treatment. *American Journal of Psychotherapy*, 1977, *31*, 284–293.

Goorney, A. B. Psychological measures in aircrew-normative data. *Aerospace Medicine*, 1970, *41*, 87–91.

Goorney, A. B., & O'Connor, P. J. Anxiety associated with flying. *British Journal of Psychiatry*, 1971, *119*, 159–166.

Gormally, J., Sipps, G., Raphael, R., Edwin, D., & Varvil-Weld, D. The relationship between maladaptive cognitions and social anxiety. *Journal of Consulting and Clinical Psychology*, 1981, *49*, 300–301.

Gormally, J., Varvil-Weld, D., Raphael, R., & Sipps, G. Treatment of socially anxious college men using cognitive counseling and skills training. *Journal of Counseling Psychology*, 1981, *28*, 147–157.

Gottman, J. M. *Marital interaction: Experimental investigations*. New York: Academic Press, 1979.

Gray, J. A. *Elements of a two-process theory of learning*. New York: Academic Press, 1975.

Grayson, J. B., & Borkovec, T. D. The effects of expectancy and imagined response to phobic stimuli on fear reduction. *Cognitive Therapy and Research*, 1978, *2*, 11–24.

Graziano, A. M., & De Giovanni, I. S. The clinical significance of childhood phobias: A note on the proportion of child-clinical referrals for the treatment of children's fears. *Behaviour Research and Therapy*, 1979, *17*, 161–162.

Graziano, A. M., De Giovanni, I. S., & Garcia, K. A. Behavioral treatment of children's fears: A review. *Psychological Bulletin*, 1979, *86*, 804–830.

Grinker, R., & Spiegel, J. *Men under stress*. Philadelphia: Blakiston, 1945.

Gross, R. T., & Fremouw, W. J. *Cognitive restructuring and progressive relaxation for treatment of empirical subtypes of speech anxious subjects*. Paper presented to American Association of Behavior Therapy, New York, November 1980.

Grossberg, J. M., & Wilson, H. K. Physiological changes accompanying the visualization of fearful and neutral situations. *Journal of Personality and Social Psychology*, 1968, *10*, 124–133.

Guidry, L. S., & Randolph, D. L. Covert reinforcement in the treatment of test anxiety. *Journal of Counseling Psychology*, 1974, *21*, 260–264.

Haaijman, W. P., van Veelen, C. W. M., & Storm van Leeuwen, W. Behandeling van dwangpatiënten, effect van neurochirurgische procedures. In A. Jennekens-Schinkel (Ed.), *Neuropsychologie in Nederland*. Deventer: van Loghum Slaterus, 1980.

Hackmann, A., & McLean, C. A. A comparison of flooding and thought stopping in the treatment of obsessional neurosis. *Behaviour Research and Therapy*, 1975, *13*, 263–269.

Hafner, R. J., & Marks, I. M. Exposure *in vivo* of agoraphobics: Contributions of diazepam, group exposure, and anxiety evocation. *Psychological Medicine*, 1976, *6*, 71–88.

Hafner, R. J. The husbands of agoraphobic women: Assortative mating or pathogenic interaction? *British Journal of Psychiatry*, 1977, *130*, 233–239.

Hafner, R. J., & Milton, F. The influence of propranolol on the exposure *in vivo* of agoraphobics. *Psychological Medicine*, 1977, *7*, 419–425.

Hagman, C. A study of fear in pre-school children. *Journal of Experimental Psychology*, 1932, *1*, 110–130.

Hain, J. D., Butcher, H. C., & Stevenson, I. Systematic desensitization therapy: An analysis of results in twenty-seven patients. *British Journal of Psychiatry*, 1966, *112*, 295–307.

Hall, R., & Goldberg, D. The role of social anxiety in social interaction difficulties. *British Journal of Psychiatry*, 1977, *131*, 610–615.

Hallam, R. S., & Hafner, R. J. Fears of phobic patients: Factor analyses of self report data. *Behaviour Research and Therapy*, 1978, *16*, 1–6.

Hallam, R. S., & Rachman, S. Current status of aversion therapy. In M. Hersen, R. M. Eisler, & P. M. Miller (Eds.), *Progress in behavior modification*, (Vol 2). New York: Academic Press, 1976.

Hamilton, V. Perceptual and personality dynamics in reactions to ambiguity. *British Journal of Psychology*, 1957, *48*, 200–215.

Hammen, C. L., Jacobs, M., Mayol, A., & Cochran, S. D. Dysfunctional cognitions and the effectiveness of skills and cognitive-behavioral assertion training. *Journal of Consulting and Clinical Psychology*, 1980, *48*, 685–695.

Hand, I., & Lamontagne, Y. The exacerbation of interpersonal problems after rapid phobia-removal. *Psychotherapy: Theory, Research and Practice*, 1976, *13*, 405–411.

Hand, I., & Tichatzky, M. Behavioral group therapy for obsessions and compulsions: First results of a pilot study. In P. O. Sjöden, S. Bates, & W. S. Dockens (Eds.), *Trends in behavior therapy*. New York. Academic Press, 1979.

Hand, I., Lamontagne, Y., & Marks, I. M. Group exposure (flooding) *in vivo* for agoraphobics. *British Journal of Psychiatry*, 1974, *124*, 588–602.

Hand, I., Spoehring, B., & Stanik, E. Treatment of obsessions, compulsions and phobias as hidden couple-counseling. In J. C. Boulougouris & A. D. Rabavilas (Eds.), *The treatment of phobic and obsessive-compulsive disorders*. New York: Pergamon Press, 1977.

Hardt, J., & Kamiya, J. Anxiety change through electroencephalographic alpha feedback seen only in high anxiety subjects. *Science*, 1978, *201*, 79–81.

Harris, G., & Bennett-Johnson, S. Comparison of individualized covert modeling, self-control desensitization, and study skills training for alleviation of test anxiety. *Journal of Consulting and Clinical Psychology*, 1980, *48*, 186–194.

Hayes, S. C. The role of approach contingencies in phobic behavior. *Behavior Therapy*, 1976, *7*, 28–36.

Haynes, S. N., Moseley, D., & McGowan, W. T. Relaxation training and biofeedback in the reduction of frontalis muscle tension. *Psychophysiology*, 1975, *12*, 547–552.

Heimberg, R. G. Comment on "Evaluation of a clinically relevant target behavior for analog outcome research." *Behavior Therapy*, 1977, *8*, 492–493.

Hekmat, H. Systematic versus semantic desensitization and implosive therapy: A comparative study. *Journal of Consulting and Clinical Psychology*, 1973, *40*, 202–209.

Hepner, A., & Cauthen, N. R. Effect of subject control and graduated exposure on snake phobias. *Journal of Consulting and Clinical Psychology*, 1975, *43*, 297–304.

Herrnstein, R. J. Method and theory in the study of avoidance. *Psychological Review*, 1969, *76*, 49–69.

Herrnstein, R. J., & Hineline, P. N. Negative reinforcement as shock-frequency reduction. *Journal of the Experimental Analysis of Behavior*, 1966, *9*, 421–430.

Hersen, M. The use of behavior modification techniques within a traditional psychotherapeutic context. *American Journal of Psychotherapy*, 1970, *24*, 308–313.

Hersen, M. Self-assessment of fear. *Behavior Therapy*, 1973, *4*, 241–257.

Hersen, M., & Bellack, A. S. (Eds.). *Behavioral assessment: A practical handbook*. New York: Pergamon Press, 1976.

Hersen, M., Bellack, A. S., & Turner, S. M. Assessment of assertiveness in female psychiatric patients: Motor and autonomic measures. *Journal of Behavior Therapy and Experimental Psychiatry*, 1978, *9*, 11–16.

Hetherington, E. M., & Brackbill, Y. Etiology and covariation of obstinacy, orderliness, and parsimony in young children. *Child Development*, 1963, *34*, 919–943.

Heyse, H. Verhaltenstherapie bei zwangneurotiker: Vorlaufige Ergebnisse. In Brengelman & Tunner (Eds.), *Verhaltenstherapie*. Berlin: Urban und Schwarzenberg, 1973.

Hill, O. The hyperventilation syndrome. *British Journal of Psychiatry*, 1979, *135*, 367–368.

Hodes, R., Öhman, A., & Lang, P. J. *"Ontogenetic" and "philogenetic" fear-relevance of the conditioned stimulus in electrodermal and heart-rate conditioning.* Unpublished manuscript, 1979. (Cited in Öhman, 1979.)

Hodgson, R., & Rachman, S. Desynchrony in measures of fear. *Behaviour Research and Therapy*, 1974, *12*, 319–326.

Hodgson, R., Rachman, S., & Marks, I. The treatment of chronic-obsessive-compulsive neurosis: Follow-up and further findings. *Behaviour Research and Therapy*, 1972, *10*, 181–184.

Hodgson, R. J., & Rachman, S. The effects of contamination and washing in obsessional patients. *Behaviour Research and Therapy*, 1972, *10*, 111–117.

Hodgson, R. J., & Rachman, S. Obsessional-compulsive complaints. *Behaviour Research and Therapy*, 1977, *15*, 389–395.

Hodgson, R. J., Rankin, H., & Stockwell, T. R. *Introversion, obsessional personality and obsessional-compulsive complaints.* Unpublished manuscript, 1980. (Cited in Rachman & Hodgson, 1980.)

Hogan, D. R. The effectiveness of sex therapy: A review of the literature. In J. LoPiccolo & L. LoPiccolo (Eds.), *Handbook of sex therapy*. New York: Plenum Press, 1978.

Holland, H. C. Displacement activity as a form of abnormal behaviour in animals. In H. R. Beech (Ed.), *Obsessional states*. London: Methuen, 1974.

Hollandsworth, J. G., Glazesky, R. C., Kirkland, K., Jones, G. E., & Van Norman, L. R. An analysis of the nature and effects of test anxiety: Cognitive, behavioral, and physiological components. *Cognitive Therapy and Research*, 1979, *3*, 165–180.

Holroyd, K. A. Cognition and desensitization in the group treatment of test anxiety. *Journal of Consulting and Clinical Psychology*, 1976, *44*, 991–1001.

Holroyd, K. A., Westbrook, T., Wolf, M., & Bradhorn, E. Performance, cognition, and physiological responding in test anxiety. *Journal of Abnormal Psychology*, 1978, *87*, 442–451.

Hops, H., Wills, F. A., Patterson, G. R., & Weiss, R. L. *Marital interaction coding system (MICS)*. Unpublished manuscript, University of Oregon and Oregon Research Institute, 1972.

Horne, A. M., & Matson, J. L. A comparison of modeling, desensitization, flooding, study skills, and control groups for reducing test anxiety. *Behavior Therapy*, 1977, *8*, 1–8.

Hornsveld, R. H., Kraaymaat, F. W., & van Dam-Baggen, R. M. J. Anxiety/discomfort and handwashing in obsessive-compulsive and psychiatric control patients. *Behaviour Research and Therapy*, 1979, *17*, 223–228.

Hudson, B. The families of agoraphobics treated by behaviour therapy. *British Journal of Social Work*, 1974, *4*, 51–59.

Hugdahl, K., & Kärker, A. C. Biological vs. experiential factors in phobic conditioning. *Behaviour Research and Therapy*, 1981, *19*, 109–116.

Hugdahl, K., & Öhman, A. Effects of instruction on acquisition and extinction of electrodermal responses to fear-relevant stimuli. *Journal of Experimental Psychology: Human Learning and Memory*, 1977, *3*, 608–618.

Hugdahl, K., Fredrikson, M., & Öhman, A. "Preparedness" and "arousability" as determinants of electrodermal conditioning. *Behaviour Research and Therapy*, 1977, *15*, 345–353.

Hurley, A. D. Covert reinforcement: The contribution of the reinforcing stimulus to treatment outcome. *Behavior Therapy*, 1976, *7*, 374–378.

Hussain, M. Z. Desensitization and flooding (implosion) in treatment of phobias. *American Journal of Psychiatry*, 1971, *127*, 1509–1514.

Hussian, R. A., & Lawrence, P. S. The reduction of test, state, and trait anxiety by test-specific and generalized stress inoculation training. *Cognitive Therapy and Research*, 1978, *2*, 25–37.

Hutchings, D. F., Denney, D. R., Basgall, J., & Houston, B. K. Anxiety management and applied relaxation in reducing general anxiety. *Behaviour Research and Therapy*, 1980, *18*, 181–190.

Hygge, S., & Öhman, A. Conditioning of electrodermal responses through perceived threat to a performer. *Scandinavian Journal of Psychology*, 1976, *17*, 65–72.

Ingram, I. M., & McAdam, W. A. The electroencephalogram, obsessional illness and obsessional personality. *Journal of Mental Science*, 1960, *106*, 686–691.

Jain, V. K., Swinson, R. P., & Thomas, J. G. Phenelzine in obsessional neurosis. *British Journal of Psychiatry*, 1970, *117*, 237–238.

Jannoun, L., Munby, M., Catalan, J., & Gelder, M. A home-based treatment program for agoraphobia: Replication and controlled evaluation. *Behavior Therapy*, 1980, *11*, 294–305.

Jasin, S. E., & Turner, R. M. *Multivariate analysis of agoraphobics', anxiety neurotics', and depressive neurotics' responses to the MMPI and Beck Depression Inventory*. Paper presented to the American Association of Behavior Therapy Convention, New York, November 1980.

Jessup, B. A., & Neufeld, R. W. J. Effects of biofeedback and "autogenic relaxation" techniques on physiological and subjective responses in psychiatric patients: A preliminary analysis. *Behavior Therapy*, 1977, *8*, 160–167.

Johnson, J. H., & Sarason, I. G. Life stress, depression and anxiety: Internal-external control as a moderator variable. *Journal of Psychosomatic Research*, 1978, *22*, 205–208.

Johnston, D. W., & Gath, D. Arousal levels and attribution effects in diazepam-assisted flooding. *British Journal of Psychiatry*, 1973, *123*, 463–466.

Johnston, D. W., Lancashire, M., Mathews, A. M., Munby, M., Shaw, P. M., & Gelder, M. G. Imaginal flooding and exposure to real phobic situations: Changes during treatment. *British Journal of Psychiatry*, 1976, *129*, 372–377.

Johnstone, E. C., Crow, T. J., Deakin, J. F. W., Frith, C. D., Lawler, P., McPherson, K., & Stevens, M. *A double-blind study of 8 real versus 8 simulated ECT in depressed inpatients*. Paper presented to the Third World Congress of Biological Psychiatry, Stockholm, July 1981.

Kane, J. M., Woerner, M., Zeldis, S., Kramer, R., & Saravay, S. Panic and phobic disorders in patients with mitral valve prolapse. In D. F. Klein & J. Rabkin (Eds.), *Anxiety: New research and changing concepts*. New York: Raven Press, 1981.

Kanfer, F. H., & Saslow, G. Behavior diagnosis. In C. M. Franks (Ed.), *Behavior Therapy: Appraisal and status*. New York: McGraw-Hill, 1969.

Kanter, N. J., & Goldfried, M. R. Relative effectiveness of rational restructuring and self-control desensitization in the reduction of interpersonal anxiety. *Behavior Therapy*, 1979, *10*, 472–490.

Kantor, J. S., Zitrin, C. M., & Zeldis, S. M. Mitral valve prolapse syndrome in agoraphobic patients. *American Journal of Psychiatry*, 1980, *137*, 467–469.

Kaplan, H. S. *The new sex therapy*. New York: Brunner/Mazel, 1974.

Karabanow, O. Double-blind controlled study in phobias and obsessions. *Journal of International Medical Research*, 1977, *5*, 42–48.

Katkin, E. S., & Silver-Hoffman, L. S. Sex differences and self-report of fear: A psychophysiological assessment. *Journal of Abnormal Psychology*, 1976, *85*, 607–610.

Kazdin, A. E., & Smith, G. A. Covert conditioning: A review and evaluation. *Advances in Behaviour Research and Therapy*, 1979, *2*, 57–98.

Kelly, D. Clinical review of beta-blockers in anxiety. *Pharmakopsychiatry,* 1980, *13,* 259–266.

Kelly, D., Guirguis, W., Frommer, E., Mitchell-Heggs, N., & Sargant, W. Treatment of phobic states with antidepressants, a retrospective study of 246 patients. *British Journal of Psychiatry,* 1970, *116,* 387–398.

Kelly, D., Richardson, A., Mitchell-Heggs, N., Greenup, J., Chen, C., & Hafner, R. J. Stereotactic limbic leucotomy: A preliminary report on forty patients. *British Journal of Psychiatry,* 1973, *123,* 141–148.

Kelly, D. H., Walter, M., Heggs, N., & Sargant, W. Modified leucotomy assessed clinically, physiologically and psychologically at six weeks and eighteen months. *British Journal of Psychiatry,* 1972, *120,* 19–29.

Kelly, G. A. *Psychology of personal constructs.* New York: Norton, 1955.

Kendell, R. E., & diScipio, W. J. Obsessional symptoms and obsessional personality traits in patients with depressive illnesses. *Psychological Medicine,* 1970, *1,* 65–72.

Kenny, F. T., Mowbray, R. M., & Lalani, S. Faradic disruption of obsessive ideation in the treatment of obsessive neurosis: A controlled study. *Behavior Therapy,* 1978, *9,* 209–221.

Kenny, F. T., Solyom, C., & Solyom, L. Faradic disruption of obsessive ideation in the treatment of obsessive neurosis. *Behavior Therapy,* 1973, *4,* 448–457.

Kipper, D. A. Behavior therapy for fears brought on by war experiences. *Journal of Clinical and Consulting Psychology,* 1977, *45,* 216–221.

Kirkland, K., & Hollandsworth, J. G. Effective test-taking: Skills-acquisition versus anxiety-reduction techniques. *Journal of Consulting and Clinical Psychology,* 1980, *48,* 431–439.

Kirsch, I., & Henry, D. Extinction versus credibility in the desensitization of speech anxiety. *Journal of Consulting and Clinical Psychology,* 1977, *45,* 1052–1059.

Kirsch, I., & Henry, D. Self-desensitization and meditation in the reduction of public speaking anxiety. *Journal of Consulting and Clinical Psychology,* 1979, *47,* 536–541.

Kirsch, I., Wolpin, M., & Knutson, J. L. A comparison of in vivo methods for rapid reduction of "stage fright" in the college classroom: A field experiment. *Behavior Therapy,* 1975, *6,* 165–171.

Klein, D. F. Delineation of two-drug responsive anxiety syndromes. *Psychopharamcologia,* 1964, *5,* 397–408.

Klein, D. F., & Fink, M. Psychiatric reaction patterns to imipramine. *American Journal of Psychiatry,* 1962, *119,* 432–438.

Kline, P. Obsessional traits and emotional instability in a normal population. *British Journal of Medical Psychology,* 1967, *40,* 153–157.

Kline, P. Obsessional traits, obsessional symptoms, and anal eroticism. *British Journal of Medical Psychology,* 1968, *41,* 299–305.

Kockott, G., Dittmar, F., & Nusselt, L. Systematic desensitization and erectile impotence: A controlled study. *Archives of Sexual Behavior,* 1975, *4,* 493–500.

Kockott, G., Feil, W., Revenstorf, D., Aldenhoff, J., & Besinger, U. Symptomatology and psychological aspects of male sexual inadequacy: Results of an experimental study. *Archives of Sexual Behavior,* 1980, *9,* 457–475.

Koczkas, S., Holmberg, G., & Wedin, L. *A pilot study of the effect of the 5-HT-uptake inhibitor, zimelidine, on phobic anxiety.* Paper presented to the Depression Symposium, Corfu, April 1980.

Kostka, M. P., & Galassi, J. P. Group systematic desensitization versus covert positive reinforcement in the reduction of test anxiety. *Journal of Counseling Psychology,* 1974, *21,* 464–468.

Kringlen, E. Obsessional neurotics: A long-term follow-up. *British Journal of Psychiatry,* 1965, *111,* 709–722.

Kushner, M., & Sandler, J. Aversion therapy and the concept of punishment. *Behaviour Research and Therapy*, 1966, *4*, 179–186.

Lacey, J. I. Psychophysiological approaches to the evaluation of psychotherapeutic process and outcome. In F. Rubinstein & M. B. Parloff (Eds.), *Research in psychotherapy* (Vol II). Washington D.C.: American Psychological Association, 1962.

Lachman, S. J. *Psychosomatic disorders: A behavioristic interpretation*. New York: Wiley, 1972.

Lader, M. H. Palmar conductance measures in anxiety and phobic states. *Journal of Psychosomatic Research*, 1967, *11*, 271–281.

Lader, M. H., & Mathews, A. M. A physiological model of phobic anxiety and desensitization. *Behaviour Research and Therapy*, 1968, *6*, 411–421.

Lader, M. H., & Wing, L. *Physiological Measures, Sedative Drugs, and Morbid Anxiety*. London: Oxford University Press, 1966.

Ladouceur, R. An experimental test of the learning paradigm of covert positive reinforcement in deconditioning anxiety. *Journal of Behavior Therapy and Experimental Psychiatry*, 1974, *5*, 3–6.

Ladouceur, R. Rationale of covert positive reinforcement: Additional evidence. *Psychological Reports*, 1977, *41*, 547–550.

Ladouceur, R. Rationale of systematic desensitization and covert positive reinforcement. *Behaviour Research and Therapy*, 1978, *16*, 411–420.

Lamb, D. Use of behavioral measures in anxiety research. *Psychological Reports*, 1978, *43*, 1079–1085.

Lambourn, J., & Gill, D. A controlled comparison of simulated and real ECT. *British Journal of Psychiatry*, 1978, *133*, 514–519.

Lang, P. J. Fear reduction and fear behavior: Problems in treating a construct. In J. M. Shlien (Ed.), *Research in psychotherapy* (Vol III). Washington, D.C.: American Psychological Association, 1968.

Lang, P. J. The mechanics of desensitization and the laboratory study of human fear. In C. M. Franks (Ed.), *Behavior therapy: Appraisal and status*. New York: McGraw-Hill, 1969.

Lang, P. J. The application of psychophysiological methods to the study of psychotherapy and behavior modification. In A. E. Bergin & S. L. Garfield (Eds.), *Handbook of psychotherapy and behavior change*. New York: Wiley, 1971.

Lang, P. J. Imagery in therapy: An information processing analysis of fear. *Behavior Therapy*, 1977, *8*, 862–886.

Lang, P. J. A bio-informational theory of emotional imagery. *Psychophysiology*, 1979, *16*, 495–512.

Lang, P. J., Kozak, M. J., Miller, G. A., Levin, D. N., & McLean, A. Emotional imagery: Conceptual structure and pattern of somatic-visceral response. *Psychophysiology*, 1980, *17*, 179–192.

Lapouse, R., & Monk, M. A. Fears and worries in representative sample of children. *American Journal of Orthopsychiatry*, 1959, *29*, 803–818.

Lautch, H. Video tape-recordings as an aid to behaviour therapy. *British Journal of Psychiatry*, 1970, *117*, 207–208.

Lautch, H. Dental phobia. *British Journal of Psychiatry*, 1971, *119*, 151–158.

Lavallee, Y. J., Lamontagne, Y., Pinard, G., Annable, L., & Tetreault, L. Effects on EMG feedback, diazepam and their combination of chronic anxiety. *Journal of Psychosomatic Research*, 1977, *21*, 65–71.

Lazare, A., Klerman, G. L., & Armor, D. J. Oral, obsessive, and hysterical personality patterns: An investigation of psychoanalytic concepts by means of factor analysis. *Archives of General Psychiatry*, 1966, *14*, 624–630.

Lazare, A., Klerman, G. L., & Armor, D. J. Oral, obsessive and hysterical personality patterns: Replication of factor analysis in an independent sample. *Journal of Psychiatric Research*, 1970, *7*, 275–290.

Lazarus, A. A. *Behavior therapy and beyond.* New York: McGraw-Hill, 1971.

Lazarus, A. A. Multimodal behavior therapy: Treating the "Basic Id." *Journal of Nervous and Mental Disease*, 1973, *156*, 404–411.

Le Boeuf, A. An automated aversion device in the treatment of a compulsive hand-washing ritual. *Journal of Behavior Therapy and Experimental Psychiatry*, 1974, *5*, 267–270.

Ledwidge, B. Cognitive behavior modification: A step in the wrong direction? *Psychological Bulletin*, 1978, *85*, 353–375.

Leger, L. A. Spurious and actual improvement in the treatment of preoccupying thoughts by thought-stopping. *British Journal of Social and Clinical Psychology*, 1978, *17*, 373–377.

Leger, L. A. An outcome measure for thought-stopping examined in three case studies. *Journal of Behavior Therapy and Experimental Psychiatry*, 1979, *10*, 115–120.

Leitenberg, H., Agras, W. S., Allen, R., Butz, R., & Edwards, J. Feedback and therapist praise during treatment of phobia. *Journal of Consulting and Clinical Psychology*, 1975, *43*, 396–404.

Leitenberg, H., Agras, S., Butz, R., & Wincze, J. Relationship between heart rate and behavioral change during the treatment of phobias. *Journal of Abnormal Psychology*, 1971, *78*, 59–68.

Leitenberg, H., & Callahan, E. J. Reinforced practice and reduction of different kinds of fear in adults and children. *Behaviour Research and Therapy*, 1973, *11*, 19–30.

Lent, R. W., Crimmings, A. M., & Russell, R. K. Subconscious reconditioning: Evaluation of a placebo strategy for outcome research. *Behavior Therapy*, 1981, *12*, 138–143.

Lent, R. W., Russell, R. K., & Zamostny, K. P. Comparison of cue-controlled desensitization, rational restructuring, and a credible placebo in the treatment of speech anxiety. *Journal of Consulting and Clinical Psychology*, 1981, *49*, 608–610.

Levine, S. B., & Agle, D. The effectiveness of sex therapy for chronic secondary psychological impotence. *Journal of Sex and Marital Therapy*, 1978, *4*, 235–258.

Levis, D. J., & Hare, A. A review of the theoretical rationale and empirical support for the extinction approach of implosive (flooding) therapy. In M. Hersen, R. M. Eisler, & P. M. Miller (Eds.), *Progress in behavior modification* (Vol. 4). New York: Academic Press, 1977, 300–376.

Lewis, A. Incidence of neurosis in England under war conditions. *Lancet*, 1942, *2*, 175–183.

Lewis, S. A comparison of behavior therapy techniques in the reduction of fearful avoidance behavior. *Behavior Therapy*, 1974, *5*, 648–655.

Lick, J. Expectancy, false galvanic skin response feedback, and systematic desensitization in the modification of phobic behavior. *Journal of Consulting and Clinical Psychology*, 1975, *43*, 557–567.

Lick, J. R., & Katkin, E. S. Assessment of anxiety and fear. In M. Hersen & A. S. Bellack (Eds.), *Behavioral assessment: A practical handbook.* New York: Pergamon Press, 1976.

Lick, J. R., Sushinsky, L. W., & Malow, R. Specificity of fear survey schedule items and the prediction of avoidance behavior. *Behavior Modification*, 1977, *1*, 195–203.

Lick, J. R., & Unger, T. E. The external validity of behavioral fear assessment. *Behavior Modification*, 1977, *1*, 283–307.

Liddell, A., & Lyons, M. Thunderstorm phobias. *Behaviour Research and Therapy*, 1978, *16*, 306–308.

Liebert, R. M., & Morris, L. W. Cognitive and emotional components of test anxiety: A distinction and some initial data. *Psychological Reports*, 1967, *20*, 975–978.

Lietaer, G. Nederlandstalige revisie van Barrett-Lennard's Relationship Inventory voor individueel therapeutische relaties. *Psychologia Belgica*. 1976, *16*, 73–94.

Linehan, M. M., Goldfried, M. R., & Goldfried, A. Assertion therapy: Skills training or cognitive restructuring. *Behavior Therapy*, 1979, *10*, 372–388.

Lipsedge, M. S., Hajioff, J., Huggins, P., Napier, L., Pearce, J., Pike, D. J., & Rich, M. The management of severe agoraphobia: A comparison of iproniazid and systematic desensitization. *Psychopharmacologia*, 1973, *32*, 67–88.

Little, S., & Jackson, B. The treatment of test anxiety through attentional and relaxation training. *Psychotherapy: Theory, Research and Practice*, 1974, *11*, 175–178.

Litvak, S. B. A comparison of two brief group behavior therapy techniques on the reduction of avoidance behavior. *Psychological Record*, 1969, *19*, 329–334.

Locke, H., & Wallace, K. Short marital-adjustment and prediction tests: Their reliability and validity. *Marriage and Family Living*, 1959, *21*, 251–255.

Lombardo, T. W., & Turner, S. M. Thought-stopping in the control of obsessive ruminations. *Behavior Modification*, 1979, *3*, 267–272.

Lo Piccolo, J., & Lobitz, W. C. The role of masturbation in the treatment of orgasmic dysfunction. *Archives of Sexual Behavior*, 1972, *2*, 163–172.

Lo Piccolo, J., & Lo Piccolo, L. (Eds.) *Handbook of sex therapy*. New York: Plenum Press, 1978.

Maccoby, E., & Jacklin, C. *The psychology of sex differences*. Stanford, Calif.: Stanford University Press, 1974.

Mack, B., & Schröder, G. Geslechts-spezifisches Angstverhalten bei Kindern im Fragebogen und in der realen Situation. *Diagnostica*, 1979, *25*, 365–375.

Mac Nab, B. I. E., Nieuwenhuijse, B., Jansweijer, W. N. H., & Kuiper, A. Height/distance ratio as a predictor of perceived openess-enclosure of space and emotional responses in normal and phobic subjects. *Nederlands Tijdschrift voor de Psychologie*, 1978, *33*, 375–388.

Mahoney, M. J. The self-management of covert behavior: A case study. *Behavior Therapy*, 1971, *2*, 575–578.

Makhlouf-Norris, F., Jones, H. G., & Norris, H. Articulation of the conceptual structure in obsessional neurosis. *British Journal of Social and Clinical Psychology*, 1970, *9*, 264–274.

Mandel, N. M., & Shrauger, J. S. The effects of self-evaluative statements on heterosocial approach in shy and nonshy males. *Cognitive Therapy and Research*, 1980, *4*, 369–381.

Marchetti, A., McGlynn, F. D., & Patterson, A. S. Effects of cue-controlled relaxation, a placebo treatment, and no treatment on changes in self-reported and psychophysiological indices of test anxiety among college students. *Behavior Modification*, 1977, *1*, 47–72.

Marcia, J. E., Rubin, B. M., & Efran, J. S. Systematic desensitization: Expectancy change or counter-conditioning? *Journal of Abnormal Psychology*, 1969, *74*, 382–387.

Marks, I. Phobias and obsessions. In J. D. Maser & M. E. P. Seligman (Eds.), *Psychopathology: Experimental models*. San Francisco: Freeman, 1977.

Marks, I. M. *Fears and phobias*. New York: Academic Press, 1969.

Marks, I. M. Phobic disorders four years after treatment: A prospective follow-up. *British Journal of Psychiatry*, 1971, *118*, 683–686.

Marks, I. M. Behavioural treatments of phobic and obsessive-compulsive disorders: A critical appraisal. In M. Hersen, R. M. Eisler, & P. M. Miller (Eds.), *Progress in behavior modification* (Vol. 1). New York: Academic Press, 1975.

Marks, I. Space "phobia": A pseudo-agoraphobic syndrome. *Journal of Neurology, Neurosurgery, and Psychiatry*, 1981, *44*, 387–391 (a).

Marks, I. M. *Cure and care of neurosis*. New York: Wiley, 1981 (b).

Marks, I. M., & Bebbington, P. Spacephobia: Syndrome or agoraphobic variant. *British Medical Journal*, 1976, *2*, 345–347.

Marks, I. M., & Gelder, M. G. A controlled retrospective study of behaviour therapy in phobic patients. *British Journal of Psychiatry*, 1965, *111*, 571–573.

Marks, I. M., & Herst, E. R. A survey of 1200 agoraphobics in Britain. *Social Psychiatry*, 1970, *5*, 16–24.

Marks, I. M., & Huson, J. Physiological aspects of neutral and phobic imagery: Further observations. *British Journal of Psychiatry*, 1973, *122*, 567–572.

Marks, I. M., & Mathews, A. M. Brief standard self-rating for phobic patients. *Behaviour Research and Therapy*, 1979, *17*, 263–267.

Marks, I. M., Gelder, M. G., & Edwards, J. G. Hypnosis and desensitization for phobias: A controlled prospective trial. *British Journal of Psychiatry*, 1968, *114*, 1263–1274.

Marks, I. M., Crowe, M., Drewe, E., Young, J., & Dewhurst, W. G. Obsessive-compulsive neurosis in identical twins. *British Journal of Psychiatry*, 1969, *115*, 991–998.

Marks, I. M., Boulougouris, J., & Marset, P. Flooding versus desensitization in the treatment of phobic patients: A cross-over study. *British Journal of Psychiatry*, 1971, *119*, 353–375.

Marks, I. M., Viswanathan, R., Lipsedge, M. S., & Gardner, R. Enhanced relief of phobias by flooding during waning diazepam effect. *British Journal of Psychiatry*, 1972, *121*, 493–506.

Marks, I. M., Hodgson, R., & Rachman, S. Treatment of chronic obsessive-compulsive neurosis by in vivo exposure. *British Journal of Psychiatry*, 1975, *127*, 349–364.

Marks, I., Hallam, R. S., Connolly, J., & Philpott, R. *Nursing in behavioural psychotherapy*. London: Research Series of Royal College of Nursing, 1977.

Marks, I. M., Stern, R. S., Mawson, D., Cobb, J., & McDonald, R. Clomipramine and exposure for obsessive-compulsive rituals: I. *British Journal of Psychiatry*, 1980, *136*, 1–25.

Marks, I. M., Gray, S., Cohen, S. D., Hill, R., Mawson, D., Ramm, L., & Stern, R. S. *Imipramine and brief therapist-aided exposure in agoraphobics having self-exposure homework: A controlled trial.* Unpublished manuscript, 1982.

Marshall, P. G., Keltner, A. A., & Marshall, W. L. Anxiety reduction, assertive training and enactment of consequences: A comparative treatment study in the modification of nonassertion and social fears. *Behavior Modification*, 1981, *5*, 85–102.

Marshall, W. K. Treatment of obsessional illness and phobic anxiety states with clomipramine. *British Journal of Psychiatry*, 1971, *119*, 467–468.

Marshall, W. L., Boutilier, J., & Minnes, P. The modification of phobic behavior by covert reinforcement. *Behavior Therapy*, 1974, *5*, 469–480.

Marshall, W. L., Gauthier, J., Christie, M. M., Currie, D. W., & Gordon, A. Flooding therapy: Effectiveness, stimulus characteristics, and the value of brief in vivo exposure. *Behaviour Research and Therapy*, 1977, *15*, 79–87.

Marzillier, J. S., Carroll, D., & Newland, J. R. Self-report and physiological changes accompanying repeated imagining of a phobic scene. *Behaviour Research and Therapy*, 1979, *17*, 71–77.

Marzillier, J. S., Lambert, C., & Kellett, J. A controlled evaluation of systematic desensitization and social skills training for social inadequate psychiatric patients. *Behaviour Research and Therapy*, 1976, *14*, 225–228.

Mash, E. J., & Terdal, L. G. (Eds.). *Behavior therapy assessment*. New York: Springer, 1976.

Masters, W. H., & Johnson, V. E. *Human sexual inadequacy*. Boston: Little, Brown, 1970.

Mathews, A., Jannoun, L., & Gelder, M. *Self-help methods in agoraphobia*. Paper presented at the conference of the European Association of Behavior Therapy, Paris, September 1979.

Mathews, A. M., & Shaw, P. M. Emotional arousal and persuasion effects in flooding. *Behaviour Research and Therapy*, 1973, *11*, 587–598.

Mathews, A. M., & Rezin, V. Treatment of dental fears by imaginal flooding and rehearsal of coping behaviour. *Behaviour Research and Therapy*, 1977, *15*, 321–328.

Mathews, A. M., Johnston, D. W., Shaw, P. M., & Gelder, M. G. Process variables and the prediction of outcome in behavior therapy. *British Journal of Psychiatry*, 1973, *123*, 445–462.

Mathews, A. M., Bancroft, J., Whitehead, A., Hackmann, A., Julier, D., Bancroft, J., Gath, D., & Shaw, P. The behavioural treatment of sexual inadequacy: A comparative study. *Behaviour Research and Therapy*, 1976, *14*, 427–436.

Mathews, A. M., Johnston, D. W., Lancashire, M., Munby, M., Shaw, P. M., & Gelder, M. G. Imaginal flooding and exposure to real phobic situations: Treatment outcome with agoraphobic patients. *British Journal of Psychiatry*, 1976, *129*, 362–371.

Mathews, A. M., Teasdale, J. D., Munby, M., Johnston, D. W., & Shaw, P. M. A home-based treatment program for agoraphobia. *Behavior Therapy*, 1977, *8*, 915–924.

Mathews, R. W., Paulus, P. B., & Baron, R. A. Physical aggression after being crowded. *Journal of Nonverbal Behavior*, 1979, *4*, 5–17.

Matussek, P., Grigat, R., Haiböck, H., Halback, G., Kemmler, R., Mantell, D., Triebel, A., Vardy, M., & Wedel, G. *Die Konzentrationslagerhaft und ihre Folgen*. New York: Springer, 1971.

May, J. R., & Johnson, J. Physiological activity to internally elicited arousal and inhibitory thoughts. *Journal of Abnormal Psychology*, 1973, *82*, 239–245.

McCutcheon, B. A., & Adams, H. E. The physiological basis of implosive therapy. *Behaviour Research and Therapy*, 1975, *13*, 93–100.

McGlynn, F. D. Experimental desensitization following three types of instructions. *Behaviour Research and Therapy*, 1971, *9*, 367–369.

McGlynn, F. D., & McDonell, R. M. Subjective ratings of credibility following brief exposures to desensitization and pseudotherapy. *Behaviour Research and Therapy*, 1974, *12*, 141–146.

McGlynn, F. D., Reynolds, E. J., & Linder, L. H. Experimental desensitization following therapeutically oriented and physiologically oriented instructions. *Journal of Behavior Therapy and Experimental Psychiatry*, 1971, *2*, 13–18.

McGlynn, F. D., Gaynor, R., & Puhr, J. Experimental desensitization of snake-avoidance after an instructional manipulation. *Journal of Clinical Psychology*, 1972, *28*, 224–227.

McGlynn, F. D., Puhr, J. J., Gaynor, R., & Perry, J. W. Skin conductance responses to real and imagined snakes among avoidant and non-avoidant college students. *Behaviour Research and Therapy*, 1973, *11*, 417–426.

McGlynn, F. D., Kinjo, K., & Doherty, G. Effects of cue-controlled relaxation, a placebo treatment, and no-treatment on changes in self-reported test anxiety among college students. *Journal of Clinical Psychology*, 1978, *34*, 707–714.

McMullen, S., & Rosen, R. C. Self-administered masturbation training in the treatment of primary orgasmic dysfunction. *Journal of Consulting and Clinical Psychology*, 1979, *47*, 912–918.

McPherson, F. M., Brougham, L., & McLaren, S. Maintenance of improvement in agoraphobic patients treated by behavioural methods—a four-year follow-up. *Behaviour Research and Therapy*, 1980, *18*, 150–152.

McReynolds, W. T., & Grizzard, R. H. A comparison of three fear reduction procedures. *Psychotherapy: Theory, Research and Practice*, 1971, *8*, 264–268.

McReynolds, W. T., Barnes, A. R., Brooks, S., & Rehagen, N. J. The role of attention-placebo influences in the efficacy of systematic desensitization. *Journal of Consulting and Clinical Psychology*, 1973, *41*, 86–92.

Mealiea, W. L., & Nawas, M. M. The comparative effectiveness of systematic desensitization and implosive therapy in the treatment of snake phobia. *Journal of Behavior Therapy and Experimental Psychiatry*, 1971, *2*, 185–194.

Meares, R. Obsessionality, the Sandler-Hazari Scale and spasmodic torticollis. *British Journal of Medical Psychology*, 1971, *44*, 181–182.

Meichenbaum, D. H. Examination of model characteristics in reducing avoidance behavior. *Journal of Personality and Social Psychology*, 1971, *17*, 298–307.

Meichenbaum, D. H. Cognitive modification of test anxious college students. *Journal of Consulting and Clinical Psychology*, 1972, *39*, 370–380.

Meichenbaum, D. H. Self instructional methods. In F. H. Kanfer & A. P. Goldstein (Eds.), *Helping people change*. New York: Pergamon, 1975.

Meichenbaum, D. H., Gilmore, J. B., & Fedoravicius, A. Group insight versus group desensitization in treating speech anxiety. *Journal of Consulting and Clinical Psychology*, 1971, *36*, 410–421.

Melnick, J. A. A comparison of replication techniques in the modification of minimal dating behavior. *Journal of Abnormal Psychology*, 1973, *81*, 51–59.

Meursing, K. De rol van angst bij het ontstaan en de behandeling van sexuele problemen. Unpublished manuscript, University of Groningen, 1980.

Meyer, V. Modification of expectations in cases with obsessional rituals. *Behaviour Research and Therapy*, 1966, *4*, 273–280.

Meyer, V., & Crisp, A. H. Some problems in behavior therapy. *British Journal of Psychiatry*, 1966, *112*, 367–381.

Meyer, V., & Gelder, M. G. Behaviour therapy and phobic disorders. *British Journal of Psychiatry*, 1963, *109*, 19–28.

Meyer, V., & Levy, R. Behavioural treatment of a homosexual with compulsive rituals. *British Journal of Medical Psychology*, 1980, *43*, 63–67.

Meyer, V., & Turkat, I. D. Behavioral analysis of clinical cases. *Journal of Behavioral Assessment*, 1979, *1*, 259–270.

Meyer, V., Levy, R., & Schnurer, A. The behavioural treatment of obsessive-compulsive disorder. In H. R. Beech (Ed.), *Obsessional states*. London: Methuen, 1974.

Miles, H., Barrabee, E., & Finesinger, J. Evaluation of psychotherapy: With a follow-up study of 62 cases of anxiety neurosis. *Psychosomatic Medicine*, 1951, *13*, 83–106.

Millar, D. G. A repertory grid study of obsessionality: Distinctive cognitive structure or distinctive cognitive content? *British Journal of Medical Psychology*, 1980, *53*, 59–66.

Miller, B. C., & Levis, D. J. The effects of varying short visual exposure time to a phobic test stimulus on subsequent avoidance behavior. *Behaviour Research and Therapy*, 1971, *9*, 17–21.

Miller, L. C., Barrett, C. L., & Hampe, E. Phobias of childhood in a prescientific era. In A. Davids (Ed.), *Child personality and psychopathology: Current topics* (Vol. 1). New York: Wiley, 1974.

Miller, L. C., Barrett, C. L., Hampe, E., & Noble, H. Factor structure of childhood fears. *Journal of Consulting and Clinical Psychology*, 1972, *39*, 264–268.

Millner, A. D., Beech, H. R., & Walker, V. Decision processes and obsessional behaviour. *British Journal of Social and Clinical Psychology*, 1971, *10*, 88–89.

Mills, H. L., Agras, W. S., Barlow, D. H., & Mills, J. R. Compulsive rituals treated by response prevention. *Archives of General Psychiatry*, 1973, *28*, 524–530.

Milton, F., & Hafner, J. The outcome of behavior therapy for agoraphobia in relation to marital adjustment. *Archives of General Psychiatry*, 1979, *36*, 807–811.

Mitchell-Heggs, N., Kelly, D., & Richardson, A. Stereotactic limbic leucotomy—a follow-up at 16 months. *British Journal of Psychiatry*, 1976, *128*, 226–240.

Morris, R. J., & Suckerman, K. R. The importance of the therapeutic relationship in systematic desensitization. *Journal of Consulting and Clinical Psychology*, 1974, *42*, 147. (a)

Morris, R. J., & Suckerman, K. R. Therapist warmth as a factor in automated systematic desensitization. *Journal of Consulting and Clinical Psychology*, 1974, *42*, 244–250. (b)

Mountjoy, C. Q., Roth, M., Garside, R. F., & Leith, I. M. A clinical trial of phenelzine in anxiety depressive and phobic neuroses. *British Journal of Psychiatry*, 1977, *131*, 486–492.

Mowrer, O. H. *Learning theory and behavior.* New York: Wiley, 1960.

Munby, M., & Johnston, D. W. Agoraphobia: The long-term follow-up of behavioural treatment. *British Journal of Psychiatry*, 1980, *137*, 418–427.

Munjack, D., Cristol, A., Goldstein, A., Phillips, D., Goldberg, A., Whipple, K., Staples, F., & Kanno, P. Behavioural treatment of orgasmic dysfunction: A controlled study. *British Journal of Psychiatry*, 1976, *129*, 497–502.

Murphy, C. V., & Mikulas, W. L. Behavioral features and deficiences of the Masters and Johnson Program. *Psychological Record*, 1974, *24*, 221–227.

Murray, E. J., & Foote, F. The origins of fear of snakes. *Behaviour Research and Therapy*, 1979, *17*, 489–493.

Murray, R. M., Cooper, J. E., & Smith, A. The Leyton Obsessional Inventory: An analysis of the responses of 73 obsessional patients. *Psychological Medicine*, 1979, *9*, 305–311.

Mylar, J. L., & Clement, P. W. Prediction and comparison of outcome in systematic desensitization and implosion. *Behaviour Research and Therapy*, 1972, *10*, 235–246.

Nagera, H. *Obsessional Neuroses: Developmental Psychopathology.* New York: Jason Aronson, 1976.

Nagler, S. H. Clinical and EEG studies in obsessive-compulsive states. *American Journal of Psychiatry*, 1944, *100*, 830–838.

Nau, S. D., Caputo, J. A., & Borkovec, T. D. The relationship between therapy credibility and simulated therapy response. *Journal of Behavior Therapy and Experimental Psychiatry*, 1974, *5*, 129–134.

Nemetz, G. H., Craig, K. H., & Reith, G. Treatment of female sexual dysfunction through symbolic modeling. *Journal of Consulting and Clinical Psychology*, 1978, *46*, 62–73.

Nesse, R. M., Curtis, G. C., Brown, G. M., & Rubin, R. T. Anxiety induced by flooding therapy for phobias does not elicit prolactin secretory response. *Psychosomatic Medicine*, 1980, *42*, 25–31.

Newman, A., & Brand, E. Coping response training versus in vivo desensitization in fear reduction. *Cognitive Therapy and Research*, 1980, *4*, 397–407.

Noyes, R., Kathol, R., Clancy, J., & Crowe, R. R. Antianxiety effects of propranolol: A review of clinical studies. In D. F. Klein & J. Rabkin (Eds.), *Anxiety: New research and changing concepts.* New York: Raven Press, 1981.

Nunes, J. S., & Marks, I. M. Feedback of true heart rate during exposure *in vivo. Archives of General Psychiatry*, 1975, *32*, 933–936.

Nunes, J. S., & Marks, I. M. Feedback of true heart rate during exposure *in vivo*: Partial replication with methodological improvement. *Archives of General Psychiatry*, 1976, *33*, 1346–1350.

Obler, M. Systematic desensitization in sexual disorders. *Journal of Behavior Therapy and Experimental Psychiatry*, 1973, *4*, 93–101.

Obler, M. *An experimental analysis of a modified version of systematic desensitization in the treatment of sexual dysfunctions.* Unpublished doctoral dissertation, 1978.

O'Brien, T. P., & Kelley, J. E. A comparison of self-directed and therapist-directed practice for fear reduction. *Behaviour Research and Therapy*, 1980, *18*, 573–579.

Odom, J. V., Nelson, R. O., & Wein, K. S. The differential effectiveness of five treatment procedures on three response systems in a snake phobia analog study. *Behavior Therapy*, 1978, *9*, 936–942.

Öhman, A. Fear relevance, autonomic conditioning, and phobias: A laboratory model. In D. O. Sjöden, S. Bates, & W. S. Dockens (Eds.), *Trends in behavior therapy.* New York: Academic Press, 1979.

Öhman, A., & Dimberg, U. Facial expressions as conditioned stimuli for electrodermal responses: A case of "preparedness"? Unpublished manuscript, 1979. (Cited in Öhman, 1979.)

Öhman, A., Eriksson, A., & Olofsson, C. One trial learning and superior resistance to extinction of autonomic responses conditioned to potentially phobic stimuli. *Journal of Comparative and Physiological Psychology,* 1975, *88,* 619–627.

Öhman, A., Erixon, G., & Löfberg, I. Phobias and preparedness: Phobic versus neutral pictures as conditioned stimuli for human autonomic responses. *Journal of Abnormal Psychology,* 1975, *84,* 41–45.

Öhman, A., Fredrikson, M., Hugdahl, K., & Rimmö, P. A. The premise of equipotentiality in human classical conditioning: Conditioned electrodermal responses to potentially phobic stimuli. *Journal of Experimental Psychology: General,* 1976, *105,* 313–337.

Öhman, A., Fredrikson, M., & Hugdahl, K. Towards an experimental model of simple phobic reactions. *Behavioural Analysis and Modification,* 1978, *2,* 97–114.

Olley, M., & McAllister, H. A comment on treatment analogues for phobic anxiety states. *Psychological Medicine,* 1974, *4,* 463–469.

Orenstein, H., & Carr, J. Implosion therapy by tape-recording. *Behaviour Research and Therapy,* 1975, *13,* 177–182.

Orme, J. E. The relationship of obsessional traits to general emotional instability. *British Journal of Medical Psychology,* 1965, *38,* 269–270.

Öst, L. G., Jerremalm, A., & Johansson, J. Individual response patterns and the effects of different behavioral methods in the treatment of social phobia. *Behaviour Research and Therapy,* 1981, *19,* 1–16.

Pacella, B. L., Polatin, P., & Nagler, S. H. Clinical and EEG studies in obsessive-compulsive states. *American Journal of Psychiatry,* 1949, *100,* 830–838.

Pare, C. M. B. Side-effects and toxic effects of antidepressants. *Proceedings of Royal Society of Medicine,* 1964, *57,* 757–758.

Pariser, S. F., Pinta, B. R., & Jones, B. A. Mitral valve prolapse syndrome and anxiety neurosis/panic disorder. *American Journal of Psychiatry,* 1978, *135,* 246–247.

Parker, G. Cyclone Tracy and Darwin evacuees: On the restoration of the species. *British Journal of Psychiatry,* 1977, *130,* 548–555.

Parker, G. Reported parental characteristics of agoraphobics and social phobics. *British Journal of Psychiatry,* 1979, *135,* 555–560.

Parker, G., Tupling, H., & Brown, L. B. A parental bonding instrument. *British Journal of Medical Psychology,* 1979, *52,* 1–10.

Parker, N. Close identification in twins discordant for obsessional neurosis. *British Journal of Psychiatry,* 1964, *110,* 496–504.

Parkinson, L., & Rachman, S. Are intrusive thoughts subject to habituation? *Behaviour Research and Therapy,* 1980, *18,* 409–418.

Pauls, D. L., Crowe, R. R., & Noyes, R. Distribution of ancestral secondary cases in anxiety neurosis (panic disorder). *Journal of Affective Disorders,* 1979, *1,* 287–290.

Pauls, D. L., Noyes, R., & Crowe, R. R. The familial prevalence in second-degree relatives of patients with anxiety neurosis (panic disorders). *Journal of Affective Disorders,* 1979, *1,* 279–285.

Paykel, E. S., & Prusoff, B. A. Relationships between personality dimensions: Neuroticism and extroversion against obsessive, hysterical, and oral personality. *British Journal of Social and Clinical Psychology,* 1973, *12,* 309–318.

Perris, C. J., Jacobsson, H., Lindströnn, H., von Knorring, L., & Perris, H. Development of a new inventory for assessing memories of parental rearing behaviour. *Acta Psychiatria Scandinavia*, 1980, *61*, 265–274.

Petrie, J. F., & Haans, H. H. M. Enkele recente ervaringen met "behaviour therapy." *Nederlands Tijdschrift voor de Psychologie*, 1969, *24*, 391–404.

Pfeffer, J. M. The aetiology of the hyperventilation syndrome. *Psychotherapy and Psychosomatics*, 1978, *30*, 47–55.

Plotkin, W. B., & Rice, K. M. Biofeedback as a placebo: Anxiety reduction facilitated by training in either suppression or enhancement of alpha brainwaves. *Journal of Consulting and Clinical Psychology*, 1981, *49*, 590–596.

Pollak, J. M. Obsessive-compulsive personality: A review. *Psychological Bulletin*, 1979, *86*, 225–241.

Prochaska, J. O. Symptom and dynamic cues in the implosive treatment of test anxiety. *Journal of Abnormal Psychology*, 1971, *77*, 133–142.

Rabavilas, A. D., & Boulougouris, J. C. Physiological accompaniments of ruminations, flooding and thought-stopping in obsessive patients. *Behaviour Research and Therapy*, 1974, *12*, 239–243.

Rabavilas, A. D., & Boulougouris, J. C. Mood changes and flooding outcome in obsessive-compulsive patients: Report of a 2-year follow-up. *Journal of Nervous and Mental Disease*, 1979, *167*, 495–496.

Rabavilas, A. D., Boulougouris, J. C., & Stefanis C. Duration of flooding sessions in the treatment of obsessive-compulsive patients. *Behaviour Research and Therapy*, 1976, *14*, 349–355.

Rabavilas, A. D., Boulougouris, J. C., Stefanis, C., & Vaidakis, N. Psychophysiological accompaniments of threat anticipation in obsessive-compulsive patients. In C. D. Spielberger & I. G. Sarason (Eds.), *Stress and anxiety* (Vol. 4). New York: Wiley, 1977.

Rabavilas, A. D., Boulougouris, J. C., & Perissaki, C. Therapist qualities related to outcome with exposure *in vivo* in neurotic patients. *Journal of Behavior Therapy and Experimental Psychiatry*, 1979, *10*, 293–294.

Rabavilas, A. D., Boulougouris, J. C., Perissaki, C., & Stefanis, C. The effects of peripheral beta-blockade on psychophysiologic responses in obsessional neurotics. *Comprehensive Psychiatry*, 1979, *20*, 378–383.

Rachman, S. Obsessional ruminations. *Behaviour Research and Therapy*, 1971, *9*, 229–235.

Rachman, S. The passing of the two-stage theory of fear and avoidance: Fresh possibilities. *Behaviour Research and Therapy*, 1976, *14*, 125–134. (a)

Rachman, S. Obsessional-compulsive checking. *Behaviour Research and Therapy*, 1976, *14*, 269–277. (b)

Rachman, S. The modification of obsessions: A new formulation. *Behaviour Research and Therapy*, 1976, *14*, 437–443. (c)

Rachman, S. The conditioning theory of fear-acquisition: A critical examination. *Behaviour Research and Therapy*, 1977, *15*, 375–387.

Rachman, S. An anatomy of obsessions. *Behaviour Analysis and Modification*, 1978, *2*, 253–278.

Rachman, S. Emotional processing. *Behaviour Research and Therapy*, 1980, *18*, 51–60.

Rachman, S. Obstacles to the successful treatment of obsessions. In E. B. Foa & P. M. G. Emmelkamp (Eds.), *Failures in behavior therapy*. New York: Wiley, 1982.

Rachman, S., & de Silva, P. Abnormal and normal obsessions. *Behaviour Research and Therapy*, 1978, *16*, 233–248.

Rachman, S., & Hodgson, R. Synchrony and desynchrony in fear and avoidance. *Behaviour Research and Therapy*, 1974, *12*, 311–318.

Rachman, S., & Hodgson, R. J. *Obsessions and compulsions*. Englewood Cliffs, N. J.: Prentice-Hall, 1980.

Rachman, S., & Seligman, M. Unprepared phobias: Be prepared. *Behaviour Research and Therapy*, 1976, *14*, 333–338.

Rachman, S., Hodgson, R., & Marks, I. The treatment of chronic obsessive-compulsive neurosis. *Behaviour Research and Therapy*, 1971, *9*, 237–247.

Rachman, S., Marks, I., & Hodgson, R. The treatment of obsessive-compulsive neurotics by modelling and flooding in vivo. *Behaviour Research and Therapy*, 1973, *11*, 463–471.

Rachman, S., de Silva, P., & Röper, G. The spontaneous decay of compulsive urges. *Behaviour Research and Therapy*, 1976, *14*, 445–453.

Rachman, S., Cobb, J., Grey, S., McDonald, B., Mawson, D., Sartory, G., & Stern, R. The behavioural treatment of obsessional-compulsive disorders with and without clomipramine. *Behaviour Research and Therapy*, 1979, *17*, 467–478.

Rainey, C. A. An obsessive-compulsive neurosis treated by flooding in vivo. *Journal of Behavior Therapy and Experimental Psychiatry*, 1972, *3*, 117–121.

Ramsay, R. W. Bereavement: A behavioral treatment of pathological grief. In P. O. Sjöden, S. Bates, & W. S. Dockens (Eds.), *Trends in behavior therapy*. New York: Academic Press, 1979.

Ramsay, R. W., & Sikkel, R. J. Behavior therapy and obsessive-compulsive neurosis. In L. C. Brengelman & W. Tunner (Eds.), *Verhaltenstherapie*. Berlin: Urban und Schwarzenberg, 1973.

Rankin, H. Are models necessary? *Behaviour Research and Therapy*, 1976, *14*, 181–183.

Rapaport, H. Modification of avoidance behavior: Expectancy, autonomic reactivity, and verbal report. *Journal of Consulting and Clinical Psychology*, 1972, *39*, 404–414.

Rapoport, J., Elkins, R., Langer, D. H., Sceery, W., Buchsbaum, M. S., Gillin, J. C., Murphy, D. L., Zahn, T. P., Lake, R., Ludlow, C., & Mendelson, W. Childhood obsessive-compulsive disorder. *American Journal of Psychiatry*, 1982, *12*, 1545–1555.

Raskin, M., Bali, L. R., & Peeke, H. V. Muscle biofeedback and transcendental meditation. *Archives of General Psychiatry*, 1980, *37*, 93–97.

Reed, G. F. Some formal qualities of obsessional thinking. *Psychiatria Clinica*, 1968, *1*, 382–392.

Reed, G. F. "Under-inclusion"—a characteristic of obsessional personality disorder: I. *British Journal of Psychiatry*, 1969, *115*, 781–785. (a)

Reed, G. F. "Under-inclusion"—a characteristic of obsessional personality disorder: II. *British Journal of Psychiatry*, 1969, *115*, 787–790. (b)

Reed, G. F. Obsessional cognition: Performance on two numerical tasks. *British Journal of* 1969, *115*, 205–209. (c)

Reed, G. F. Indecisiveness in obsessional-compulsive disorder. *British Journal of Social and Clinical Psychology*, 1976, *15*, 443–445.

Reed, G. F. Obsessional cognition: performance on two numerical tasks. *British Journal of Psychiatry*, 1977, *130*, 184–185.

Reed, M., & Saslow, C. The effects of relaxation instructions and EMG biofeedback on test anxiety, general anxiety and locus of control. *Journal of Clinical Psychology*, 1980, *36*, 683–690.

Reinking, R. H., & Kohl, M. L. Effects of various forms of relaxation training on physiological and self-report measures of relaxation. *Journal of Consulting and Clinical Psychology*, 1975, *43*, 595–600.

Reiss, S., & McNally, R. J. *The preparedness theory of phobia and human safety-signal conditioning*. Paper presented at the 14th annual American Association of Behavior Therapy Convention, New York, November 1980.

Rigby, B., Clarren, S., & Kelly, D. A psychological and physiological evaluation of the effects of intravenous clomipramine (Anafranil). *Journal of International Medical Research*, 1973, *1*, 308–316.

Rimm, D., & Litvak, S. Self-verbalization and emotion arousal. *Journal of Abnormal Psychology*, 1969, *74*, 181–187.

Rimm, D. C., Janda, L. H., Lancaster, D. W., Nahl, M., & Dittmar, K. An exploratory investigation of the origin and maintenance of phobias. *Behaviour Research and Therapy*, 1977, *15*, 231–238.

Ritter, B. The use of contact desensitization, demonstration-plus-participation and demonstration alone in the treatment of acrophobia. *Behaviour Research and Therapy*, 1969, *7*, 157–164.

Robert, A. H. House-bound housewives: A follow-up study of a phobic anxiety state. *British Journal of Psychiatry*, 1964, *110*, 191–197.

Rockwell, F. V., & Simons, D. J. The electroencephalogram and personality organization in the obsessive-compulsive reactions. *Archives of Neurology and Psychiatry*, 1947, *57*, 71–77.

Rogers, T., & Craighead, W. E. Physiological responses to self-statements: The effects of statement valence and discrepancy. *Cognitive Therapy and Research*, 1977, *1*, 99–119.

Romano, J. L., & Cabianca, W. A. EMG biofeedback training versus systematic desensitization for test anxiety reduction. *Journal of Counseling Psychology*, 1978, *25*, 8–13.

Röper, G., & Rachman, S. Obsessional compulsive checking: Experimental replication and development. *Behaviour Research and Therapy*, 1976, *14*, 25–32.

Röper, G., Rachman, S., & Hodgson, R. An experiment on obsessional checking. *Behaviour Research and Therapy*, 1973, *11*, 271–277.

Röper, G., Rachman, S., & Marks, I. M. Passive and participant modelling in exposure treatment of obsessive-compulsive neurotics. *Behaviour Research and Therapy*, 1975, *13*, 271–279.

Rosen, G. M. Therapy set: Its effect on subjects' involvement in systematic desensitization and treatment outcome. *Journal of Abnormal Psychology*, 1974, *83*, 291–300.

Rosen, G. M., Glasgow, R. C., & Barrera, M. A two year follow-up on self-administered desensitization with data pertaining to the external validity of laboratory fear assessment. *Journal of Consulting and Clinical Psychology*, 1977, *45*, 1188–1189.

Ross, J. The use of former phobics in the treatment of phobias. *American Journal of Psychiatry*, 1980, *137*, 715–717.

Rotter, J. B. Generalized expectancies for internal vs. external control of reinforcement. *Psychological Monographs*, 1966, *80*, 1–28.

Roy, A. Obsessive-compulsive neurosis: Phenomenology, outcome and a comparison with hysterical neurosis. *Comprehensive Psychiatry*, 1979, *20*, 528–531.

Rüdin, E. Ein Beitrag zur Frage der Zwangskrankheit, insbesondere ihrere hereditären Beziehungen. *Archiv für Psychiatrie und Nervenkrankheiten*, 1953, *191*, 14–54.

Russell, P. L., & Brandsma, J. M. A theoretical and empirical integration of the rational emotive and classical conditioning theories. *Journal of Consulting and Clinical Psychology*, 1974, *42*, 389–397.

Russell, R. K., & Sipich, J. F. Cue-controlled relaxation in the treatment of test anxiety. *Journal of Behavior Therapy and Experimental Psychiatry*, 1973, *4*, 47–49.

Rutner, I. T. The effects of feedback and instructions on phobic behavior. *Behavior Therapy*, 1973, *4*, 338–348.

Rutter, M., Tizard, J., & Whitmore, S. *Education, health and behavior*. London: Longmans, 1970.

Ryan, V. L., & Moses, J. A. Therapist warmth and status in the systematic desensitization of test anxiety. *Psychotherapy: Theory, Research and Practice*, 1979, *16*, 178–184.

Samaan, J. Thought-stopping and flooding in a case of hallucinations, obsessions and homicidal-suicidal behavior. *Journal of Behavior Therapy and Experimental Psychiatry*, 1975, *6*, 65–67.

Sandler, J., & Hazari, A. The obsessional: On the psychological classification of obsessional character traits and symptoms. *British Journal of Medical Psychology*, 1960, *33*, 113–122.

Sartory, G., Rachman, S., & Grey, S. An investigation of the relation between reported fear and heart-rate. *Behaviour Research and Therapy*, 1977, *15*, 433–438.

Schachter, S., & Singer, J. C. Cognitive, social and physiological determinants of emotional state. *Psychological Review*, 1962, *69*, 379–399.

Schandler, S. L., & Grings, W. W. An examination of methods for producing relaxation during short-term laboratory sessions. *Behavior Research and Therapy*, 1976, *14*, 419–426.

Schilder, P. The organic background of obsessions and compulsions. *American Journal of Psychiatry*, 1938, *94*, 1397–1413.

Segal, Z., & Marshall, W. L. *Actual versus predicted expectancies and their influence in flooding therapy.* Paper presented to American Association of Behavior Therapy, New York, November 1980.

Seligman, M. E. P. On the generality of the laws of learning. *Psychological Review*, 1970, *77*, 406–418.

Seligman, M. E. P. Phobias and preparedness. *Behavior Therapy*, 1971, *2*, 307–320.

Seligman, M. E. P., & Hager, J. L. (Eds.), *Biological boundaries of learning*. New York: Appleton-Century-Crofts, 1972.

Seligman, M. E. P., & Johnston, J. A cognitive theory of avoidance learning. In F. S. McGuigan & D. Lumsden (Eds.), *Contemporary approaches to conditioning and learning*. Washington D. C.: Winston, 1973.

Shahar, A., & Merbaum, M. The interaction between subject characteristics and self-control procedures in the treatment of interpersonal anxiety. *Cognitive Therapy and Research*, 1981, *5*, 221–224.

Shapiro, M. B. An experimental approach to diagnostic psychological testing. *Journal of Mental Science*, 1951, *97*, 748–764.

Shaw, P. M. *A comparison of three behaviour therapies in the treatment of social phobia.* Paper read at the British Association for Behavioral Psychotherapy, Exeter, 1976.

Sheehan, D. V., Ballenger, J., & Jacobson, G. Relative efficacy of monomamine oxidase inhibitors and tricyclic antidepressants in the treatment of endogenous anxiety. In D. F. Klein & J. Rabkin (Eds.), *Anxiety: New research and changing concepts.* New York: Raven Press, 1981.

Sherman, A. R. Real-life exposure as a primary therapeutic factor in the desensitization treatment of fear. *Journal of Abnormal Psychology*, 1972, *79*, 19–28.

Shepherd, G. W., & Watts, F. N. Heart rate control in psychiatric patients. *Behavior Therapy*, 1974, *5*, 153–154.

Silverman, L. H., Frank, S. G., & Dachinger, P. A psychoanalytic reinterpretation of the effectiveness of systematic desensitization: Experimental data bearing on the role of merging fantasies. *Journal of Abnormal Psychology*, 1974, *83*, 313–318.

Sinnott, A., Jones, R. B., Scott-Fordham, A., & Woodward, R. Augmentation of in vivo exposure treatment for agoraphobia by the formation of neighbourhood self-help groups. *Behaviour Research and Therapy*, 1981, *19*, 539–347.

Sjöqvist, F. Interaction between mono-amine oxidase inhibitors and other substances. *Proceedings of the Royal Society of Medicine*, 1963, *58*, 967–978.

Slade, P. D. Psychometric studies of obsessional illness and obsessional personality. In H. R. Beech (Ed.), *Obsessional states*. London: Methuen. 1974.

Slater, E., & Shields, J. Genetical aspects of anxiety. In M. J. Lader (Ed.), *Studies of Anxiety.*
    British Journal of Psychiatry, Special Publication, No. 3, 1969.
Smith, G. P., & Coleman, R. E. Processes underlying generalization through participant
    modeling with self-directed practice. *Behaviour Research and Therapy,* 1977, *15,*
    204–206.
Smith, R. E., & Nye, S. L. A comparison of implosive therapy and systematic desensitization
    in the treatment of test anxiety. *Journal of Consulting and Clinical Psychology,* 1973, *44,*
    37–42.
Smith, R. E., Diener, E., & Beaman, A. Demand characteristics and the behavioral avoid-
    ance measures of fear in behavior therapy analogue research. *Behavior Therapy,* 1974,
    5, 172–182.
Snowdon, J. A comparison of written and postbox forms of the Leyton Obsessional Inven-
    tory. *Psychological Medicine,* 1980, *10,* 165–170.
Snyder, A. L., & Deffenbacher, J. L. Comparison of relaxation as self-control and system-
    atic desensitization in the treatment of test anxiety. *Journal of Consulting and Clinical
    Psychology,* 1977, *45,* 1202–1203.
Solomon, K., & Hart, R. Pitfalls and prospects in clinical research on antianxiety drugs:
    Benzodiazepines and placebo—A research review. *Journal of Clinical Psychiatry,* 1978,
    823–831.
Solomon, R. L., & Wynne, L. C. Traumatic avoidance learning: The principles of anxiety
    conservation and partial irreversibility. *Psychological Review,* 1954, *61,* 353–385.
Solyom, C., Solyom, L., La Pierre, Y., Pecknold, J. C., & Morton, L. Phenelzine and
    exposure in the treatment of phobias. *Journal of Biological Psychiatry,* 1981, *16,*
    239–248.
Solyom, L., Zamanzadeh, D., Ledwidge, B., & Kenny, F. Aversion relief treatment of
    obsessive neurosis. In R. D. Rubin (Ed.), *Advances in behavior therapy.* New York:
    Academic Press, 1971.
Solyom, L., McClure, D. J., Heseltine, G. F. D., Ledwidge, B., & Solyom, C. Variables in the
    aversion relief therapy of phobics. *Behavior Therapy,* 1972, *3,* 21–28.
Solyom, L., & Kingstone, F. An obsessive neurosis following morning glory seed ingestion
    treated by aversion relief. *Journal of Behavior Therapy and Experimental Psychiatry,* 1973,
    4, 293–295.
Solyom, L., Beck, P., Solyom, C., & Hugel, R. Some etiological factors in phobic neurosis.
    Canadian Psychiatric Association Journal, 1974, *19,* 69–78.
Solyom, L., Silberfeld, M., & Solyom, C. Maternal overprotection in the etiology of agora-
    phobia. *Canadian Psychiatric Association Journal,* 1976, *21,* 109–113.
Solyom, L., Heseltine, G. F. D., McClure, D. J., Solyom, C., Ledwidge, B., & Steinberg, S.
    Behaviour therapy versus drug therapy in the treatment of phobic neurosis. *Canadian
    Psychiatric Association Journal,* 1973, *18,* 25–31.
Sookman, D., & Solyom, L. The effectiveness of four behaviour therapies in the treatment
    of obsessive neurosis. In J. C. Boulougouris & A. D. Rabavilas (Eds.), *The treatment of
    phobic and obsessive-compulsive disorders.* New York: Pergamon Press, 1977.
Sorgatz, H., & Prümm, N. Feeling of improvement in flooding: Some analogue data.
    Psychological Reports, 1978, *42,* 1187–1191.
Sotile, W. M., & Kilmann, P. R. Effects of group systematic desensitization on female
    orgasmic dysfunction. *Archives of Sexual Behavior,* 1978, *7,* 477–491.
Sotile, W. M., Kilmann, P., & Follingstad, D. R. A sexual-enhancement workshop: Beyond
    group systematic desensitization for women's sexual anxiety. *Journal of Sex and Marital
    therapy,* 1977, *3,* 249–255.

Speltz, M. L., & Bernstein, D. A. Sex differences in fearfulness: Verbal report, overt avoidance and demand characteristics. *Journal of Behavior Therapy and Experimental Psychiatry*, 1976, *7*, 117–122.

Spiegler, M. D., Cooley, E. J., Marshall, G. J., Prince, H. T., Puckett, S. P., & Skenazy, J. A. A self-control versus a counterconditioning paradigm for systematic desensitization: An experimental comparison. *Journal of Counseling Psychology*, 1976, *23*, 83–86.

Stampfl, T. G., & Levis, D. J. Essentials of implosive therapy: A learning-theory-based psychodynamic behavioral therapy. *Journal of Abnormal Psychology*, 1967, *72*, 496–503.

Stampfl, T. G., & Levis, D. J. Implosive therapy: A behavioral therapy? *Behaviour Research and Therapy*. 1968, *6*, 31–36.

Steiner, J. A questionnaire study of risk taking in psychiatric patients. *British Journal of Medical Psychology*, 1972, *45*, 365–374.

Stern, R. Treatment of a case of obsessional neurosis using thought-stopping technique. *British Journal of Psychiatry*, 1970, *117*, 441–442.

Stern, R., & Marks, I. M. Brief and prolonged flooding: A comparison in agoraphobic patients. *Archives of General Psychiatry*, 1973, *28*, 270–276.

Stern, R. S. Obsessive thoughts: The problem of therapy. *British Journal of Psychiatry*, 1978, *132*, 200–205.

Stern, R. S., & Cobb, J. P. Phenomenology of obsessive-compulsive neurosis. *British Journal of Psychiatry*, 1978, *132*, 233–239.

Stern, R. S., Lipsedge, M. S., & Marks, I. M. Obsessive ruminations: A controlled trial of thought-stopping technique. *Behaviour Research and Therapy*, 1973, *11*, 659–662.

Sternberg, M. Physical treatments in obsessional disorders. In H. R. Beech (Ed.), *Obsessional states*. London: Methuen, 1974.

Suarez, Y., Adams, H. E., & McCutcheon, B. A. Flooding and systematic desensitization: Efficacy in subclinical phobics as a function of arousal. *Journal of Consulting and Clinical Psychology*, 1976, *44*, 872.

Suinn, R. M. Anxiety management training to control general anxiety. In J. D. Krumboltz & C. E. Thorensen (Eds.), *Counseling methods*. New York: Holt, Rinehart & Winston, 1976.

Suinn, R. M., & Richardson, F. Anxiety management training: A non-specific behavior therapy program for anxiety control. *Behavior Therapy*, 1971, *2*, 498–511.

Sullivan, B. J., & Denney, D. R. Expectancy and phobic level: Effects on desensitization. *Journal of Consulting and Clinical Psychology*, 1977, *45*, 763–771.

Sutton-Simon, K., & Goldfried, M. R. Faulty thinking patterns in two types of anxiety. *Cognitive Therapy and Research*, 1979, *3*, 193–203.

Swan, G. E., & MacDonald, M. L. Behavior therapy in practice: A national survey of behavior therapists. *Behavior Therapy*, 1978, *9*, 799–807.

Tan, E., Marks, I. M., & Marset, P. Bimedial leucotomy in obsessive-compulsive neurosis: A controlled serial enquiry. *British Journal of Psychiatry*, 1971, *118*, 155–164.

Tanner, B. A. A case report on the use of relaxations and systematic desensitization to control multiple compulsive behavior. *Journal of Behavior Therapy and Experimental Psychiatry*, 1971, *2*, 267–272.

Taylor, J. A. A personality scale of manifest anxiety. *Journal of Abnormal and Social Psychology*, 1953, *48*, 285–290.

Teasdale, J. D. Learning models of obsessional-compulsive disorder. In H. R. Beech (Ed.), *Obsessional States*. London: Methuen, 1974.

Teasdale, J. D., & Rezin, V. Effect of thought-stopping on thoughts, mood and corrugator EMG in depressed patients. *Behaviour Research and Therapy*, 1978, *16*, 97–102.

Teasdale, J. D., Walsh, P. A., Lancashire, M., & Mathews, A. M. Group exposure for agoraphobics: A replication study. *British Journal of Psychiatry*, 1977, *130*, 186–193.

Terhune, W. M. The phobic syndrome. *Archives of Neurology and Psychiatry*, 1949, *62*, 162–172.

Thase, M. E., & Moss, M. K. The relative efficacy of covert modeling procedures and guided participant modeling in the reduction of avoidance behavior. *Journal of Behavior Therapy and Experimental Psychiatry*, 1976, *7*, 7–12.

Thorén, P., Åsberg, M., Cronholm, B., Jörnestedt, L., & Träskman, L. Clomipramine treatment of obsessive-compulsive disorder. *Archives of General Psychiatry*, 1980, *37*, 1281–1285.

Thorpe, G. L. Desensitization, behavior rehearsal, self-instructional training and placebo effects on assertive-refusal behavior. *European Journal of Behavioural Analysis and Modification*, 1975, *1*, 30–44.

Thorpe, G. L., Amatu, H. I., Blakey, R. S., & Burns, L. E. Contributions of overt instructional rehearsal and "specific insight" to the effectiveness of self-instructional training: A preliminary study. *Behavior Therapy*, 1976, *7*, 504–511.

Tiegerman, S., & Kassinove, H. Effects of assertive training and cognitive components of rational therapy on assertive behavior and interpersonal anxiety. *Psychological Reports*, 1977, *40*, 535–542.

Torgersen, S. The nature and origin of common phobic fears. *British Journal of Psychiatry*, 1979, *134*, 343–351.

Torgersen, S. The oral, obsessive, and hysterical personality syndromes. *Archives of General Psychiatry*, 1980, *37*, 1272–1277.

Tori, C., & Worell, L. Reduction of human avoidant behavior: A comparison of counterconditioning, expectancy and cognitive information approaches. *Journal of Consulting and Clinical Psychology*, 1973, *41*, 269–278.

Townsend, R. E., House, J. F., & Addario, D. A. A comparison of biofeedback mediated relaxation and group therapy in the treatment of chronic anxiety. *American Journal of Psychiatry*, 1975, *32*, 598–601.

Trethowan, W. H., & Scott, P. A. L. Chlorpromazine in obesessive-compulsive and allied disorders. *The Lancet*, April, 1955, pp. 781–785.

Trower, P., Yardley, K., Bryant, B. M., & Shaw, P. The treatment of social failure: A comparison of anxiety-reduction and skills-acquisition procedures on two social problems. *Behavior Modification*, 1978, *2*, 41–60.

Tucker, W. I. Diagnosis and treatment of the phobic reaction. *American Journal of Psychiatry*, 1956, *112*, 825–830.

Turner, R. M., Steketee, G. S., & Foa, E. B. Fear of criticism in washers, checkers and phobics. *Behaviour Research and Therapy*, 1979, *17*, 79–81.

Turner, S. M., Hersen, M., Bellack, A. S., & Wells, K. C. Behavioral treatment of obsessive-compulsive neurosis. *Behaviour Research and Therapy*, 1979, *17*, 95–106.

Turner, S. M., Hersen, M., Bellack, A. S., Andrasik, F., & Capparell, H. V. Behavioral and pharmacological treatment of obsessive-compulsive disorders. *Journal of Nervous and Mental Disease*, 1980, *168*, 651–657.

Tyrer, P., Candy, J., & Kelly, D. A study of the clinical effects of phenelzine and placebo in the treatment of phobic anxiety. *Psychopharmacologica*, 1973, *32*, 237–254.

Tyrer, P. J., & Lader, M. H. Central and peripheral correlates of anxiety: A comparative study. *The Journal of Nervous and Mental disease*, 1976, *162*, 99–104.

Ullrich, R., Ullrich, R., Crombach, G., & Peikert, V. Three flooding procedures in the treatment of agoraphobics. Paper read at the European Conference on Behaviour Modification, Wexford, Ireland, 1972.

Van den Berg, P. J., & Helstone, F. S. Oral, obsessive and hysterical personality patterns: A Dutch replication. *Journal of Psychiatric Research*, 1975, *12*, 319–327.

Van Son, M. J. M. *Sociale vaardigheidstherapie*. Amsterdam: Swets und Zeitlinger, 1978.

Vila, J., & Beech, H. R. Vulnerability and conditioning in relation to the human menstrual cycle. *British Journal of Social and Clinical Psychology*, 1977, *16*, 69–75.

Vila, J., & Beech, H. R. Vulnerability and defensive reactions in relation to the human menstrual cycle. *British Journal of Social and Clinical Psychology*, 1978, *17*, 93–100.

Visser, K. Ademhalingstherapie bij hyperventilerende agorafobici. Unpublished manuscript, University of Utrecht, 1978.

Volans, P. J. Styles of decision-making and probability appraisal in selected obsessional and phobic patients. *British Journal of Social and Clinical Psychology*, 1976, *15*, 305–317.

Walker, V. J. *An investigation of ritualistic behaviour in obsessional patients*. Unpublished Ph.D. thesis, University of London, 1967.

Wallander, J. L., Conger, A. J., Mariotto, M. J., Curran, J. P., & Farrell, A. D. Comparability of selection instruments in studies of heterosexual-social problem behaviors. *Behavior Therapy*, 1980, *11*, 548–560.

Walton, D. The relevance of learning theory to the treatment of an obsessive-compulsive state. In H. J. Eysenck (Ed.), *Behaviour therapy and the neurosis*. Oxford: Pergamon Press, 1960.

Walton, D., & Mather, M. D. The application of learning principles to the treatment of obsessive-compulsive states in acute and chronic phases of the illness. *Behaviour Research and Therapy*, 1963, *1*, 163–174.

Watson, J., & Rayner, R. Conditioned emotional reactions. *Journal of Experimental Psychology*, 1920, *3*, 1–22.

Watson, J. P., Gaind, R., & Marks, I. M. Physiological habituation to continuous phobic stimulation. *Behaviour Research and Therapy*, 1972, *10*, 269–278.

Watson, J. P., & Marks, I. M. Relevant and irrelevant fear in flooding—A crossover study of phobic patients. *Behavior Therapy*, 1971, *2*, 275–293.

Watson, J. P., Mullett, G. E., & Pilley, H. The effects of prolonged exposure to phobic situations upon agoraphobic patients treated in groups. *Behaviour Research and Therapy*, 1973, *11*, 531–546.

Waxman, D. A clinical trial of clomipramine and diazepam in the treatment of phobic and obsessional illness. *Journal International Medical Research*, 1977, *5*, 99–109.

Webster, A. S. The development of phobias in married women. *Psychological Monographs*, 1953, *67*, No. 367.

Weimann, G. *Das Hyperventilationsyndrom*. Munich: Urban und Schwarzenberg, 1968.

Weinberger, D. A., Schwartz, G. E., & Davidson, R. J. Low-anxious, high-anxious, and repressive coping styles: Psychometric patterns and behavioral and physiological responses to stress. *Journal of Abnormal Psychology*, 1979, *88*, 369–380.

Weissberg, M. A comparison of direct and vicarious treatments of speech anxiety: Desensitization, desensitization with coping imagery, and cognitive modification. *Behavior Therapy*, 1977, *8*, 606–620.

Welner, A., Reich, T., Robins, E., Fishman, R., & van Doren, T. Obsessive-compulsive neurosis: Record, follow-up, and family studies. I. Inpatient record study. *Comprehensive Psychiatry*, 1976, *17*, 527–539.

Whitehead, W. E., Robinson, A., Blackwell, B., & Stulz, R. M. Flooding treatment of phobias: Does chronic diazepam increase effectiveness? *Journal of Behavior Therapy and Experimental Psychiatry*, 1978, *9*, 219–226.

Wickramasekera, I. Heart rate feedback and the management of cardiac neurosis. *Journal of Abnormal Psychology*, 1974, *83*, 578–580.

Wilkins, W. Expectancy of therapeutic gain: An empirical and conceptual critique. *Journal of Consulting and Clinical Psychology*, 1973, *40*, 69–77.

Wilkins, W. Expectancies and therapy effectiveness: Emmelkamp versus Davison and Wilson. *Behavioural Analysis and Modification*, 1979, *3*, 109–116. (a)

Wilkins, W. Expectancies in therapy research: Discriminating among heterogeneous non-specifics. *Journal of Consulting and Clinical Psychology*, 1979, *47*, 837–845. (b)

Williams, S. L., & Rappoport, J. A. *Behavioral practice with and without thought modification.* Paper presented at the American Psychological Association convention, Montreal, September 1980.

Willis, R. W., & Edwards, J. A. A study of the comparative effectiveness of systematic desensitization and implosive therapy. *Behaviour Research and Therapy*, 1969, *7*, 387–395.

Wilson, H. Mental reactions to air raids. *Lancet*, 1942, *1*, 284–287.

Wincze, J. P., & Caird, W. K. The effects of systematic desensitization and video desensitization in the treatment of essential sexual dysfunction in women. *Behavior Therapy*, 1976, *7*, 335–342.

Windheuser, H. J. Anxious mothers as models for coping with anxiety. *Behavioural Analysis and Modification*, 1977, *1*, 39–58.

Wishnoff, R. Modeling effects of explicit and nonexplicit sexual stimuli on the sexual anxiety and behavior of women. *Archives of Sexual Behavior*, 1978, *7*, 455–461.

Wisocki, P. A. Treatment of obsessive-compulsive behaviour by covert sensitization and covert reinforcement: A case report. *Journal of Behavior Therapy and Experimental Psychiatry*, 1970, *1*, 233–239.

Wolfe, J. L., & Fodor, I. G. Modifying assertive behavior in women: A comparison of three approaches. *Behavior Therapy*, 1977, *8*, 567–574.

Wolowitz, H. M. Therapist warmth: Necessary or sufficient condition in behavioral desensitization? *Journal of Consulting and Clinical Psychology*, 1975, *43*, 584–586.

Wolpe, J. *Psychotherapy and reciprocal inhibition.* Stanford: Stanford University Press, 1958.

Wolpe, J. Quantitative relationships in the systematic desensitization of phobias. *American Journal of Psychiatry*, 1963, *119*, 1062–1068.

Wolpe, J. Behaviour therapy in complex neurotic states. *British Journal of Psychiatry*, 1964, *110*, 28–34.

Wolpe, J. *The practice of behavior therapy.* New York: Pergamon, 1973.

Wolpe, J. Inadequate behavior analysis: The Achilles heel of outcome research in behavior therapy. *Journal of Behavior Therapy and Experimental Psychiatry*, 1977, *8*, 1–3.

Wolpe, J., & Lang, P. J. A Fear Survey Schedule for use in behavior therapy. *Behaviour Research and Therapy*, 1964, *2*, 27–30.

Wonneberger, M., Henkel, D., Arentewicz, G., & Hasse, A. Studie zu einem Selbsthilfe-programm für Zwangneurotische Patienten. *Zeitschrift für Klinische Psychologie*, 1975, *4*, 124–136.

Woodruff, R., & Pitts, F. N. Monozygotic twins with obsessional neurosis. *American Journal of Psychiatry*, 1964, *120*, 1075–1080.

Worsley, J. L. Behaviour therapy and obsessionality. In H. Freeman (Ed.), *Progress in behaviour therapy*. Bristol: John Wright, 1968.

Worsley, J. L. The causation and treatment of obsessionality. In L. E. Burns & J. L. Worsley (Eds.), *Behaviour therapy in the 1970's*. Bristol, England: John Wright, 1970.

Wyndowe, J., Solyom, L., & Ananth, J. Anafranil in obsessive compulsive neurosis. *Current Therapeutic Research*, 1975, *18*, 611–617.

Yamagami, T. Treatment of an obsession by thought-stopping. *Journal of Behavior Therapy and Experimental Psychiatry*, 1971, *2*, 133–135.

Yaruyra-Tobias, J. A. Obsessive-compulsive disorders: A serotonergic hypothesis. *Journal of Orthomolecular Psychiatry*, 1977, 6, 1–10.

Yaruyra-Tobias, J. A., & Bhagavan, H. N. L-Tryptophan in obsessive-compulsive disorders. *American Journal of Psychiatry*, 1977, 134, 1298–1299.

Yaryura-Tobias, J. A., & Neziroglu, F. The action of chlorimipramine in obsessive-compulsive neurosis: A pilot study. *Current Therapeutic Research*, 1975, 17, 111–116.

Yaryura-Tobias, J. A., Neziroglu, F., & Bergman, L. Chlorimipramine, for obsessive-compulsive neurosis: An organic approach. *Current Therapeutic Research*, 1976, 20, 541–548.

Yates, A. J. *Behavior therapy*. New York: Wiley, 1970.

Yorkston, N. J., Sergeant, H. G. S., & Rachman, S. Methohexitone relaxation for desensitizing agoraphobic patients. *Lancet*, 1968, 2, 651–653.

Young, J. P. R., Fenton, G. W., & Lader, M. J. The inheritance of neurotic traits: A twin study of the Middlesex Hospital Questionnaire. *British Journal of Psychiatry*, 1971, 119, 393–398.

Zaworka, W., & Hand, I. Phänomenologie (Dimensionalität) der Zwangssymptomatik. *Archiv für Psychiatrie und Nervenkrankheiten*, 1980, 228, 257–273.

Zemore, R. Systematic desensitization as a method of teaching a general anxiety-reducing skill. *Journal of Consulting and Clinical Psychology*, 1975, 43, 157–161.

Zitrin, C. M., Klein, D. F., & Woerner, M. G. Behavior therapy, supportive psychotherapy, imipramine, and phobias. *Archives of General Psychiatry*, 1978, 35, 307–316.

Zitrin, C. M., Klein, D. F., & Woerner, M. G. Treatment of agoraphobia with group exposure in vivo and imipramine. *Archives of General Psychiatry*, 1980, 37, 63–72.

Zitrin, C. M., Woerner, M. G., & Klein, D. F. Differentiation of panic anxiety from anticipatory anxiety and avoidance behavior. In D. F. Klein & J. Rabkin (Eds.), *Anxiety: New research and changing concepts*. New York: Raven Press, 1981.

Zung, W. W. K. A Self-Rating Depression Scale. *Archives of General Psychiatry*, 1965, 12, 63–70.

Index

351